SEAMUS HEANEY IN CONTEXT

Few poets have captured the imagination of the world like Seamus Heaney. Recognized as one of the truly outstanding poets of our time, Heaney's work is both critically acclaimed and popular with the general reader. It is taught in classrooms across the globe and has been translated into more than twenty-seven languages. Presenting original research from an international field of scholars, *Seamus Heaney in Context* offers new pathways to explore the places, times and influences that made Heaney a poet. Drawing on newly available archival and print sources, these essays situate Heaney in a multitude of contexts that help readers navigate received ideas about his life and work. In mapping intersecting themes in the current terrain of Heaney criticism, this study also signposts new directions for understanding Heaney's poetry in future contexts.

GERALDINE HIGGINS is Associate Professor of English and Director of Irish Studies at Emory University in Atlanta, GA. Her publications include works on Yeats and other Revival writers, Yeats and popular culture, Brian Friel, and Seamus Heaney. She is the curator of the National Library of Ireland's acclaimed exhibition, 'Seamus Heaney: Listen Now Again', open at the Bank of Ireland Cultural and Heritage Centre in Dublin until 2023. A former director of the W. B. Yeats Summer School in Sligo, Ireland, she was Emory's Massee-Martin/NEH distinguished teaching chair from 2015 to 2018.

SEAMUS HEANEY IN CONTEXT

EDITED BY
GERALDINE HIGGINS
Emory University

CAMBRIDGE
UNIVERSITY PRESS

CAMBRIDGE
UNIVERSITY PRESS

Shaftesbury Road, Cambridge CB2 8EA, United Kingdom

One Liberty Plaza, 20th Floor, New York, NY 10006, USA

477 Williamstown Road, Port Melbourne, VIC 3207, Australia

314–321, 3rd Floor, Plot 3, Splendor Forum, Jasola District Centre, New Delhi – 110025, India

103 Penang Road, #05–06/07, Visioncrest Commercial, Singapore 238467

Cambridge University Press is part of Cambridge University Press & Assessment, a department of the University of Cambridge.

We share the University's mission to contribute to society through the pursuit of education, learning and research at the highest international levels of excellence.

www.cambridge.org
Information on this title: www.cambridge.org/9781107180147

DOI: 10.1017/9781316841372

First published 2021

A catalogue record for this publication is available from the British Library

Library of Congress Cataloging-in-Publication data
NAMES: Higgins, Geraldine, editor.
TITLE: Seamus Heaney in context / edited by Geraldine Higgins.
DESCRIPTION: Cambridge ; New York, NY : Cambridge University Press, 2020. | Includes bibliographical references and index.
IDENTIFIERS: LCCN 2020022791 (print) | LCCN 2020022792 (ebook) | ISBN 9781107180147 (hardback) | ISBN 9781316632017 (paperback) | ISBN 9781316841372 (epub)
SUBJECTS: LCSH: Heaney, Seamus, 1939–2013–Criticism and interpretation.
CLASSIFICATION: LCC PR6058.E2 Z884 2020 (print) | LCC PR6058.E2 (ebook) | DDC 821/.914–dc23
LC record available at https://lccn.loc.gov/2020022791
LC ebook record available at https://lccn.loc.gov/2020022792

ISBN 978-1-107-18014-7 Hardback

For my sisters and brothers, Roisín, Vincent, Peter,
and Claire – GRMA.

Contents

Contributors

Nicholas Allen, University of Georgia
Jonathan Allison, University of Kentucky
Deepika Bahri, Emory University
Sarah Bennett, University of Oxford
Rand Brandes, Lenoir-Rhyne University
Matthew Campbell, University of York
Heather Clark, University of Huddersfield
Catriona Clutterbuck, University College Dublin
Brendan Corcoran, Indiana State University
Patrick Crotty, University of Aberdeen, Emeritus
Margaret Greaves, Skidmore College
Vona Groarke, University of Manchester
Margaret Mills Harper, University of Limerick
Geraldine Higgins, Emory University
Florence Impens, University of Manchester
Simon B. Kress, Attorney, WilmerHale, Boston
Rosie Lavan, Trinity College Dublin
John McAuliffe, University of Manchester and Carcanet Press
Chris Morash, Trinity College Dublin
Laura O'Connor, University of California, Irvine
Bernard O'Donoghue, University of Oxford, Emeritus
Aidan O'Malley, University of Rijeka
Fintan O'Toole, Literary Editor, *Irish Times*
Kieran Quinlan, University of Alabama at Birmingham
Justin Quinn, University of West Bohemia, Czech Republic
John Redmond, University of Liverpool

Stephen Regan, Durham University
Marilynn Richtarik, Georgia State University
Richard Rankin Russell, Baylor University
Ronald Schuchard, Emory University, Emeritus
Nathan Suhr-Sytsma, Emory University
Kevin Whelan, University of Notre Dame

Acknowledgements

It is perhaps a truth universally acknowledged that no one reads acknowledgements unless they might find themselves in them. However, acknowledgement is much too formal a word for the immense gratitude I feel towards the many people who helped to bring this book to life.

So, thank you to Ray Ryan for commissioning and guiding this volume to completion. At Cambridge University Press, I would also like to thank Senior Editorial Assistant Edgar Mendez, Senior Content Manager Victoria Parrin, and freelance copy-editor Damian Love.

Next, I am of course extremely grateful to the wonderful contributors who responded so generously to my invitation to write on Seamus Heaney for this distinguished series.

Much of that generosity is due to Heaney himself as a beloved icon of Irish poetry and indeed Irish life. In donating his papers to the National Library of Ireland, Heaney and his family entrusted scholars with an extraordinary gift of not just access, but new pathways to understanding his work. I am so grateful to Marie, Mick, Christopher and Catherine for that gift and for their friendship, hospitality and help. Thanks also to the Seamus Heaney estate to and Faber and Faber for permission to quote from Heaney's work.

My deepest thanks go to Maggie Greaves, editorial assistant beyond compare, who made every aspect of this project better, sharper and more convivial despite living far away in Saratoga Springs.

Working on two exhibitions about Heaney in two different locations deepened my appreciation of Heaney and his poetry and opened many fruitful avenues of exploration and collaboration. Had I not worked with these amazing exhibition teams, the scope and shape of this book would have been far less visible to me. At *Seamus Heaney: The Music of What Happens* (Emory University, 2014), I'd like to thank my brilliant curatorial assistants, Maggie Greaves and Emily Leithauser, and the Rose Library exhibitions team, Kathy Dixson, John Klingler and Gretchen Warner.

At *Seamus Heaney: Listen Now Again* (National Library of Ireland, 2018), I had the wonderful experience of working with Sandra Collins, Katherine McSharry, Vincent O'Shea, and Sara Smyth to curate the NLI's public exhibition at the Bank of Ireland's new Cultural and Heritage Centre on College Green.

Living in Dublin from 2015–2017 brought me back to my extended Higgins family and I would like to thank them and the friends who helped immeasurably with our lives there, especially Suzanne McElligott, Selina Guinness, and Colin Graham.

Emory University is my home away from home and it also houses Heaney's amazing archive of correspondence. I am grateful to many friends and colleagues in the English department and the Stuart A. Rose Library, particularly Deepika Bahri, Pat Cahill, Rosemary Magee and Ron Schuchard. Thanks also to Rand Brandes, Heaney's bibliographer, for his advice and support. For the leave of absence granted to work at the NLI, I would like to thank Deans Michael Elliott and Carla Freeman.

Rob, Liadan and Conor – I am ever grateful to you three for sharing the road wherever it leads.

Abbreviations

Titles of books frequently referred to, especially volumes of poetry and the four collected volumes of prose essays. Unless otherwise stated, these abbreviations refer to the first editions published in London by Faber and Faber.

B	*Beowulf* (1999)
BT	*The Burial at Thebes* (2004)
CP	*Crediting Poetry* (1995)
CT	*The Cure at Troy* (1990)
DC	*District and Circle* (2006)
DD	*Door into the Dark* (1969)
DN	*Death of a Naturalist* (1966)
EL	*Electric Light* (2001)
FK	*Finders Keepers* (2002)
FW	*Field Work* (1979)
GT	*The Government of the Tongue* (1988)
HC	*Human Chain* (2010)
HL	*The Haw Lantern* (1987)
N	*North* (1975)
OG	*Opened Ground: Poems 1966–1996* (1998)
OL	*An Open Letter* (Derry: Field Day, 1983)
P	*Preoccupations* (1980)
RP	*The Redress of Poetry* (1995)
SA	*Sweeney Astray* (1984)
SI	*Station Island* (1984)
SL	*The Spirit Level* (1996)
ST	*Seeing Things* (1991)
WO	*Wintering Out* (1972)
SS	*Stepping Stones* (2008)

Introduction

Geraldine Higgins

In later life, the phrase 'born on a farm in County Derry in 1939' made Seamus Heaney roll his eyes. He had read it so often in the many thousands of 'Notes on Contributors' featuring his biography that it had become both overly familiar and unreal. In fact, the outline of Heaney's biography is so well known that it has become part of his poetic mythology – the gifted son of Bellaghy elevated to winner of the Nobel Prize for literature and international acclaim. From the outset, Heaney's work emerged from and merged into a complex set of historical and political contextual circumstances. The thirty-two original essays in this volume combine historicizing scholarship with critical depth and insightful new readings of Heaney's work.

Over the course of a career spanning fifty years, Heaney became one of the most celebrated poets writing in the English language and was also a distinguished essayist, playwright, translator, professor and literary critic. His publications include twelve volumes of original poetry (plus four Selected Poems), three volumes of prose (plus one Selected edition), two plays, two anthologies (edited with Ted Hughes), thirteen translations (including *Beowulf* and the posthumous *Aeneid Book VI*) and numerous limited editions and broadsides.[1]

Unusually, Heaney's poetry is both critically acclaimed and popular with the general reader, appearing on syllabi across the globe and translated into more than twenty-seven languages.[2] His work resonates with a wide readership outside of Ireland and has influenced poets around the world, from the United States (where he encountered and taught many prominent poets) to the Caribbean and Japan. During his lifetime, Heaney received many honours, culminating in the Nobel Prize for literature in 1995 'for works of lyrical beauty and ethical depth, which exalt everyday miracles and the living past'.[3] This citation acknowledges Heaney's position not just as a pre-eminent international poet but also as cultural conserver and conscience of his society.

In the poem 'Traditions', Heaney recalls the scene in Joyce's *Ulysses* in which Leopold Bloom is challenged about his nationality – 'What is your nation?' – and replies, 'Ireland. I was born here. Ireland' (*WO* 21). Heaney inhabited and wrote out of the real island of Ireland – an island that can be mapped as a topographical, historical, political and cultural entity. Yet the map that dominated Heaney's schoolroom showed only the six counties of Northern Ireland (*SS* 246), the site of a bloody thirty-year conflict (1968–98) known as 'the Troubles'. This conflict, variously defined as a civil war, a sectarian conflict or a hangover of British colonialism, underpins much of Heaney's life and work. In Heaney's prose he describes 'the lines of sectarian antagonism and affiliation [that] followed the boundaries of the land' (*P* 20). This 'realm of division' is inscribed by place names drawn from the Irish, Scottish and English languages, such as Anahorish, Broagh and Castledawson, that mark it as contested territory. For Heaney, this territory is deeply connected to his sense of history – both ancient and modern – and of language as a tool of excavation.

Heaney's experience as a Northern Irish writer from a nationalist, Catholic background informed his work from the beginning. In the 'mud grenades' of the threatening frogs in 'Death of a Naturalist'(*DN* 3–4), the pen 'snug as a gun' in 'Digging' (*DN* 1), and the constable's bicycle that 'ticked, ticked, ticked' in 'A Constable Calls' (*N* 67), it is possible to sense the undercurrents of violence that would erupt in the late 1960s. Yet Heaney resisted the public's urge to look to him as a spokesman during the Troubles. He wanted neither to be co-opted to defend republican violence nor to be part of what he called 'the good news brigade' endorsing the status quo of the Northern Irish polity. In 'Whatever You Say, Say Nothing' (*N* 50–3), he captures the ambivalence expressed by many of his fellow poets about commenting on 'the Irish thing'. Echoing W. B. Yeats's search for 'befitting emblems of adversity', a decisive turning point for Heaney came when, as he writes in 'Feeling into Words', the 'problems of poetry moved from being simply a matter of achieving the satisfactory verbal icon to being a search for images and symbols adequate to our predicament' (*P* 56). Although some critics ascribed to Heaney an unwavering stance of non-intervention on the subject of Northern Irish politics, he agonized over every incident and each political statement.

W. B. Yeats, the 'Everest' of Irish poetry, looms large in Heaney criticism, particularly after Robert Lowell's 1975 review of *North* anointing Heaney as 'the best Irish poet since W. B. Yeats'.[4] Heaney engaged extensively with Yeats as an 'exemplar' in lectures and essays as well as in his Nobel lecture, 'Crediting Poetry'. Since Heaney's death in August

2013, there have been many more comparisons made between Ireland's two Nobel prize-winning poets (including the fact that 1939 was the year of Yeats's death and Heaney's birth). Both poets wrestled with the responsibilities of the artist to the demands of violent conflict, both resisted the call of propaganda and both became spokesmen for a civic and cultural agenda in public life. But examining the differences in biography, history, poetics and politics in Yeats and Heaney underscores the importance of contextual criticism in understanding their work. Heaney is not a 'Catholic Yeats' repackaged for troubled times and a new generation of post-nationalist Irish readers. His work is most fruitfully read in the context of the personal, historical and political circumstances of its composition.

Heaney lived in a time of accelerated judgement and instant celebrity. Arguably, he faced greater scrutiny in his own lifetime than any other Irish writer. His reputation for generosity and affability fed a relentless appetite for public readings, media appearances, openings and lectures. As Bernard O'Donoghue points out in his comparison of Yeats and Heaney in *The Cambridge Companion to Seamus Heaney*, when Yeats won the Nobel Prize for literature in 1923, there was no critical study of his work in existence.[5] In contrast, since his 1966 debut *Death of a Naturalist*, Heaney's work has emerged into the full glare of critical attention and when he won the Nobel in 1995, there were countless monographs, articles, edited collections, interviews and reviews extant. Indeed, when the *Cambridge Companion to Seamus Heaney* was published in 2009, no other living poet had ever been the subject of such an appraisal. Attempts to sum up his achievement and legacy will soon mirror the industrial scale of critical evaluations of his work during his lifetime.

At the time of publication, there is as yet no official biography of Seamus Heaney,[6] although *Stepping Stones*, the linked interviews by the late Dennis O'Driscoll published in 2008, is as close as the poet came to writing an autobiography. Many of the essays in this collection include insights gleaned from *Stepping Stones*, but it is important to remember that these are Heaney's (written) reflections, composed in hindsight. In fact, Heaney guided perceptions and assessments of his own work not only in this invaluable collaboration with O'Driscoll but also in the many interviews given over the course of half a century of a writing life, almost all of it in the public eye.

Heaney's poem 'Exposure' highlights his own ambivalence about living in the public eye and perhaps hints at one of the tropes of Heaney criticism – that he was over-exposed. The title also suggests the revelation of hidden things while the poem itself explores the need for artistic camouflage, 'Taking protective colouring / from bole and bark, feeling / every wind that blows' (*N* 73). Heaney was of course much photographed and in the early part of his career was also a regular television presenter on BBC NI and later on RTÉ. Over the course of his life, he also sat for at least ten portraits. The first, Edward McGuire's 1974 portrait (now in the Ulster Museum), appeared on the back cover of *North* in 1975, breaking Faber and Faber's house style which Heaney reminds us 'had never featured author photographs or jacket art'. Of the artists who followed McGuire, Heaney said, they were confronted with an older face and 'a sitter more used to being inspected' (*SS* 329).

Seamus Heaney in Context occupies a unique moment in Heaney criticism. Appearing just over seven years since the poet's death, and eleven years after the *Cambridge Companion*, it considers the contexts of Heaney's work while his literary reputation is not finally settled. This is not to suggest that Heaney's reputation will fluctuate wildly; rather, it is to draw attention to the relationship between the works in print, the writer's archive and future publishing projects. The unpublished correspondence acquired by Emory University in 2003 and the vast literary archive donated by the Heaney family to the National Library of Ireland in 2011 will continue to change the landscape of Heaney criticism. *Seamus Heaney in Context* joins the critical conversation at what might be called Heaney's archival moment, a moment that contributes to the formation of the writer's afterlife in print. As his work enters its posthumous phase, new projects like a collected poems, prose and letters will inevitably shape our understanding of Heaney's place in the pantheon.[7] The essays published here offer intersecting themes and critical concerns in the current terrain of Heaney studies while suggesting new directions for reading Heaney's poetry in future contexts.

In seven overlapping sections, *Seamus Heaney in Context* establishes the historical, conceptual and literary criteria through which Heaney's work can be usefully understood. The first two sections, 'Mapping' and 'Influences and Traditions', develop Heaney's much-quoted line that he became a poet when his 'roots were crossed with his reading' (*P* 37). These essays map the places that featured most prominently in Heaney's imaginative landscape as well as the literary influences that shaped his development. Sections III and IV, 'Poetics' and 'Publishing', feature discussions of the poet's craft and the contexts of his literary production in print. Sections V and VI, 'Frameworks' and 'Critical Contexts', explore the intellectual frameworks and ideologies that informed his writing and reception. The final section, 'Legacy', examines the material traces of Heaney's legacy in public exhibitions, contemporary Irish poetry and the paper trail of the archive itself.

I Mapping

Mapping the world of Heaney's poetry involves real places, mythical timeframes and the spaces of the imagination. We move from Mossbawn to the 'man-killing parishes' of Jutland to the utopian 'Republic of Conscience'. Images of the real and the imagined Ireland permeate Heaney's work; one critic estimates that three quarters of his poems are set within a 10 mile radius of his birthplace. Heaney's places of writing, from Bellaghy to Belfast, and from Glanmore to Dublin, each mark a stepping stone in claiming his poetic territory. Since Ireland as a location and a theme has been covered so thoroughly in Heaney criticism, it is not treated as a discrete chapter here. Instead, the opening sequence of chapters situates Heaney's work in four other important geographical contexts. Heaney's description of his life as 'a series of ripples widening out from an original centre'[8] is reflected in essays that move beyond Ireland to Scotland and England before considering Eastern Europe and America.

Looking across the Irish Sea to Scotland, Patrick Crotty accounts for Heaney's intense linguistic engagement and personal empathy with Scottish writers. Apart from Heaney's admiration for Robert Burns, Robert Henryson and the anthologized Jacobite poems of his youth, Crotty explores his close ties to contemporary Scottish poets, especially Hugh MacDiarmid. In fact, shortly before his death, Heaney was working on a translation (and animation) from the Scots of Robert Henryson's *The Testament of Cresseid and Seven Fables*. Continuing south, John McAuliffe examines how England figures in Heaney's work and the continuing applicability of his 1976 essay 'Englands of the Mind' (*P* 150–69). McAuliffe discusses how Heaney's poems engage with English places and poets, as settings and exemplars for younger poets such as Simon Armitage and Alice Oswald. Moving outside the framework of Britain and Ireland, Margaret Greaves contextualizes Heaney's fascination with Eastern Europe in the intersecting political climates of the Cold War and the Troubles. She demonstrates how Heaney turns to Eastern European poets to sketch crucial differences between the 'Irish' lyric and the 'Anglo-American' lyric – a move that chimes with a broader Cold War-era tendency to justify lyric poetry in political terms. Finally, Sarah Bennett considers the profound effect of Heaney's academic sojourns in America – initially at Berkeley in California in 1970–1 and then for several decades as a distinguished visiting professor at Harvard. She shows that, despite the dearth of overt references to America in his poetry, Heaney's American experience is reflected in his assessment of American poetics together with his public statements and personal relationships.

II Influences and Traditions

'Influences and Traditions' challenges Richard Ellmann's famous assessment of influence that 'writers move upon other writers not as genial successors but as violent expropriators ... they do not borrow, they override'.[9] Harold Bloom later adds Freudian psychodrama to this model of misreading that informs his theory of the anxiety of influence.[10] The chapters that follow show Heaney less as a 'violent expropriator' than as an intertextual 'corroborator' with his precursors in the construction of his own literary pedigree and in his exploration of form.

In Heaney's essay 'Something to Write Home About', he talks about growing up 'in-between' not just the two traditions in Northern Ireland but also between the English and Irish literary traditions (*FK* 53). Heaney created his own lineage of ancestral poets offering sustaining models of form, rhythm and subject matter. This section is necessarily selective, and difficult editorial decisions had to be made. For example, Heaney's endorsements of Patrick Kavanagh's affirmatively parochial stance and Robert Frost's veneration of nature are well established and therefore not revisited here. I also excluded the influence of Heaney's friendships with contemporary poets such as Lowell, Hughes, Longley, Miłosz, Walcott and Muldoon (although many of these poets feature in other chapters). Instead, the essays examine Heaney's construction of his own heritable poetic tradition through a consideration of the poetics of Wordsworth, Hardy and Eliot as well as new assessments of Yeats and MacNeice.

Matthew Campbell begins by assessing Heaney's poetic chain of continuity with (mainly male) literary precursors through what he called a 'primal reach into the physical'. Focusing on Wordsworth as Heaney's indispensable figure of Romantic poetics, Campbell's chapter compares their gendered poetry of origin and selfhood. Ron Schuchard goes on to show how Thomas Hardy helped Heaney to define and redefine his own aesthetic of the ordinary world against the magical and religious traditions of Yeats and Eliot. Heaney's full engagement with the moderns was accompanied by what Schuchard calls 'regular retreats into his Hardy haven'. Stephen Regan looks at the ways in which Heaney learns from Eliot, including how he is alerted to his own complex relationship with tradition and later develops an acute appreciation of what Eliot memorably termed 'the auditory imagination'. In Margaret Mills Harper's consideration of Heaney and Yeats, she moves away from the idea of influence to one of poetic confluence, tracing the connections between two surprising poem pairings. She proposes that intertextuality moves in multiple directions so that we now encounter Heaney's Yeats as much as we consider Yeats as a precursor to the younger poet. Catriona Clutterbuck concludes this section with her close reading of Heaney's engagement with the poetry of Louis MacNeice, particularly in its renewal of the relationship between immutable reality and the alterity of dream life.

III Poetics

Heaney's mastery of the lyric form and his distinctive poetic style evolved from the narrow stanzas of the bog poems through the longer, agricultural rhythms of the 'Glanmore Sonnets' into 'a poetics of airy listening' in his later career. This section explores the stylistic innovations – the forms, sounds and shapes of Heaney's poetry – that have contributed so much to his wide critical readership. John Redmond reads the formal evolution of Heaney's poetry as a partial return to the kind of poet he was in his early career. Devoting most attention to the final two collections, *District and Circle* and *Human Chain*, Redmond argues that in returning to the 'weight' of his early work, Heaney is in search of a style that is 'universal and permanent'. Bernard O'Donoghue picks up his incisive discussion of Heaney's poetic language where his 1994 book, *The Language of Seamus Heaney*, left off, just after *Seeing Things*. Here he recognizes a shift in Heaney's use of linguistic terminology in the later work to show how the instinctive observation of objects and experiences underlies language: what he calls 'raids on the prearticulate'. Heaney's work as the master elegist informs Brendan Corcoran's piece on how the elegiac poems represent and comprehend the ways in which loss defines the contours of human life. Starting with Heaney's childhood intimacy with death, Corcoran considers how the ordering principle of 'grief and metre' allows Heaney's poetry to engage and challenge death's rupturing force. Discussing Heaney's deployment of music and its cognate terms – song, chorus, rhythm, note – Simon Kress explores how Heaney adopts the figure of music to reckon with what it means to be an Irish lyric poet. Vona Groarke throws down a trail of fairytale breadcrumbs in her piece on Heaney's nouns. From anvil to underground, from Conway Stewart to harvest bow, from skylight to tinsmith's scoop, she shows how these nouns in their respective poems resonate as a kind of linguistic and imagistic tuning fork in Heaney's work.

IV Publishing

Shortly after Karl Miller published three of Heaney's poems in the *New Statesman* in 1964, Heaney received a letter from the editor of Faber and Faber, Charles Monteith, inviting him to submit a manuscript. Heaney later said that it was 'like getting a letter from God the Father'. In *Stepping Stones*, Heaney describes the moment when he received his six free copies of *Death of a Naturalist* in 1966: 'The actual book looked very good: a lime-green and solid-pink dust jacket, and on the back a list of the Faber poets. Fabulous names: Auden, Eliot, Hughes, Larkin, Lowell, MacNeice, Spender' (*SS* 61). This section examines the literary and material publishing contexts of Heaney's work, beginning with Heather Clark's account of collaboration and competition in Heaney's earliest writing group: Philip Hobsbawn's loose confederation of poets known as the 'Belfast Group'. Nathan Suhr-Sytsma deepens our understanding of how Heaney's engagement with the publication of his own books in material form both expressed and furthered his faith in literature. Drawing extensively on archival material, Marilynn Richtarik's essay on Field Day takes us back into the 1980s with a renewed sense of how Brian Friel, Seamus Deane and Heaney conceived of Field Day's intervention in the Irish cultural landscape. Aidan O'Malley examines Heaney's theory and practice of translation across texts and languages, suggesting how Frost's notion of the 'sound of sense' lay both at the root of his poetry and his mode of 'impure translation'. As a result, translational fidelity, for Heaney, privileged the uncovering of echoes that might capture and recreate the sound of the original text.

V Frameworks

These chapters consider the wider social-historical frameworks that were often experienced simultaneously in Heaney's life and work. As such, the discussions here of Heaney's Catholicism, and his multiple roles as a teacher, broadcaster and translator, subtend the predominant context of the political situation in Northern Ireland from the Troubles to the peace process. Kieran Quinlan follows Heaney's progression from faithful and engaged Catholic to a more sceptical stance in the years following Vatican II. Reading *Station Island* (1984) as the key volume in which Heaney's disbelief is fully acknowledged, he nevertheless shows that Heaney remained steeped in the language, rituals and transcendental mysteries of Catholicism even when he was no longer a believer. Florence Impens examines Heaney's fifty-year engagement with classical texts, whether as adaptations or as intertextual allusions in his own poems. Ultimately, Impens argues that Heaney revisits Ireland as a classical and secular space reflecting political, social and cultural changes on the island. In an interview with Seamus Deane in 1977, Heaney described how the poems in *North* 'arose out of a necessity to shape and give palpable linguistic form' to the 'urgency' he felt regarding Northern Ireland's political complexity in the mid-1970s.[11] Jonathan Allison explores Heaney's alert awareness of sectarianism and the different kinds of political poems that form his aesthetic response to thirty years of the Troubles. A professional teacher before he was a professional poet, Heaney was acutely conscious of different kinds of learning. Rosie Lavan's essay considers the interaction between Heaney's roles as broadcaster and as educator as well as his enduring commitment to the 'advancement of learning'. Finally, Richard Rankin Russell evaluates Heaney's interest in both war and peace in poems that address the two world wars as well as the conflict in Northern Ireland. He concludes with the Heaney of reconciliation in the elegiac and affirmative poems of his last volume, *Human Chain*.

VI Critical Contexts

Turning to the critical reception of Heaney's work in several key areas, this section begins with Laura O'Connor's contextualization of Heaney's gendered poetry and feminist responses to it. O'Connor places Heaney in the Irish patrilineal canon and then examines the *aisling* (dream-vision poem) as a flashpoint both for the critical controversy surrounding *North* (1975) and for the ensuing feminist critique of patriarchal poetry and of gendered nationalist iconography. Kevin Whelan's essay complicates readings of Heaney's poetry that divide it into two phases of bog and body and later, air and spirit. He examines a third phase of late Heaney poems that no longer treat body or spirit as a binary but explore the catalytic relationship between them. Justin Quinn draws attention to the dynamic of Heaney's different constituencies (Irish, British and American), and the ways in which these critical audiences affected his work. Quinn also considers how the Cold War conditioned the postcolonial reading of Heaney's poems, especially in the United States. Expanding the context of contemporary theories of postcolonialism, Deepika Bahri's essay situates Heaney's work in theories of transnational poetics ranging from the border to the broader world of global politics. Finally, Nicholas Allen argues for a reconsideration of water and liquidity in Heaney's work as a counterbalance to the familiar trope of earthiness. Reading a series of texts across the breadth of his career, Allen engages Heaney's work with critical conversations in archipelagic literature.

VII Legacy

This section traces Heaney's impact as a 'smiling public man' in Ireland's cultural life and begins to consider his legacy. Fintan O'Toole opens this discussion by remembering Heaney in the National Museum of Ireland in 2013, speaking as a public figure who wished 'not to be part of "Irish heritage", not to be "inherited" as an asset but to be "handed down" with the sensation of human contact'. In a close reading of an early poem, 'The Last Mummer', O'Toole examines the tension in Heaney's work between the public need for a response to the political crisis and the private need to be true to his poetic impulse. In showing the importance of Heaney's archive to new interpretations of his work, Rand Brandes follows the paper trail of the archives from the prenatal attic to the postmortem reading room and into the afterlife of textual studies. Geraldine Higgins draws on the experience of curating two exhibitions on Heaney to chart the transition from the private space of the writer's room to the public place of the exhibition while probing the relationship between texts, contexts and objects in Heaney's work. The final essay in the volume, by Chris Morash, considers Heaney's legacy as a poet and global public figure. Moving from the outpouring of grief in newspapers and elegies written by his poet-peers, Morash discusses 'Clearances 3', better known as 'When all the others were away at Mass', voted in 2015 Ireland's favourite poem of the past one hundred years.

The central questions of *Seamus Heaney in Context* are Heaney's own, raised in his first volume of prose, *Preoccupations* (1980): 'How should a poet properly live and write? What is his relationship to be to his own voice, his own place, his literary heritage and his contemporary world?' (*P* 13). Heaney spent his writing life wrestling with these questions, but as the essays here demonstrate, the answers are flexible rather than fixed. The manifold contexts of Heaney's 'life and times' enrich our understanding of the poetry and ultimately, it is as poet or *file* that he asks to be judged. In the title essay of *The Government of the Tongue*, Heaney sets out the terms by which poetry itself must be measured:

> The fact is that poetry is its own reality and no matter how much a poet may concede to the corrective pressures of social, moral, political and historical reality, the ultimate fidelity must be to the demands and promise of the artistic event . . . In one sense the efficacy of poetry is nil – no lyric has ever stopped a tank. In another sense, it is unlimited. It is like writing in the sand in the face of which accusers and accused are left speechless and renewed. (*GT* 107)

Notes

1 Rand Brandes and Michael J. Durkan, *Seamus Heaney: A Bibliography 1959–2003* (London: Faber and Faber, 2008.) Brandes and Durkan list over 2,000 items in this bibliography (Brandes is currently updating this edition). See also Rand Brandes, 'Secondary Sources: A Gloss on the Critical Reception of Seamus Heaney 1965–1993', *Colby Quarterly*, 30/1 (March 1994), 63–77.

2 See the website of the Seamus Heaney estate: www.seamusheaney.com.

3 Swedish Academy, 'The Nobel Prize in Literature 1995', press release, 5 October 1995.

4 Robert Lowell, 'Books of the Year', *Observer*, 14 December 1975, p. 19.

5 Bernard O'Donoghue (ed.), *The Cambridge Companion to Seamus Heaney* (Cambridge University Press, 2009).

6 In November 2017, the *Irish Times* announced that Faber and Faber had appointed Fintan O'Toole to write Heaney's official biography.

7 Forthcoming publications include *Selected Letters*, ed. Christopher Reid; an official biography by Fintan O'Toole; and a *Collected Poems*, ed. Bernard O'Donoghue and Rosie Lavan. Also of note is the BBC2 Arena Documentary, *Seamus Heaney and the Music of What Happens*, dir. Adam Low (2019).

8 Seamus Heaney, 'The Art of Poetry No. 75', interviewed by Henri Cole in May 1994, *Paris Review*, 144 (Fall 1997), www.theparisreview.org/interviews/1217/the-art-of-poetry-no-75-seamus-heaney.

9 Richard Ellmann, *Eminent Domain: Yeats among Wilde, Joyce, Pound, Eliot, and Auden* (Oxford University Press, 1967), p. 3. For further discussion of 'influence', see Neil Corcoran, 'Question Me Again: Reflections on W. B. Yeats and Seamus Heaney', *Yeats Annual*, 18 (2013), 215–38.

10 Harold Bloom, *The Anxiety of Influence: A Theory of Poetry* (Oxford University Press, 1973), p. 153.

11 Seamus Deane, 'Unhappy and at Home: Interview with Seamus Heaney', *Crane Bag*, 1/1 (Spring 1977), 61–7.

1

Mapping

CHAPTER 1

Scotland

Patrick Crotty

Seamus Heaney was exceptional among Irish intellectuals in his awareness of Scotland and his sponsorship of Scottish literature. As poet, critic, translator and editor he celebrated Scottish poetry, in its three main languages, over more or less the entire span of his career. Towards the end of his life he wrote of the 'hidden Scotland at the back of [his] ear'. That adaptation of the title of Daniel Corkery's celebrated study of the poetry of Gaelic Munster, *The Hidden Ireland* (1924), occurs both in *Stepping Stones* (365) and in the introduction to *The Testament of Cresseid and Seven Fables*, a book that presents Heaney's versions of poems by the fifteenth-century 'makar' Robert Henryson side by side with the originals. It might have been expected that he would figure the affinity between himself and his Scottish forerunner as a matter of the instinct for ordinary life and evocative rendering of homely detail that characterise both their oeuvres; in the event he appears to have thought of it primarily in linguistic terms, as a function of a shared acoustic inheritance:

> I enjoyed the work because Henryson's language led me back into what might be called 'the hidden Scotland' at the back of my own ear. The speech I grew up with in mid-Ulster carried more than a trace of Scottish vocabulary and as a youngster I was familiar with Ulster Scots idioms and pronunciations across the River Bann in County Antrim. I was therefore entirely at home with Henryson's 'sound of sense', so much in tune with his note and his pace and his pitch that I developed a strong inclination to hum along with him.[1]

Heaney's hummings along with a small chorus of predecessors and older contemporaries from Scotland provide the focus of this essay. As the range and subtlety of his responses to their work can be fully appreciated only when set against the reactions of other Irish writers to Scottish language and literature, it will be necessary to begin by sketching some of the most prominent among these. Heaney's fellow Ulsterman, co-religionist and

'Station Island' alter ego William Carleton was born to Irish-speaking parents in the Clogher Valley in 1794. Attempting to represent the speech of the rural poor in *Traits and Stories of the Irish Peasantry*, he forged a would-be universal Hiberno-English that gave unsuspecting readers to believe that Irish country people spoke in the same way all over the island, with no variation between the tonalities of Tipperary and Tyrone. To achieve this national standard, Carleton had to exclude from his dialogue the Scots elements prominent in the English of his native region. He was proud to do so, boasting in the preface to the first (1830) edition of *Traits and Stories* that he had 'studiously avoided ... that intolerable Scoto-Hibernic jargon which pierces the ear so unmercifully'.[2] Heaney's ear, fortunately, was made of sterner – or more hospitable – stuff.

Scots was brought to Ireland by Presbyterian Lowlanders who came to Ulster in two great waves, in the Plantation at the beginning of the seventeenth century and in a more spontaneous influx eight decades later. The expropriation of Gaelic Catholics effected by the Plantation, along with the bloody anti-Planter uprising of 1641, made relations between speakers of Irish and Scots problematic in a way that is reflected in the continuing sectarian divisions of Northern Ireland. Language is ultimately no respecter of religious, ethnic or political boundaries, however, and the English now native to communities on both sides of the Reformation fault line in the nine counties of Ulster and in adjoining regions of Connaught and Leinster retains significant elements of Scots. Though they diminish in frequency as they radiate west and south from Antrim, vestiges of Lowland lexis and idiom can be found all over the northern third or so of Ireland, and feature more strongly in literature than is generally acknowledged. The recourse of Shawn Keogh and Michael James Flaherty in J.M. Synge's *The Playboy of the Western World* to the Scots verb 'liefer' (for *rather*, *prefer to*) is entirely credible, given the play's Mayo setting (though whether a Munster native such as Christy Mahon would protest 'I'm a pot-boy in this place, and it's here I'd liefer stay'[3] must be considered doubtful). The literature of the Revival boasts one pre-eminent, if stubbornly unrecognised, instance of Scots vocabulary, a quotidian common noun disguised by dubious orthography. The *Scottish National Dictionary* offers five spellings for *pirn*, the term for the spool a weaver uses to hold his weft yarn in the shuttle. That notoriously poor speller W. B. Yeats managed to come up not just with a sixth but a seventh way of representing it. The word first appears in his work as a noun, with more or less its customary meaning, in 'Shepherd and Goatherd', one of the poems added to the British and American edition of *The Wild Swans at Coole* (1919), where it is spelled P-E-R-N.

By 1921, in the *Michael Robartes and the Dancer* poem 'Demon and Beast', it has become a verb, given in present participle form: 'Now gyring here and perning there'. The verb famously recurs in the imperative – 'Come from the holy fire, perne in a gyre' – in the opening poem of *The Tower* (1928), where it has acquired a second 'e' and travelled all the way from Scotland to Byzantium. A note in the *Wild Swans* volume reproduced in his 1933 *Collected Poems* suggests that Yeats saw *pern* as an item of dialect peculiar to Sligo, and was ignorant of its Scottish provenance.[4]

Yeats was to some degree suspicious of Scotland. A passage from *The Celtic Twilight* (1893) intimates that his suspicion may have been connected to a variety of sectarian feeling rarely spoken of but persistent in Irish literary history from Swift to Beckett – distaste towards northern Presbyterians on the part of southerners of Church of Ireland background: 'In Scotland you are too theological, too gloomy . . . You have burnt all the witches. In Ireland we have left them alone. To be sure, the "loyal minority" knocked out the eye of one with a cabbage stump on the 31st of March 1711, in the town of Carrickfergus. But then the "loyal minority" is half Scottish.'[5] 'A Remonstrance with Scotsmen for Having Soured the Disposition of their Ghosts and Faeries' was originally published in Edinburgh on 2 March 1889 in W.E. Henley's *Scots Observer*, under the tactfully anodyne title 'Scots and Irish Fairies'.[6] There was nothing anodyne about Yeats's attacks on his Rhymers' Club rival John Davidson (1858–1909), whom he accused of 'Scots jealousy' and 'Scottish roughness and exasperation'.[7] One might be forgiven for concluding that W. B. harboured an inclination to remonstrate with Scotsmen over the mere fact of their being Scotsmen.

Curiously perhaps, the only major Irish writer to exhibit as deep an interest in Scottish culture as Heaney's shared the latter's Catholic, though not his northern background. Glasgow was the first place outside Ireland James Joyce visited, at the age of twelve in 1894, and the city hovers as a locus of ambiguous opulence – residence of the soak Freddy Malins's sister and mother – in the background of his early masterpiece, 'The Dead'. Scotland is hailed as a sibling of Ireland in the satirical poem 'Gas from a Burner' (1912), albeit a sibling in treachery: 'Poor sister Scotland! Her doom is fell; / She cannot find any more Stuarts to sell.'[8] Joyce was so beguiled by the fact that his mother's maiden name – Murray – was one of the surnames regarded as indigenous to both countries that he had himself photographed in 1930 sporting a tie made of Murray tartan. By that stage of his career Scottish references were being systematically woven into the fabric of his prose. Scots is one of the languages drawn upon for the multilingual puns of *Finnegans Wake*, a book that repeatedly cites Macpherson's *Ossian*, Hogg's *Private Memoirs and Confessions of a Justified Sinner*, Stevenson's *Strange Case of Dr Jekyll and Mr Hyde* and the poetry of Burns.[9] These works are used both to add intertextual enrichment to the depiction of the antagonistic mutual dependence of Shem and Shaun, and to highlight the to-and-fro nature of population movements between Ireland and Scotland, with the inward drive represented by the Ulster Plantation figured as a counterpart to the outward thrust embodied in the settlement of Antrim Gaels in Argyll twelve centuries earlier. The novel's introduction to the character of Shem the Penman includes an apparent allusion to an immediately contemporary Scottish opus, MacDiarmid's *A Drunk Man Looks at the Thistle* (1926). If Joyce does indeed nod to the future author of *In Memoriam James Joyce* (1955), he evokes him by his C.M. Grieve patronym rather than his MacDiarmid nom de guerre: 'when playing with thistlewords in their garden nursery, Griefotrofio . . .'[10]

Between Joyce's time and our own, such attention to Scottish matters as has featured in Irish writing has been found mainly in the work of northerners. Louis MacNeice's *I Crossed the Minch* (1938), a bemused account of a two-part 1937 tour of the Hebrides, is remembered today chiefly for its rambunctious interpolated lyric 'Bagpipe Music', a poem in which the clubbable middlebrow in MacNeice all too predictably trumps the empathetic observer, with the result that what might have been an illuminating portrait of a marginalized culture ends up as a snigger of metropolitan disdain. The New York born, Tyrone-raised John Montague published verse and prose on MacDiarmid, and oversaw the spoken word series at Claddagh Records that includes albums by that writer as well as by Sorley MacLean, Norman MacCaig, Sydney Goodsir Smith, Hamish Henderson and George Mackay Brown.[11] Michael Longley's poems about Scottish archipelagos – the Western Isles ('The Hebrides', from *No Continuing City*, 1969), Orkneys ('Skara Brae' and 'Ghost Town', from *An Exploded View*, 1973) and Shetlands ('On the Shetlands', 'Whalsay' and 'Shetland Mouse-ear', from *A Hundred Doors*, 2011) – marry ecological attentiveness to an acute sense of the transience of the civilizations associated with those remote locations. The most resolute mining of the Scots seam in Hiberno-English by a serious poet, meanwhile, has been undertaken by Tom Paulin, particularly in his 1983 collection *Liberty Tree*.

Heaney differs from these northern predecessors and contemporaries in the scale and range of his engagement with Scottish materials. If he thought of his kinship with Henryson in terms of intimacy with how the makar's words sounded, the roots of many of his other Caledonian interests may likewise be traced to a primal fascination with language. The etymological cast of his imagination – a trait he shared with Joyce – meant that his sense of history was rarely separable from his sense of linguistic history. Of the half dozen or so poems about language in *Wintering Out* (1972), two – 'Traditions' and 'Broagh' – explore the implications of the encounter between English, Scots and Irish in the poet's native locality. Most unusually, and in a way that directly challenges unionist and nationalist identity narratives, 'Broagh' apprehends Northern Ireland's mixed linguistic inheritance as a matter of richness rather than division. Heaney's sense of the wealth of South Derry verbal resource facilitates the political optimism – as obstinate as it is clear-eyed and tentative – adumbrated in that tiny but explosive lyric constructed out of Irish, English and Scots elements of diction. Much of his subsequent achievement as translator, editor and critic can be understood as a working out of his debt to each of the three languages that meet on the canopied pad leading down to the ford.

The poet's 1999 translation of *Beowulf* raises fascinating questions about cultural politics and about the tripartite linguistic inheritance invoked in 'Broagh' and revisited in explicitly autobiographical terms in the introduction to his rendition of the Anglo-Saxon epic. Heaney was fond of joking that if the Field Day Theatre Company had been serious about its anti-colonial enterprise it would have produced *The Field Day Anthology* of *English* rather than of *Irish* writing, and there is doubtless a mischievous, subaltern aspect to his undertaking a Hiberno-English version of the poem that has come – however questionably – to be seen as the foundational text of the literature of England. The translation exhibits more sonic heft and a surer sense of voice than the one by the (Scottish, coincidentally) poet Edwin Morgan it was commissioned to replace in *The Norton Anthology of Poetry*. Its power derives from Heaney's playing a ghost of the original's alliterative metre off against a mode of speech that is convincingly localised and colloquial, if weighted slightly towards formality. Instances of Scots-derived vocabulary in the translation are in fact rare,[12] though when they occur they do indeed exhibit the particular 'body and force' claimed for them in the introduction (*B* xxx).

Seamus Heaney's rapid ascent to canonicity and his pre-eminence in what one might be tempted to call the NATO Alliance of modern and contemporary poetry – a decisively Anglo-American formation that can deal with only one Irish writer at a time (Yeats, Heaney) and that relegates from consideration Scotland, Wales and the English regions along with many of the art's other socio-geographical constituencies – have been the subject of sometimes disgruntled speculation. What has perhaps been insufficiently recognized is the extent to which he used his position within that formation to challenge institutional complacencies and act as advocate for poets and varieties of poetry overlooked at the canon-building centres of power. Thus the pantheon erected in his lectures as Oxford Professor of Poetry includes the eighteenth-century Gaelic libertarian Brian Merriman and the Scots republican separatist MacDiarmid, than whom a less establishmentarian or Oxbridge-friendly pair of writers can scarcely be imagined. (The fact that their work embodies unexpected late flowerings of the two lesser-used languages of 'Broagh' should be noted.) A woodkernish undermining of customary attitudes and demarcations similarly infuses the comparison between 'To a Mouse' and 'An Bonnán Buí' ('The Yellow Bittern') in Heaney's lecture commemorating the bicentenary of the death of Robert Burns.[13] No one familiar with the codes of Ulster community relations will miss the egalitarian insistence behind his linking the impoverished Catholic Cathal Buí Mac Giolla Ghunna (1680–1756) to the Presbyterian and in some respects brashly masonic Burns.

If the slightly oppositional element there works against rather than for the cited Scottish figure, that is because the status of Burns is assured. The lyric achievement of the Bard's twentieth-century compatriots, conversely, has gone more or less unnoticed in the world furth of Scotland, so it should come as no surprise to find Heaney subverting conventional associations to memorialize some of the foremost among them. The Oxford-visiting speaker of '"Would They Had Stay'd"' (*EL* 68) is in the poem's first two sections startled in turn by the sudden appearance of the resident herd of fallow deer at Magdalen College and by their reminding him of Norman MacCaig, the mere thought of whom seems out of place in that most English of settings. Iain Crichton Smith, Sorley MacLean and George Mackay Brown, three other Scottish poets who died in the second half of the 1990s, are saluted in the sections that follow, each evoked through an adaptation of the deer motif to figuration characteristic of his poems. Heaney works his key reversal of expectation through playing with the associations of his Shakespearean title, which quotes the protagonist's dismayed response to the abrupt vanishing of the three weird sisters in *Macbeth* (1.3.83). Not only does the poet view his Scottish topic from an English location and through the prism of an English text popularly if misleadingly known as 'the Scottish play', he implicitly likens his speaker to the murderous protagonist and his quartet of mourned poets to the trio of 'secret, black, and midnight hags' (4.1.48) who are among Shakespeare's most terrifyingly repulsive creations.[14] The unsettling juxtapositions expedite the poem's sense of shocked sorrow that MacCaig, MacLean, Crichton Smith and Mackay Brown have melted, as Macbeth says of the weird sisters (in the first half of the line the second half of which supplies the title) 'As breath into the wind', along with its expression of wonder at the miracle of their having been 'inhabitants o'th' earth' (1.3.44) in the first instance, and of gratitude for the poet's having known them.

Heaney's acquaintance with MacCaig and MacLean spanned more than three decades, and he paid tribute to them in various ways in his work. A perceptive and amusing preface written for a 1995 Italian edition of the poems of the former is reprinted in *Finders Keepers*. Four somewhat overlapping articles on the latter published between 1986 and 1996 remain uncollected, as does the text of the first Sorley MacLean Memorial Lecture, delivered at the Edinburgh Festival in 2002.[15] That same year saw the appearance as a limited edition pamphlet of the most famous of MacLean's later poems, 'Hallaig', with a new facing-page translation by Heaney.[16] The translator's excellent command of Scottish Gaelic's sister language, Irish, about which he was characteristically modest, equipped him to identify key assonances and verbal chimes in MacLean's text, if not necessarily to comprehend its furthest subtleties of implication. While making no attempt to replicate the intricate though irregular rhyming of the original, Heaney deploys a series of understated rhymes to recreate its ballad-like movement. MacLean's own English rendering, though scrupulously attentive to the literal sense of the Gaelic, is by contrast stiff and declamatory.[17] Heaney's loose-limbed stanzas restore the eerie, spectral quality of a poem that envisages the cleared Raasay village of the title simultaneously in an abandoned and populated state:

> Between The Leac and Fearns
> The road is plush with moss
> And the girls in a noiseless procession
> Going to Clachan as always
>
> And coming back from Clachan
> And Suisnish, their land of the living,
> Still lightsome and unheartbroken,
> Their stories only beginning.

'Unheartbroken' constitutes a notable instance in the series of negative adjectives (epithets with the prefix *un-*) that, as Neil Corcoran has pointed out, occur at key moments in Heaney's career.[18]

The MacCaig preface recounts how enthralled the author was to be introduced in 1973 to the late Gavin Muir, son of the Orcadian poet

Edwin Muir. As I have noted elsewhere, Heaney's early collections share with Muir's verse and autobiographical prose a concern with the transition 'from a childhood world of immemorial custom to a chastened state of knowledge identified with modernity, sexuality and an awareness of time'.[19] Muir's poems have not worn well, as a consequence perhaps of their unadventurous rhythms and somewhat heraldic figuration. Their fall from the high status they enjoyed at the time of their author's death in 1959 may account for the fact that Heaney's 1988 commemorative lecture is to a greater extent than most of his critical forays a work of advocacy: the inclusion of an edited version of it in *Finders Keepers* is a further earnest of his loyalty to a writer whose leading editor and interpreter was P.H. Butter, professor and head of the English department at Queen's University during Heaney's undergraduate years.[20]

The ease of the poet's intimacy with Scottish literature is illustrated by his decision to cast his most discursive poem, the still uncollected Field Day pamphlet *An Open Letter* (1983), in Standard Habbie (the so-called 'Burns stanza'). By couching its repudiation of Britishness in the most distinctively Scottish of all stanza forms, 'An Open Letter' ironizes essentialist identity politics even as it asserts the author's Irishness. 'In the Attic' (*HC* 83), which may come to be seen as Heaney's last major lyric, reaches with comparable naturalness to Robert Louis Stevenson's *Treasure Island* to set up its meditation on the nominal aphasia that presages old age. (Stevenson's famous adventure story, admittedly, for all its gestation in the Highland village of Braemar on the author's return to his homeland to be reconciled to his family after his marriage in the United States, is among the least obviously Scottish of his novels.)

The most pervasive and deeply inter-stitched Caledonian presence in Heaney's work is undoubtedly that of Hugh MacDiarmid. The poet suggested that the sense of linguistic affinity that attracted him to the older writer was less with the literary Scots to which MacDiarmid committed the best of his notoriously uneven output than with the demotic Scots he used in unguarded moments: 'I loved the fact that I was talking to a great poet who spoke what they'd call in Ulster Scots 'the hamely tongue'. There he was beside the hob smoking his pipe and saying 'aye, aye, aye' to himself, for all the world like one of my father's cousins in Ballyscullion' (*SS* 364). The number of readers who consider MacDiarmid a great rather than merely a major poet may be small but it is almost exactly coterminous with the number who have closely attended to his Scots verse. Though Heaney had joined their ranks by the closing decades of his life, a chronological survey of his published comments indicates that he had to overcome significant inner resistance on his way to doing so. The short, slightly tentative 1972 *Hibernia* review of *The Hugh MacDiarmid Anthology* collected in *Preoccupations* was followed by the still cautious 1980 interview belatedly printed in Nancy K. Gish's *MacDiarmid: Man and Poet* (1992).[21] The lyric memoir 'An Invocation' (*SL* 27), which marked the 11 August 1992 centenary of MacDiarmid's birth in both the *London Review of Books* and the *Guardian*, is notably warmer than these and includes an admission that the young Heaney had underestimated the Scot's 'far-out, blathering genius'. The Oxford lecture 'A Torchlight Procession of One' attempts a full-scale revaluation, balancing the prodigious linguistic and imaginative resourcefulness of the Scots poetry of the 1920s and early 1930s – and particularly of *A Drunk Man* – against the 'megalomaniac fantasy' (*RP* 118) of a later output that 'gave [MacDiarmid's] detractors plenty to work with' (*RP* 120). The lecture ends with what may be seen as a rare critical misstep when it identifies an underlying Christianity in the post-Christian (and indeed post-humanist) materialism of the verse of the middle and later 1930s. It is as if the terrifyingly unconsoled vision of 'On a Raised Beach' and related utterances was so at odds with Heaney's aesthetic of resolution that he hesitated to recognize it for what it was. His commitment to the earlier work, however, was by that stage deep-rooted and even evangelical. He wanted to include a long, continuous extract from *A Drunk Man* in *The School Bag* (1997) but was overruled by his co-editor Ted Hughes, to whose royalist instincts MacDiarmid's republican enthusiasms were anathema. 'The Shining Streams',[22] delivered as a lecture in MacDiarmid's home town of Langholm on 17 August 2002, maintains a celebratory tone by restricting its comments mainly to the Scots work. Heaney devotes considerable space in *Stepping Stones* (362–5) to tracing the evolution of his attitude to MacDiarmid, and cites him twice in the introduction to the 2009 Henryson book (xi–xii, xvi).

Heaney's growing regard for MacDiarmid is reflected in his creative work. Surprisingly perhaps, it is not the Scots poems from the mid-1920s or the lyric resurgence of 1931 and 1932 – those areas of the achievement where 'A Torchlight Procession of One' locates its characteristic excellence – that are drawn upon but rather the rag-bag English and Scots volume *Stony Limits and Other Poems* (1934). One of two striking instances of Heaney–MacDiarmid intertextuality is a direct quotation. A suite of ten numbered 'Shetland Lyrics' featured among the bounty brought back by the Scottish poet from a week-long and legendarily sleepless working trip round the Shetlands aboard the sailing drifter the *Research* in May 1933. The first poem in the suite, 'With the Herring Fishers', includes the following stanzas:

O it's ane o' the bonniest sichts in the warld
To watch the herrin' come walkin' on board
In the wee sma''oors o' a simmer's mornin'
As if o' their ain accord.

For this is the way that God sees life,
The hail jing-bang o's appearin'
Up owre frae the edge o' naethingness
– It's his happy cries I'm hearin'.[23]

'The Turnip-Snedder', the opening lyric of *District and Circle* (2006), quotes simultaneously the farm machine of the title and MacDiarmid's poem in the following, appropriately Scots-inflected lines:

'This is the way that God sees life,'
it said, 'from seedling-braird to snedder'

as the handle turned
and turnip-heads were let fall and fed

to the juiced-up inner blades . . .

The allusion to the Shetland fishery scene here, along with the transfer from sea to land of the depiction of ultimately violent processes of food production, adds depth of field to Heaney's poem, while enhancing its sense that the life God sees is the same life everywhere. There is no question of the MacDiarmid echo being an unconscious one, given that the relevant stanza of 'With the Herring Fishers' is singled out for praise in 'The Shining Streams', where we are told that 'jing-bang' featured in the vocabulary of Heaney's mother.[24] The relationship between the two lyrics, nevertheless, might be said to be incidental rather than essential. The poet's other citation of MacDiarmid is by contrast crucial to the meaning of one of his most ambitious poems, 'Keeping Going' (*SL* 10). The opening salute to Heaney's brother Hugh comically measures itself against one of the oddest passages in the Scottish poet's work, the closing verse paragraph of the six-hundred-line 'Lament for the Great Music', where MacDiarmid combines a sort of vatic grandeur with an over-the-top and uncharacteristic romanticism that cannot be said to avoid sentimentality. 'Keeping Going' is a tale of two Hughs, Hugh MacDiarmid and Hugh Heaney, the former representing high-falutin' overstrain, the latter the down-to-earth virtues of good humour and resilience. The necessary context of the Irish poet's genial childhood reminiscence –

The piper coming from far away is you
With a whitewash brush for a sporran
Wobbling round you, a kitchen chair
Upside down on your shoulder, your right arm
Pretending to tuck the bag beneath your elbow,
Your pop-eyes and big cheeks nearly bursting
With laughter, but keeping the drone going on
Interminably, between catches of breath

– is provided by his Scottish predecessor's climactic address to the seventeenth-century MacCrimmons, hereditary pipers to Macleod of Macleod of Skye:

I dare not leap to you now . . .

******

My duty done, I will try to follow you on the last day of the world,
And pray I may see you all standing shoulder to shoulder
With Patrick Mor MacCrimmon and Duncan Ban MacCrimmon
in the centre
In the hollow at Boreraig or in front of Dunvegan Castle
Or on the lip of the broken graves in Kilmuir Kirkyard,
While, the living stricken ghastly in the eternal light
And the rest of the dead all risen blue-faced from their graves
(Though, the pipes to your hand, you will be once more
Perfectly at ease, and as you were in your prime)
All ever born crowd the islands and the West Coast of Scotland
Which has standing room for them all, and the air curdled with angels . . .

. . .

And you playing: 'Farewell to Scotland, and the rest of the Earth,'
The only fit music there can be for that day
– And I will leap then and hide behind one of you,
A's caismeachd phìob-mòra bras-shròiceadh am puirt.
Look! Is that only the setting sun again?
Or a piper coming from far away?[25]

Notes

1 Seamus Heaney, 'Introduction', in Robert Henryson, *The Testament of Cresseid and Seven Fables,* trans. Seamus Heaney (London: Faber and Faber, 2009), pp. xiii–xiv.
2 William Carleton, *Traits and Stories of the Irish Peasantry*, 2 vols. (Dublin: William Curry, 1830), Preface, vol. 1, p. xi.

3 J. M. Synge, *The Playboy of the Western World*, in *Collected Works IV: Plays, Book 2*, ed. Ann Saddlemyer (Gerrards Cross: Colin Smythe, 1982), p. 91. For use of the verb by Shawn Keogh and Michael James, see pp. 155 and 157.

4 The note is reprinted in W. B. Yeats, *Yeats's Poems*, 3rd edn, ed. A. Norman Jeffares (Basingstoke: Macmillan, 1996), p. 756.

5 W. B. Yeats, *Mythologies* (London: Macmillan, 1959), p. 107.

6 See W. B. Yeats, *Writings on Irish Folklore, Legend and Myth*, ed. Robert Welch (London: Penguin, 1993), p. 399.

7 W. B. Yeats, *Autobiographies* (London: Macmillan, 1955), pp. 316, 168.

8 James Joyce, *Poems and Shorter Writings*, ed. Richard Ellmann, A. Walton Litz and John Whittier-Ferguson (London: Faber and Faber, 1991), p. 105. The poem is put in the mouth of George Roberts, the Ulster Presbyterian manager of Maunsel & Co., the Dublin publishers who after much prevarication refused to issue *Dubliners* in the text submitted by Joyce; consequently it is arguable that in the quoted couplet Scotland is seen as Ireland's sibling from an Ulster Scots rather than an authorial perspective.

9 See Richard Barlow, *The Celtic Unconscious: Joyce and Scottish Culture* (Notre Dame, IN: University of Notre Dame Press, 2017).

10 James Joyce, *Finnegans Wake*, 3rd edn (London: Faber and Faber, 1964), p. 169. In conversation with the present writer in March 1976 MacDiarmid claimed that the novelist and publisher Robert McAlmon (1895–1956), chiefly remembered for *Being Geniuses Together* (1938), told him that during the course of a visit to London he had purchased a copy of *A Drunk Man Looks at the Thistle* to bring back to Paris as a gift for Joyce, who 'greatly enjoyed' the book.

11 See 'Scotia: i.m. Hugh MacDiarmid', in John Montague, *Mount Eagle* (Oldcastle: Gallery, 1988), p. 60, a poem which also memorializes MacCaig and MacLean, both still living at the time of publication. 'Scotia' appears neither in Montague's *Collected Poems* (Oldcastle: Gallery, 1995) nor *New Collected Poems* (Oldcastle: Gallery, 2012), though it is reprinted in a slightly longer version in his *The Figure in the Cave and Other Essays*, ed. Antoinette Quinn (Dublin: Lilliput, 1989), p. 162, where it is appended to the 1967 essay 'Hugh MacDiarmid: The Seamless Garment and the Muse'.

12 There are seven in all – *thole*, *graith*, *hirpling*, *wean*, *reek*, *howe*, *hoked*.

13 See 'Burns's Art Speech', *FK* 353–5.

14 An early version of 'Would They Had Stay'd', privately published as a Christmas card in 1997, matched the number of poets to the number of witches. The ten lines on Iain Crichton Smith were inserted as the central section after the death of that author on 15 October 1998. Their quotation from *Macbeth* makes the informing conceit of the poem explicit and identifies the provenance of a title that might otherwise have left readers baffled.

15 See Seamus Heaney, 'Introduction', in Raymond J. Ross and Joy Hendry (eds.), *Sorley MacLean: Critical Essays* (Edinburgh: Scottish Academic Press, 1986), pp. 1–7; 'Seamus Heaney Praises the Scottish Poet Sorley MacLean', *London Review of Books*, 8/19 (6 November 1986), 6–7; 'The Voice of a Bard',

Antaeus, 60 (1988), 297–306; and '"He saved Gaelic poetry in this century, before he saved it for all time": A Tribute to Sorley MacLean', *West Highland Free Press*, 6 December 1996. An abridged version of the memorial lecture appeared in the Review section of the *Guardian*, pp. 4–6, on 30 November 2002 as 'The Trance and the Translation'.

16 Somhairle MacGill-Eain, *Hallaig*, trans. Seamus Heaney (Edinburgh: Urrus Shomhairle / The Sorley MacLean Trust, 2002).

17 See Somhairle MacGill-Eain / Sorley MacLean, *Caoir Gheal Leumraich / White Leaping Flame: Collected Poems in Gaelic with English Translations*, ed. Christopher Whyte and Emma Dymock (Edinburgh: Polygon, 2011), pp. 231–5.

18 See Neil Corcoran, 'The Melt of the Real Thing', *Irish Review*, 49–50 (Winter–Spring 2014–15), 5–18.

19 Patrick Crotty, 'The Context of Heaney's Reception', in Bernard O'Donoghue (ed.), *The Cambridge Companion to Seamus Heaney* (Cambridge University Press, 2009), pp. 37–55 (at 46).

20 'Edwin Muir' (*FK* 246–56) was originally delivered as the Alexander Stone Lecture in Bibliophily at the University of Glasgow in November 1988.

21 Nancy K. Gish, 'Interview with Seamus Heaney 1980', in Gish (ed.), *Hugh MacDiarmid: Man and Poet* (Edinburgh University Press, 1992), pp. 63–70.

22 Seamus Heaney, 'The Shining Streams: A Tribute to MacDiarmid', *Dark Horse*, 15 (Summer 2003), 8–18.

23 Hugh MacDiarmid, *The Complete Poems of Hugh MacDiarmid*, vol. 1, ed. Michael Grieve and W.R. Aitken (Manchester: Carcanet, 1993), pp. 437–8.

24 'Shining Streams', p. 13.

25 MacDiarmid, *Complete Poems*, pp. 481–2.

CHAPTER 2

England

John McAuliffe

In 1962, after a term of teaching practice at a secondary school in Ballymurphy, Seamus Heaney took a summer job in the British Passport Office in Petty France, a short street in the City of Westminster and just two miles south of the Queen Square offices of Faber and Faber, which would go on to publish all of his major work (*SS* xxi–xxii). Two years later, the *New Statesman* published three of his poems, beginning a long and illustrious relationship with the young poet. There, and also in the *Listener*, the *Guardian*, the *Times Literary Supplement*, the *Observer*, the *Poetry Review* and later *PN Review*, the *New Review*, the *London Review of Books* and many other more or less obscure journals, his work would be published, reviewed and debated by critics and poets including, among many others, John Carey, Ted Hughes, Blake Morrison, Andrew Motion and Christopher Ricks.[1] He became England's best-selling poet, too, and yet England is, despite its extensive reception for his work and for all the time he spent there, an incidental subject for his poems. Initially attached imaginatively to history and colonialism, England's meaning for his poems changes as he develops a broader conception of a world literature.

When England is first mentioned, it is not the Passport Office but another of those London offices of state which figures, in 'For the Commander of the "Eliza"', whose speaker disparages the sympathy of one James Dombrain: 'Sir James, I understand, urged free relief / For famine victims in the Westport Sector / And earned tart reprimand from good Whitehall. / Let natives prosper by their own exertions' (*DN* 35). That ironic 'good Whitehall' is typical of the way that Heaney's early books read England's relationship with Ireland: the colonial nature of the state is overridingly present in his use of English material. In another poem, 'Traditions', the plural title and archly condescending tone of the speaker signal the historically pointed argument Heaney insists on: 'some cherished archaicisms / are correct Shakespearean' (*WO* 21).

Heaney's bog poems involved a more thoroughgoing *setting* of his Irish subjects in relation to another context, but they rarely land in England. Contemporary scenes are set in Madrid, Wicklow and Dublin, which join Scandinavia and Northern Ireland, while one memorable sequence in 'The Ministry of Fear' tracks the poet from Bogside to Brandywell, the Lecky Road, 'Then Belfast, and then Berkeley' (*N* 58). But England remains the subject of a more rhetorical, historical argument: in 'Ocean's Love to Ireland', Walter Ralegh is jammed into place as both imperial and regional, 'Speaking broad Devonshire, / Ralegh has backed the maid to a tree' and, later, as a reminder that imperial power was based on bloody plunder: 'In London his name will rise on water, and on those dark seepings: // Smerwick sowed with the mouthing corpses' (*N* 40). In the same mode, 'Leavings' is weighed down by historical symbols, as D.H. Lawrence's countryside gives way to Thomas Cromwell and a 'broken statue's head' (*FW* 57). As these poems touch on English subjects, they – like the work of migrant writers of other nationalities, and in other genres too – almost instinctively refer their landscapes and personal encounters to the larger history of the English state. Heaney's engagement with English dominion in Ireland, and the English language as inheritance and opportunity, negotiates these postcolonial encounters with great complexity, especially in 'Broagh' and the etymological poems of *Wintering Out* with their combinations of different registers and idioms.

On occasion, too, as his aesthetic evolved, English history offers not difference but common ground, as worked out most carefully and sympathetically in his portrait of the artist as Caedmon in 'Whitby-sur-Moyola', 'with his full bucket / And armfuls of clean straw, the perfect yardman, / unabsorbed in what he had to do / But doing it perfectly, and watching you' (*SL* 41). In the sequence 'Bone Dreams', Heaney reflects more widely on his historical pickings and choosings from England's poets, writing of a bone he finds, 'I touch it again, / I wind it in // the sling of mind / to pitch it at England', and what follows is his first sustained work with a contemporary English setting. Initially, this suggests the kind of common ground he had negotiated in the place name poems of *Wintering Out*: beyond 'Elizabethan canopies, / Norman devices, // the erotic mayflowers / of Provence / and the ivied Latins / of churchmen', he finds 'the scop's twang, the iron / flash of consonants / cleaving the line' (*N* 20). His identification with the scop, like his later portrait of Caedmon, suggests a common territory for Irish and English poets. But as the sequence 'Bone Dreams' comes back up to date, power (as elsewhere in *North*) is seen most clearly in sexual terms: 'we end up / cradling each other / between the lips / of an earthwork' (21), before the poem switches tack, with swift mastery, from the Roman wall in the North of England to an Iron Age fort in Dorset: 'I have begun to pace / the Hadrian's Wall / of her shoulder, dreaming / of Maiden Castle' (22). The poem, more exploratory and dramatic than any of Heaney's previous 'English' poems, is still written out of a binary model of colonial discourse.

Heaney's closing image in the sequence is of a dead mole (an animal not native to Ireland), in whose shoulders he touches 'small distant Pennines, / a pelt of grass and grain / running south' (23). It is the beginning of a more complex calibration of the aesthetic and the ethical in his response to England, as both state and poetic tradition, a calibration Heaney works out in a series of suggestive essays.

In 'Extending the Alphabet', he reframes the terms of his reading of English imperial poetry:

> But even so it still seems an abdication of critical responsibility to be swayed by these desperately overdue correctives [of the pretensions of Renaissance humanism] to a point where imaginative literature is read simply and solely as a function of an oppressive discourse, or as a reprehensible masking. (FK 268)

Even more explicitly, in his essay 'Through-Other Places, Through-Other Times: The Irish Poet in Britain', he writes, 'What I am getting around to saying is that any account of the Irish poet and Britain must get past politics and into poetry itself' (*FK* 373).

Prose Settings

The Englishness of particular writers becomes less prominent or anyway more complex in Heaney's discussion of them, as is clear in the Beckman Lecture he delivered at Berkeley in 1976. Its original title, 'Now and in England', echoed T.S. Eliot's formulations in Little Gidding, where 'Now and in England' soon becomes 'History is now and England.'[2] The lecture, subsequently published in *Critical Inquiry*, was retitled 'Englands of the Mind' for publication in *Preoccupations* (1980). It notably squares away the work of Heaney's English peers, reading them in light of his own interest in diversifying English-language poetry. While he singles out Hill, Hughes and Larkin as the country's pre-eminent poets, he also subjects them to a regional framework they may not have welcomed. And although he refers to them as poets of the 'mother culture', he refuses to grant them centrality:

> All three treat England as a region – or rather treat their region as England – in different and complementary ways . . . The poets of the mother culture,

> I feel, are now possessed of that defensive love of their territory which was once shared only by those poets whom we might call colonial – Yeats, MacDiarmid, Carlos Williams. (P 150–1)

While Heaney allows for an English poetry he values *as poetry*, he is still careful here to insist that it must be one poetry among many, that it take its place as one part of world literature. Or as he put it in a later essay, 'John Clare's Prog', 'The dream of a world culture, after all is a dream of a world where no language will be relegated, a world where the ancient rural province of Boeotia . . . will be on an equal footing with the city-state of Athens' (*FK* 292).

Translation

Translations necessarily reflect on history, language and nation – among many other matters – and in his translation of *Beowulf*, Heaney's critical, historical arguments about England discover a productively creative match. As he balanced the source Old English text with his own aesthetic, he found an original way, as any epic translation must, to combine the present and the past, 'now' and 'England'. The translation does double work, then, contributing to a translation history of its source text, but – in its representations of England – also developing or broadening his readers' sense of how an outside figure, an Irish poet, seeks authority, or centrality, or relevance as he situates his concerns in the mainstream of the English literary tradition. *Beowulf* is also one of the most visible ways in which his work has affected younger generations of English poets.

In England, *Beowulf* won the overall Whitbread Prize and was a best-seller on its appearance in 1999. Dedicated to his friend Ted Hughes, the book seemed to arise from Heaney's interest in destabilizing simple identifications between nation and poet, that subject he addressed in 'Englands of the Mind' where he had identified the potential *and* the difficulty of seeing the past in the present and the present in the past, particularly in Hughes and Hill. Like Thomas Kinsella's great translation of *The Tain* before it, *Beowulf* is an act of recovery and reinvention that is set at an angle to the culture it is usually defined by. Heaney's version emulates elements of the Anglo-Saxon in its use of alliteration, kenning and enjambment, but reviewers noted most its strongly contemporary language (though its emulation of the poem's formal elements has too a distinctly contemporary meaning). Heaney's introduction provides a present-day 'backstory' relating *Beowulf* to his own poems' long-standing, obviously political interest in polyglot, bridge-crossing language. In his study of Heaney and medieval poetry, Conor McCarthy very usefully calls Heaney's version 'stereoscopic', a word he borrows from studies of Proust to indicate how Heaney's translation offers 'depth of field' in its account of ancient events that have a distinctly modern resonance.[3] This sense of a 'stereoscopic', a *dramatic* translation, allows for the originality of Heaney's translation while acknowledging its honouring of the source text's otherness.

Heaney's stereoscopic rendition of *Beowulf* reads it as a poem about community, violence and the replacement of the old order: this postcolonial reading regenerates its status as a foundational poem for the canon of a distinctively varied English, *world* poetry. Heaney particularly attends to the poem's mixture of languages, an attention that stems, he writes, from finding *his* Derry language making its multicultural odyssey into Scottish, English and American poems and places. In this sense, he coins the phrase 'voice-right' to explain his claim on the poem, and commits himself to the occasional use of a particular local vocabulary of 'bawns and scullions and hoking' (*B* xxiii). Conor McCarthy argues that this makes the translation 'bear on contemporary issues and in particular the problems that afflicted Northern Ireland from 1969–1994',[4] but it can be argued that Heaney's *Beowulf* expands its subject, as Heaney had done in his use of England and English places, in order to emphasize how regional *and* transnational *and* universal the poem could be.

In his introduction, Heaney conjures up numerous analogies and readings of the poem, which indicate his translation's purchase on the contemporary world. The mourning Geat women put him in mind of Rwanda or Kosovo (*B* xxi), and he describes Beowulf's gold-hugging compatriot dragon as a 'fourth of July effulgence fireworking its path across the night sky' (*B* xix). His translation, then, operates at once as a faithful school text – to be used in university Old English courses, *and* as an intervention, a steer on his own changing aesthetic, and an original contribution to debates about language and community in an increasingly multicultural country, in the way that every Western European country is now becoming to some extent a 'world' country.

Of course the poem is larger than Heaney's arguments about it, or his introduction's attempts to corral it into his own ethical and aesthetic vision. Heaney acknowledges this at the close of his introduction:

> Indeed, every time I read the lovely interlude that tells of the minstrel singing in Heorot just before the first attacks of Grendel, I cannot help thinking of Edmund Spenser in Kilcolman Castle, reading the early cantos of *The Faerie Queene* to Sir Walter Raleigh, just before the Irish would burn the castle and drive Spenser out of Munster back to the Elizabethan court.

In an earlier poem, 'Exposure', Heaney saw himself in a figure from Spenser's imagination of the native Irish, 'a *wood-kerne* / Escaped from the massacre, / Taking protective colouring / From bole and bark, feeling / Every wind that blows' (*N* 67). Now he seems to transform Grendel into the wood kerne, a Caliban of postcolonial imagination, declaring his opposition to the 'minstrel' aesthetic of a court poet. It is a contrary, enlivening discontinuity, with the most stable and heroic figures of the Old English epic becoming soft wax he presses into new service. That is, having asserted continuities between his interests and the 'national' interests of the source text throughout the introduction, his shift in emphasis throws the pluralist liberalism of the introduction into question and begins to identify him with just one, disturbing element in the poem's social weave.

Perhaps the most obvious English responses to Heaney are mediated through Heaney's *Beowulf*, which started a fashion for translations, often 'from the English' into English, which includes work by Ciaran Carson, Lavinia Greenlaw, Vona Groarke, Sean O'Brien, Don Paterson, Simon Armitage and Alice Oswald: it is the latter pair who show most clearly how Heaney's anxiety about nation and national traditions plays out in England.

Simon Armitage's *Sir Gawain and the Green Knight* is, like Heaney's *Beowulf*, a convincing, driving narrative translation.[5] Like Heaney, he adopts – with some flexibility – the earlier poem's form, the alliterative pattern and bob and wheel stanza, saying its alliterative patterning combines 'meaning with feeling', though unlike Heaney he writes the poem (which was published simultaneously in the US and the UK) closer to Standard English, even as he emphasizes the poem's Northern provenance and has experimented with Yorkshire dialect across his individual collections.

More significantly, he follows Heaney in making his translation an act of appropriation, but the charge is very different for Armitage and flags up one interesting way in which Heaney's example changes as it is reabsorbed into England's poetry. Armitage's introduction *also* casts his translation as autobiography *and* political intervention, but whereas Heaney's essay challenges existing ideas about the 'national', English poem, carefully identifying the original, non-English elements his translation brings *to* the original, Armitage offers not so much a dramatic, stereoscopic reading of the poem as a kind of *ur* version of it. He describes the poem's author, like himself, as 'broadly speaking, a Northerner' and locates its 'linguistic epicentre' (vi) in northern England (although – as stated – the poem's vocabulary is *not* rendered as 'Northern' in his translation). Armitage also speculates that 'Lud's Church' in Derbyshire may be the site of the green chapel, arguing that its location there may have been what 'legitimised the vocabulary' of the poem (vi). He records visiting one particular mossy cleft near there 'that cannot have changed that much over the centuries'. Here and elsewhere in the introduction, Armitage seems to argue that the poem is less *an intervention* than a 'natural' or organic project, and when he calls the poem 'one of the jewels in the crown of English Literature' as it 'sits in the British Library under conditions of high security and controlled humidity' (v) – its hypotaxic projection of continuity feels like a conjuring trick, and at some distance from Heaney's centrifugal dispersal of a centralizing authority in his work.

Armitage's contemporary, Alice Oswald, responds to Homer's *Iliad* in *Memorial*, which begins with an alienating cast of characters, all in capitals.[6] While Heaney and, after him, Armitage, focus on their fidelity to the originals' narrative line, Oswald omits, as she puts it in her brief introduction, 'seven eighths' (2) of the *Iliad* and splits what's left into, her words, 'paraphrased biographies' and 'translated similes' (1), until we get to the closing dozen pages which consist entirely of similes, without names attached. Oswald's *Iliad* is not so much epic as a rendering of the epic, which transforms Homer's poem into something closer to lyric. No longer are we focused on particular heroes on whose fate nations depend. Instead Oswald presents the capitalized names of the dead, now illustrated by a gesture or by telling us of their family life, generating pathos as their killers move in to block off these tributaries from a larger social life.

Her presentation of the material is novel too, although like Heaney and Armitage she is at pains in her brief preface to assert her formal authority, contrasting the compressed similes with the metre of the lament-like biographies. One of her innovations is to repeat each simile, an effect that forces us to reread the poem even as we read it for the first time and seems, by the way, to offer up an argument about translation and repetition: is each repetition an exact translation of the simile or doesn't the same simile seem to change and assume authority as it is repeated? If anything the poem relishes its discontinuities, its use of non-epic but distinctively Greek poetic effects (the lyric, the lament and the chorus) and its refusal to focus on heroes or any kind of narrative. In this way Oswald's poem resembles Heaney's 'stereoscopic' translation, offering 'depth of field' in the way it accesses both ancient and contemporary references. And *Memorial* can, like Armitage's and Heaney's translations, be read in relation to her other work: she projects her concerns with the interrelationships between people and environments onto the epic material she translates, just as Armitage's concern with masculinity, the body and violence are mapped onto his *Gawain*.

Heaney's influence on English translator-poets is not unproblematic, and is just one part of his legacy to them, alongside his commitment to the public reading and lecture, to the value of traditional forms, and the way in which English poetry opened up to regional voices in his generation of poets, after the 1944 Butler Education Act and the Education (Northern Ireland) Act 1947, whose other beneficiaries included his Northern Irish contemporaries, but also Northern English and Midlands poets like Hill and Hughes and Tony Harrison, Jeffrey Wainwright, Roy Fisher and Ken Smith.

Geography

Heaney's historical approach to English material changes in his later work, which moves less guardedly across, in particular, London terrain. His worldly perspective touches down on English places in poems that become more geographical and less historical, a stopping-off point rather than a destination: 'Brancardier' represents Heaney as a 'pilgrim', in the age of steam: 'Derry, Dun Laoghaire, Dover, Rue du Bac' (*DC* 72). The mysterious parable, 'A Royal Prospect', also sets its characters in motion, as it places its speakers on a barge on the Thames, while the morning train of 'Electric Light' finds Heaney writing, 'To Southwark too I came, / from Tube-mouth into sunlight, / Moyola-breath by Thames's "straunge stronde".'[7] The Tube, in fact, and the underground more generally, become the defining location for Heaney's English poems. Heaney cherishes the metaphorical implications, the way that the Underground conjures Hades, Hell, the burial chamber. But his choice of a metropolitan, London setting is also useful for how Heaney's later work frames its representations of war and violence as *world* issues, or issues of modernity, rather than local to the Ireland with which he was most often associated. In 'The Underground', the poet is still on the move, 'a trail / Between the Underground and the Albert Hall' (*SI* 13), a young husband who is also Hansel and Orpheus and whose situation opens up the road to the land of the dead which will be central to *Station Island*: 'a draughty lamplit station / After the trains have gone, the wet track / Bared and tensed as I am, all attention / For your step following and damned if I look back' (*SI* 13).

His most substantial England poem is the title sequence of *District and Circle* (2006). The poem mutated from a resurrection of the Tollund Man to an extended self-portrait occasioned by a glimpse of a busker who resembled his father, another addition to the complex, thorny poems he wrote about that relationship (as well as an elaboration on the Bayswater stanza of Patrick Kavanagh's 'Memory of my father'). But, as he explained to Dennis O'Driscoll, news of the 7/7 bombings added momentum to the sequence's darker imaginings (*SS* 410). That bigger canvas allows Heaney to introduce the war machinery that characterizes the entire collection: the poem's sunbathers seem anomalous and innocently doomed from the speaker's underground perspective: 'Parks at lunchtime where the sunners lay / On body-heated mown grass regardless.' If that 'body-heated' does not trigger the poem's sinister undertones, what follows brackets its seemingly idyllic scene as a mere interlude in a Bosch-like landscape: 'A resurrection scene minutes before / The resurrection, habitués / Of their garden of delights, of staggered summer' (*DC* 18).

The sequence continues, beautifully, to combine its sense of an imminent warzone with a sensuously exact representation of Tube travel ('a monotonous slight rocking in the works', *DC* 18), the confrontation with the father which is still grounded in farm life ('strap-hanging, / My lofted arm a-swivel like a flail, / My father's glazed face in my own waning / And craning', *DC* 21). The setting for this overlapping set of co-ordinates is a London in which the speaker is an unestranged soul: 'And so by night and day to be transported / Through galleried earth with them, the only relict / Of all that I belonged to, hurtled forward' (*DC* 21). The poet here is as at home in T.S. Eliot's unreal city as he is in the Virgilian afterlife to which he would return in *Human Chain*.

If London figures unobtrusively as an extension of his imagined underworld in *District and Circle*, something equally unexpected happens in his late poem, 'Eelworks', where not for the first time, he aligns himself with that amphibian creature, the eel, slipping easily between different traditions, from Lough Neagh to England's South Downs:

A lawn beyond French windows
And downs in the middle distance)
'That tree, saw it once

Struck by lightning... The bark –
In his accent the ba-aak –
'The bark came off it

Like a girl taking off her petticoat'
White linen eblouissante
In a breath of air,

Sylph-flash made flesh,
Eelwork.

(HC 31)

'Eelworks', then, as well as revisiting this creature of in-between-ness, offers a brilliant gloss on the reactive, unstable, linguistic patchwork of 'Broagh' and *its* paradoxical iteration of difference: the earlier '*gh*' sound that strangers found 'difficult to manage' (*OG* 54) is now placed in the mouth of Walter de la Mare, where it has become an image of a beguiling sexuality, a difference to which the speaker is drawn. The poem, *stereoscopically* caught between its French windows and its downs, gathers different kinds of English which are not to be resolved, but whose untranslated differences co-exist and inform how we read them. Although it is a typically original flourish when the English scene of 'Eelworks' calls forth, dazzlingly, the French word, *eblouissante*.

Notes

1 See Rand Brandes, *Seamus Heaney: A Bibliography 1959–2003* (London: Faber and Faber, 2008).
2 T.S. Eliot, *Collected Poems 1909–1962* (London: Faber and Faber, 1963), pp. 215, 222.
3 Conor McCarthy, *Seamus Heaney and Medieval Poetry* (Woodbridge: D.S. Brewer, 2008), p. 112.
4 *Ibid.*, p. 6.
5 Simon Armitage, *Sir Gawain and the Green Knight* (London: Faber and Faber, 2007).
6 Alice Oswald, *Memorial* (London: Faber and Faber, 2011).
7 Seamus Heaney, *New Selected Poems 1966–1987* (London: Faber and Faber, 1990), p. 145.

CHAPTER 3

Eastern Europe

Margaret Greaves

'I'm no Cold War hero, I'm afraid', Heaney said in 2008 in response to Dennis O'Driscoll's inquiries about the extent of his association with Eastern European poets (*SS* 299). This wry remark underscores Heaney's awareness of his distance from the historical circumstances of Eastern Europe. From 1970 on, Heaney read, promoted and sometimes translated poets from Russia, the Czech Republic, Poland and Romania. He was particularly captivated by Osip Mandelstam, Miroslav Holub, Zbigniew Herbert and, above all, Czesław Miłosz, admiring their dual commitment to aesthetic autonomy and historical responsibility. Yet Heaney knew that, as Justin Quinn has put it, he 'was more likely to be found with heads of state than in a prison compound', making identification with Eastern European poets precarious.[1] But if Heaney was 'no Cold War hero', he was in many ways a Cold War poet, sharing the period's preoccupations with privacy and exposure, the individual and the collective, and the role of the self in the lyric poem. Heaney evokes Eastern European poets at strategic moments in his career as he navigates the strangely entangled politics of the Troubles and the politics of Anglo-American institutions.[2] Drawing parallels between Eastern Europe and Ireland allowed Heaney to distinguish the 'Irish' lyric from the Anglo-American lyric, even as his turn to Eastern Europe must be understood within a transnational Cold War-era anxiety about poetry's relationship to politics and history.

Heaney's work has little investment in Eastern Europe as a geography. While literary functions brought him to the Balkans, Lithuania, Russia and Poland between 1978 and 2004, and while he had more than a general knowledge of twentieth-century upheavals across the European continent, Heaney's work rarely records specific locations or incidents in Eastern Europe. The elision of Eastern European landscapes from most of Heaney's poems is related to a language barrier. Heaney's poetry awakens landscapes through the textures and origins of words, a technique that was simply unavailable to him when it came to a region whose languages he did not know. Not only did Heaney not study these languages, he was also tellingly uninterested in pursuing their soundscapes. He was satisfied he understood enough of Mandelstam's prosody, for instance, through Joseph Brodsky's remark, 'When you are listening to Mandelstam in Russian you have to think something like late Yeats.'[3] This may sound too offhand in an internationally renowned translator, but translation was not the point of his encounter with Eastern Europe: reading poetry that he could not access through his signature channels led Heaney into more abstract engagements with poetics. Sequestered from his 'word-hoard', Heaney's Eastern Europe rarely materializes into a place; instead, it becomes a set of intellectually, aesthetically and morally enticing ideas related to the role of the poet during political strife.

Heaney did occasionally translate Eastern European writers, though never the poets most important to him. Using crib sheets, he reworked poems from the Romanian of Marin Sorescu (1987) and Ana Blandiana (1996); his versions of Sorescu's 'The First Words' and 'Proper Names' suggest his translator's craving for etymology even without access to the source language. 'Proper Names', for instance, evokes the *dinnseanchas* tradition, pairing Sorescu's resistance to Nicolae Ceaușescu's repressive regime with cultural reclamation of Irish land from British occupation in early poems like 'Anahorish'.[4] From the Polish, Heaney never translated his much-admired Miłosz and Herbert, but he did collaborate with the Polish translator of his own work, Stanisław Barańczak, on the *Laments* of sixteenth-century Polish poet Jan Kochanowski[5] – a project he undertook because Kochanowski's elegies for his daughter Ursula resonated with the death of his younger brother Christopher (*SS* 427). These few examples aside, Heaney overwhelmingly approached Eastern European poetry as a creative reader rather than as a translator.

This abstract reading practice is key to the tricky issue of 'influence'. Magdalena Kay's comprehensive study of Heaney's Eastern Europe suggests that this influence was so extensive and ineffable that it can be credited with leading Heaney to revise his relationship with Anglo-American lyric practices. Heaney particularly admired Eastern European poets' serious pursuit of lofty concepts like 'faith, hope, justice, spirit, love' – ones that both New Criticism and high theory, battling it out in American institutions in the later years of the Cold War, deemed 'embarrassing'.[6] In fact, Heaney's attraction to Eastern European poets was in part a reaction against the same Anglo-American poetic and academic climate that alerted Heaney to their existence.

Heaney's first American academic position at Berkeley in 1970–1 coincided with a burst of Anglo-American fascination with literature from behind the Iron Curtain. This Cold War-era fervour would endure through the late 1970s and 1980s, when Heaney held a returning post at Harvard. Heaney had read Miłosz's anthology *Postwar Polish Poetry* (1965) while still at Queen's University Belfast. But his captivation with Eastern European poetry solidified through his American-made connections, many of which were transnational: the American university brought Heaney into contact not only with Miłosz but also with Russian exile Joseph Brodsky and Saint Lucian-born Derek Walcott.[7] The enthusiasms of Heaney, Brodsky and Walcott reinforced the popularity of some of the Eastern European writers who were becoming available to a wide anglophone readership from the 1960s to 1980s. During this period, the Penguin Modern European Poets series brought the work of many Russian, Polish and Czech poets into English, while Philip Roth's Writers from the Other Europe series bolstered the popularity of Eastern European fiction. On the other side of the Atlantic, Ted Hughes and Daniel Weissbort edited and promoted the journal *Modern Poetry in Translation* (founded in 1965), leading British poets to take an active role in Poetry International Festivals starting in 1967. Through publications and public events, Eastern European poetry became increasingly visible and influential internationally.

As Eastern European poetry enjoyed its Western heyday, Heaney's appointments at Berkeley and Harvard overlapped with the escalating violence of the Troubles. Heaney's Eastern European turn was partly a reaction against the poetic and critical aesthetic he encountered in American universities, which he found to be at odds with the political situation in Northern Ireland. In a climate in which white American poets enviously regarded Eastern Europeans as creators of more serious, important poetry than they had the historical experience to write,[8] Heaney was happy to confirm this sense. His oft-quoted declaration in his 1986 essay 'The Impact of Translation' sounds almost triumphant: 'Poets in English have felt compelled to turn their gaze East and have been encouraged to concede that the locus of greatness is shifting away from their language' (*GT* 38).[9] In the same essay, Heaney recalls the 'feeling of collusion' he experienced when Robert Pinsky read aloud a translation of Miłosz's 'Incantation' in the privacy of his Berkeley home, describing the samizdat-style intrigue of 'enjoying a poem which did things forbidden' in the American poetry scene (*GT* 37). In an academic climate governed by Pound's warning to 'go in fear of abstraction', Miłosz's didactic and moralistic style came as a refreshing jolt. As Heaney worked to distance himself from some Anglo-American critical positions, his essays of the late 1970s and 1980s collected in *The Government of the Tongue* overstate the distance between the 'historically aware, hard-bitten eastern-European aesthetic' and the 'ahistorical, hedonistic aesthetic' of American poetry (*SS* 114–15) – an exaggeration that helped him to distinguish the 'Irish' lyric from its Anglo-American cousin. He repeatedly finds English and American poets lacking compared to the Eastern Europeans, from Wilfred Owen's commitment to the pity of war at the expense of the perfection of craft to Sylvia Plath's appropriation of history for the amplification of the ego. T.S. Eliot is also found wanting; Zbigniew Herbert 'has seen more broken columns with his eyes than most literary people have seen in their imaginations' (*GT* 58). Yet challenging this Eastern European/Anglo-American dichotomy is the fact that, in Heaney's words, by the 1980s Miłosz 'more or less counted as an American poet' (*SS* 283).

Ted Hughes's influence further complicates the geography and politics of Heaney's attraction to Eastern Europe. Hughes is rarely acknowledged for his impact on Heaney's Eastern European imagination, perhaps because Hughes's nationality muddies the postcolonial parallel between Northern Ireland and Soviet bloc nations as contested victims of internal European colonization. Yet in addition to drawing Heaney's attention to Eastern European poetry through *Modern Poetry in Translation* and international poetry festivals, Hughes was a model for transforming Eastern European source material into far-reaching aesthetic and theoretical principles. For instance, Hughes likely exposed Heaney to the Romanian scholar Mircea Eliade, who deepened Heaney's preoccupation with sacred and profane space (*SS* 309). Eliade reverberates in lines that recur in *The Haw Lantern* and *Station Island* (both published during the Eastern European literary vogue of the 1980s): 'round and round a space, / utterly empty, utterly a source' (*SI* 68).[10] These lines also echo one of Heaney's favourite passages from Hughes's *Crow*, a volume indebted to Eliade and the Serbian poet Vasko Popa: 'at the bottom of all things, / Utterly worn out utterly clear'.[11] Sparked by Pinsky's reading of Miłosz, deepened by Hughes and personalized by Brodsky, Heaney's turn to Eastern Europe is a complex transnational story.

While Heaney's attraction to Eastern Europe should be read as part of this larger transnational vogue, Heaney also took care to emphasize the Irish dimensions of his interest. As he frames it, 'there is something in [Eastern European poets'] situation that makes them attractive to a reader whose formative experience has been largely Irish' (*GT* xx). Quinn has demonstrated how these poets helped Heaney to navigate Ireland's complexly postcolonial situation through their meditation on the ancient imperial examples of Greece and Rome.[12] Heaney also claimed that 'historically and culturally, the Poles and the Irish have a lot in common' due to their shared Catholic sense of sin and the sacred (*SS* 300). Kay has also noted 'the deep communal rootedness of the paradigmatic poet in Ireland and Eastern Europe',[13] a sense Heaney echoes in likening the poetry scene in 1994 Kraków to the Belfast Group in its 'mixture of close-knit friendships and commitment to poetry' (*SS* 300). Moreover, Eastern Europe and Ireland are often imagined together as regions of the 'other' Europe: places at the margins of the European continent that resist incorporation into modernity. Heaney's reading of Eastern European poetry provided an alternative idea of Europe that makes Irish experience central, rather than marginal, to the European imaginary.[14] Heaney's late villanelle 'Beacons at Bealtaine', written for the 2004 European Enlargement Ceremony in Dublin that marked the induction of eight Eastern European nations into the EU, takes its cue from Miłosz's 'Child of Europe'.[15]

These Irish contexts mix strangely with Anglo-American ones. For instance, the politics of the American academy and the politics of the Troubles echo one another unexpectedly in Heaney's work. Compared to American poets, for instance, Heaney finds the Eastern Europeans to be 'a tonic to somebody who had grown up in Northern Ireland, where the quiet surface covered up profound faults and disturbances' (*SS* 297). The remark recalls the well-crafted poem of the New Critics: a work whose quiet surface ripples with concealed tensions for the savvy reader to uncover. The Irish and Anglo-American contexts, then, symbiotically enhanced the appeal of Eastern European poets for Heaney. And, as the Troubles intensified, demands on Northern Irish poets would prove incompatible with Anglo-American notions of the lyric, leading Heaney to finesse fundamental aspects of his poetics.

Heaney returned from Berkeley in August 1971, the same week the British Army enacted internment in Northern Ireland. This timing of events emphasized his distance from the American poets 'at bay in prosperity and freedom' who found it difficult to '[escape] from the arena of the first-person singular'.[16] Eastern European poets helped Heaney to avoid conflating what he thought of as the 'necessary inwardness' (*SS* 336) of lyric poetry with the apparently self-absorbed, ahistorical American poem dominated by a lyric 'I'. For a poet who believed the lyric enterprise relied on maintaining a lyric 'I', Eastern European poets demonstrated how writing from a position of 'I' could itself be a political act, as Clare Cavanagh has argued.[17] At the same time, Heaney found affirmation of a plural, communally attuned lyric 'we' that first appears in *Door into the Dark* (1969) in his readings of Eastern European poetry. Strategic vacillation between 'I' and 'we' in his poetry allowed him, as he put it, to resist 'herd-speak' by trusting that 'the integrity of the polis is guarded as much by the solitariness of [the lyric poet's] enterprise as by other people's solidarities' (*SS* 382). Eastern European poets helped to bridge the private, insular Anglo-American models of the lyric with the political realities of Northern Ireland in the 1970s and 1980s; they also led Heaney to assert the idea of a distinctly 'Irish' lyric as he taught in American universities.

During the early years of the Troubles, Heaney turned first to Mandelstam's example. A Russian contemporary of T.S. Eliot frequently imprisoned for anti-Soviet views, Mandelstam died in a transit camp in Russia a year before Heaney's birth. Their biographical and generational differences perhaps made him a less daunting figure than poets like Holub and Herbert, who wrote through upheavals contemporary with the Troubles. In 'Exposure', Heaney describes Mandelstam as 'a hero / On some muddy compound' (*N* 67) and worries that his differing decision to '[escape] from the massacre' by moving from Northern Ireland to the Republic has made him miss the fullness of Mandelstam's vision (68). While Heaney acknowledged the 'inflation' of relating Mandelstam's situation to his own, he also remarked, 'insofar as I was being asked what bogs had to do with Bogside, there was a correspondence' (*SS* 175). The Mandelstam of *North* is responsive both to national politics and the politics of poetry, serving as 'a reminder that the anchor of poetry . . . should drag a certain amount of your inwardness up along with it . . . That a politically correct purpose was neither here nor there when it came to saving your poetic soul' (*SS* 175–6). In *Station Island*, Heaney's poetic persona shares more in common with another Russian: in 'Chekhov on Sakhalin', Chekhov is determined to face the suffering in the prisons on Sakhalin Island but falters at the final moment. In the end, he 'walk[s] away from floggings' and, rather than making his own way, 'shadow[s] a convict guide through Sakhalin' (*SI* 19) as Heaney himself shadows his Eastern European models.

During the 1980s, these main exemplars shifted from the Russians to the Poles. Miłosz in particular would become Heaney's mentor as he sought poetry 'strong enough to help' during the Troubles (*SS* 190). He was alert to Miłosz's challenge 'What is poetry that doesn't save nations / Or people?' and kept as a 'mantra' a passage from Miłosz that he quotes in 'Away from It All': 'I was stretched between contemplation of a motionless point and the command to participate actively in history' (*SS* 304, 260) – a revision of Eliot's 'still point of the turning world'. Miłosz is also 'the master' in *Station Island*'s poem of that name. Heaney's first meeting with Miłosz (at a Berkeley restaurant in 1983, the summer before Heaney would publish *An Open Letter*) morphs into Sweeney approaching a master in an 'unroofed tower' for instruction (*SI* 110). The tower setting, of course, also signals the 'Irish master', whose influence Heaney qualified with Miłosz's. Unlike Yeats, Heaney declares, Miłosz's 'intellect wasn't forced to choose between "perfection of the life or of the work"' (*SS* 301). In fact, Heaney reflects, Miłosz's biography and the history he lived through were inseparable. Miłosz's lived experience of negotiating life and art, poetry and politics, made him a touchstone for Heaney's meditations on the relationship between personal and poetic responsibility.

These Miłosz-inspired principles are encapsulated in the Amnesty International Award named after Heaney's poem 'From the Republic of Conscience'. (In a near convergence of politics and poetry, Heaney would present the Republic of Conscience Award to Václav Havel in the Abbey Theatre in 2001.) Reversing Plato's banishment of the poet from the republic, Heaney likens the poet to a citizen of the Republic of Conscience, where 'no ambassador would ever be relieved' (*HL* 12). The poem is one of many allegorical works in *The Haw Lantern*, which resounds with Zbigniew Herbert's influence as a moralist.[18] Heaney describes these poems as metaphorical 'translations of an imagined original' (*SS* 181), acknowledging that their 'plainspoken, translated feel' means 'their provenance is likely to be found in the Penguin Modern European Poets series' (*SS* 293). The opening poem of *The Haw Lantern*, 'Alphabets', likens learning to write in one's first language as a child to translation, alluding to Miłosz in its depiction of learning Latin declensions. Composed for Harvard's 1984 Phi Beta Kappa ceremony, 'Alphabets' drew its inspiration from Miłosz's poem 'The World', also told from a child's perspective (*SS* 291). The 'new calligraphy that felt like home' (*HL* 2) conjures the sense of recognition that Heaney found in Miłosz, as 'calligraphy' was a word Heaney associated with Miłosz's question, 'What is poetry that does not save / Nations, or people?' (Heaney suggests one response is 'in the obstinate espousal of beauty and order – the calligraphy – as [Miłosz] once called it – of poems', *SS* 381). And, on his decision to elegize 9/11 through a translation of Horace in 'Anything Can Happen', Heaney credits Miłosz's insight that during the Warsaw Uprising, the poet needed 'something like a calligraphic stroke that responded truly but in a different register' (*SS* 242). As Heaney's international reputation grew, he enacted Miłosz's ABCs as a counterweight to what he calls 'the poetic ABCs' of Pound's legacy (*GT* 37).

Cooling international interest in Eastern European poetry followed the official disbanding of the USSR in 1991, coincidentally the same year that *Seeing Things* registered Heaney's turn to the 'marvellous'. From 1991 through his death, Heaney's relationship with Eastern European poetry became increasingly spiritual and personal. Heaney's volume marking the new millennium, *Electric Light* (2001), sustains the revelations of *Seeing Things* while taking a backward look at Eastern European poetry with its elegies for Joseph Brodsky and Zbigniew Herbert.

Electric Light also contains Heaney's only poem that directly engages with a history-making event in Eastern Europe. 'Known World' should be understood not only in terms of Heaney's fascination with Eastern Europe, but also as part of his increasing tendency to write poems about international conflicts – including 9/11 and the 2005 London Tube bombings – following his public post-Nobel life. Using his trip to Macedonia for the Struga Poetry Festival in 1978 as a frame narrative, the central section of 'Known World' addresses the 1998 Kosovo War. (A draft version comprised solely of the Kosovo section, with the title 'Kosovo Summer' evoking the Prague Spring, is dated May 1998, just a month after the Good Friday Agreement.[19]) The young Heaney of 1978 finds parallels between the Balkans and Ireland, from 'mosaics and madonnas' (*EL* 19) to 'kin groups' of 'Congregations blackening the length / And breadth of summer roads' (*EL* 20), leading the speaker to think, naively, that he has found his version of Yeats's Byzantium: 'In Belgrade I had found my west-in-east.' But the congregations en route to mass transform in the middle section to a flood of Albanian Kosovar refugees forming a 'coil . . . like a syrup of Styx'. Heaney undercuts the smooth east–west comparisons of the 1978 trip by drawing a contorted contrast between the ethnic conflicts of the Balkans and Northern Ireland, while also calling into question the Eastern European-inflected allegorical tendencies of poems like those in *The Haw Lantern*: 'Allegory, I say, but who's to know / How to read sorrow rightly, or at all?' he asks of his attempts to 'read' events beyond his 'known world' (*EL* 21). This is a vulnerable moment, calling into question the poet's enterprise: if figuration and abstraction are suspect, poetry's tools may be the wrong ones to confront suffering.

But one of Heaney's final Eastern European-themed poems extols rather than doubts the tools of poetry. His elegy for Miłosz, 'Out of This World' (2004), draws on the poets' shared backgrounds as European Catholics, beginning with an elegiac catechism: '*Q. Do you renounce the world? / A. I do renounce it*' (*DC* 48). By the poem's end, Miłosz's memory moves Heaney not to question but to affirm 'the untranscendent music of the saw', which he knows Miłosz 'would not have renounced, however paltry' (*DC* 49). The saw's paltry music recalls the 'tentative art' of 'Casualty' that leads the poet to conclude, 'Question me again' (*FW* 22, 23); Miłosz puts questions about the worth of poetry to rest. Near the end of his own life,

Heaney reflected on what poetry had 'taught' him. His answers turn the Eastern-European-inflected Irish poem into a far-reaching standard for the lyric: 'that there's such a thing as truth . . . that subjectivity is not to be theorized away . . . that poetry itself has virtue' (*SS* 467).

Notes

1 Justin Quinn, 'Heaney and Eastern Europe', in Bernard O'Donoghue (ed.), *The Cambridge Companion to Seamus Heaney* (Cambridge University Press, 2009), pp. 92–105 (at 99).

2 Justin Quinn's *Between Two Fires: Transnationalism and Cold War Poetry* (Oxford University Press, 2015) addresses the Cold War politics of Anglo-American institutions in depth. See especially pp. 178–82 for a discussion of Heaney within this argument.

3 Robert Hass and Seamus Heaney, *Sounding Lines: The Art of Translating Poetry* (Berkeley, CA: Townsend Center for the Humanities, 2000), p. 14.

4 Marin Sorescu, *The Biggest Egg in the World* (Newcastle-upon-Tyne: Bloodaxe, 1987), pp. 71–2 ; John Fairleigh, *When the Tunnels Meet: Contemporary Romanian Poetry* (Newcastle-upon-Tyne: Bloodaxe, 1996). Fairleigh's volume paired Irish and Romanian poets to translate one another's work. Heaney also wrote the introductions for translations of Sorescu's selected poems into English (Oberlin College Press, 1991) and Irish (Coiscéim, 2000).

5 Barańczak translated 44 of Heaney's poems into Polish in 1994, for which Heaney attended the launch ceremony in Kraków in 1994; he later translated a number of Heaney's later poems and some prose selections. Heaney has been most extensively translated into Polish of all the Slavic languages and was inducted into the Polish Academy of Arts and Sciences in 2007.

6 Magdalena Kay, *In Gratitude for All the Gifts: Seamus Heaney and Eastern Europe* (University of Toronto Press, 2012), p. 19.

7 Justin Quinn reads the American reception of Heaney, Brodsky and Walcott in terms of Cold War dynamics, arguing that Heaney and Walcott made the postcolonial 'safe' for America. See *Between Two Fires*, pp. 143–94.

8 See Clare Cavanagh, *Lyric Poetry and Modern Politics: Russia, Poland, and the West* (New Haven, CT: Yale University Press, 2009), p. 2.

9 *GT* in this chapter refers to the American edition: Seamus Heaney, *The Government of the Tongue: Selected Prose 1978–1987* (New York: Farrar, Straus and Giroux, 1988).

10 *SI* in this chapter refers to the American edition: Seamus Heaney, *Station Island* (New York: Farrar, Straus and Giroux, 1985). This passage is reworked in 'Clearances' (*HL* 32).

11 Ted Hughes, *Collected Poems*, ed. Paul Keegan (New York: Farrar, Straus and Giroux, 2005), p. 258.

12 Quinn, 'Heaney and Eastern Europe'.

13 Kay, *In Gratitude*, p. 52.

14 For a sustained treatment of Miłosz's influence on Heaney's idea of Europe, see Peggy O'Brien, *Writing Lough Derg: From William Carleton to Seamus Heaney* (Syracuse University Press, 2006), pp. 232–67. Also writing on 'Station Island', Michael Parker analyses Miłosz's influence on Heaney's response to the hunger strikes in 'Czeslaw Milosz and His Impact on Seamus Heaney's Poetry', *Textual Practice*, 5/1 (2013), 839–49.

15 See Margaret Greaves, 'Punishing the Lyric: Seamus Heaney and the Poetics of a Communal Europe', in *Éire-Ireland*, 51/3–4 (Fall/Winter 2016), 217–43.

16 Quoted in Dennis O'Driscoll, 'Heaney in Public', in O'Donoghue (ed.) *Cambridge Companion*, pp. 56–72 (at 66–7).

17 Cavanagh, *Lyric Poetry*, pp. 20–1.

18 For more on Herbert's influence as a moralist, see Kay, 'ZH and the Moral Imperative', in *In Gratitude*, pp. 86–123.

19 Seamus Heaney, typescript of 'Kosovo Summer', May 1998, box 98, folder 14, Seamus Heaney papers, MS 960, 98/14. Rose Library, Emory University.

CHAPTER 4

America

Sarah Bennett

Heaney's preoccupation with place was most strenuously directed towards the peculiar relationship between a writer and their home region. In *The Place of Writing* he describes the 'urge' to inquire into the 'inspiration and foundation which place affords in the creative process', and begins with the assumption that 'the writer stands in some directly expressive or interpretative relationship' to the place and society from which they emerge.[1] In his most famous articulation of the Irish writer's feeling for place, the 1977 lecture 'The Sense of Place', Heaney defends the legacy of the Celtic Revivalists' reanimation of the Irish legendary landscape with a line from the American novelist Carson McCullers: 'to know who you are, you have to have a place to come from' (*P* 135). This is one of a number of instances in Heaney's writing where an idea of American place, its mythologies, its geography and its cultural legibility, is brought into apposition or contrast with the sense of Irish place. It is to the foundational myths of the American literary consciousness, the 'frontier and the west', that Heaney looks when, in 'Feeling into Words', he describes the discovery of an 'original accent' in his 1969 poem 'Bogland' (*P* 43). From its opening line, 'We have no prairies / To slice a big sun at evening' (*DD* 41), 'Bogland' stakes a defence of the peculiar experience of Irish place in answer to the radiant mythology of the American landscape. Horizontal space is met with immersive depth, as 'the eye concedes to / Encroaching horizon, / Is wooed into the cyclops' eye / Of a tarn' (41). The competition is overt, but the very 'discovery' and achieved 'signature' that 'Bogland' represents in Heaney's narrative of poetic development reveals a collusion with this myth-making. National definition – what the Irish landscape is and is not – has been stridently formed by transatlantic comparison, but this drive is interrupted in the final lines: 'The bogholes might be Atlantic seepage. / The wet centre is bottomless' (42). The acknowledgment of possible contamination, of a poetic signature brightened by the self-definition of another nation, is treated with reflective optimism.

As his early writing reveals, Heaney's sense of American place was in the first instance literate, shaped by expressions of American regional identity (notably Theodore Roethke's 'In Praise of Prairies') and the literature of the American dream that he taught at Queen's in the late 1960s. The transatlantic contest of 'Bogland', the closing poem of *Door into the Dark*, anticipates Heaney's acquaintance with America as an actual, social and political environment. He made his first visit in 1969, on a reading invitation to Richmond, Virginia. When he took up a Visiting Lectureship at the University of California, Berkeley, in 1970, Heaney and his family embarked upon their first extended period outside of Northern Ireland. Heaney has spoken of this as a transformative year in his career as poet and academic: one of expanded confidence in his writing, and rich intellectual communion with the Berkeley faculty and surrounding San Francisco writers. This was the beginning of an involvement with institutional America that would last until he resigned from his position as Poet-in-Residence at Harvard in 2007. Berkeley in the 1960s and early 1970s was the nexus of student activism in Free Speech and Civil Rights, and an environment of unprecedented student freedoms. In interviews Heaney recalled 'the time of the loose garment and the long hair; of pot in the air and sex on the waterbed' as the corollary to the grimmer realities of American youth: 'the draft card and the water cannon' (*SS* 137).

The American academic invitation also afforded greater comfort and financial stability for the Irish poet; in 'The Sense of Place' Heaney invokes John Montague's description of the 'sunlit campus' and 'heated pool' as a breezy modern alternative to the purer happiness of experiencing 'prehistoric timelessness' on the slopes of Sliabh Gullion (*P* 140). His lecture endorses this antithesis, as modern institutional America, an extension of the expansionist mythology of the American Dream, again serves to bring the historical profundity of the Irish landscape into relief. Although Heaney had a full teaching load, the novelty and eccentricity of life at Berkeley (preserved in 'The Flight Path' as 'Laid-back Tiburon. / Burgers at Sam's, deck-tables and champagne', *SL* 23), formed a sharp contrast to institutional life at Queen's. In the *Stepping Stones* interviews, however, Heaney shows himself capable of responding to this institutional landscape with visionary zeal. Reflecting on 'intimations of immortality', he describes a moment on the balcony of the Berkeley English Department:

> The bricks were already warm in the sun, it was clear and summery and light-drenched; you could see the white terraces and tower blocks of San Francisco across the bay and the green trace of trees and gardens in between, and I had this visitation of – well, I don't know what to call

> it . . . Humanist joy? Awe? A tremendous sense of what human beings had achieved on earth. (*SS* 32)

As he remembers Berkeley, we see Heaney recognizing the poetic possibilities of the audacious conflation of manmade and natural spectacle in the American landscape.

It has surprised many of Heaney's readers that these moments of reflection on American place are rare in his work, and largely absent from the poetry. The manuscript for *Wintering Out* (1972) was completed in September 1971, on Heaney's return from California. Yet the volume betrays no assurance that the distance and novelty afforded by a year in California are earned freedoms. Irish language and history are persistent themes in Part One; 'Anahorish', 'Toome' and Broagh' perform the anxious sounding out of Irish place names in their anglicized form. These poems establish an intimacy between speech and place in a language that is both proudly possessive and estranged. In 'Traditions', a poem for Heaney's Berkeley colleague Tom Flanagan, the 'guttural muse' of the Irish language is remembered behind the English traditions that supplanted it. Part Two of *Wintering Out* culminates in California, a destination reached through a series of local penances. Guilt, betrayal and blame are resonant themes within these poems, from the bruising marital argument of 'Summer Home' to the 'maiden daughter' who flees naked from her family in 'A Winter's Tale' (*WO* 52), to the mother who has drowned her illegitimate child 'under / The sign of her cross' (58). The final poem, 'Westering', was in fact the first poem Heaney wrote in America. It describes another 'turning away' from the responsibilities of faith and community, this time in the long westward passage that has terminated, according to the poem's subtitle, 'In California', 'under Rand McNally's / "Official Map of the Moon"' (*WO* 67).

The speed with which this poem's gaze turned from California back to Ireland irritated some contemporary reviewers.[2] Disappointment at Heaney's unwillingness to *look* at his American landscape is in part a product of expectations: the Faber blurb boasts of 'a noticeable widening of poetic landscapes'.[3] However, by the second quatrain of 'Westering', we are recalled to another West, the 'empty amphitheatre' of Donegal, where 'Summer had been a free fall' (*WO* 67). Rand McNally's map, which charted and described the surface of the moon American astronauts had walked upon the year before Heaney's visit to Berkeley, agitates memories of the shadow cast on 'the whitewash / From her bony shine' in Donegal (67). Lunar imagery and mythology is, as a number of critics have noticed, thoroughly internalized in the language of *Wintering Out*.[4] The 'official' American (and territorially masculine) reproduction of the moon is a pale prelude to the recollected experience of feminized moonlight on a summer evening. Yet there is a common 'weightlessness' to the 'free fall[ing]' summer in the West of Ireland, the further West of California, and the moonwalking Apollo mission: all terminals operating, like the speechless child confined to a henhouse in 'Bye-Child', at 'lunar distances' from a centre of gravity (*WO* 60). The journey that 'Westering' describes begins from this centre of gravity, a point of 'home', and on a holy day – 'Good Friday / We had started out' (67) – in an allusion to John Donne's poem of bodily and spiritual conflict drawn along the poles of divine East and aberrant West, '*Goodfriday*, 1613. *Riding Westward*'. Any suggestion of defiant passage is diminished, however, by the self-deprecating appraisal of the travellers' status as a 'dwindling interruption' to the solemnity of 'clappers smack[ing]' and 'congregations ben[ding]'. 'Dwindling' forms part of a series of verbs denoting decline and descent in this poem, which closes with 'A loosening gravity, / Christ weighing by his hands' (68). This conflicted act – imagining both the loosened binds of home and a consequent vulnerability to judgement – reveals the poem's discomfort with distances.

In *Wintering Out* Heaney is not interested in looking long at America: poems such as 'Westering' and the preceding 'Travel' challenge the notion of achieving distance from a troubled Northern Ireland. Heaney described the volume as an inquiry into the 'active signals and loyalties' found in the language and history of Northern Ireland, and the 'I' of the volume consciously participates in community loyalties and pieties as it investigates them, colluding in the suspicion of the outsider.[5] In the seasonal schema of *Wintering Out*, an academic year in California is reduced to a summer vacation, one that is not fully submitted to.

Whilst it is possible to understand such a diminishment of America as a consequence of the larger 'geographical inquiry' of his early volumes, it is difficult to ignore the parallel between the light impress of America on the poetry, and the imputations of insubstantiality that seep into Heaney's treatments of American poetry in the 1970s and 1980s. When writing about his encounter with American poetry in California, Heaney is again prone to antithesis: the green-eared author of 'thin cross-legged quatrains' arrives in California and is thrown into a hotbed of open-form experiment (*SS* 16). This experience is amplified in Heaney's reflections on his friend Czesław Miłosz's path to Berkeley. He describes the strange cultural leap that carried Miłosz from an education rooted in medieval Catholicism, through various forms of exile from oppressive Nazi and Soviet regimes and a direct encounter with Marxist orthodoxy, to the 'free gravity-less modernity' of California in the 1960s.[6] Elmer Kennedy-Andrews has noticed a tendency in Heaney's prose and interviews to pit the 'gravity' of Eastern European poetry, born in conditions of cultural jeopardy, against the more free-wheeling American alternative. In 'Current Unstated Assumptions about Poetry' (1981), Heaney assumes a tricky plural pronoun in writing about the 'impatience' and 'unease' 'we' experience as readers in the face of excessive 'talkiness' and 'metrical wooliness' in a 'self-regarding poetry' of 'the enclosed psyche'.[7] In contrast, 'we' are attracted to the 'extreme statements and images' surrounding the production of Osip Mandelstam's poetry in peril and exile. Heaney is ostensibly offering a broad comparison between the poetry of Britain, Ireland and America and the poetry of Eastern Europe, but it is American examples – James Wright, Allen Ginsberg – that furnish his argument. A few years later, in an interview with Rand Brandes, Heaney exercises a similarly antithetical comparison with a more candid acknowledgement of his own prejudices, describing the differences between the European poetry he feels sympathy for and the American poetry he struggles to appreciate. In self-consciously generalized terms, Heaney speaks of the American cadence that is 'fluid and spread', in contrast to a poetry he practises and prefers, that 'contains' and confines its forces.[8]

The hugely diverse and divisive poetry scene Heaney entered in the 1970s provides one context for the polarized terms he applies to American poetry. He was confronted first-hand with the 'Redskin versus Paleface' poetic divide, a tension between the rough-necked West Coast poetry scene and the more genteel New England verse-making. Robert Lowell reformulated this in terms of 'cooked' and 'raw' poetries in his 1960 National Book Award acceptance speech; in the same year the 'raw' side of the divide was represented in Donald Allen's influential counter-canonical anthology *The New American Poetry 1945–1960*. The lore of 'Redskin versus Paleface' held currency in the discourse of Philip Hobsbaum's workshop in Belfast in the 1960s, and Heaney has declared his partisan alignment with the 'Redskin/Lowell camp' (*SS* 218). The positioning of Lowell the patrician New Englander, one-time disciple of the Southern Agrarians, on the side of the 'raw' is itself problematic, however, requiring an understanding of the shift in Lowell's career from the tight metrical forms of the early poetry to the freer forms and speech experiments from *Life Studies* (1959) onwards. Lowell's approach was in part motivated by an admiration for William Carlos Williams, whose handling of plain speech and wielding of the American subject he praised in several essays. In Heaney's accounts of his Berkeley education in

American poetry, Williams, one of the forefathers of Allen's 'New American Poetry', emerges as a significant discovery. Efforts to come to terms with Charles Olson's 'projective verse' and Robert Duncan's mysticism went without reward, but Heaney left California 'with a leather hat on his head and a short William Carlos Williams line in his ear' (*SS* 137). This short line, previewed in 'Bogland', has an insistent force in Heaney's post-Berkeley volumes. It can be seen in the first part of *Wintering Out* and in the poems from *North* that most memorably realize his politicized bogland aesthetic: 'Bog Queen', 'The Grauballe Man' and 'Punishment'. Responding to the music of Williams's two-beat line, Heaney invested this spare, frequently enjambed form with a violence and fragility fully suited to his subject.

Heaney's politicization of the Williams aesthetic speaks to the deeper legacy that the political climate in San Francisco left in his work. In contemporary dispatches to the *Listener* he was critical of the inflammatory language of social protest in America; in December 1970 he offered his own exasperated slogan: 'While Berkeley shouts, Belfast burns.'[9] Yet in a later interview he described the galvanizing atmosphere of possibility surrounding the Civil Rights Movement as the most important influence of his time at Berkeley, supporting a belief that 'poetry was a force, almost a mode of power, certainly a mode of resistance'.[10] Robert Bly, Gary Snyder and Robert Duncan were San Francisco poets on the front line of the anti-war protest scene, and Heaney attended a number of their readings. These poets' earnest engagement with the contemporary climate, and their rejection of ironic commentary in favour of an inquiry into regional history, nature and mythology, impressed him. The mythological mode in Bly, Snyder and Duncan's poetry was broad and promiscuous: Chinese poetry and Native American texts were brought to bear on contemporary American culture in Snyder's *Myths and Texts* (1960), and the verse line in Bly's *Silence in the Snowy Fields* (1962) was adapted from Arthur Waley's Chinese translations, and from Frank O'Connor's translations of Celtic poetry. While Heaney's appreciation of these poets' mythological and spiritual 'doctrine' was qualified, their solidarity with a minority American culture presented resonant parallels with the situation in Northern Ireland, and suggested 'new ways of handling' his experience.[11] Part of this legacy was the formal process these poets were engaged in: an active and candid search for new forms suitable for new political and cultural situations. Bly adapted the long line of Whitman and Blake for his Vietnam War poem, 'The Teeth-Mother Naked at Last' (1970), in pursuit of a form adequate to the subject of political power and rhetoric. Heaney's adaptation of the short Williams line in his political poetry of the early 1970s, and his return to a longer line and 'a more social voice' in *Field Work* (1979), follows the example of the San Francisco poets.[12] During his year at Berkeley Heaney also experimented with prose poems, inspired by Bly's renowned ventures in the form; these later appeared in the pamphlet *Stations* (1975). The various political and formal influences Heaney came under at Berkeley give us a broader view of his depreciative remarks about America's lightweight poetics, remarks he later dismissed as the product of a youthful defensiveness of Irish traditions. Variety is more widely operative here: the American scene Heaney entered in the 1970s resisted generalization.

Harvard, where Heaney first arrived for a spring semester in 1979, was the site of a number of formative friendships. The critic Helen Vendler, one of Heaney's earliest American admirers, joined the English Department in 1981. Robert Lowell and Elizabeth Bishop were Heaney's predecessors as creative writing lecturers. Lowell had died suddenly in September 1977, and Bishop was mandatorily retired in the same year. Heaney and his family befriended Bishop during that first period in Cambridge, in the months before her death. His acquaintance with Lowell was of longer standing; they had met in London in the early 1970s, when Lowell was based in Kent. In 1976 Lowell presented Heaney with the Duff Cooper Memorial Award for *North* at a ceremony in the University of London, against the wishes of his doctors (he was at that time hospitalized for depression). Lowell's contention that Heaney was 'the best Irish poet since Yeats' went on public record, quoted in the *Guardian* when *North* won the W.H. Smith award, and becoming legendary in Heaney criticism.[13] Heaney's admiration for Lowell, in turn, was persistent. It matured from a youthful enthusiasm for the conflicted 'Redskin' of *Life Studies* (1959) and *Imitations* (1961) to an appreciation and emulation of Lowell's copious blank-verse sonnets from the volumes of 1973, *For Lizzie and Harriet*, *History* and *The Dolphin*, and a conviction, expressed in a lecture of 1986, that the 'gentler, autumnal' poems in Lowell's final collection *Day by Day* (1977) were among his best (*FK* 212). Heaney, by his own standards, dignifies Lowell in that lecture by comparing him to Osip Mandelstam for the weight of his moral conscience: in his public stance as conscientious objector Lowell, like Mandelstam throughout his life, rose to 'the demands of the historical moment' (206).

Heaney delivered a eulogy at Lowell's memorial service in London in 1977. 'Elegy', his poetic tribute to Lowell, was published the following year in a limited-edition pamphlet for Deerfield Press, the Massachusetts-based imprint co-founded by Peter Fallon and the American painter Tim Engelland, demonstrating the increasingly transatlantic reach of Heaney's poetry. 'Elegy' honours Lowell as *il miglior fabbro* in naming him 'master elegist', and the arrogated authority both of Lowell's lyric gift and his position in American culture is acknowledged with gentle irony: 'what was not within your empery?' (*FW* 31). Crediting Lowell as a 'welder of English', Heaney suggests that a capacity for a poetry that joins traditions and languages – a capacity sometimes indistinguishable from base manipulation – is a central facet of his legacy. This is crucial to Lowell's Americanness. A cry at the centre of the poem – 'You drank America / like the heart's / iron vodka' (*FW* 31) – links a life of dangerous excess to an attempt to channel the American experience. Heaney's portrait of Lowell as the American master-welder of poetic traditions is strongly reminiscent of Lowell's characterization of William Carlos Williams's gift as a weird and hybrid craft that broke through the stagnancy of an English literature education at Harvard: 'It was as though some homemade ship, part Spanish galleon, part paddle-wheels, kitchen poets and elastic bands and worked by hand, had anchored to a filling station.'[14] Heaney's elegy is built upon a similar metaphor, as Lowell is cast as 'our night ferry / thudding in a big sea, / the whole craft ringing / with an armourer's music / the course set wilfully across / the ungovernable and dangerous' (*FW* 32). Heaney's tribute to Lowell evinces a sensitive understanding of the polarized late twentieth-century world of American poetry, by identifying him with the energetic, peremptory and hybrid poetics that Lowell praised in Williams as '*the American style*'.[15]

Heaney's spring semester in Harvard led to a temporary contract on a part-time arrangement in 1982, and his election two years later as the Boylston Chair of Rhetoric and Oratory. The chair was a significant honour for an Irish poet in mid-career; he was the first non-American to hold the post, and the first incumbent not to have been a Harvard graduate. From 1982 until 1996, Heaney sustained what Lowell once described as a 'commuter's professorship', his years divided between a semester in residence at Harvard's Adams House and eight months at home in Dublin.[16] On resigning the chair in 1996, Heaney retained his Harvard association as Ralph Waldo Emerson Poet-in-Residence, a post with lighter residency requirements of six weeks every alternate year. 'The Flight Path', from *The Spirit Level* (1996), speaks of the excitement and the strain of a transatlantic existence of entrances, departures and re-entrances. The meandering path of 'westering[s]' and 'eastering[s]' leads to Harvard 'Yard', a name that promises a meeting point between farm and campus life. This destination heralds a 'tauten[ing]' of purchase but not quite a point of arrival: it remains 'a holding pattern' (*SL* 24). In that poem the return to Ireland north and south of the border represents the exhilaration of homecoming, and the resumption of the risks and scrutiny of writing. Lines of separation between a teaching life and writing life are visibly drawn. And while significant sections of Heaney's work were completed in America – notably the *Sweeney Astray* revisions during the summer of 1979 at Tom Flanagan's Long Island home – Heaney has spoken of the more entrenched division of working energies during his time at Harvard, between the 'executive self' of the Boylston Professor, and the summer self, 'versing' with relish in Ireland (*SS* 272).

Heaney's involvement in Harvard life is documented in two occasional poems, 'Alphabets' (1984), his contribution to the Phi Beta Kappa ceremony in his inaugural year as Boylston Professor, and 'Villanelle for an Anniversary' (1986), commissioned for the 350th anniversary of Harvard's founding. In their common themes of learning, progress and opportunity, these poems offer self-reflexive comment on the distance between Heaney's Mossbawn origins and his position of institutional privilege in America. In 'Villanelle for an Anniversary', John Harvard (disputed 'founder' of Harvard College) is imagined 'walk[ing] the yard' in which his statue now sits, ghosted by a 'verb in hibernation', the verb 'to find' (*OG* 289). In its refrain, 'The books stood open and the gates unbarred', the poem dwells upon the moment between discovery and the potential for discovery. The concluding quatrain beseeches 'Find yourself or founder', and Heaney, who now finds himself walking Harvard Yard, is finding himself in the history of the college, discovering a connection with the émigré son of a butcher and cattle trader, and with the original schoolhouse which was built beside cattle sheds. As the critic Michael Allen observed, Heaney's portrayal of John Harvard's progress is a surprising recapitulation of the mythology of the American dream that sparked competition in Heaney's poetry of the 1960s.[17] The bravado of the American pioneering drive has been succeeded, however, by an enthusiasm akin to the 'humanist joy' Heaney described on encountering the view from the Berkeley English Department. Heaney is content to align himself with this American mythology in 'Villanelle for an Anniversary', however insistently he retains an awareness of origins.

In 2011 Heaney contributed an introduction to *Explore Harvard: The Yard and Beyond*, a collection of photographs commemorating the University's 375th anniversary. He described the composite picture of these images from Harvard's history as 'neither one of light-headedness on high nor of delving below: it is more about an in-between condition we might call buoyancy'.[18] Buoyancy and in-betweenness aptly describe the state of being-in-America that is evoked across Heaney's work. This condition is at odds with the rooted self-knowledge that Heaney theorized in his essays on the writer and the home place; the poetry of the early

1970s reveals that buoyancy was not always a condition he embraced. Yet it describes the American social attitude Heaney identified during his time at Berkeley, poised between serious-mindedness and exuberance, an attitude he saw replicated in the political poetry of Snyder and Bly, and the hybrid poetics of Williams and Lowell. It has left its mark in the gradual loosening and adapting of forms that began with *Wintering Out*, and an increased tolerance, in volumes like *The Spirit Level* and *Electric Light*, for a 'talkiness' Heaney once rejected. 'Canopy', a poem from Heaney's final volume, *Human Chain* (2011), is a tribute to the buoyancy he associated with Harvard and America.[19] It depicts Harvard Yard in 1994 transformed by a sound installation from the British artist-in-residence David Ward, in which speakers playing recorded voices were suspended from trees. This moment of 'Words being given new airs' occasions an unusually lingering meditation on the visual and aural experience of American place, and a celebration of discovery, innovation and collaboration in the American institution (*HC* 45).

Notes

1 Seamus Heaney, *The Place of Writing* (Atlanta: Scholars Press, 1989), pp. 19–20.
2 See Patricia Beer, 'Seamus Heaney's Third Book of Poems', *Listener*, 88/2280 (December 1972), 795.
3 *Ibid.*, 795.
4 See Neil Corcoran, *The Poetry of Seamus Heaney: A Critical Study* (London: Faber and Faber, 1998), 50; and Daniel Tobin, *Passage to the Center: Imagination and the Sacred in the Poetry of Seamus Heaney* (Lexington: University Press of Kentucky, 1999), pp. 99–100.
5 See James Randall, 'An Interview with Seamus Heaney', *Ploughshares*, 5/3 (1979), 7–22 (at p. 17).
6 Rand Brandes, 'Seamus Heaney: An Interview', *Salmagundi*, 80 (Fall 1988), 4–21 (at p. 9).
7 Seamus Heaney, 'Current Unstated Assumptions about Poetry', *Critical Inquiry*, 7/7 (Summer 1981), 645–51 (at p. 646).
8 Brandes, 'Seamus Heaney: An Interview', p. 17.
9 Heaney, 'Views', *Listener* 84/2179 (31 December 1970), 903.
10 Randall, 'Interview with Seamus Heaney', 19–20.
11 *Ibid.*, 20.
12 *Ibid.*, 15.
13 Lowell, quoted in W.L. Webb, 'Irish poet wins £1000 award', *Guardian*, 16 November 1976, 5.
14 Robert Lowell, 'Dr. Williams', in *Collected Prose*, ed. Robert Giroux (London: Faber and Faber, 1987), p. 40.

15 *Ibid.*, 43.
16 Robert Lowell, Letter to Ezra and Dorothy Pound, 18 March 1962, *The Letters of Robert Lowell*, ed. Saskia Hamilton (New York: Farrar, Straus and Giroux, 2005).
17 Michael Allen, 'The Parish and the Dream: Heaney and America, 1969–1987', *Southern Review* 31/3 (Summer 1995), 726–38.
18 Heaney, 'Introduction', in *Explore Harvard: The Yard and Beyond* (Cambridge, MA: Harvard University Press, 2011), n.p.
19 'Canopy' was first published in David Ward, *Canopy: A Work for Voice and Light in Harvard Yard*, ed. Ivan Gaskell (Cambridge, MA: Busch-Reisinger Museum, Harvard University, 1997).

II

Influences and Traditions

CHAPTER 5

Wordsworth and Romanticism

Matthew Campbell

In his conversations with Dennis O'Driscoll in *Stepping Stones* (2008), Seamus Heaney was asked to address O'Driscoll's observation that Frost 'seems to have provided you with an entire philosophy of poetry'. The answer is partly as expected – Heaney says he 'felt at home in the world of his poetry' and mentions farms and haystacks and Frost's accuracy and inwardness with country living. But he also offers an understanding of Frost across two perceptions. One is of 'a highly literary poet' who has 'seriousness, an inner core of hard intelligence', and a second quality balancing that: 'Frost was at home in the high cultural context of the university courses, but he still gave you a link back down in to what you stored in your own intimate child-body, the tramping of hay. So I responded immediately to that primal reach into the physical' (*SS* 453). For all that he was using the word 'primal' in conversation, Heaney approved it in print, and he allows its usage in two senses. One would be understandable by Frost, as 'belonging to the earliest time, original, first . . . primitive, primeval' (*OED* 2a). The other sense was only beginning to come into English through psychotherapy in Frost's time and might be said to have reached its apogee about the time that Heaney lived in 1970s San Francisco in the company of poets like Gary Snyder and Robert Bly (*SS* 141), where the word 'primal' would refer to something at the origins of the emotional life, 'primal therapy' though not (this being Seamus Heaney) the 'primal scream' (*OED* 2b). If a 'primal reach into the physical' is offered here as one of the things to which Heaney responds in poetry, then the primal is positioned both as utterly of the individual and at the end of 'a link back down', a sort of archaeology of continuity with literary precursors,

In Heaney's retrospective mode, 'primal reach' becomes something figured as a personal and textual history which grants a certain authority to the peculiarities of individual lived experience. In this case it is rural, conducted in the social norms of everyday speech and subject matter, syntactically and formally traditional but also recognizably aware of the physicality of the human body working in nature, affected by seasonal as much as historical or cultural patterns. This amounts to a state of being, an ontology, which is not merely the literary construction of the bucolic or Pastoral – no matter that Virgil's *Georgics* are playing in the background. In his thinking about poetry and poets as well as in his own poetic practice, Heaney seeks individuation not just in the sense that he is the possessor of an authentic self, but in his companionship with others who shared that same sense of authenticity. Tradition – in its broadest sense across twentieth-century post-Romantic poetics, encompassing both ideas of high culture and a continuously renewed engagement with folklife – is work of shared experience and association, antiquity and innovation, whether it be the agricultural or the 'high literary', the Ivy League seminar or the South Derry field.

In his criticism and conversation, and in the allusiveness of his poetry, Heaney continually returned to other writers who stand along this archaeological 'link back down' (and indeed back up) between and before Frost and him: Gerard Manley Hopkins, Edward Thomas and Patrick Kavanagh and then Michael Longley and Paul Muldoon. What these writers share is a set of problematic relations with something that literary history has called 'Romanticism', a word more distinctive for the range of its possible definitions than in its precision. In *The All-Sustaining Air*, a study about the persistence of Romanticism in modern poetry, Michael O'Neill worries over the possibility of a stock definition of a literary concept which is 'notoriously a protean term and post-facto construction'. He first offers us Friedrich Schlegel: 'The romantic kind of poetry . . . recognizes as its first commandment that the will of the poet can tolerate no law above itself.' But he then offers us the posterity of that will in the drama of the self and society told in the Romantic poem: 'Above all, its affirmations, about the self and its innate and potential grandeur, about the mind's capacity to enter into relationship with and to transform understanding of reality, and about the significance of poetry and the imagination, can be seen to involve themselves in a poetically productive drama.'[1] Even more so than Frost, it is in the first place Heaney's reading in William Wordsworth that provides his source for such a drama of affirmation, relation and the self, a primal reach enacted both as a principle of individuation rooted in the environmental and social, and as the source of creativity.

For Fiona Stafford, writing about the grounding influence of Wordsworth on Heaney, 'Wordsworth was the earliest writer to understand fully the necessary connections between the poet and his "first place".'[2] And already in Wordsworth, that sense of reaching back – as in

Frost, as in Heaney – is of a doubleness, an original voice coded by the linguistic and literary necessity that determines any act of adult retrospect into 'the intimate child-body' of the origins and continuity of the emotional life. The early sections of Wordsworth's *Prelude* (1798–1850) tell of this as a doubling of self, of 'Two consciousnesses':

> And is there one, the wisest and the best
> Of all mankind, who does not sometimes wish
> For things which cannot be, who would not give,
> If so he might, to duty and to truth
> The eagerness of infantine desire?
> A tranquillizing spirit presses now
> On my corporeal frame: so wide appears
> The vacancy between me and those days
> Which yet have such self-presence in my mind
> That, sometimes, when I think of them, I seem
> Two consciousnesses, conscious of myself
> And of some other being.[3]

Thus in Heaney's signature poem, 'Digging' (1966), childhood memories of smell and touch are awoken by 'the curt cuts of an edge / Through living roots' (*OG* 3). Cutting through roots is no destructive act: it is necessary for growth, for planting, harvesting, and, in the broadest sense, husbandry. Heaney's poem had sought to collapse the difference between the writer's and the farmer's labour – between his occupation then and now – in order to maintain 'living roots' by digging with a pen which is spade, gun and phallus in one. But the Wordsworthian 'Two consciousnesses' inevitably surface, both here and in the poetry which followed, where 'The eagerness of infantine desire' strives to inhabit, to give presence to, 'The vacancy between me and those days'. In Heaney, the influence is marked by his consistent sense of arguing against scepticism for 'living roots' given a belief in, and desire for, 'self-presence'.

In autobiographical mode, Heaney's poetry replays a Wordsworthian attachment to origins and location, while offering a similar anxiety about growth and dislocation. A 1984 lecture which was given at Dove Cottage is subtitled 'Recent Poetry from Northern Ireland', but its main title 'Place and Displacement', along with the location of delivery, allows Heaney to open with an extensive passage from *The Prelude* on a conflict within the self, when personal politics means supporting the other side, an Englishman supporting revolutionary French ideals. Heaney's gloss is lengthy and politically astute, aware that he too has a personal political conflict at issue when dealing with notions of home and sovereignty, rooting both for Ireland and poetry in English. He concludes with the Wordsworthian solution to the suffering caused by such a conflicted self, given the poet's recourse to the writing of a self that knows that it suffers:

> Wordsworth's case is symptomatic of the historical moment, but it is not paraded as being representative: the pressure of the poem's occasion launches it beyond allegory and exemplum. Its principle of development and its structural and rhetorical life are to be found not in any designs he has upon a readership, not in self-exculpation or self-dramatization, but in the autonomous habits of the poet's mind and practice. The 'I' of the poem is at the eye of the storm within the 'I' of the poet. (FK 114–15)

It is a poet's solution and one that Heaney knew would assist him in the conflicting urges that are felt through his and his contemporaries' poetry of the preceding decade, the 1970s: given they were writing in terrible times, of whether to embrace or resist the allegorical and the exemplary. Writing about the 1790s, Wordsworth's *Prelude* bears witness to a similar dilemma, telling of its author's life in times of ideological conflict and national war, while obeying an artistic necessity, to retain the autonomy of poet and poem, 'beyond allegory and exemplum'. Heaney's contemporary, the critic Edna Longley, would pronounce a year after Heaney's Dove Cottage lecture, in 1985, that 'Poetry and politics like church and state should be separated.'[4] Heaney is not quite enlisting Wordsworth in a similar cause, but he is suggesting that the 'I' in poet and poem, while never entirely the same person, would do better to follow the ways of Wordsworth or his contemporary Schlegel: 'the will of the poet can tolerate no law above itself'.

Heaney was, of course, touching on large issues in the political responsibility of the poet given the then seemingly insoluble problem of violence in his home place of Northern Ireland in the early 1980s. He too had become 'displaced', in class as much as geography, from both the actuality if never quite the idea of 'home'. In 1981 he was an active founding member of the Field Day Theatre Company, at that time beginning to mount a strong critique of the cultures of imperialism that were diagnosed as at the roots of Britain's ongoing Irish problem. Nevertheless, accusations were made of political evasion or irresponsibility, a prizing of the aesthetic considerations of a poetry which appeared to resist one requirement – that it be 'representative' – while embracing another – that it be 'autonomous'.[5] Hugh Haughton shows that while Heaney's (and Field Day's) thinking here coincided with a new cultural materialism in literary criticism, such as Jerome McGann's highly influential 1983 book, *Romantic Ideology*, there was a creative identification with Wordsworthian 'displacement'. Haughton points out that Heaney 'draws attention to the ways in which

Wordsworth's idea of the "good place", like his own, may be seen as a product of trauma, a strategy for psychic survival, rather than evasion'.[6] Running throughout Heaney's career that sense of the home place as psychically supportive – no matter how divided its 'two communities' – borrows much from the Wordsworthian idea of the immersion of the self in the home place, an environment (in the broadest sense) more of nurture and growth than trauma. What Heaney adds to Wordsworth is a sense that the poetry is oriented from present trauma to a long past. Yet such poetry is also preoccupied with the future of its subject (self and location), as told in the present tense of the 'I' of the poem. Heaney's place name poems in the crucial early volume *Wintering Out* explore this multiple sense of the places of the history of the self which also function in a poetic of emergence, or, as Neil Corcoran memorably remarks, 'the promised future work is almost as satisfying as the recognition of present achievement'.[7]

For both poets any sense of getting back to the land also involves the primal reach of memory into the strongly physicalized bodily experience of growing up, both in the temporal span of their own lives and in a longer grasp of roots and origins. Except this is frequently not a matter of getting back to land: rather it is getting back to water, for Wordsworth the Lake District and for Heaney the land around Lough Neagh and Lough Beg, connected as they are by the River Bann which is straddled by the town of Toome (or Toomebridge as it is often called). In his classic *Irish Names of Places*, P.W. Joyce tells us that Toome was originally called *Fearsat Tuama*, the faucet or ford of the toome, which is a mound and a burial place, a tumulus, a tomb.[8] The place name tells of a long history that is both linguistic and geological, Gaelic, Latin and Iron Age, the bog which is both land and water at once. Heaney's immersion in such watery land is at once linguistic, archaeological and biological. 'Anahorish' is a 'place of clear water'; 'Broagh' is a riverbank; in 'Gifts of Rain', 'The tawny guttural water / spells itself: Moyola.' The poem 'Toome' is about saying its own title: the word is sounded under the tongue until it becomes a prehistory of place. Situated as the poem is, between Wordsworth and Heaney, a second influence comes in, that of Charles Darwin, who tells of time before the flood, of the human organism travelling forward through personal, family and local history, and watery biological origins from before the primal. It ends with

> flints, musket-balls,
> fragmented ware
> torcs and fish-bones,
> till I am sleeved in

alluvial mud that shelves
suddenly under
bogwater and tributaries,
and elvers tail my hair.
(OG 53)

There is something a little silly, maybe even dated, about this: to borrow a phrase from another poem about watery places, 'Personal Helicon', if it isn't 'beneath all adult dignity' (*OG* 15), it is unkempt, long-haired, folky-Celtic and slightly hippy (the poem was published in 1972, after all). But other interests of the time are in evidence, such as archaeology, anthropology and psychoanalysis.

The poem goes not so much on an archaeological dig as a dive backwards through history to prehistory, from flints to fish-bones. It ends in both the primeval and the primordial, swamped and then submerged, turned from clothed male human ('sleeved') to inchoate, sexless elver. As described in an earlier poem of Heaney's, 'Lough Neagh Sequence' (1969), the eel is an ancient denizen, as well as the product farmed by a long-standing human industry, in and around Lough Neagh and the River Bann. That poem told of the life cycle of the adult eel, but the elvers here are young eels which have yet to develop reproductive organs. Weaving elvers into his Californian hair, Heaney promulgates a myth of a retrograde evolution or even de-evolution back to the swamp, as well as a more psychically graspable return, to the amniotic fluid of the womb. The moment at the end may even be that before conception, where the elvers are like sperm before conception or gender. Whether or not Heaney's long hair itself is a sign of the diminution of gender difference, it is more than a matter of 1970s fashion: in 'Exposure' (1975) he describes himself as 'grown long-haired / And thoughtful, a wood-kerne // Escaped from the massacre'. This is not so much counter-cultural fashion statement as philosopher-insurgent on the run: the wood-kernes who harried the colonizing English in the sixteenth and seventeenth centuries were regularly depicted as savagely unkempt.

A history of such watery immersion as a savagery tricked out of Jean-Jacques Rousseau via Wordsworth's 'eagerness of infantine desire' runs through Heaney's own autobiographical writing. In his reading of *The Prelude*, the emergence from water and then the return to it is imagined as a sort of initiation into male sexuality. Take this extraordinary paragraph from the 1978 memoir of his home place, 'Omphalos':

> To this day, green, wet corners, flooded wastes, soft rushy bottoms, any place with the invitation of watery ground and tundra vegetation, even glimpsed from a car or a train, possess an immediate and deeply peaceful

> attraction. It is as if I am betrothed to them, and my betrothal happened one summer evening, thirty years ago, when another boy and myself stripped to the white country skin and bathed in a moss-hole, treading the liver-thick mud, unsettling a smoky muck off the bottom and coming out smeared and weedy and darkened. We dressed again and went home in our wet clothes, smelling of the ground and the standing pool, somehow initiated. (*FK* 5)

This is a strange primal confession of initiation with the land. The two boys are at first virginal and subsequently betrothed, though not to each other. It is not quite the consummation of the homosocial as a betrothal with earth and water and mud. The result is a sort of rebirth.

There is a similar childhood skinny-dipping moment in Book One of *The Prelude*, just before the celebrated accounts of the boat-stealing and ice-skating adventures of the young boy. For Heaney's Bann read Wordsworth's Derwent, although the river itself is playmate enough for Wordsworth.

> Oh! many a time have I, a five years' Child,
> A naked Boy, in one delightful Rill,
> A little Mill-race severed from his stream,
> Made one long bathing of a summer's day,
> Basked in the sun, and plunged, and basked again
> Alternate all a summer's day, or coursed
> Over the sandy fields, leaping through groves
> Of yellow grunsel, or when crag and hill,
> The woods, and distant Skiddaw's lofty height,
> Were bronzed with a deep radiance, stood alone
> Beneath the sky, as if I had been born
> On Indian Plains, and from my Mother's hut
> Had run abroad in wantonness, to sport,
> A naked Savage, in the thunder shower.

Wordsworth's next verse paragraph rounds back on the notions which are implicit here, of immersion, baptism into nature, and (repeated) self-initiations. 'Fair seed-time had my soul' he goes on to say, 'Fostered alike by beauty and by fear'.[9] The germination of the seed of the soul needs water and sun and earth. From 'naked Boy' to the 'naked Savage', the imagined Indian other-self is a creature out of Rousseau delivered directly from a Nature which both nurtures and teaches by dispensing beauty and fear.

In Heaney's earlier poetry and criticism he sought recourse to a gendered language which answered for his own masculine experience, his own boyhood, and which accepted the passivity of the gendered figurations of a colonized Irish culture, as manifest in the *aisling* tradition of Irish Jacobite poetry. Its persistence into the adulthood of his poetry has not gone unremarked,[10] and it does seem that given the strength of the critique of some exceptionable statements made by Heaney in the 1960s and 1970s about gender, nation and language – male consonant / female vowel, male earth / female water, masculine English / feminine Gaelic – meant their removal from the poet's readjustment of his canon in selected editions in his lifetime. This is most notable in the omission of the colonization-as-rape poem 'Ocean's Love to Ireland' from *Opened Ground* and the loss of the section on a gendered national linguistics from the 'Belfast' section of *Preoccupations* from *Finders Keepers*. His essay on Hopkins's 'masculine' consonantal music was not republished.[11] Acts of revision may be self-censorship, the acceptance of correction, or even just changing one's mind: in this case they seem to have been one result of a sort of textual conversation with the audience, the recognition of a certain kind of generational gender-blindness.

Heaney's development of these ideas of submersion, loss of self and disappearance back into the amorphousness of the thing, involved a conversation with Romantic precursors who explored extreme acts of self-negation in the act of perception. Reading both Wordsworth and Heaney, the critic Guinn Batten has suggested that what she calls 'swallowing of the source' is associated with the maternal – and indeed its loss. Heaney's later poetry, much of it in elegiac mode, is not only displaced from the home place but also aware of the displacement of family itself, the vacancy or emptiness which has been left at the place of origin, memorably figured as 'utterly empty, utterly a source' which occurs first as 'like the idea of sound' in the 'Station Island' (1984) sequence and then a felled chestnut tree in the last sonnet of 'Clearances' (1987) (*OG* 248, 314). For Batten, the fact of loss works itself out as a corresponding incorporation:

> place (or Nature) is, through the active engagement of the senses, displaced into the self that will both preserve and imitate her power. Indeed, the self is already imitative of Nature or 'place' precisely in being a *place* that swallows (in bog-like fashion) and that which, in turn, is pursued or even swallowed by the entity that has been imaginatively incorporated: see, for example Wordsworth's 'Boy of Winander' or Heaney's 'Toome'.[12]

Implicit in some of the imagery I have been discussing above is a return to land and water as a desire for return to a place before individuation, perhaps the womb. Moynagh Sullivan has even found 'unmarked transvestitism' (the '"redress" of poetry' as she puts it) in Heaney's assumption of the maternal in his writing about the divided nation.[13] Batten insists that in a poem like 'Toome' the shock of the poem is in its wilful delight in its own imaginative incorporation by its source material.

Heaney's contribution to an ongoing development of these 'Romantic' ideas in modern poetry and through his own writing, is focused in his reading of the boy of Winander story in Book Five of *The Prelude*, as a means of approaching the poetry of Sylvia Plath in the lecture 'The Indefatigable Hoof-Taps' (1986). Wordsworth tells of a friend of the poet who could imitate owls so well that when he started hooting at them they would answer back. The result is cacophonous echo, then silence, and then this:

> the visible scene
> Would enter unawares into his mind
> With all its solemn imagery, its rocks,
> Its woods, and that uncertain heaven received
> Into the bosom of the steady lake.[14]

This is the mutuality of the steady lake of nature and the steady lake of the mind: mind and heaven are mirrored in and mirrored by the lake. It is a poetic event that Heaney glosses as having 'that degree of imaginative access where we feel the poem as a gift arising or descending beyond the poet's control'. In relation to Plath, in terms of unqualified praise, this is 'somnambulist poetic certitude'. The subsequent knowing that is uniquely achieved by the poet is 'what determines the ultimate human value of the act of poetry' (*FK* 227, 230).

These are high claims indeed, and this passage joins Plath's *Ariel* volume, in particular a poem like 'Edge', as representative of the third of three stages of poetical development. Heaney's reading in Plath tries to shake off the terrible knowledge of her biography, more than half in love with easeful death as she was. But it seeks also the strength of a justification of the value of poetry through her writing. The story in Wordsworth exemplifies these three stages which are given through the account of Plath – and the account I have given here of the younger Heaney's own poetry. The first stage is imitation of owls, the primal reach, or as Heaney says, 'the satisfaction and justification implicit in the primary act of sounding forth'. The second is 'the poetry of relation, of ripple-and-wave effect upon audience . . . ways by which distinctively personal subjects and emotional necessities can be made a common possession of the readers'. And finally, the stage reached by the end of Wordsworth's passage, 'the poem's absolute business . . . an unconceding pursuit of poetic insight and poetic knowledge' (*FK* 220, 223–4, 226). We might shrink these stages down to imitation, communication and autonomy. Much of Heaney's autobiographical poetry delights in the first stage, yet it is the relation between the latter two which he works out for himself in poetry and criticism, going beyond virtuosity and enjoyment in its power to the metaphysics of the later career. In a way it amounts to a lifting off, a walking on air.

Robert Frost is at a mid-point in this conversation between the poets, in particular his 'The Most of It', a poem which retains a more sceptical view of Wordsworth's boy of Winander, and the limits of Heaney's second stage of poetry, the social relation with audience. Frost's poem begins with a character who 'thought he kept the universe alone': 'He would cry out on life, that what it wants / Is not its own love back in copy speech, / But counter-love, original response.'[15] Writing about the conversation opened up with Wordsworth in Frost's poem, Michael O'Neill sees that 'the dialogue that takes place between Romantic and post-Romantic poems' reveals 'an unexpectedly disturbed and disturbing presence'.[16] The character in Frost's poem is disappointed in its seeking for original response. The 'great buck' which becomes the 'embodiment' of this character's calling into nature looks like the thing that Keats termed the opposite of his 'negative capability', 'the egotistical sublime', which in Frost is abruptly, incommunicably, masculine. It is also ultimately unproductive, leaving nothing after it bar its bullying presence: 'and that was all' are the deflated last words of his poem. By Keats's time Wordsworth had ultimately become the model for the poetic category of the egotistical sublime, keeping the universe alone. Heaney's contribution to this discussion between writers is maybe less worried, eventually focused on creativity. The 'ultimate human value of the act of poetry' offered at the end of the lecture is a statement of social and sociable productivity: 'That act remains free, self-governing, self-seeking, but the worth of the booty it brings back from its raid upon the inarticulate will depend upon the emotional capacity, intellectual resource and general civilization which the articulate poet maintains between the raids' (*FK* 230–1). If Heaney's poetry brings back booty from a raid on the inarticulate, it was presented to the 'general civilization'. If he never 'kept the universe alone' – some readers do sometimes find themselves confronted by a 'great buck'.

Such a result could be, as O'Neill says, disturbed and disturbing, and these essays announce a necessary change in style for the mid-1980s onward, as sensed then by a poet approaching fifty. When the change was first tried out it brought this typically wry response from Heaney's (and Frost's) follower Paul Muldoon, who writes that in 1992 he received 'a Christmas poem from Doctor Heaney'. Muldoon's view was that 'the great physician of the earth / is waxing metaphysical, has taken to "walking on air"; / as Goethe termed it, *Surf und Turf*'.'[17] The joke was a good one in the 1990s (has the Californian food fad survived?) and the water and earth of Heaney's early milieu gave way to airiness and the marvellous in the volumes that followed. The conversations with dead precursors in the later writing come out of Dante and Virgil rather than Wordsworth and Frost.

That phrase, 'walk on air', occurs in 'The Gravel Walks' (1996). It is a poem about earth and water, leisure and music, but before it all, a primordial scene: 'River gravel. In the beginning that.' The poem is a record of a summer walk and an allegory of the need to occupy a place 'somewhere in between' Wordsworth's uncertain heaven and steady lake, where gravel is both produce of the river and the solid result of culture: footpath, road, a way forward if never in itself a destination. The last stanza has provided Heaney's epitaph, and it tends to the location of its culture, the memory of the Irish reel 'The Gravel Walks' and the primal reach of memory into water and earth: 'So walk on air against your better judgement / Establishing yourself somewhere in between / Those solid batches mixed with green cement / And a tune called "The Gravel Walks" that conjures green' (*OG* 423–4).

Notes

1 Michel O'Neill, *The All-Sustaining Air: Romantic Legacies and Renewals in British, American and Irish Poetry since 1900* (Oxford University Press, 2007), pp. 2, 5.
2 Fiona Stafford, *Local Attachments: The Province of Poetry* (Oxford University Press, 2010), p. 38.
3 *William Wordsworth*, ed. Stephen Gill (Oxford University Press, 2010), here *Prelude* (1805), 11.21–32. Gill uses the Cornell edition.
4 Edna Longley, 'Poetry and Politics in Northern Ireland', *Crane Bag*, 9/1 (1985), 26–40.
5 See, for instance, the encounter with the ideologue in 'The Flight Path': 'When, for fuck's sake are you going to write / Something for us?' 'When I do write something, / Whatever it is, I'll be writing for myself' (*OG* 413).
6 Hugh Haughton, 'Power and Hiding Places: Wordsworth and Seamus Heaney', in Damian Walford Davies and Ricard Marggraf Turley (eds.), *The Monstrous Debt: Modalities of Influence in Twentieth-Century Literature* (Detroit, MI: Wayne State Universiy Press, 2006), p. 75.
7 Neil Corcoran, *Seamus Heaney* (London: Faber and Faber, 1986), p. 72.
8 P.W. Joyce, *Irish Names of Places*, 4th edn (Dublin: McGlashan & Gill, 1875), p. 334.
9 *Prelude*, 1.290–306.

10 See for instance, Patricia Coughlan, '"Bog Queens": The Representation of Women in the Poetry of John Montague and Seamus Heaney', in Toni O'Brien Johnston and David Cairns (eds.), *Gender in Irish Writing* (Milton Keynes: Open University Press, 1991), pp. 88–111; and Moynagh Sullivan, 'The Treachery of Wetness', *Irish Studies Review*, 13/4 (November 2005), 451–568.

11 See also Fran Brearton, 'Heaney and the Feminine', in Bernard O'Donoghue (ed.), *The Cambridge Companion to Seamus Heaney* (Cambridge University Press, 2009), pp. 73–91.

12 Guinn Batten, 'Heaney's Wordsworth and the Poetics of Displacement', in O'Donoghue (ed.) *Cambridge Companion*, pp. 178–91 (at p. 181).

13 Sullivan, 'Treachery of Wetness', p. 456.

14 *Prelude*, v.388–413.

15 Robert Frost, *The Poetry of Robert Frost*, ed. Edward Lathem (London: Cape, 1971), p. 338.

16 O'Neill, *All-Sustaining Air*, p. 5.

17 Paul Muldoon, *The Prince of the Quotidian* (Oldcastle: Gallery, 1994), p. 14.

CHAPTER 6

Thomas Hardy

Ronald Schuchard

Hardy's birthplace in Bockhampton in 1840 was very like Heaney's birthplace in Mossbawn in 1939 – thatched, whitewashed, pre-electric, its three rooms lit by candle and oil lamps, the horse, ploughs and harvest tools in an attached shed, cows in the byre a few yards away – and in the early 1940s the mechanized modern world was only beginning to impinge upon the Heaney home and farm. 'My father was a creature of the archaic world, really', wrote Heaney. 'His side of the family belonged to a traditional rural Ireland . . . I suppose you could say that my father's world was Thomas Hardy and my mother's D. H. Lawrence.'[1] Both birthplaces became places of lifelong departure and return for Heaney as he attempted to comprehend the mystery of his poetic gift and ground his art within them. He wrote 'The Birthplace' (1982) not only because it 'reminded me of Mossbawn', but because 'Hardy's novels and poems were so much part of me by the time I got there. In fact, the grave in Stinsford churchyard and the home in Upper Bockhampton are literary "stations" I keep going back to' (*SS* 252).

Heaney has often referred to the 'den-life' of his early years in Mossbawn (*OG* 415), of the dreamworld that enwrapped him there in his 'secret nests' (the forks of various trees, a boxwood hedge), and of the importance of the radio set for expanding his sense of the outside world, including Hardy's poetry. 'I remember hearing the poem "Weathers" read on the BBC radio when I was eleven or twelve and never forgetting it':[2] 'This is the weather the cuckoo likes, / And so do I; / When showers betumble the chestnut spikes, / and nestlings fly.'[3] With few books in his house, his access to them came from his paternal aunt and godmother, Sarah (known as Aunt Sally), a schoolteacher who had on her shelves a complete set of Hardy's novels and an anthology containing his poems, including 'The Oxen'.[4] 'From the moment I read "The Oxen"', he wrote, 'the moment I read the opening chapters of *Return of the Native*, I was at home with him – something about the vestigial ballad atmosphere, the intimacy, the oldness behind and inside the work, the peering and puzzlement and solitude . . . I loved the oddity and previousness of the English in it. "The lonely barton by yonder comb" – that can still make me feel sad and taken care of all at once.'[5] Elsewhere he described the poem as one that 'feels like a pre-natal possession. Probably because I learnt it by heart early on.'[6] Through his early memorization of Hardy's poems, Heaney began to create his word-hoard and memory bank.

Scenes from Hardy's novels would also make their way into Heaney's own poems, as late as in 'The Loose Box' (2001), about a box of miscellaneous objects at the back of their stable, the memory of which triggers an early epiphany:

> Stable child, grown stabler when I read
> In adolescence Thomas *dolens* Hardy –
> Not, oddly enough, his Christmas eve night-piece
> About the oxen in their bedded stall
> But the threshing scene in *Tess of the D'Ubervilles* –
> That magnified my soul.
>
> (EL 15)

I postpone for the moment Heaney's use of the Latin '*dolens*' in describing Hardy to look at that indelibly remembered scene in which Tess is given the exhausting and debilitating task of feeding sheaves of wheat into the buzzing mechanical thresher owned by the indifferent 'engineer'. What magnifies Heaney's soul is Hardy's description of the old bystanders who hate the machine and remember the communal days 'when they had been accustomed to thresh with flails on the oaken barn-floor; when everything, even to the winnowing, was effected by hand-labour, which to their thinking, though slow, produced better results'. As an efficient but heartless mechanization intrudes upon the harvest, Hardy diligently records the lost communal attachment of a displaced ancestral ritual. Heaney took it to heart.

In larding his later poetry and prose with remembered moments from his early reading of Hardy, Heaney slowly retraces the trail of revelations that formed his 'lurking' *ars poetica* as he sought to discover his poetic voice. In the preface to the first issue of the new Irish poetry periodical, *Soundings* (1972), we find Heaney as editor asserting that the authors selected for the issue 'can be viewed as part of a poetic drift all over the world . . . all involved in a retrieval of ancestry . . . an attempt to make poetry once again an act of faith in the land and language that the poet shares with his dead';[7] we find it in 'Poet's Chair', where he remembers sitting as an 'all-seeing' boy in the centre of a field, his back against a thorn tree, watching his father ploughing: 'I am all foreknowledge. / Of the poem as a ploughshare that turns time / Up and over . . . Of being here for good in every sense' (*OG* 399); and yet we find it nowhere more directly than in an uncollected essay, 'The Sense of the Past' (1993), which he prefaces with the printing of Hardy's 'The Garden Seat',[8] a sitting place for generations of ancestors. 'Hardy's poem', writes Heaney, 'embodies a way of feeling and thinking about the past which significantly amplifies our consciousness':

> It is about the ghost life that hovers over the furniture of our lives, of the way objects can become temples of the spirit. To an imaginative person, an inherited possession like a garden seat is not just an object, an antique, an item on an inventory; rather it becomes a point of entry into a common emotional ground of memory and belonging. It can transmit the climate of a lost world and keep alive in us a domestic intimacy with realities that might otherwise have vanished.[9]

In Heaney's aesthetic of ancestral and personal objects, the many poems about them are excavations from memory for the creation of a poetic 'country of the mind' and a 'temple of the spirit'. As he writes of Mossbawn in 'The Earth House' (1990): 'Out of that earth house I inherited / A stack of singular, cold memory-weights / To load me, hand and foot, in the scale of things.'[10] The successive volumes of poetry become increasingly weighted with those inherited objects, 'capsules of the past' he calls them. With remembered objects he writes a vanished culture back into the world.

The birthplaces of Bockhampton and Mossbawn are thus seen as the sources of poetic consciousness and renewal and of being mysteriously grounded in the ordinary world. Heaney's earliest recovered memory is of the cot he slept in as a small child, placed in the kitchen, and the sensation of touching his feet to the cement floor: 'When my feet touched the floor, I knew I was on my way somewhere, but at the time I could not have said exactly where. Nowadays I would say it was to poetic discovery' (*SS* 55–6). When he recounted his memory of the cot for Dennis O'Driscoll in *Stepping Stones* (2008), of how the bottom was made of removable boards so that he could pull some up and put his feet on the floor, he described himself as 'Antaeus Óg, just touching base' (*SS* 15). By the time the pre-reflective child found his bearings in the poems of *Death of a Naturalist* (1966), he had made the mythical Antaeus, the giant who was invincible while touching the ground, his alter ego. He wrote the poem 'Antaeus' on acceptance of the volume, too late for inclusion; he withheld it from a volume until the appearance of *North* nine years later (1975), but when he prepared his *Opened Ground: Selected Poems 1966–1996* (1988) he restored it below the bracketed composition date at the end of *Death of a Naturalist* (*OG* 15). It is at once a declaration of his stance as a poet, one in which he 'cannot be weaned / Off the earth's long contour . . . cradled in the dark that wombed me', and a defensive challenge to those 'sky-born' modernists who would demean his Hardyesque pastoral world in seeking their 'golden apples and Atlas'.

Heaney's *Death of a Naturalist* signalled the birth of a poet, born into and confidently defending his grounded aesthetic against the intellectual and visionary suppositions of modernist poetry: 'I learned', he said in an interview, 'that my local County Derry experiences, which I had considered archaic and irrelevant to "the modern world", were to be trusted.'[11]

Heaney returns to the myth in 'Hercules and Antaeus' (also in *North*), where the mind of Hercules is again 'big with golden apples, / his future hung with trophies', having lifted Antaeus 'out of his element / into a dream of loss / and origins'. In his own nightmare, the poet dreams that all of Antaeus's grounded strengths have been 'bequeathed to elegists' and scorned by triumphant Hercules as 'pap for the dispossessed' (*OG* 121–2). And then, twenty-four years later, on his seventieth birthday in April 2009, just after the publication of *Human Chain*, Heaney delivered on RTÉ a speech on the importance that the myth of Antaeus and Hercules had played in his writing life. 'In Greek mythology', he began, 'Antaeus was a giant who was born out of the earth and who consequently derived all his strength and prowess from contact with the earth':

> I identified with this earthman because I saw myself as something of an earthman, somebody with his poetic feet very much on the local ground . . . But at the same time I was also aware that Antaeus, for all his strength, was far from invulnerable; I knew indeed that he would be defeated in the end by another hero, the mighty Hercules.[12]

In the long run of his poetry, Heaney would finally encounter Hercules.

Aunt Sally soon presented another poet to her nephew, for her bookshelf contained not only Hardy's novels but a three-volume set of Yeats's poems, plays and stories. And when he turned sixteen in 1955 she gave him Eliot's *Collected Poems 1909–1935*, with all the poems through 'Burnt Norton'. 'For a long time', he later wrote in 'Learning from Eliot' (1988), 'that book represented to me my distance from the mystery and my unfittedness – as a reader or writer – for the vocation it represented . . . one did not need to know any literary thing in particular in the 1950s in order to know that Eliot was the way, the truth and the light, and that until one had found him one had not entered the kingdom of poetry' (*FK* 28–9). It would also be a while before he wrote the interrogative essay 'Yeats as an Example?' (1978), but he had at hand as a schoolboy the great leaders of the divided Romantic and classical traditions of modern literature to which one or the other of his favourite new authors belonged. On his twenty-first birthday, on the eve of graduating from Queen's University Belfast, Aunt Sally gave him his first bookcase, the contents of which became the canonical subject of a poem, 'The Bookcase', including on its shelves 'Macmillan's / Collected Yeats. And their Collected Hardy. / Yeats of "Memory." Hardy of "The Voice"' (*EL* 51).

As Heaney worked his way towards the separate kingdoms of Yeats and Eliot, Hardy remained the presiding spirit through whom he filtered his discovery of new poets; Hardy serves as the measure for Heaney's criticism and comparison of those poets as he writes about them.

His reading of Patrick Kavanagh is a case in point. Heaney wryly remembers Kavanagh's suspicion when he met him in a Dublin pub and asked what he thought of Hardy: he 'replied ex cathedra, as obliquely and authoritatively as a Yeats, "Pope's a good poet." And that was me in my box' (*SS* 73). Brushing off Kavanagh's put-down, Heaney went on to devote two essays and part of a poem to Kavanagh's achievement in Hardyesque terms. In writing of his admiration of the 'inner freedom' of Kavanagh's poetry, it is as though Heaney seeks to define himself in what he finds there: 'It is', he says, 'an example of self-conquest, a style discovered to express this poet's unique response to his universal ordinariness, a way of re-establishing the authenticity of personal experience and surviving as a credible being' (*FK* 157).

The modest emotional transport of Heaney's earth-rooted poems at this time is similar to that of Hardy, who had his ear to the ground and who certainly mistrusted, and led other poets to mistrust, the claim that the poet can transcend linear or historical time through mystical, magical, visionary, religious or prophetic constructs, as poets such as Blake, Yeats, Eliot and others aim to do in certain poems. Both poets have visions of reality, which are not the same as supernatural visions; both are content to accept Wordsworth's 'spots of time', which Heaney describes as 'moments at the very edge of consciousness which had lain for years in the unconscious as active lodes or nodes'.[13] His recollections of his early childhood experiences are just such 'spots of time'. For both Heaney and Hardy the emotional/intellectual heightening or exaltation that the poem brings is a personal epiphany, a sensation of revelation, a sweetness of mind, as in the secular Joycean sense of 'a sudden spiritual manifestation', to be recorded in the poem as 'the most delicate and evanescent of moments'.

Heaney's lucent epiphanies, like Hardy's, arise from echoes emanating from the darkness of the self and from the sounding of subconscious memories, aspects of a creative process strikingly confirmed in the poem 'North', where the poet hears the voices of drowned Nordic seamen rising out of their 'violence and epiphany' to speak in warning through the 'swimming tongue' of their sunken ship: 'It said, "Lie down / in the word-hoard, burrow / the coil and gleam / of your furrowed brain. / Compose in darkness. / Expect aurora borealis / in the long foray / but no cascade of light. / Keep your eye clear ... trust the feel of what nubbed treasure / your hands have known"' (*OG* 98–9). Yes, in the long poetic raid upon the darkness and word-hoard of the self, expect epiphanies, like the luminous phenomena of the low-lying northern lights (aurora borealis), but no supernatural 'cascade' of visionary light or prophetic revelation, no golden apples, no still points of the turning world, no visionary spirits from the gong-tormented sea. And in knowledge of the limits of poetic creativity, trust in the 'nubbed treasure' of the earthbound self. 'Glimmerings are what the soul's composed of', Heaney affirms in 'Old Pewter', 'And a whole late-flooding thaw of ancestors' (*SI* 22–3).

Standing behind the appearance of *North*, of course, are the Troubles, from the battle of the Bogside in 1969 to Bloody Sunday in Derry and Bloody Friday in Belfast in 1972, all causing violent upheavals in poetry as well as culture. By the publication of *North*, one of Heaney's main preoccupations was the difficult relation of 'violence and epiphany', of his inner freedom as a poet and the public's expected response to the extreme political crisis brought on by the continuing Troubles, a dilemma that perplexed him until he found resolution in his Nobel speech, 'Crediting Poetry' (1995), in his realization through Yeats and Eastern European poets writing under political oppression that there can be an order of poetry 'true to the impact of external reality and ... sensitive to the inner laws of the poet's being' at the same time (*OG* 420). The violence brought him closer to Yeats, who was utterly indifferent to Hardy; it led him to take as a new poetic motto Yeats's attempt 'to hold in a single thought reality and justice'; it made him a student of Yeats's 'Meditations in Time of Civil War', longing himself 'to exalt a lonely mind' with 'Befitting emblems of adversity'. The violence brought about a stylistic and thematic shift in volumes from *Field Work* (1979) to *The Haw Lantern* (1987), filled as they are with killings, funeral rites, elegies and a guilty conscience over the poetry not yet being equal to the historical crisis, the objects in

Mossbawn landscapes seemingly displaced by Derry and Belfast bombscapes. But not entirely.

In 1972 Heaney resigned his lectureship at Queen's University Belfast and moved his family to Glanmore cottage in Co. Wicklow. It was a move from the burnt-black city back into the countryside, a rebirth place, a haven, a move to recover his inner freedom and to weigh his previous commitments as a poet in relation to the Troubles. He was not to be diverted by the Troubles from his original poetic: fully half of all his poems are set within ten miles of his birthplace.

And yet, significant expansions were taking place. He had been silently learning from Eliot; however, there was no modern poet more unsympathetic to Hardy than Eliot, who had written to Pound about the Swinburnian and Georgian poets: 'I am as blind to the merits of these people as I am to Thomas Hardy',[14] and he would continue to write diminishingly of Hardy's poetry and fiction. As he did with Yeats, Heaney had to find a way of reconciling Eliot's high modernity and distaste for his master with his own aesthetic. What he found in Eliot's poetry was not an external landscape but an internal soundscape, what Eliot called the 'auditory imagination'; Heaney's fascination with its power in poetry became his critical point of reference for discussing the poems of Eliot and others in future essays.

We see Heaney moving deliberately between the Romantic and classical traditions of Yeats and Eliot, open to both, taking from each what most benefited and expanded his poetic and critical consciousness, but in the midst of such ventures he would invariably sound a retreat to Hardy. As Glanmore cottage was a haven from Belfast violence, Hardy was a haven from modernist poetics. When an interviewer asked, 'Did some influences from [your] reading, like Hardy . . . prove more durable havens . . . than others?' Heaney replied, 'Well, haven is a great word for it . . . Hardy is a haven, all right.'[15] And in that haven he searched for other poets who had discovered and embraced Hardy on their own as his natural heirs, members of a Hardy rank and file that moved like an underground fifth column against the dominant modernist movement. There was Auden, who declared Hardy his master for three years before he finally surrendered to Eliot; there was Dylan Thomas, who said that Yeats was the greatest but that he admired Hardy more than any poet of the century. There were numerous compatriots, but the most important to Heaney was Philip Larkin.

Larkin's first volume, *The North Ship* (1945), was filled with images and lines derivative of his first master, Yeats. When the volume was reissued in

1966 he declared that shortly after the initial publication he discovered Hardy, adding to the reissue a Hardyesque poem of the period to show the transformation and a 'postscript' to describe his conversion. 'When I came to Hardy', Larkin wrote in later reflection, having dissociated himself from what he called 'the myth-kitty' of Yeats and Eliot, 'it was with the sense of relief that I didn't have to try and jack myself up to a concept of poetry that lay outside my own life – this is perhaps what I felt Yeats was trying to make me do . . . Hardy taught one to feel rather than to write . . . and he taught one as well to have confidence in what one felt.'[16] Heaney locked on to Larkin as a model of the emerging Hardy tradition, stating that 'Larkin's antiheroics, and his absconding from anything visionary or bold did have its effect.'[17] In his first appreciative essay on Larkin, 'The Main of Light' (1982), he discussed the power of Larkin's Hardyesque treatment of the sadness of contemporary life, of his 'disillusioned compassion' for his countrymen.

This brings us back to Heaney's description in 'The Loose Box' of 'Thomas *dolens* Hardy'. Heaney saw more deeply into Hardy than Larkin, knew that Hardy's darker side was secondary to his primary quest for joy, love, beauty, zest and radiance in a tragic world, some of the most recurring words and concepts in Hardy's poetry. To Heaney, Hardy was not only an Antaeus figure but an Atlas figure who bore the weight of the ordinary world on his shoulders, voicing his *dolens*, his great sadness and sorrow, over the silent suffering of men and women in the ordinary world of Dorset; he felt their sense of loss and loneliness over lost love and lovers, their uncomprehending experience of mischance and missed chances. Heaney echoes Hardy's Brueghel-like vision in the late poem 'Known World', in which he voices 'That old sense of a tragedy going on / Uncomprehended, at the very edge / Of the usual, it never left me once' (*EL* 21). Heaney frequently quoted Hardy's defence of his tragic melancholy in 'In Tenebris II' – 'if way to the Better there be, it exacts a full look at the Worst'[18] – in full knowledge that readiness is all.

Deeply aware of Hardy's ability to break through tragedy into joy, Heaney turns to one of his favourite poems, 'The Darkling Thrush', written on the eve of the twentieth century when, to Hardy, 'every spirit upon earth' seemed 'fervourless as I'. Suddenly the poet sees and hears a beleaguered, 'blast beruffled' thrush break out 'In a full-hearted evensong / Of joy illimited', flinging his soul 'Upon the growing gloom'.[19] Heaney writes:

> We might say that Hardy, at this moment, experienced what Yeats says he experienced in the writing of *A Vision*: he too was simply overwhelmed by miracle whilst in the midst of it. But this, for sure, is not the Hardy to whom Larkin was converted after the strong enchantments of Yeats had

> failed for him. At that crucial point in his artistic development, Larkin turned to Hardy, the poet of human sadness, rather than to Hardy, the witness of irrational hope. (FK 348–9).

In speaking of Hardy and Yeats being 'overwhelmed by miracle' in the midst of a poem, Heaney at fifty was himself beginning to see things in a new light, if not of the miraculous, then surely of the marvellous, as marked in a transitional poem titled 'Fosterling', in which he announces a turn from an habitual 'heaviness' of mind and a poetry become 'sluggish' in the ordinary: 'Me waiting until I was nearly fifty / To credit marvels . . . So long for air to brighten, / Time to be dazzled and the heart to lighten' (*OG* 331). It is clear that Heaney had had his day of reckoning with Hercules: 'The import of the story about Hercules and Antaeus', he wrote, 'is complicated but potent. It tells us that we are made to live in at least two places at one time . . . We should keep our feet on the ground to signify that nothing is beneath us, but we should also lift up our eyes to say nothing is beyond us.'[20] While celebrating the reality of the marvellous in *Seeing Things* (1991), in making space in his reckoning and imagining 'for the marvellous as well as the murderous', as he described it in his Nobel speech (*OG* 423), he wrote two new sonnets about Hardy, one many years in conception, from childhood days in the Mossbawn scullery watching ripples moving outward in a pail of water. In discovering his new self in his old self, Heaney imagines Hardy as a child experimenting with infinity while lying on the ground in a field of sheep 'waiting / For sky to make it sing the perfect pitch / Of his dumb being, and that stir he caused / In the fleece-hustle was the original / Of a ripple that would travel eighty years / Outward from there, to be the same ripple / Inside him at its last circumference' (*OG* 336).[21] The poem comes in tribute to Hardy's own 're-illumed' transformation in poems like 'For Life I Had Never Cared Greatly', in which he describes his turn from the 'evasions' of his earlier poetry to the point when his life suddenly 'uncloaked a star . . . And showed its beams burning from pole to horizon': 'And so, the rough highway forgetting, / I pace hill and dale / Regarding the sky, / Regarding the vision on high, / And thus re-illumed have no humour for letting / My pilgrimage fail':[22] that long and stressful pilgrimage to joy and love and radiant beauty.

Heaney's transformation not only led him to admit the marvellous into his poetry, but to justify it in his criticism, particularly through Hardy. In the introduction to *The Redress of Poetry* (1995), his lectures as Oxford Professor of Poetry, he focuses on Hardy's 'Afterwards', a poem written in wonderment of what his country neighbours would say of him after his death. Hardy portrays them speaking in platitudes about his striking descriptions of objects in the natural world: 'If it be in the dusk when, like an eyelid's soundless blink / The dewfall-hawk comes crossing the shades to alight / Upon the wind-warped upland thorn, a gazer might think, / "To him this must have been a familiar sight".'[23] 'In one way', says Heaney, 'this is an expression of solidarity with the ordinary world where people stand around after the news of a death . . . and repeat conventional decencies': 'But then consciousness is given access to a dimension beyond the frontier where an overbrimming, totally resourceful expressiveness suddenly becomes available; and this entry into a condition of illuminated rightness becomes an entry into poetry itself' (*RP* xvii). That is Heaney fully in the heartland of the ordinary *and* the extraordinary, both, he now discovers, essential to the fully achieved poem, a position arrived at over a lifetime of listening to and reading Hardy ever more closely.

The symbolic drama of Antaeus and Hercules in Heaney's poetry plays itself out not in defeat or victory but in reconciliation, in a conjoining of ordinary and extraordinary worlds. For half of his career there was no stronger proponent or defender of Hardy than Heaney, as he shaped his earthbound aesthetic with Hardy's poetry and novels. Even as he openly explored and resisted the separate visionary kingdoms and traditions of Yeats and Eliot, he repeatedly returned to Hardy for nourishment and self-definition. But in 'the long foray', as he calls the poetic journey, he credited Yeats and Eliot with liberating him into the realm of the miraculous and marvellous, in the exhilarating recognition that the balance of earth and lift is essential to the greatest poetry. What is finally remarkable about Heaney's lifelong reading of Hardy is that in discovering the extraordinary in himself, he discovers it in Hardy as well, and shows us its workings in the poems.

Notes

1 Seamus Heaney, 'The Art of Poetry No. 75', interviewed by Henri Cole in May 1994, *Paris Review*, 144 (Fall 1997), 88–138 (at pp. 93–4).
2 *Ibid.*, p. 127.
3 Thomas Hardy, *The Complete Poems of Thomas Hardy* (New York: Macmillan, 1976), p. 563.
4 *Ibid.*, p. 468.
5 Heaney, 'Art of Poetry', p. 127.
6 John Brown, *In the Chair: Interviews with Poets from the North of Ireland* (Cliffs of Moher: Salmon, 2002), p. 77.
7 Heaney, 'Editor's Note', *Soundings '72: An Annual Anthology of New Irish Poetry* (Belfast: Blackstaff Press, 1972), pp. 5–6 (at p. 5).

8 Hardy, *Complete Poems*, p. 567.
9 Heaney, 'The Sense of the Past', *History Ireland*, 1/4 (Winter 1993), 33–37 (at p. 33). Heaney had earlier quoted the poem with similar commentary at the beginning of 'Place, Pastness, Poems: A Triptych', an essay in which he also discusses Hardy's 'Channel Firing'. *Salmagundi*, 68–69 (Fall 1985 – Winter 1986), 30–47.
10 *The Earth House* (Cheltenham: Wittington Press, printed for the Friends of the Cheltenham Festival of Literature, 1990): the first separate publication of one of the untitled sonnets (xl) in the 'Squarings' section of *Seeing Things* (1991) (*OG* 358).
11 Heaney, 'Talk with Seamus Heaney', interview with Seamus Deane, *New York Times*, 2 December 1979, 12.
12 'Seamus Heaney's Birthday Speech', Irish Museum of Modern Art, 13 April 2009, RTÉ: 'Heaney at 70'. www.rte.ie/heaneyat70/media/Heaney_Speech_13April09.pdf.
13 Heaney, *Stations* (Belfast: Ulsterman, 1975), p. 3.
14 *The Letters of T. S. Eliot*, vol. II: 1923–1925, ed. Valerie Eliot and Hugh Haughton (London: Faber and Faber, 2009), p. 557.
15 Brown, *In the Chair*, p. 77.
16 Philip Larkin, 'The Poetry of Hardy', *Required Writing: Miscellaneous Pieces 1955–1982* (London: Faber and Faber, 1983), pp. 175–6. Larkin also included more poems by Hardy than any other poet in his edition of *The Oxford Book of Twentieth-Century English Verse* (1973).
17 Heaney, 'Art of Poetry', 114.
18 Hardy, *Complete Poems*, p. 168.
19 *Ibid.*, p. 150.
20 Heaney, 'Birthday Speech', p. 4.
21 In the second poem Heaney corrects his misremembrance of the scene in the ewe-leaze and portrays Hardy 'in renowned old age / When sometimes he imagined himself a ghost / And circulated with that new perspective' (*OG* 337).
22 Hardy, *Complete Poems*, p. 537.
23 *Ibid.*, p. 553.

CHAPTER 7

W. B. Yeats

Margaret Mills Harper

For a number of years, Seamus Heaney came as often as he could to the Yeats Summer School, giving electrifying readings, attending lectures, joining discussions, and adding good company to the annual fortnightly 'Yeats camp'.[1] He was in Sligo as early as 1970. He would have been a regular by 1975, when Helen Vendler heard him read for the first time.[2] By the time I was invited to lecture in the 1990s, the summer school was deeply inflected by Heaney's presence. During the same decades, any number of academic readers of the two writers were drawn to the obvious and strong links between Heaney and Yeats. Buttressed by Bloomian theories of anxious influence, the temptations or necessities of canon formation, and issues in political literary history, and in response to Heaney's own obvious affiliations with the older poet, a substantial body of critical discourse developed analysing Heaney's debts to his predecessor.[3] That body of work continues to expand, one sign that a comparison between the two writers, as Bernard O'Donoghue points out on the first page of his Introduction to *The Cambridge Companion to Seamus Heaney*, 'has been found hard to avoid' on any number of occasions.[4]

I want to use these two phenomena – Seamus Heaney in Sligo, on the one hand, and a bibliography on the other – as something like directional signals for the remarks that follow, which meditate on the relationship between these two poets. Such a relationship, understood in a context that derives a good deal of its intellectual energy from thinkers like Saussure, Lévi-Strauss, Freud, and Kristeva, tends now to be labelled *intertextuality*, a word that seems almost to have replaced *influence* as the term of art most useful for understanding how texts derive from, lead to, echo, or presume other texts. Unsatisfied with the authoritarian presumptions in the notion of influence, the idea that earlier texts exert power over later ones, paradigms suggesting (re)circulation, dia- or polylogue are now more common. The recycling of words and texts is expressed using other terms as well, like those of Gérard Genette, who names the many ways texts respond to each other, from genre to quotation to imitation to bibliographic codes, in his trilogy of aptly named books: *The Architext*, *Paratexts*, and *Palimpsests.* Whatever terms are used, I am tempted to agree with Michael Riffaterre (though not exactly in the way he intended) that 'Intertextuality is . . . the mechanism specific to literary reading. It alone, in fact, produces significance, while linear reading, common to literary and nonliterary texts, produces only meaning.'[5] Signs and not only meaning: Riffaterre's distinction between 'significance' and 'meaning' is particularly appropriate for the unrepentant symbolist Yeats, for whom, as he wrote in an early essay, 'all things are shadows of spiritual things'.[6] Heaney, 'seeing things' with a sensibility attuned to medieval notions of the sign, also links the physical world and an indwelling numinosity. Augustine's definition of the sign in *De doctrina Christiana* is Heaneyesque: 'Signum est enim res praeter speciem quam ingerit sensibus aliud aliquid ex se faciens in cogitationem venire' ('a sign is something which, besides the impression it offers to the senses, conveys something other to the mind').[7]

Words do not flow in one direction, as the etymology of *influence* suggests, but the old word *fluere* still does good work. The presence (or present absence) of one text in another, the trace of one writer in the work of another, is less like a *tractus* than a watercourse in a tidal zone, where incoming and outgoing flows turn and mingle in interstitial space. Poets read and respond to earlier poets, and what the later ones say expresses and forms them. In this incoming formation, the rising tide I am symbolizing by that pile of books and articles on Yeats and Heaney, the later poet both appropriates and extends the vitality of the earlier. Auden's elegy for Yeats comes to mind in this regard, though Auden uses a range of metaphors in addition to water: Yeats's words have indeed been 'modified' in 'the guts' of readers like Heaney, chewed and digested and changed into the energy of the later writing. Neil Corcoran is one of many to whom Auden's 'In Memory of W. B. Yeats' has seemed apt, noting that 'One of the admirers Yeats has most crucially become is Seamus Heaney.'[8]

The transformation of poet into admirer runs counter to chronology, too, in the sense that history, or the past that has attained a form available for the present, is constructed in and from the present. Posterity creates forebears; later words nourish and vivify those that have come before them.[9] This other direction is symbolized for me by Seamus Heaney's contribution to the creation of who and what Yeats has become since Heaney began reading him. This effluence, if you will, includes Heaney's criticism of Yeats, his choice of Yeatsian subjects for attention, and his friendship with a generation of Yeatsian critics, including Ann Saddlemyer and Helen Vendler, both of whom made crucial differences in Heaney's life and work. As Heaney notes of the relationship between Eliot and Dante, 'Eliot was recreating Dante in his own image' (*FK* 173). Similarly, for readers of at least a generation, Heaney has been recreating Yeats.

In fact, I want to suggest that a distinctive poetic place may be located where the Yeatsian Heaney and the Heaneyan Yeats meet. The appraisal that follows will follow the structure I have been suggesting: the influx of Yeats into Heaney, then the receding and exposing tide of Heaney into Yeats, and in conclusion, a few remarks about a zone that does not follow one or another trajectory. I will begin with a brief overview of what Yeats did for Heaney, particularly in his latter years, given that much work has already been done on earlier points of connection. A second section will suggest what Heaney has done for Yeats. A third section reflects upon a pair of poems: Yeats's 'The Cold Heaven' and Heaney's 'Lightenings' i, from the sequence 'Squarings'. I will not remain in the foursquare structure provided by the direct connections between the poems but conclude with remarks that are crossings, to use Heaney's metaphor, or the unstable but most dynamic point at the ends of gyres, to use Yeats's.

Influence: Yeats to Heaney

Based merely on the number of references to Yeats in Heaney's work, a reader might decide that Yeats represents for Heaney perhaps the most important of the many poetic predecessors and peers that become expressive touchstones, tried against the ideas and voice of someone whom Helen Vendler describes as 'among the most learned of contemporary poets'.[10] Major essays by Heaney focus on Yeats, and important poems speak to poems by Yeats.[11] Even when writing about other poets, Heaney may well have recourse to Yeats's words, as when he describes Dante as belonging to 'the rag-and-bone shop of Eliot's middle-ageing heart', Hill's 'indomitable Englishry', Kavanagh's having 'cleared a space where, in Yeats's words, "The soul recovers radical innocence, / And learns at last that it is self-delighting, / Self-appeasing, self-affrighting, / And that its own sweet will is Heaven's will"', or Plath's ability to access a place beyond conscious control – 'whatever place a poem like Yeats's "Long-Legged Fly" emerges from' (*FK* 31–2, 90, 144, 227). Heaney's many quotations from Yeats include single words and turns of phrase that arise seemingly spontaneously, as if Yeats's language were embedded in Heaney's poetic DNA. Other poetry, such as the *Aeneid*, occurs on a similar almost cellular level in Heaney, but Yeats (unlike, for example, Virgil, Dante, or even other

English-language poets like Wordsworth) speaks a language close in time and space to Heaney's own. Yeats's language, as it were, is one of the primary colours in the palette with which Heaney paints.

In general, Yeats seems to have given Heaney early permission to express emotion more directly and musically than he might otherwise have received, given where and when he came of age. Yeats's commitment to and experimentation with traditional form, as well as powerful aural resonance, clearly gave Heaney material to raid for technical possibility.[12] Yeats also gave Heaney models (both exemplary and cautionary) in treating history or myth and responding artistically and ethically to unstable and violent times. Paradoxically enough, given that Heaney's voice is more inclined towards the demotic than the hierophantic, more Keatsian-receptive than Nietzschean-dramatic, the example of Yeats's voice has been most bracing in several different ways. Yeats's flexible confessional voice, whether as a love poet, an active creator in cultural politics, or an ambivalent witness to ageing, was a helpful module in Heaney's singing school.

Yeats is one of the poets whose work shadows Heaney's engagement with the issue of public voice, the carefully calibrated though seemingly undeliberated persona or mask that is an unavoidable aspect of the modern lyric voice. A poet, as Yeats famously put it, is never the 'bundle of accident and incoherence that sits down to breakfast; he has been reborn as an idea, something intended, complete'.[13] As Dennis O'Driscoll notes, Heaney quoted this statement frequently (*SS* 197). Heaney responded to the suggestion that the poem, once written, is independent of the poet, but it is clear from iterations of the statement in other essays (notably 'Feeling into Words' and 'Yeats as an Example?') that he appreciated the independence, or at least privacy, that this formulation of art also granted to the artist. Poets who are reborn as ideas are safer from intrusion. An introverted Yeats lived behind his personae, a fact that explains some of the energy behind his theories of the mask – as well as the intensity of the poetry in which he seems to drop it. When Heaney writes about other poets or himself, he too uses 'exposure' to powerful effect, as well as masks from Incertus to Northman to Sweeney to authoritative man of letters to Nobel laureate. He also crafted the arc of a career and life that is yet another marvel to credit, as if he couldn't have written it better. Early themes and settings were reprised in his last volumes, and a sense of unexpected pattern was part of the blow of his loss. Kevin Young spoke for many in his elegy for Heaney: 'I hear *Noli timere* / everywhere. . . .'[14]

Effluence: Heaney to Yeats

Yeats's last decade or so 'as himself', on the other hand, was a fractious mess, full of depression and anger over politics, unbecoming sexual adventures, personae that spit with vitriol and artistic pronouncements that were far out of the mainstream (in his notorious editing of the *Oxford Book of Modern Verse*, for example). Meanwhile, the Yeats who had become his admirers was lionized in academic and cultural circles. Only after the 1960s, following the death of Mrs Yeats, when the fiftieth anniversary of the Easter Rising was itself history and Irish politics was being overturned by the violence in the North, did this Yeats begin in earnest to be dismantled, the unassailably Great Irish Poet at last tugged into some disarray. Conor Cruise O'Brien's pivotal essay 'Passion and Cunning: An Essay on the Politics of W. B. Yeats' (1965) was followed by such voices as Seamus Deane, W. J. McCormack, and David Lloyd. Thus, when Heaney was first writing about Yeats in the late 1970s, he spoke into a complicated political space. But Heaney was adept at speaking carefully in risky discursive settings, and three essays from this period outline Yeats's poetic merit as well as measuring his failings. For example, in 'A Tale of Two Islands: Reflections on the Irish Literary Revival', Heaney criticizes Yeats's Protestant politics (and quotes in full one of Yeats's least successful late poems) but also recognizes something 'artistically proper and exhilarating' in the romanticism of the Anglo-Irish Revival: 'Writers need images and situations which release in them whatever is latent and submerged and allow them to appease their perhaps unconscious yearnings and tensions.'[15] 'The Makings of a Music: Reflections on Wordsworth and Yeats' compares the practices of the two poets in terms of different negotiations with inspiration and formal control. Most importantly, 'Yeats as an Example?' finds an admirable continuum in Yeats's intransigences with regard to his occult spirituality, cultural nationalist politics, and self-assertive theatricality. The essay concludes with an argument that extends the implicit essentialist gendering of the earlier essay (Wordsworth in the feminine position, Yeats in the masculine) to a strikingly gendered conclusion. Yeats's late best work, Heaney argues, bends from its 'priapic' qualities (*FK* 98) towards the 'maternal', laying aside the patriarchal 'great fur coat of attitude' for an image of honey-bees and stare's nest in 'Meditations in Time of Civil War', and ending in the strange 'motherly kindness' of the ritual described in 'Cuchulain Comforted' (*FK* 110–11).

Heaney's observations about Cuchulain in Yeats's poem bring to mind Heaney's own St Kevin, who provides his own house for a stare in 'a poem deeply at one with the weak and the strong of this earth ... but also unflinching in its belief in the propriety and beauty of life transcended into art, song, words' (111). 'St Kevin and the Blackbird', published nearly twenty years after Heaney's early essays on Yeats, owes something to Heaney's awareness of Yeats's spiritual life, especially in his late years (after his marriage and the arrival of the automatic script through George Yeats, and also after his renewed study of Hindu and Buddhist philosophies). The converse is also true: although Heaney was not the only voice urging for reappraisals of a stereotypically masculine Yeats, striding commandingly through Irish and modernist poetry, Heaney's persuasive critical prose and allusive poems have worked in recent decades to nudge changes along these lines in dominant perceptions of Yeats. The battles of the 1970s and 1980s are no longer actively waged. Heaney (along with other poets, notable among them Michael Longley and Eavan Boland) found something salutary about the mess as well as the mastery of Yeats, and this Yeats is one that has increasingly found purchase. This Yeats is characterized by 'sweetness flowing into the breast' (*FK* 146) as well as toughmindedness: this Yeats is one whose foul rag-and-bone shop and cold-eyed viewer of horseman rub against each other, gyre inside as well as outside complementary gyre.[16]

Fluence: Intertidal Zones

In fact, Heaney takes pains to make sure that his essays on Yeats do not fall into the simple binaries my own may so far have inferred: tough-minded or sweet-hearted, controlled or vulnerable, active or passive, made or found, reality or justice, joy or night (the terms invoked by the title of a later essay on Yeats and Larkin).[17] The art to which Heaney is drawn and to which he aspires undergoes a kind of alchemical reaction in which 'deliberation can be so intensified that it becomes synonymous with inspiration' (*FK* 107), skill metamorphosed into a kind of letting go. The Yeats he invents in his earlier essays is exemplary in the integrity of his lifelong commitment to art conceived as (in Yeats's words) a 'vision of reality'[18] with the emphasis on 'vision' as much as 'reality'. Heaney's later Yeats does not need to push so hard against the possibility of doubt or refusal to the status of art; instead, this Yeats reaches for something beyond his own masterful achievements in late works like 'Man and the Echo' or 'Cuchulain Comforted'. (These differing portrayals of Yeats of course reflect the maker of the portraits at different points in his career; I suspect Heaney was well aware of this point, which is after all like the one he makes about the different Dantes of Eliot and Mandelstam in the essay 'Envies and Identifications: Dante and the Modern Poet', *FK* 168–79.)

I will let Dante guide me to my final observations, which use as examples two poems, one by Yeats and one by Heaney, which in very different ways also treat the state of the soul. In an essay entitled 'Sixth Sense, Seventh Heaven', published in the *Dublin Review* in 2002, Heaney discusses what he calls his 'unconscious dialogue' with Yeats's poem 'The Cold Heaven' while writing the poem 'Lightenings' i, from the sequence 'Squarings'. Heaney writes:

> The first draft was written down in the Reading Room of the National Library in Dublin on an afternoon in August 1988, on the day I completed the long task of annotating a selection of Yeats's poems for *The Field Day Anthology of Irish Writing*. ... [T]here was a definite sense of release. ... A great sense too of the dimensions of Yeats's achievement, the boldness of his imagining, the extravagance of his concerns with life after death, with the adventures of the soul when it leaves the body, with its 'shiftings', as he calls it one place.

Heaney's poem begins with the striking line 'Shifting brilliancies', a phrase that can serve as synecdoche for the metamorphosis Yeats's poem undergoes in Heaney's reading of it. 'The Cold Heaven' is terrifying, and Yeats was terrified as he drafted the poem in February 1911, on a train en route to an amateur performance of his play *The Countess Cathleen* in Norwich. As Deirdre Toomey has noted, the journey was bound to bring back memories of Maud Gonne. In the mid-1940s, Gonne told A. Norman Jeffares in an interview that the poem came from feelings of loneliness and responsibility for past mistakes, leading to what Jeffares calls 'a momentary intensity of dream-like perception'.[19] (Heaney mentions that Jeffares alerted him to Gonne's recollection of Yeats saying that the poem 'was his attempt to describe the feeling roused in him by the cold detached sky in winter').[20] An image of ice burning is called forth from the poet's sense that he is to blame for the pain he has caused in his life. In Yeats's way of thinking, any great and lasting psychic pain must be worked out, and in the poem, the speaker is caught up and swept away in long, seemingly unstoppable lines, 'riddled with light' as if the truth had him against a wall facing a firing-squad or were peppering him with unanswerable questions. The final two lines of Yeats's poem wonder about a ghost's horrible loneliness and absolute exposure, 'sent out on the roads for punishment'.

Heaney, inspired by an image of an elderly beggar and an abandoned homestead, and fortified by Yeats, writes a poem also about judgement, but one which moves beyond blame into 'Unroofed scope. Knowledge-freshening wind'. Yeats's focus on a 'rook-delighting heaven' morphs into Heaney's attention to open sky. That sky, which symbolizes the soul's doom, is cold but also bracing to the later poet, who is psychically ready to face what follows 'particular judgement': a 'soul-free cloud life'. Yeats's speaker 'took all the blame out of all sense and reason', the repetition of the word *all* in the just-too-long hexameter line hammering in his head like Emily Dickinson's boots in 'I felt a funeral in my brain'. The roofless walls of Heaney's loose pentameter hold the poet so that he can face the 'old truth dawning: there is no next-time-round'. Both poems are twelve lines long, but while Yeats's feels like a truncated sonnet, Heaney, as he describes in the *Dublin Review* essay, felt that 'The great thing about the twelve lines I've been discussing is that they felt both finished and ready to be expanded upon'. Writing it set him going on the remarkable sequence 'Squarings' – several poems of which notably address and (mis)quote Yeats.[21]

Heaney provides another wilful reading of Yeats's poem in the later essay 'Joy or Night: Last Things in the Poetry of W. B. Yeats and Philip Larkin'. This essay finds 'The Cold Heaven' finally suggesting 'that there is an overall purpose to life' even while describing the 'sudden apprehension that there is no hiding place, that the individual human life cannot be sheltered from the galactic cold' (*FK* 318). The poem does so by the 'intrinsically poetic action of its rhymes, its rhythms, and its exultant intonation', which 'create an energy and an order which promote the idea that there exists a much greater, circumambient energy and order within which we have our being' (319). In other words, Yeats's art is his traumatic topic's other gyre, and that art is an image of 'superabundant life' (321). Current thinking about Yeats is likely to share Heaney's sense of conflicting energies in Yeats's art, as well as the centrality of esotericism to Yeats's artistic achievement. Heaney's reading of Yeats also underscores the degree to which Heaney has been a strong apologist for the value of poetry to human life on both an individual and a social scale.

The poem by Heaney's Yeats, chilling and heart-shattering vision held in tension by the force of art, might be informed by another poem that begins with travel, this time in a car: Heaney's 'Postscript'.[22] 'Postscript' leads in turn to Yeats's poem 'The Wild Swans at Coole', to which it nods on several levels, including temporal and spatial in-betweenness, a setting of autumn in the west of Ireland, speaker observing water and swans, and even formal elements like rhyme (most notably, the half-rhymes *stones* and *swans*) and word choice (such as the Yeatsian *foam* and *glitter*). The speaker of 'Postscript', like the one of 'The Cold Heaven', is imaginatively between worlds, 'neither here nor there', hit by 'soft buffetings' that 'catch the heart off guard and blow it open'. Here it is less helpful to think of Yeats and Heaney in a unidirectional current but flowing in and out and into each other, like a tide or a turlough. The multiplicity of poetry is where the relationship between Heaney and Yeats leads, not to an answer so much as the question of whether we will be awake when we find these headstrong paddlers have flown away.

Notes

1 Heaney is first mentioned in the Yeats International Summer School brochure from 1970, when he gave a lecture on 'Yeats's Diction'; lectures followed in 1971 (on 'Yeats the Poet'), 1972 ('The Choice'), and 1977 ('The Wind Among the Reeds').

2 Vendler reports her response to a reading in Sligo of 'some of the most extraordinary poems I had ever heard' in the Introduction to *Seamus Heaney* (Cambridge, MA: Harvard University Press, 1998), p. 3. These are probably the poems from *North* that Heaney read from for several years before publication in 1975. See letters from Michael Longley to Heaney dated September/October 1972, Seamus Heaney papers, MSS 960, 41/11, Rose Library, Emory University.

3 Neil Corcoran has summarized the corpus of discussions of Yeats and Heaney in two versions of an essay: 'Yeats and Heaney', in Bernard O'Donoghue (ed.), *The Cambridge Companion to Seamus Heaney* (Cambridge University Press, 2009), pp. 165–77; and the expanded 'Question Me Again: Reflections on W. B. Yeats and Seamus Heaney', *Yeats Annual*, 18 (2013), 215–38.

4 O'Donoghue, 'Introduction', *Cambridge Companion to Seamus Heaney*, pp. 1–18 (at p. 1).

5 As is perhaps appropriate for an essay on intertextuality, I quote not from Riffaterre but from Genette's quotation of Riffaterre's essay 'La syllepse intertextualle', in *Palimpsests: Literature in the Second Degree*, trans. Channa Newman and Claude Doubinsky (Lincoln: University of Nebraska Press, 1997), p. 2.

6 The essay, published in the Dublin edition of the *Daily Express*, is reprinted in W. B. Yeats, *Uncollected Prose*, vol. II, ed. John P. Frayne and Colton Johnson (London: Macmillan, 1975), pp. 141–2.

7 St. Augustine, *De doctrina Christiana*, ed. R.P.H. Green (Oxford: Clarendon Press, 1995), ii.1.

8 Corcoran, 'Yeats and Heaney', p. 166, and 'Question Me Again', p. 220.

9 Fritz Senn introduced me to this idea in a workshop on Joyce and Homer at the Zürich James Joyce Foundation in 1995, considering Joyce's influence on Homer.

10 Vendler, *Seamus Heaney*, p. 4.

11 In addition to works cited by Corcoran, see Richard Rankin Russell, 'Heaney's Yeats', *Literary Imagination*, 18/3 (November 2016), 199–220;

and the sections entitled 'Falling into Dualism' and 'Joy *and* Night' from Chapters 3 and 5 of John Dennison's *Seamus Heaney and the Adequacy of Poetry* (Oxford University Press, 2015).

12 As Meg Tyler points out, '*The Princeton Encyclopedia of Poetry and Poetics* tells us "no major poet in English had used near rhyme consistently until Hopkins and Yeats"–which is itself a good reason to find it turning up in Heaney' (165). Meg Tyler, *A Singing Contest: Conventions of Sound in the Poetry of Seamus Heaney* (New York and London: Routledge, 2005).

13 W. B. Yeats, *The Collected Works*, vol. v: *Later Essays*, ed. William H. O'Donnell (New York: Macmillan, 1994), p. 204.

14 Kevin Young, *Blue Laws: Selected and Uncollected Poems 1995–2016* (New York: Knopf, 2016), p. 498.

15 Seamus Heaney, 'A Tale of Two Islands: Reflections on the Irish Literary Revival', in P. J. Drudy (ed.), *Irish Studies I* (Cambridge University Press, 1980), pp. 1–20.

16 David O'Grady argues convincingly that the speaker of Yeats's epitaph in the famous final lines of 'Under Ben Bulben' is the subject casting a cold eye, not the horseman. David O'Grady, 'Yeats's Epitaph and Esoteric Buddhism', *New Hibernia Review / Iris Éireannach Nua*, 20/3 (Fómhar/Autumn 2016), 125–40.

17 This essay, 'Joy or Night: Last Things in the Poetry of W. B. Yeats and Philip Larkin', was originally focused on Yeats alone, as Dennison notes in *Seamus Heaney and the Adequacy of Poetry*, p. 165 n99.

18 *The Variorum Edition of the Poems of W. B. Yeats*, ed. Peter Allt and Russell K. Alspach (New York and London: Macmillan, 1966), p. 369.

19 A. Norman Jeffares, *Yeats: Man and Poet* (London: Routledge & Kegan Paul, 1949), p. 175.

20 Heaney quotes loosely from Jeffares, whose description of the interview in his *Commentary* (and *New Commentary*, p. 124) is derived from recollections recorded there, in his Trinity College Dublin PhD dissertation, and in the first edition of *Man and Poet* (174–5). A. Norman Jeffares, *A New Commentary on the Poems of W. B. Yeats* (Stanford University Press, 1984).

21 Warwick Gould alerted me to the passage in Yeats's *The Trembling of the Veil* that is the source for Heaney's lines (in 'Crossings' xxiv): 'Yeats said, *To those who see spirits, human skin / For a long time afterwards appears most coarse.*' Describing his visionary dream of a naked woman shooting an arrow at a star, Yeats writes, 'I still remember the tint of that marvellous flesh which makes all human flesh seem unhealthy, and remember that others who have seen such forms have remembered the same characteristic' (*Autobiographies*, London: Macmillan, 1955), pp. 372–3.

22 See Medbh McGuckian's Yeatsian-titled 1999 pamphlet *Horsepower Pass By! A Study of the Car in the Poetry of Seamus Heaney* (Coleraine: Cranagh Press, 1999). McGuckian notes that in 'Postscript', 'It is as if the real beating heart had no protecting flesh but the car body which affords only glimpses of eternity and visions of arrested light towards which we must maintain progress and outward movement' (34–5).

CHAPTER 8

T.S. Eliot

Stephen Regan

In 'Learning from Eliot', a lecture he delivered at Harvard University in 1988, Seamus Heaney confesses to having been 'daunted by the otherness of Eliot and all that he stood for', and he admits that it was some time before he 'began to grow up to Eliot' (*FK* 26).[1] As a 'schoolboy in a Catholic boarding school in Derry' in the mid-1950s Heaney read Eliot's 'Journey of the Magi' and could readily identify with the Christmas imagery, and even (as the son of a farmer) appreciate the reek of 'actual country' in the poem, but the formal complexity and imaginative strangeness of Eliot's verse eluded him (*FK* 32). 'The Hollow Men', he tells us, was understood in terms required by the school examination system – that is, as an exploration and manifestation of loss of faith in the modern world – and its 'rare music' was only fully appreciated later. 'Ash-Wednesday', he recalls, stirred him with its sensuous passages, but only later did he perceive 'the finer tone and stricter disciplines of Eliot's poetry' (*FK* 28–9). Given the rural life and labour to which the young Heaney was accustomed, it should come as no surprise that Patrick Kavanagh, R.S. Thomas and Ted Hughes were to have a more immediate effect upon his early poetry than that of T.S. Eliot. By his own admission, what he heard in the work of these poets was 'more in tune with the actual voices of my own first world than the ironies and elegances of MacNeice and Eliot could ever have been'.[2] While Eliot's poetry was an acquired taste for Heaney, it seems that Eliot's critical essays worked upon him more immediately. However long it took Heaney to 'grow up' to Eliot, it is clear that his critical faculties were strongly responsive to Eliot as early as 1972 when he composed an essay on Hugh MacDiarmid titled 'Tradition and an Individual Talent' (*P* 195–8).

Heaney's reading of Eliot's essays during his undergraduate years at Queen's University, Belfast was clearly decisive in terms of alerting him to his own complex relationships with tradition, and sharpening his appetite for what Eliot memorably termed 'the "auditory imagination" . . . the feeling for syllable and rhythm, penetrating far below the conscious levels of thought and feeling'.[3] That notion of 'the auditory imagination' takes on a central role in Heaney's own critical vocabulary, shaping his way of reading and interpreting poetry more than any of the other critical touchstones inherited from Eliot or (for that matter) from Robert Frost or Wallace Stevens or Czesław Miłosz. The auditory imagination is a term that became popular after Eliot used it in his essay on Matthew Arnold in *The Use of Poetry and the Use of Criticism* (1933), though Neil Corcoran surmises that very likely Heaney discovered the term in John Hayward's edition of Eliot's *Selected Prose*, published by Penguin in 1953 (a supposition that Heaney confirms in the interviews with Dennis O'Driscoll in *Stepping Stones*). As Corcoran points out, though, what is most striking is the powerful way in which Heaney absorbs Eliot's poetic ideals and transforms them into a critical method of his own. Perhaps the best example of this critical transmutation is the remarkable opening paragraph of 'Englands of the Mind' (1976), his influential essay on Philip Larkin, Ted Hughes and Geoffrey Hill, in which he first gives Eliot's definition of 'the auditory imagination' and then steadily but surely makes it his own:

> I presume Eliot was thinking here about the cultural depth-charges latent in certain words and rhythms, that binding secret between words in poetry that delights not just the ear but the whole backward and abysm of mind and body; thinking of the energies beating in and between words that the poet brings into half-deliberate play; thinking of the relationship between the word as pure vocable, as articulate noise, and the word as etymological occurrence, as symptom of human history, memory and attachments. (FK 82)

Heaney applies the term 'auditory imagination' to the poetry of his near contemporaries with striking results, showing how it might enable a deeper critical thinking about Larkin, Hughes and Hill by encouraging readers to listen to their language, but he does the same with the poetry of Sylvia Plath in *The Government of the Tongue* and, somewhat audaciously, he applies the term to Eliot's own poetry in 'Learning from Eliot'. Confidently appropriating Eliot's own critical vocabulary, he draws our attention to the 'undulant cadences and dissolvings and reinings-in' of the 'Death by Water' section of *The Waste Land*, and encourages us to listen to 'the interweaving and repetition' of words that go round 'like a linked dance through the ear' in the opening lines of 'Burnt Norton' (*FK* 34–5).

Heaney claims in the *Stepping Stones* interviews that his second volume of poems, *Door into the Dark* (1969), was inspired by Eliot's idea of the 'dark embryo' that forms in the poet's consciousness and gradually takes on the form and speech of a poem.[4] A strong psychological interest in the processes of perception and imagination in that book was accompanied by a new, exploratory way of thinking about poetry and place that probably derives from *Four Quartets*. That enigmatic Eliot voice, part travelling companion, part spiritual director, can be heard drifting through some early Heaney poems, as with these lines from 'The Peninsula': 'so you will not arrive / But pass through, though always skirting landfall' (*OG* 21). At this stage in Heaney's career as a poet, however, Eliot's influence on the poetry is not strongly marked, nor is it explicit in what follows in *Wintering Out* and *North*. Even so, if the controversial Bog Poems in those volumes owe a debt to Yeats and his search for 'Befitting emblems of adversity', they also suggest Heaney's positive response to 'the mythical method' described by Eliot in '*Ulysses*, Order, and Myth' (1923). It is, of course, Yeats, as much as Joyce, that Eliot has in mind when he writes about 'a way of controlling, of ordering, of giving a shape and a significance to the immense panorama of futility and anarchy which is contemporary history'.[5]

Anthony J. Cuda has argued persuasively that Eliot was very much on Heaney's mind during the composition of *North*, even if there is little obvious textual evidence in Heaney's poetry at this time. He draws attention to an epigraph that Heaney had planned to use in *North*, comprising ten lines from *Little Gidding*, beginning with 'This is the use of memory'.[6] These lines from Eliot appear in an uncorrected proof copy of *North*, currently in the Special Collections and Archives of the Robert W. Woodruff Library at Emory University, but they were deleted from the book by Heaney before it went to press in 1975. As Cuda points out, the lines in question are highly relevant to the various uses of memory in *North*, with its candid exposure of how memory functions in ways that are both brutal and redemptive. He goes on to show how Heaney would repeatedly return to the 'use of memory' passage in *Little Gidding*, citing it in numerous essays and talks, including his memorial address for Robert Lowell at St Luke's Church in London on 5 October 1977.

A crucial part of Eliot's legacy of course, for Heaney and for other modern poets, is in transmitting the work of Dante. In 'Learning from Eliot', Heaney writes of how Eliot's 'dream processes' fed upon Dante's visionary art in the *Divine Comedy* (*FK* 31). Heaney's own turning to Dante by way of Eliot finds its most creative expression in the purgatorial 'Station Island' (1984), not least in the loosely adapted *terza rima* verse form. Heaney's conversations with the dead show the unmistakable imprint of Eliot's encounter with a ghostly figure 'In the uncertain hour before the morning' in 'Little Gidding'.[7] Heaney writes about the same 'Dantesque set-piece of the dawn patrol' in *The Government of the Tongue*

(1988), this time presenting 'Little Gidding' as an exemplary instance of how the imagination might endure the impact and destruction of war, invigorated and sustained by tradition. He notes how the 'matutinal airs' of the passage float from Dante to Shakespeare in their recollection of Hamlet confronting the ghost of his father (*GT* 43). In the poems written after *North*, Heaney now situating himself physically and mentally in Glanmore turns more and more to the meditative timbre of *Four Quartets*, especially 'Little Gidding'. Hope and anticipation, as well as trepidation, are powerfully registered in his 'Glanmore Sonnets': 'And I am quickened with a redolence / Of farmland as a dark unblown rose' (*OG* 163). If Yeats and James Clarence Mangan find a well-ploughed furrow in Heaney's *Field Work* (1979), so too does Eliot, whose symbolic rose also takes on a dark and elegiac resonance in *Four Quartets*: 'The moment of the rose and the moment of the yew-tree / Are of equal duration.'[8]

As Heaney 'grew up' to Eliot, he seemed increasingly to accommodate and emulate the mystical qualities of *Four Quartets*, most obviously in the visionary, transcendental poems of *Seeing Things* (1991). Virgil and Dante, both mediated through Eliot, are well represented in *Seeing Things*, especially in 'The Golden Bough' and 'The Crossing'. 'The Golden Bough', for instance, contains that strange word 'foresuffered', echoing Eliot's presentation of Tiresias in 'The Fire Sermon' section of *The Waste Land*: 'And I Tiresias have foresuffered all / Enacted on this same divan or bed'.[9] Eliot's example also prompts the letting in of light in *Seeing Things*. Neil Corcoran observes the 'lexicon of luminosity' in that volume with its brilliancies, radiance, blazing, dawning and brightness. He notes that this is a Dantean inheritance, but reminds us of Eliot's remarks on Dante's style: 'The style of Dante has a peculiar lucidity', says Eliot. 'The thought may be obscure, but the word is lucid, or rather translucent.' Eliot also discusses Dante's 'masterly use of that imagery of *light* which is the form of certain types of mystical experience'.[10]

In *Electric Light* (2001) and *District and Circle* (2006), Heaney circles back on his own coming to consciousness as a writer, and yet another side of Eliot's legacy emerges. The title poem of *Electric Light* alludes to the electrification of rural areas, including Co. Derry, in the 1930s and 1940s, but it also clearly signals the emergence of a new and bright conception of poetry and poetic vocation. It is as if the poet's memories are given a powerful new charge. A switch is pressed and a light shines searchingly over the long perspective of the past sixty years. As Heaney put it in the Poetry Book Society bulletin accompanying *Electric Light*: 'moments that were radiant or distressful at the time c[a]me back in the light of a more distanced and more informed consciousness'.[11] 'Electric Light' gives symbolic resonance to the light switch and the wireless knob, granting the mature writer a new way of seeing his own poetic calling, and of tuning in to the voices of his education, including those of T.S. Eliot, James Joyce and Philip Larkin.

'Electric Light' opens with a pre-electric image of candle wax, but also with the possibility of epiphany. The grandmother's mangled thumb nail, likened to the congealed 'Candle-grease ... dark-streaked with soot', is transformed by the light of imagination into a thing of beauty, 'puckered pearl' (*EL* 80). As we slip from tercet to tercet, new shapes and patterns of memory are brought into play. The 'ancient' mangled thumb is now likened to 'Rucked quartz' and leads us down the rock-strewn footpath to the Sybil's cave in Virgil's *Aeneid.* The grandmother, a modern Sybil in her unzipped 'fur-lined felt slippers', would not be out of place in *The Waste Land*, except that Heaney's attitude is one of familial warmth and attachment rather than comic condescension or ironic disdain. We are reminded here of the Sybil as she appears in the epigraph to *The Waste Land*, from the *Satyricon* of Petronius: 'Nam Sibyllam quidem Cumis ego ipse oculis meis' ('I saw with my own eyes the Sibyl at Cumae').[12] The child's vision of the grandmother has the force of revelation, occurring 'In the first house where I saw electric light'. The electric light is left 'turned on' to appease the homesick child, but what might have been a 'waste of light' is seen retrospectively to have had a productive power in shaping the growth of the poet's mind.

Like the Sibyl, the grandmother speaks in whispers, and her 'Urgent, sibilant' implorings – '"What ails you, child, / What ails you, for God's sake?"' – awaken a poetic intuition of linguistic strangeness, as well as registering the child's troubled awareness of being 'unhomed'. The adult poet's fascination with 'ails' – '*Ails*, far off and old' – recalls the similar fascination of Stephen Dedalus with the word 'tundish' in *A Portrait of the Artist as a Young Man.*[13] The phonetic equation of the grandmother's sibilant, sybilline English with the lapping of water transports us to England. The second part of the poem recalls the young poet's journeys from Belfast to London by ferry and train, in the process echoing and re-echoing the 'brow-to-glass transport' of journeys made by Philip Larkin and Louis MacNeice. The image of 'fleeting England' seen from a railway carriage emulates the vision of 'The Whitsun Weddings' with its 'backs of houses', and Heaney, like Larkin, imaginatively aligns the rural and the urban, the contemporary and the historical.[14] His 'Fields of grain' (recalling Larkin's 'squares of wheat') are brilliantly transformed into 'the Field of the Cloth of Gold', a reference to the famed meeting place of Henry VIII and Francis I in 1520. The guiding spirit in part two of 'Electric Light', however, is T.S. Eliot, and the echoes of Eliot further develop the association of poetic calling with the play of light. The artistic arrivals conjured up by 'Splashes between a ship and dock' bring to mind Eliot's 'Animula' (1929) with its startling opening quotation from Dante: '"Issues from the hand of God, the simple soul", / To a flat world of changing lights and noise, / To light, dark, dry or damp, chilly or warm'. Eliot's brilliant exploration of the innocent soul that comes alive to 'Pleasure in the wind, the sunlight and the sea' before studying 'the sunlit pattern on the floor' is, for Heaney, an exemplary instance of the young artist's coming to consciousness.[15] It perfectly adumbrates his own steady emergence into the light – his entry into England, into English, and into poetry itself. That process is aptly conveyed, as well, in the memorable London image of emerging 'From tube-mouth into sunlight' (*EL* 81). The compound 'tube-mouth' cleverly catches a number of mouths: the mouth of a baby being bottle-fed, the mouth of a river (linking his own native River Moyola to the Thames), and the mouth of the London Underground providing an exit from darkness into light. It recalls, as well, W.H. Auden's famous pronouncement on the persistence of poetry in his elegy for Yeats: 'It survives, / A way of happening, a mouth.'[16] Southwark summons the aspiring poet with its traces of Chaucer's Canterbury pilgrims and Shakespeare's Globe, but the light of inspiration in literary London is undeniably Eliot's, with Heaney re-echoing the words of St Augustine already echoed in *The Waste Land*: 'To Southwark too I came' (*EL* 81).

The child's reaching for the light switch and the wireless knob points to sources of illumination and inspiration, both of them associated with technological change, that complement and extend the other symbolic objects and places of inspiration in the early poems of *Death of a Naturalist* and *Door into the Dark*: the bog, the well, the forge. The repeated admission, 'They let me and they watched me', works as a mantra, giving concentration and emphasis to the rhythmic interplay of volition, assent and guidance by which the child acquires the light of knowledge in the adult world. The memory of the child who 'roamed at will the stations of the world' substitutes the stations of the cross with the glowing radio stations of the wireless set, without cancelling the intimations of pain and suffering that come with the passage from innocence to experience. At the same time, the phrase cunningly echoes 'the stations of the breath' in

Dylan Thomas's wartime elegy, 'A Refusal to Mourn the Death, by Fire, of a Child in London'.[17] Heaney's own wartime experience in rural Derry is recalled in 'All quiet behind the blackout', a line that both echoes the title of a well-known anti-war novel (*All Quiet on the Western Front*) and looks back to Heaney's 'Stations' (that title once again pointing to rites of passage) in which 'Behind the blackout, Germany called to lamplit kitchens through fretted baize' (the wireless set). In that same prose poem or 'station', titled 'England's Difficulty', Heaney remembers the bombing of Belfast: 'I was on somebody's shoulder, conveyed through the starlit yard to see the sky glowing over Anahorish' (*OG* 83). Here, and in 'Electric Light', the fluctuation of light and darkness sensitively records the anxieties and hopes of a child 'fostered alike by beauty and by fear'. Like the tick of the two clocks in 'Sunlight', the 'ticking' of knitting needles induces a counter-intuitive sense of time stilled while time is actually passing, but like the ticking of the bicycle in a later poem in *North*, 'A Constable Calls', it also prompts uneasiness. The child's fear is projected on to the grandmother's gashed thumbnail, but there is beauty, too, in the 'plectrum-hard, glit-glittery' nail, which becomes an art object, redolent of light and music ('glittery' nicely qualifying the slimy 'glit' of the earlier poem 'Fosterling' while keeping contact with it). More than a keepsake, 'it must still keep / Among beads and vertebrae in the Derry ground'. 'Keep' here is finely chosen, as well as deftly placed at the end of the penultimate line: 'keep' as 'remain' but 'keep' as 'due observance of some ritual', as with 'keeping the faith'. The poem whispers of immortality, recalling Eliot's meditation on 'the skull beneath the skin' and his sombre reflection on how 'our lot crawls between dry ribs / To keep our metaphysics warm'.[18] There is an afterlife here – an afterlife predicated on the preservation of objects – that takes us back to 'Bogland' at the end of *Door into the Dark*. There is also continuity and trust in the image of the 'dirt-tracked flint and fissure' of the nail, a keeping of faith with Heaney's own earlier work embedded in the darkness of the earth (*EL* 81).

From *Door into the Dark* in 1969 though to *District and Circle* in 2006, the presence of Eliot is pervasive and subtly assimilated. It manifests itself most powerfully in those poems that bear out Eliot's belief in poetry as the 'concentration' of experience rather than its recollection in tranquillity: 'a concentration which does not happen consciously or of deliberation' (*GT* 124). Heaney's manifesto poem, 'From the Frontier of Writing', published in *The Haw Lantern* in 1987, might well have been written to demonstrate this distinction. What initially looks like the recollection of a routine 'stop and search' at an army checkpoint is startlingly transformed into pure concentration as the poem asserts its own countervailing reality:

And suddenly you're through, arraigned yet freed,
as if you'd passed from behind a waterfall
on the black current of a tarmac road

past armour-plated vehicles, out between
the posted soldiers flowing and receding
like tree shadows into the polished windscreen.
(OG 297–8)

Here is that 'new thing resulting from the concentration', the poem itself 'adjacent and parallel to lived experience' (*GT* 125). What Eliot has to say about composition proves fortifying for Heaney in the midst of conflict and violence, and the tense encounter at the army checkpoint recalls Eliot's persona in 'Little Gidding' as he 'wanders through the newsreel familiarity of a blitz'. Heaney writes of that resilient persona that 'he constitutes a proof – sufficient for the imagination, at least – that an ordained and suprahistorical reality persists, and it is one of the triumphs of the poem to make such a faith provisionally tenable' (*GT* 43).

In *District and Circle*, as Heaney enters the London Underground we are made to feel close to Eliot, just as we are in the London of *Electric Light*. The director and editor at Faber, the maker of reputations and literary circles, surfaces in an elegy for Ted Hughes, in which Heaney remembers asking Hughes what it was like meeting Eliot:

'When he looked at you,'
He said, 'it was like standing on a quay
Watching the prow of the *Queen Mary*
Come towards you, very slowly.'
(DC 46)

The title of the elegy, 'Stern', cleverly catches Eliot's stern demeanour, the Stearns in Thomas Stearns Eliot (his mother's side of the family), and the stern of the boat of death in which Heaney imagines Hughes's recent departure. Here, Eliot serves as the critical medium enabling a creative dialogue between contemporary poets, and we are reminded of the legacy that Heaney attributes to Eliot in *The Government of the Tongue* when he writes of how Keith Douglas, Louis MacNeice, Dylan Thomas and Eliot himself 'all testified at different moments and in different registers in their poetry to the horror and fury of the war', but did so 'with an unbroken historical nerve'. He goes on to note that 'It was as if a kind of cultural air-raid shelter was prepared by Eliot's reinforcement of the idea of tradition itself' (*GT* 43).

Heaney's final observation in 'Learning from Eliot' is that 'in the realm of poetry, as in the realm of consciousness, there is no end to the possible learnings that can take place. Nothing is final, the most gratifying discovery is fleeting, the path of positive achievement leads to the *via negativa* (*FK* 38)'. These are all insights patiently explored and mulled over in the philosophical 'Squarings' section of *Seeing Things* (1991). Heaney does not renounce the lyric for philosophic song, as he suspects Eliot might have done, though renunciation is a powerful impulse in his work, especially after the poems of *Station Island* (1984). His verdict on Eliot's conception of the poetic life is one that aptly applies to his own serious and sustained following of his art, and it neatly encapsulates his own legacy: 'He showed how poetic vocation entails the disciplining of a habit of expression until it becomes fundamental to the whole conduct of a life' (*FK* 38).

Notes

1 'Learning from Eliot' was the T.S. Eliot Centenary Lecture, delivered by Heaney at Harvard University in 1988 and published in the *Boston Review* in October 1989. Chronologically, it belongs with the essays published in *The Government of the Tongue* (1988), which included the T.S. Eliot Memorial Lectures given by Heaney at the University of Kent in 1986.

2 Quoted by Neil Corcoran in *Seamus Heaney* (London: Faber and Faber, 1986), p. 20

3 T.S. Eliot, *The Use of Poetry and the Use of Criticism*, 2nd edn (London: Faber and Faber, 1964), pp. 118–19.

4 T.S. Eliot, 'Critical', *The Collected Poems of Harold Monro* (London: Cobden-Sanderson, 1933), p. xiii.

5 T.S. Eliot, *Selected Prose of T.S. Eliot*, ed. Frank Kermode (London: Faber and Faber, 1975), p. 177.

6 Anthony J. Cuda, 'The Use of Memory: Seamus Heaney, T. S. Eliot, and the Unpublished Epigraph to *North*', *Journal of Modern Literature*, 28/4 (2005), 152–75.

7 *The Poems of T. S. Eliot*, vol. 1: *Collected and Uncollected Poems*, ed. Christopher Ricks and Jim McCue (Baltimore, MD: Johns Hopkins University Press, 2015), p. 203.

8 *Ibid.*, p. 208.

9 *Ibid.*, p. 64.

10 Neil Corcoran, *The Poetry of Seamus Heaney: A Critical Study* (London: Faber and Faber, 1998), p. 174.

11 Seamus Heaney, 'Lux perpetua', *Poetry Book Society Supplement 2001*, n.p.

12 *Poems of Eliot*, vol. 1, p. 53. Also see the extensive notes on Eliot and the Sibyl by Christopher Ricks and Jim McCue, pp. 593–4.

13 James Joyce, *A Portrait of the Artist as a Young Man*, ed. Seamus Deane (London: Penguin, 1992), p. 204. It is worth noting that among the words that Stephen Dedalus draws attention to in confessing his unease in 'the shadow' of the speech of the Dean of Studies is 'ale' (spelled differently from 'ail' but phonetically the same): 'How different are the words *home, Christ, ale, master*, on his lips and on mine!' (p. 205).

14 Philip Larkin, *The Complete Poems*, ed. Archie Burnett (London: Faber and Faber, 2012), p. 56.

15 *Poems of Eliot*, vol. 1, p. 105.

16 *The Collected Poetry of W.H. Auden* (New York: Random House, 1945), p. 50.

17 Dylan Thomas, *Collected Poems: 1934–1952* (London: Faber and Faber, 1966), p. 94

18 *Poems of Eliot*, vol. 1, p. 48.

CHAPTER 9

Louis MacNeice

Catriona Clutterbuck

The lineage of predecessor Irish poets to which Seamus Heaney has claimed indebtedness includes pre-eminently the names of W. B. Yeats and Patrick Kavanagh, but not Louis MacNeice (1907–63). Initially, there is nothing surprising in this: MacNeice's signature identification with cosmopolitan transience and Heaney's with rooted continuity, positions them poles apart. However, MacNeice's counterpointing aesthetic signals key directions for reading Heaney's work. The submerged yet generative relationship between these two poets – aptly symbolized by the trope of the dotted line on sand left by Heaney's deceased father's stick in 'The Strand' (*SL* 62) – is directly signalled in Heaney's 1988 lecture 'The Pre-Natal Mountain: Vision and Irony in Recent Irish Poetry'.[1] Here Heaney acknowledges MacNeice as a 'vital figure' because he 'provides an example of how distance can be used as an enabling factor in the work of art in Ulster' – which work for him is 'the actual business of moving a world' through 'unwrit[ing]' as well as writing place.[2] As Neil Corcoran has pointed out, this lecture was delivered during the writing of the poems of *Seeing Things* (1991), at a period when Heaney would flex a longer-handled lever than ever before (or since) in order to mobilize this 'revealing distance' in his own work.[3] The present essay traces the influence of MacNeice's fluctuating representation as realist and fantasist on Heaney's own aesthetic move from level-headed responsibility to transformative possibility.

By his early twenties, Seamus Heaney had heard Louis MacNeice read in person and bought his *Collected Poems*, yet even though he recognized that the older poet 'thicken[ed] your sense of being alive', as a young man he couldn't respond to this famous Northern Irish predecessor because he 'just wasn't ready, didn't know the work, hadn't the ears to hear' (*SS* 50). In contrast to the direct transfusions of poetic energy offered by Patrick Kavanagh and Ted Hughes, Heaney associated MacNeice with his own unsatisfactory apprenticeship stage of 'dabbling and fiddling but not really hitting the note' (*SS* 51). Heaney's sense of distance from MacNeice is easy to contextualize. Notwithstanding the fact that his Protestant, urban, upper middle-class background meant that MacNeice's life prospects were anchored in financial, educational and social assurance, his childhood was scarred by insecurity following the loss of his mother at age five. This loss was compounded by the 'uprootability' bequeathed to MacNeice through his father's and his own enforced early dislocations.[4] Such a split between the poet's personal and social genesis is reversed in Heaney, whose Catholic, rural, lower middle-class upbringing forty miles west and forty years later, was characterized by primary security at home but branded by the political subordination of his broader community within the mid-century Northern Irish state. These biographical disparities played out in the early poetics of each writer, the young Heaney asserting concrete power where the young MacNeice emphasized yielding of control. For example, Heaney in 'Digging' shows confidence that dispossession from ancestry can be directly redeemed on individual terms: when 'cuts… Through living roots awaken in my head', he picks up his pen to 'dig with it' so as to reconnect with his forefathers' legacy (*DN* 13–14). This contrasts sharply with MacNeice's instinct that human lives are inevitably 'Drowned and drunk with the cataract that carries them and buries them'.[5] These discrepant poetics signal deeper psychological imperatives: if, as Michael Longley argues, 'MacNeice's poetry began and continued as a reaction against darkness and a search for light',[6] Heaney's began by moving from claimable light towards a door into the dark.

Their differing backgrounds and dispositions meant that Heaney, with his self-described Hopkinsesque 'devotion to the concrete and the condensed' and 'suspicion of too much up-in-the-airness' (*SS* 36, 37), could not but find MacNeice a significant challenge. After all, the Co. Derry poet for whom 'coagulated sunlight' could be 'heaped up like gilded gravel in the bowl' of art ('Churning Day', *DN* 21–2) had a very different understanding of how 'The earth compels' to that of MacNeice, who at the equivalent life stage saw 'sunlight on the garden' as proof only that 'We cannot cage the minute / Within its nets of gold' ('The Sunlight on the Garden', *Collected Poems* 57–8).

The contrast between their early priorities is spotlighted through these two poets' discrepant uses of the trope of the insect to represent tension between innocence and experience. The classic MacNeicean poetic persona is an ephemeral mayfly who, fully aware that he can only live for a day, 'Inconsequently dance[s]', flinging himself 'Up and down one among a million' in order to 'stretch' his life out 'taut and thin and ringing clear'

('Mayfly', *Collected Poems* 31–2). All the time, however, he is riven with anxiety at the mortality he defies. In direct opposition, early Heaney resists the 'smoke of flies / Drift[ing] thick in the sunset' that in their 'million collisions' threaten to infiltrate his protective coverings, infecting the speaker with a transgressive 'rash' of unwanted experience – even though he knows that in the end such experience cannot be avoided ('At Ardboe Point', *DD* 35–6). Thus MacNeice represents in form and subject matter the unstoppable but ultimately creative centrifugal forces of modernity, flux and heterogeneity (as evidenced in his poems 'Train to Dublin', 'Snow', 'Bagpipe Music', 'Variation on Heraclitus' and 'Star-Gazer', to name but a few, *Collected Poems* 17–18, 24, 95–6, 560, 607–8), whereas Heaney is associated with the more essential (and for some critics, essentialist) centripetal power of tradition, continuity and community, as variously affirmed in poems like 'Digging' (*DN* 13–14), 'Anahorish' (*WO* 16), 'Sunlight' (*N* 8–9), 'The Toome Road' (*FW* 15), 'The Harvest Bow' (*FW* 58), 'Alphabets' (*HL* 1–3), 'Keeping Going' (*SL* 10–12), 'At Toomebridge' (*EL* 3) or 'Human Chain' (*HC* 18).

However, the gap between Heaney and MacNeice – while never closed – would be bridged with ever-greater facility by the younger poet seeking out new directions for his own growth as artist. Thus, even though at aged thirty the Co. Derry poet had been anxious to excavate 'Slabs' of 'smooth weight' of originary matter ('Bann Clay') that 'holds and gluts', forty years later it would be Heaney himself who, in distinctively MacNeicean terms, advocates our need to 'Go with the flow' in order to enable optimal engagement with life in this world (*DD* 53–4; 'A Herbal', *HC* 37).

What accounts for this shift? As Heaney began to move back and forth at ever greater range across the boundaries of his own home base, he would find much of value in the example of a precursor poet who had embraced deracination as the natural outcome of a divided identity. As Heaney gradually came to accept the idea that 'Unstable is good' ('A Herbal', *HC* 37), his poetics opened to the kind of wavering, 'zig-zag hieroglyph' that MacNeice's mayfly anticipated ('Seeing Things II', *ST* 17). By the final decade of his life, Heaney had long ceased pitting innocence against experience but rather connected them as both pointing towards our larger human frailty in the face of mortality. In poem xi of 'Route 110', for example, Heaney directly embraces the early MacNeiceian 'midge-drift' of uncertainty and dream. He now sees that insect-veil as an essential component of 'the solid ground / Of the riverbank field' of this life, since he knows without question that his own participation in history is approaching the boundary of dissolution (*HC* 58). Thus for late Heaney, as for the late MacNeice of poems like 'Charon' or 'The Introduction' (*Collected*

Poems 592–3, 593), this world has become a space of 'commingl[ing]' on the brink of an unknown world, where the poet must learn to patiently 'wait . . . / Needy and ever needier for translation' (*HC* 58).

Heaney's love of tongue-and-grooved poetic carpentry was a significant component of his early resistance to MacNeice's mode of openness to the unexpected. However as he matures, Heaney's body of well-made work slowly 'swung its arc through air. . . / . . .on a druggy hinge' of recognition that conditions of stability optimally face those of instability in a complementary rather than conflictual manner ('The Bookcase', *EL* 51). MacNeice had demonstrated the scope of such growth by sketching it from the other side: by the time each of these poets had reached their late thirties, both had begun to positively imagine conditions that were opposed to their respective early identifications with flux and groundedness. For example, when we compare their two war elegies of almost the same title, Heaney's 'Casualty' (*FW* 21–4) and MacNeice's 'The Casualty' (*Collected Poems* 237–40), we see within each of these poems an Aristotelian, MacNeice-associated vision of diffusion[7] fruitfully crossing with a Platonic, Heaney-associated purpose of cohesion. In his 1943 poem, MacNeice honours his dead friend Graham Shepard (whose ship was sunk by U-boat attack) by imagining on his behalf, 'one last integration . . . a Form / Grow[ing] out of formlessness when the Atlantic hid you'. Conversely, Heaney in 1979 celebrates Louis O'Neill (a fisherman murdered after ignoring the curfew that followed Bloody Sunday) by imagining for him creative formlessness growing out of the forms that killed him. At the very moment when O'Neill is forced, by his murder, to submit to the deterministic structures of the communal political funeral he had fatally defied, that ritual – represented in the hearse's 'dawdling engine' – is subverted from within to become his own boat's engine casually heading out into Lough Neagh, offering a 'rhythm / Working you, slow mile by mile, / Into your proper haunt / Somewhere, well out, beyond . . .'.

At a little over the halfway point of his career, in the 1991-collected poem 'Seeing Things I' (*ST* 16), Heaney brings this complementarity between stability and instability to thematic centre-stage. Here the poet-speaker's discomfiture on stepping into a boat to Inishbofin suggests Heaney's concern at opening his poetics to the formal and philosophical example of MacNeice, but also his determination to take this risk. Inishbofin is located very close to Omey, the Connemara island where MacNeice's father spent his childhood in the 1870s, and which general area exerted continuing fascination on his poet-son.[8] If the boat into which Heaney steps in this later poem is that of MacNeice's craft of creative uncertainty, it is one which, from the younger poet's perspective, 'dipped and shilly-shallied / Scaresomely every time' (*ST* 16). Yet, crucially, Heaney does not turn back from this journey, even if throughout 'What guaranteed us – / That quick response and buoyancy and swim – / Kept me in agony.' By the mid-nineties, Heaney would very publicly incorporate MacNeice into his larger ideal of rhyming hope with history: in his final Oxford lecture, he celebrates MacNeice's 'bilocated extraterritorial fidelities' as the anchor point of his own ideal of an 'integrated literary tradition'. This literary tradition would serve a 'visionary Ireland' enabled through a 'political order' characterized by distinctively MacNeicean vision: an order 'tolerant of differences and capable of metamorphoses within all the multivalent possibilities of Irishness, Britishness, Europeanness, planetariness, creatureliness, whatever' (*RP* 198, 199, 200).

But the utopian sweep of Heaney's future-oriented rhetoric here masks the practical basis of his own poetry's more local 'traffic . . . in recognition' with MacNeice ('District and Circle', *DC* 17). Their exchange builds through a shared concern with renewing the relationship between immutable reality and the alterity of dream-life: Heaney as well as MacNeice knows that 'There is more than glass between the snow and the huge roses' of this divide ('Snow', *Collected Poems* 24). Both poets understand that the opposition between dream and reality can operate both for ill and for good, Heaney affirming MacNeice's ratification of 'visionary appeal . . . in spite of accustomed guardedness and irony' *along* with the older poet's awareness of 'how quickly the gleam in a romantic poet's eye could convert to the gleam in the eye of a sniper'.[9] As a result, Heaney and MacNeice are each concerned with acts of dynamic balancing between these elements, as they separately acknowledge the truism that 'life is false to [the] formula' into which either fancy or fact can slip when one is prioritized over the other.[10]

Both poets attest to the claims of realism and fantasy and share a poetic preoccupation with the task of 'mark[ing] time' whilst simultaneously ensuring time is 'held . . . open' ('Markings', *ST* 9). This is highlighted by comparing their two poems of the same title, 'The Strand'. In his 1945 poem, MacNeice walks on a beach in the West of Ireland in order that his 'steps repeat' those of his father on an earlier rare visit back to his original home ground. Yet filial testimony succeeds *because* of the fact that both sets of footsteps soon must be wiped away by the larger forces of the sea and mortality, 'and no sign // Remain of face or feet when visitors have gone home' (*Collected Poems* 263–4). Twenty-five years later, Heaney's early poem 'Follower' (*DN* 24–5) echoed MacNeice's lesson that loss swallows even as it affirms continuity. Subsequently, however, Heaney recycles MacNeice's title and core concern with elegiac father–son relations in 'The Strand' only to make the contrary claim of sustainable inheritance: in his three-line poem, 'The Strand' (*SL* 62), Heaney declares: 'The dotted line my father's ashplant made / On Sandymount Strand / Is something else the tide won't wash away.'

However, the subtext of this 1996 poem points in the direction MacNeice had signalled fifty years before: that lasting line on Heaney's strand remains vulnerable to the past tense of the verb 'to make' in which it is couched as well as to the final words of the poem – 'wash away'. As such it is exposed to the irresolvable tension with which both poets remain preoccupied: human beings can neither truly master nor transcend their corporeal material condition, yet nevertheless, they must find ways to transmute their historical situation if they are to realize themselves as subjects with power of action and intervention in this world. This same tension of counterfactual creativity embedded in the real is key to the antecedent text of both these poems: the Proteus episode of Joyce's *Ulysses*. Here, Stephen Dedalus 'walking into eternity along Sandymount strand' registers the myriad elements of the world about him as 'Signatures of all things I am here to read', by closing his eyes and radically shifting the terms by which control is claimed over given reality.[11] As we will now see, such alteration of the terms of asserted agency becomes crucial in the context of both MacNeice's and Heaney's treatments of major territorial conflict.

The same quarter-century period of the Troubles between the late sixties and early nineties during which MacNeice and Heaney separately attained recognition as major Irish writers, saw opposition between revisionism and postcolonialism grow until it came to dominate Irish letters. The antagonism between these two approaches to Irish history and culture was partly rationalized by consolidating MacNeice's and Heaney's reputations in oppositional terms. The political corollary of their characterization as laureates respectively of instability and stability, was MacNeice's association with standards of individual freedom, collective moral accountability and opposition to tribal identity politics, as validated by poems like 'Belfast', 'Valediction', 'Eclogue from Iceland', 'Neutrality', 'Autumn Journal' XVI, 'Epitaph for Liberal Poets' or 'Soap Suds' (*Collected Poems* 25, 7–10, 72–82, 224, 137–41, 231–2, 577). As Neil Corcoran put it at the time, 'MacNeice has become the name for desirable kinds of hybridity and plurality in a culture of positions often fixed into calcification.'[12] Meanwhile, Heaney was linked to values of familial responsibility, heroic individual mediation of history, and acceptance of tribal identity politics as alterable only from within – a position identifiable (though also opened for critique) in bog poems such as 'The Tollund Man' (*WO* 47–8) and 'The Grauballe Man' (*N* 35–6), where Iron Age victims of ritual violence symbolize the terrible logic of sectarian warfare in 1970s Northern Ireland.

Heaney in writing the bog poems knew that any poet who explored such a culture from inside risked equally being tainted and elevated by the rigidity of that culture. Certainly, his immersion in the worlds of violence explored in *Wintering Out* and *North* seems a world away from the detached, humane social vision attested to in MacNeice's 'Eclogue from Iceland' or 'Prayer Before Birth' (*Collected Poems* 72–82, 213–14). Here, in an earlier war context, the older poet defends tolerance and individualism within the terms of communal responsibility by challenging all tribal and racial imperatives, along with the collusive liberal ignorance that serves them. Yet the unborn speaker in 'Prayer Before Birth', in calling for protection from such ills, must also call in advance for forgiveness for his own bad faith in perpetuating them, for he himself is likely to enact those larger forces of evil on behalf of the fallen world which is his birthright (*Collected Poems* 213–14). The MacNeice who had already recognized of himself in 'Valediction' that 'I cannot be / Anyone else than what this land engendered me' (*Collected Poems* 7–10) was well-placed to teach Heaney that nobody is immune from the fault of over- or under- identification with an ideological cause, especially in times of violence – a condition which MacNeice describes as being 'a hypocrite in good faith'.[13]

This condition is anatomized in the 1944 poem 'Prayer Before Birth', where the innocent-cum-culpable unborn child is the moral antecedent of Heaney's 1970s Tollund and Grauballe men, who are similarly sinless and corrupt at once. These impenetrable half-born figures resist identification with the mutually collusive ideologies of blood sacrifice and rational modernity, to which they also succumb. On the one hand, they each have begun a journey of birth out of tribal belonging and into ethical and imaginative consciousness. On the other hand, these journeys remain incomplete. Only half-delivered as subjects, these figures mediate our necessary awareness that invoking the concepts of primitive and civilized as clear-cut binaries, only redirects us towards atavistic reversion rather than delivering us from this fate. Unable to go forward or back, both MacNeice's child and Heaney's bog bodies thereby represent not just stalled human progress, but our 'sad freedom' (*WO* 48) to open a space for conscious non-conformity with the totalizing logic of our own destiny, at the very moment that destiny is being forced upon us in new or old guise.

In an attempt to negotiate this Scylla-and-Charybdis of toxically restricted choice between tribal commitment and liberal individualism, Heaney in his 1975 volume *North* began to follow MacNeice's example by deliberately 'fac[ing] the unmagical / invitations of Iceland' ('North', *N* 19–20). MacNeice in 'Eclogue from Iceland' (1936) conducts a colloquy with a sceptical archaic Icelandic hero (the ghost of Grettir), whom MacNeice imaginatively resurrects in order to challenge the complacencies of his own ethical and aesthetic assumptions in the run-up to World War II (*Collected Poems* 72–82). However, only in the early 1980s does Heaney actively set course for the Iceland of MacNeice's imagination – that which, in 'Station Island' v (*SI* 72–4), is invoked by the spirit of Patrick Kavanagh who slyly proposes Iceland as an alternative pilgrimage to Lough Derg. This prompts our return to MacNeice's 'Postscript to Iceland' (1936), in which location the precursor poet's 'ascetic guts' are granted a vital 'Breather[] from the Latin fire' of the 'death-wish' constituted by 1930s tendencies towards purgatorial self-consciousness, idealist abstraction and evangelical religiosity.[14] MacNeice's Iceland offers a simple alternative ethic: 'Time for soul to stretch and spit' where 'lust for life prevails' (*Collected Poems* 96–8). Heaney in the *Station Island* sequence similarly claims 'lust for life' by rejecting his own traditional Catholicism as a code for an unproductively apologetic poetics. He does this, paradoxically, by engaging with some of the more radical elements of Catholic vision as symbolized by the 'eternal fountain' of St John of the Cross (a translation of whose work is incorporated into 'Station Island' xi, *SI* 89–91). That fountain reappears within a few years in Heaney's 'A Postcard from Iceland' (*HL* 37) in the form of the 'hot spring' that emerges beside 'the whole mud-slick muttering and boiling'. The poet dipping his hand into the adjacent outflowing temperate stream, relearns the power of creative intimacy between mind, body and spirit as 'the inner palm of water found my palm'. In this unlikely location of physical and symbolic extremes, Heaney is surprised anew by 'How usual [the] waft and pressure' of their integration 'felt'.

By now – the later 1980s – Heaney draws substantively upon MacNeice in order to revise his own 1970s elevated sense of vocation as 'Hamlet the Dane' (*N* 23). In 'The Mud Vision' (*HL* 48–9), he invests in a less exclusive but ultimately more rigorous portrait of self-consciousness than that found in *North*, as the postmodern entanglements of modernity and tradition now produce in his work a more positively configured understanding of the relationship between dream and reality than heretofore. In 'The Mud Vision', Heaney positions himself as one among many in his generation who had 'sleepwalked / The line between panic and formulae' as they sought answers to the crisis of incipient and actual violence through the ideal of 'div[ing] to a future', by way of authorizing their own tribal cultural and political identity. Yet as Heaney recognizes, that future had remained unfulfilled for his age-group who 'Watch[ed] ourselves at a distance, advantaged / And airy as a man on a springboard / Who keeps limbering up because the man cannot dive' (*HL* 48). Here Heaney directly borrows from MacNeice's 1942 poem 'The Springboard', in which a suicidal diver, 'High above London, naked in the night', stands 'crucified among the budding stars', poised to fulfil his cogent, yet in practical terms, delusionary vision of 'dying for the people' through one single act of 'wiping out his own original sin' (*Collected Poems* 235–6).

Because the man's utopian dive remains at once unconfirmed yet still possible through imaginary projection, MacNeice's poem balances opposed impulses to devalidate and revalidate the diver's dream, allowing scepticism and faith to compete as responses to the dream's functional illusoriness. Similarly, in Heaney's text, his generation's 'limbering up' towards change eventually gives rise to a patently fictitious – but still potentially transformative – 'mud vision' that 'Had invented itself out of the glittery damp' of their communal imperative towards self-realization. This revelation in which 'we were vouchsafed / Original clay, transfigured and spinning' operates tautologically as 'A gossamer wheel, concentric with its own hub / Of nebulous dirt, sullied yet lucent'. Such a vision, regarded as a process of verification 'That would prove us beyond expectation', inevitably must be failed through its adherents' lack of faith, even as it fails those same people. Yet the dissatisfaction attendant upon this defeat has purpose: instead of becoming dangerous 'mud-men, convinced and estranged' through literalizing utopia by enacting a blind-faith dive into religious destiny, Heaney suggests the larger community can best grow through owning the 'clarified place' of *possible* rather than claimable redemption to which they are now forced to turn (*HL* 48–9). Heaney's corrupted mud vision, like MacNeice's rebounding springboard, compellingly directs them to this alternative ethic of hopeful rather than achieved heroic identity.

MacNeice's 1954 poem 'The Once-in-Passing' (from 'A Hand of Snapshots', *Collected Poems* 503) underscores this reading of 'The Mud Vision'. Here MacNeice affirms his identity as part of the national 'permanence of what passes', not despite but *in* his equivocally claimable Irishness, anticipating Heaney's understanding in 'The Mud Vision' that dreams are not necessarily cancelled by harsh reality but more properly enter creative relationship with such circumstance. MacNeice here teaches Heaney that although mirages of organic identity may not survive the test of our real-life experience and critical awareness, nevertheless, we need to affirm our capacity to imagine conditions other than those given us in history. This is a lesson well learned by the Nobel prize winner who would deliver in Stockholm the powerful address 'Crediting Poetry'.

Both poets allow dreams to be realized in temporary form as empowering instances of 'time out of time'. Thus MacNeice's 1946 poem 'The Cyclist', which celebrates a boy's short-lived experience of 'Freewheeling' downhill in summer (*Collected Poems* 270–71), may have prompted Heaney in the 1990-collected 'Wheels within Wheels' (*ST* 46–7) to credit his own boyhood memory of turning by hand the back wheel of an upturned bike until 'the space between the hub and the rim / Hummed with transparency'. Just as MacNeice's cyclist is made 'one with the sky', Heaney's is granted an 'access of free power' through a powerful vision of '*Perpetuum mobile.* Sheer pirouette'. Notwithstanding the fact that inevitably, 'the hub jammed, rims rusted, the chain snapped', this vision henceforth will allow Heaney to ask, 'Who ever saw / The limit in the given anyhow?' (*ST* 47, 46).

Heaney's poetry draws from the wellspring of MacNeice's intuition that we have greatest power to transform the world and ourselves be transformed, when we remain attached within fallen history. Both poets therefore teach us to trust those 'freshets and rivulets / Starting from nowhere, capillaries of joy // Frittered and flittering' in the midst of our human experience of loss and (self) betrayal ('Late in the Day', *EL* 70–71). If their affinity has remained muted in Irish critical consciousness, MacNeice's 'Coda' suggests that 'Maybe we shall know each other better / When the tunnels meet beneath the mountain' of that compacted literary landscape (*Collected Poems* 610). Certainly the dotted line between these two poets leads towards a place conceived by Heaney in almost exactly the same terms as MacNeice: that place 'where all the names converge / underneath the mountain and where (some day) / they are going to start to mine the ore of truth' ('Parable Island I', *HL* 10).

Notes

1 Seamus Heaney, *The Place of Writing* (Atlanta, GA: Scholars Press, 1989), pp. 41–7.
2 *Ibid.*, pp. 46–7.
3 *Ibid.*, p. 43; Neil Corcoran, *Poets of Modern Ireland* (Cardiff: University of Wales Press, 1999), p. 61.

4 See Jon Stallworthy, *Louis MacNeice* (London: Faber and Faber, 1995), pp. 3–6; *Selected Prose of Louis MacNeice*, ed. Alan Heuser (Oxford: Clarendon Press, 1990), pp. 61, 88.

5 Louis MacNeice, 'A Cataract Conceived as the March of Corpses', in *Collected Poems*, ed. Peter McDonald (London: Faber and Faber, 2007), p. 623. All further references are given in the body of the text as *Collected Poems*.

6 Michael Longley, 'The Neolithic Night: A Note on the Irishness of Louis MacNeice', in Douglas Dunn (ed.), *Two Decades of Irish Writing: A Critical Survey* (Manchester: Carcanet, 1975), p. 103.

7 MacNeice's early orientation towards Aristotle and away from Plato is noted in his essay 'When I was Twenty-One: 1928' in MacNeice, *Selected Prose*, p. 232.

8 Stallworthy, *Louis MacNeice*, pp. 3–4; Heaney, *Place of Writing*, p. 44.

9 Heaney, *Place of Writing*, p. 44.

10 MacNeice, *Selected Prose*, p. 76.

11 James Joyce, *Ulysses* (London: Penguin, 1992), p. 45.

12 Neil Corcoran, *After Yeats and Joyce: Reading Modern Irish Literature* (Oxford University Press, 1997), p. 133.

13 MacNeice, *Selected Prose*, p. 180.

14 This supports Neil Corcoran's argument that 'Postcript to Iceland' was one of the intertexts of *North*. See Corcoran, *Poets of Modern Ireland*, p. 60.

III

Poetics

CHAPTER 10

Lyric Form

John Redmond

'I am a Saturn', Italo Calvino wrote, 'who dreams of being a Mercury ... everything I write reflects these two impulses.'[1] Many writers have wished to be mercurial, to achieve 'the poetic equivalent of walking on air', a slightly envious description once applied by Seamus Heaney to Paul Muldoon, the great Mercury of Irish poetry.[2] Many writers have wished to be another kind of writer altogether – and to recognize this desire is often critical to understanding their canon. At various points in his career, Heaney has seemed to want to be another poet – Kavanagh, Hughes, Lowell, Herbert, Milosz – and, as a consequence, sharp changes in his style have been detectable. It is the contention of this essay that, during a substantial phase of his career, Heaney sought a style which was 'light and airborne, astute, agile, adaptable, free and easy' – to adopt, in other words, the attributes of Calvino's 'Mercury'.[3]

From the beginning of his poetic career, the Irish poet has been regarded as a formal conservative – a judgement sometimes shading into a suggestion of old-fashionedness or backwardness. Worrying about the Irish poet's lack of modernist credentials, Al Alvarez, in a review of *Field Work*, wondered if Heaney was 'really the best we can do'.[4] Certainly Heaney was not frankly experimental like Auden or Ashbery. From *Death of a Naturalist* to *Human Chain* his collections are organized in a recognizably regular fashion, even if the type of regularity varies.

Nevertheless, although we do not identify him with extensive formal restlessness we do associate him with formal change. In this essay, I view Heaney's formal strategies in relation to the conclusion of his poetic journey, directing most attention towards his last two collections, *District and Circle* and *Human Chain*. In particular, I view *Human Chain*, in its use of refrains, tercets and short lines, as a kind of formal last word – a self-conscious return to some of the poet's earlier methods. In these collections, Heaney contemplates his position as an ageing poet by dwelling on – and implicitly aligning himself with – people and objects characterized as permanent and immemorial. While the book bears evidence of Heaney's stylistic changes, it marks a partial return to the kind of poet he was towards the beginning of his career.

In referring to himself as a 'Saturn', Calvino has in mind an inward writer – 'melancholy, contemplative, and solitary'.[5] While Heaney has sometimes appeared to be that kind of poet, I think it better to align him with another member of Calvino's classical scheme – Vulcan, 'a god who does not roam the heavens but lurks at the bottom of craters, shut up in his smithy, where he tirelessly forges objects which are the last word in refinement: jewels and ornaments for the gods and goddesses, weapons, shields, nets, traps'.[6] In drawing this analogy with Heaney's poetic disposition, the emphasis on craftsmanship, the litany of instruments and the somewhat furtive underground mode of operation all seem appropriate – Heaney is a Vulcan who dreams of being a Mercury.

As regards formal choices, I want to lay particular stress on his treatment of line-length. Heaney has seemed most at home with the so-called 'skinny stanza' (in Edna Longley's formulation) which he began to use in *Door into the Dark* and of which he made extensive use in the landmark collection, *Wintering Out*. The short line has also been prominent in his translations and versions of medieval Irish poetry. As with any short-line poem, increasing the number of line-breaks relative to the number of words slows the reader's movement through the poem. This is one of the formal means by which Heaney's poems generate an impression of weight. Many of the poems are dense with modifiers – a conventional way of retarding the reader's 'progress'. Here, in a description of his favourite bog-landscape, is a typical example of the 'skinny stanza' in operation in *North*:

> Earth-pantry, bone-vault,
> sun-bank, embalmer
> Of votive goods
> And sabred fugitives.
>
> (N 41)

In poems of this period, the nouns are frequently compounds and arranged in small chains, making them even more formidable as 'obstacles'. This poem is slowed down by other devices too – the elliptical syntax demands more of an effort by the reader, who must labour to work out what the sense is. The lines are packed with stresses, making them seem 'firmer'. The unusual diction – turning a noun 'sabre' into an unconventional adjective – also provides a reason to pause.

A similar strategy of slowing down can be discerned when Heaney encourages the poem to orbit around a single word. This is the celebrated procedure of the place-name poems in *Wintering Out*, but other poems are (perhaps less noticeably) organized in this way - 'The Toome Road', for example, gravitates towards the single word 'omphalos', while 'Fosterage' moves towards 'obols' (*FW* 7). We can see this process in operation in *Human Chain* in the architecture of the poem 'Slack', where the final three tercets are designed to concentrate acoustic pressure on a single word:

> Stand in the unlit
> Coalhouse door
> And take in
>
> Its violet blet
> Its wet sand weight,
> Remembering it
>
> Tipped and slushed
> *Catharsis*
> From the bag.
>
> (HC 34)

Characteristically, this focus on a single word is designed to bring out its various meanings. The reader is forced to consider the rightness of this level of emphasis, as well as the artfulness of the one-word line reversing the stress-pattern of the lines before and after. Deriving its etymology from the Greek word for 'clean', a sense humorously opposed, of course, to the material stored in the coalhouse, 'Catharsis' has a primary literary meaning drawn from Aristotle's *Poetics*, but it also has secondary meanings relating to psychological and biological states. By arranging his lines in this clipped manner, the word effectively concentrates the force of the poem. It is also worth pointing out that this picks up on a movement in an earlier poem, 'Seeing Things', where Heaney similarly put the spotlight on a word from the classical past: '*Claritas*. The dry-eyed Latin word / is perfect for the carved stone of the water.' Writing in his journals, W.H. Auden characterized this approach to poetic composition as a reliance on 'the picked word', giving as an example Shakespeare's phrase 'antres vast and deserts idle'. Suspicious of how such diction drew attention to itself, Auden characterized it as 'egoistic'.[7] It is suggestive that Calvino links Vulcan (and Saturn from whom he descends) with the schizophrenic realm of 'egocentric isolation'.

Through his poetry and criticism Heaney has encouraged schematic treatments of his work – Hercules vs. Antaeus, male vs. female, vowel vs. consonant. One of the best known of these schemes is the notion that his first four books – from *Death of a Naturalist* to *North* – may be considered as one book and that thereafter the poetry changes in an aerial direction: 'I'm certain that up to *North*, that was one book; in a way it grows together and goes together.'[8] This aerial direction, in which the volume *Field Work* plays a transitional role, is associated with other changes of style and substance – for example an embrace of more cosmopolitan subject matter, a greater reliance on abstract categories and a more ready deployment of some of the classic forms of English poetry (the widespread adoption, for example, of the five-beat line and the sonnet in *Field Work*).

The sense of weight in Heaney's early work was of course partly generated by its subject matter. By favouring the sense of touch, Heaney's poems often record the presence of an object through an up-close intimacy. When 'Bogland', for example, draws attention to an extinct creature – the Great Irish Elk – the poem asks the reader to consider the effort of retrieving its skeleton from a bog ('An astounding crate full of air', *DD* 55). Always a poet who respects the practical and the tangible, Heaney's early poems evoked the solidity of such instruments as 'a tinsmith's scoop / sunk past its gleam / in the meal-bin' (*N* 8). A lengthy litany of such objects, including buckets, pumps, forks, spades, would be easy to construct. As he once put it in interview, 'My head is furnished with medieval tools like sledgehammers and iron spikes to drive into walls and horse collars and so on . . . something in me that responds very physically and emotionally to them'.[9]

But for an extended period in mid-career, roughly from *The Haw Lantern* to *Electric Light*, Heaney wanted to remove such weight from his writing. As he put it in the concluding line of 'Fosterling': 'Time to be dazzled and the heart to lighten' (*OG* 357). Heaney's turn to a more aerial perspective is especially emphatic in the volume *Seeing Things* where it is associated with the preoccupations of advancing age, dealing with the deaths of loved ones and the contemplation of one's own mortality. As Helen Vendler puts it, 'The airiness of *Seeing Things* occurs because Heaney is contemplating the physical through the scrim of extinction.'[10] The attempt at lightness is also evident in *Electric Light*. In line with this vision, the poem 'Ballynahinch Lake', for example, invokes a 'captivating brightness' and 'spring-cleaning light', while the next poem in the book, 'The Clothes Shrine', invokes 'Light white muslin blouses / On a see-through nylon line' (*EL* 26, 27).

But in pursuing this style, Heaney encountered problems. We can see some of these in the poem 'The Pitchfork' from *Seeing Things*:

> then when he thought of probes that reached the farthest,
> He would see the shaft of a pitchfork sailing past

Evenly, imperturbably through space,
Its prongs starlit and absolutely soundless –

But has learned at last to follow that simple lead
Past its own aim, out to an other side
Where perfection – or nearness to it – is imagined
Not in the aiming but the opening hand.

(25)

There is a marked contrast with an earlier poem like 'Nerthus' (also about a fork). The later poem is a good deal longer, and much more determined to explain itself. The elevation of the pitchfork introduces it to a dimension – outer space – where it has no weight, having escaped the gravity of our planet altogether. But this image of the pitchfork as a kind of spaceship strikes a note of (unintended) comedy, which undermines the poem's earnest conclusion. Here is Vulcan operating uncomfortably in the realm of Mercury.

As though recognizing that the attempt at lightness was not a success, *District and Circle* represented a 'return to weight'. Glancing at events like 9/11 and 7/7, and framing contemporary violence against incidents from his childhood, it compares favourably with those 'mercurial' middle collections. The vulcanic figures of Heaney's early work make a return. Heaney has always been fascinated with the supposed virility of the blacksmith's realm, generally linking it, as in 'The Forge', to expressions of male sexuality: 'The anvil must be somewhere in the centre, / Horned as a unicorn' (*DD* 19). In 'Poet to Blacksmith', for instance, he translates the instructions of the eighteenth-century Irish poet, Eoghan Rua Ó Súilleabháin, to Seamus MacGearailt for the forging of a 'side-arm', a digging tool: 'No trace of the hammer to show on the sheen of the blade, / The thing to have purchase and spring and be fit for the strain' (*DC* 25). This association of poet and blacksmith is also made in 'A Midnight Anvil' and 'The Harrow-Pin', the latter a poem resonant with the sound of 'hammered iron' (*DC* 24).

In *District and Circle*, Heaney's evocations of virile male craftsmen from his childhood shade into his various identifications with great twentieth-century male poets (Seferis, Auden, Rilke, Cavafy, Neruda). The implication that the reader is asked to draw is that Heaney is 'one of them', a permanent fixture, a writer for all times. To a considerable degree, this concern with literary durability makes *District and Circle* an anxious book. By extension, the poet's fascination with aged objects – a harrow-pin fixed in the wall, for instance – can readily be associated with the poet's wish for his own permanency, with attaining a 'vulcanic' condition of concentrated, lasting power.

In one of the most vulcanic moments in *District and Circle*, Heaney makes an explicit connection between a stove-lid remembered from childhood and the eponymous object in Auden's tough Cold War poem 'The Shield of Achilles'. Above the poem is a direct quotation from Auden: 'The mass and majesty of this world, all / That carries weight and always weighs the same'. It is notable that, in classical myth, this shield was forged for Achilles by Vulcan, and that Heaney's mulling-over of the object leads to a moment of 'egocentric isolation':

So one more time
I tote it, hell-mouth stopper, flat-earth disc,
And replace it safely. Wherefore rake and rattle,
Watch sparks die in the ashcan, poke again,
Think of dark matter in the starlit coalhouse.
(DC 71)

These lines chime with Calvino's intuition that Vulcan is one who prefers to operate in a concealed environment. While looking back to poems of meditative isolation like 'Bye-Child' and 'Exposure', this poem looks ahead to his last collection in its balanced acceptance of the poet's mortality.

The final poem in *District and Circle*, 'The Blackbird of Glanmore', can be read as Heaney's version of the golden bird in Yeats's 'Sailing to Byzantium', another permanent and egoistic icon. Even here, Heaney's identification is characteristically feline. While the blackbird stares from the ivy at the end of the book, a permanent presence looking on at 'what is past, or passing, or to come', we are invited to conclude (but are not *told*) that Heaney is there too – permanently:

Hedge-hop, I am absolute
For you, your ready talkback,
Your each stand-offish comeback,
Your picky, nervy goldbeak —
On the grass when I arrive,

In the ivy when I leave.
(*DC* 76)

Philip Hobsbaum once opined that Heaney was too fond of the 'loose quatrain', a way of organizing the poem which Hobsbaum thought came from Patrick Kavanagh. He added that it 'all too often circumscribes itself into a four-line stanza, and the effect is that of a good poet on his best behaviour'.[11] Marking the distance between his first and last collections, it is noticeable how many key poems in *Death of a Naturalist* are written in quatrains ('Follower', 'The Diviner', 'The Barn', 'Antaeus', 'Personal Helicon') and how the vast majority of work in *Human Chain* is written in tercets. The older poet appears to know what form suits him best, and it is not the form that he used at the beginning of his career. The one-word line is also extensively used. One of the persistent motifs in the book is that of ash – and this is formally matched by the way the tercets convey a sense of fragmentation, a return to bits and pieces.

One of the particularly striking poems in *Human Chain* is the sequence called 'A Herbal'. This is a vision of an 'elsewhere world' – a kind of afterlife – 'Where all is woven into // And of itself, like a nest / Of crosshatched grass blades' (*HC* 53). While this reaches back to some of Heaney's own earlier work – for example, to 'Fodder', the opening poem in *Wintering Out*, where the poet dwelt on 'tumbled / swathes of grass / and meadowsweet' (*WO* 13) – Heaney may also have had in mind the most grass-oriented of all of Muldoon's collections, *Hay*. In that book Muldoon – increasingly preoccupied with song over the course of his career – experimented with similar-sounding types of refrain. Linked partly through the title of the book, poems like 'The Bangle' and 'The Bangle (Slight Return)' play with nonsensical exclamations like 'hey', 'ho' and 'heigh ho'.

Such exclamations also appear in *Human Chain* where the emphasis on attractive-sounding nonsense terms is noticeable. In providing lines that could readily be set to music, Heaney aims at a type of poetry 'for all times' – a kind of poem which has the permanence of Shakespearean songs like 'When icicles hang by the wall'. Two examples of this short-line form are 'An Old Refrain' and 'Derry Derry Down'. The former represents one of Heaney's many oblique treatments of sexuality, where he plays on the idea of the oak grove (in the translation of 'Doire'). The title comes from a traditional song called 'The Keeper', which is itself a thinly disguised treatment of sexuality through the metaphor of hunting. The geographical metaphor is slightly deepened by the inclusion of the names of two counties in the title.

In a manner reminiscent of his contemporary Michael Longley, Heaney uses an alternative name for a flower, 'Robin-run-the-hedge', to begin 'The Old Refrain'. This phrase also reaches back to one of the most celebrated passages in the work of Edward Thomas, the alternative names for the immemorial character evoked by the poem 'Lob': 'Young Jack, or old Jack, or Jack What-d'ye-call, / Jack-in-the-hedge, or Robin-run-by-the-wall'.

Fully in line with the diplomatic instincts he has always shown, but which are especially obvious in the latter part of his career, Heaney's poem is in part a reaching out to England, as though locating a space where the two poetic traditions can peacefully co-exist. Just as 'Lob' imagines an England before the coming of roads, 'The Old Refrain' evokes a premodern world largely shorn of obvious signs of technology. One suggestion of such poems is that all our differences may be dissolved in pastoral, erased into a kind of etymological peace. Of course these two poems also invoke Shakespeare, with the explicit use of the refrain of 'It was a lover and his lass' from *As You Like It* ('with a hey, and a ho, and a hey nonino'). We might think of both examples as forming parts of Heaney's movement towards the immemorial.

At one point, 'The Old Refrain' refers to 'A fading straggle // Of Lincoln green' (*HC* 19). This depends on a slightly obscure sense of the word 'fading' which describes a dance. In its definition of 'nonny-nonny', the *OED* quotes *Harper's Magazine* in 1881: 'The fading is the name of an Irish dance, but "with a fading" seems to have been used as a burden to various songs, in the same way as "Derry down", "Hey nonny nonny no" etc.' One rather suspects that Heaney used this *OED* reference as a point of departure in the book.

In line with a tendency in Heaney's last two books to revisit earlier parts of his canon, ''Derry Derry Down' reintroduces the figure of Annie Devlin who featured in 'A Drink of Water'. In *Stepping Stones*, Heaney gives a relatively expansive account of this neighbour, referring to her as an 'ancient': 'I'm thinking of Thomas Hardy's use of the word to mean an older country person formed within older, more reticent, more stoical rules and codes ... old vestals living beside an open hearth, with a dog that barked at you from behind the gate' (*SS* 173).

Certainly, the old woman is described in 'A Drink of Water' in frankly unflattering terms – 'an old bat staggering up the field' – and one of the objects which is foregrounded by the poem is the enamel bucket which she carries:

> I recall
> Her grey apron, the pocked white enamel
> Of the brimming bucket, and the treble
> Creak of her voice like the pump's handle.
> (*OG* 151)

Like many other mid-period poems by Heaney, there is a concern to explain the situation of the woman, a drive to be explicit, even as the poem builds a level of adjectival density. Writing about Elizabeth Bishop, the critic David Kalstone observed that one of her prime aims was to turn a descriptive poem into a narrative. In Heaney's poetry we find a similar kind of technical tension – the poet is smitten with description, but feels an urge to condition the reader's interpretation. In *Human Chain*, it is noticeable how narrative becomes relatively muted.

'A Drink of Water' follows a simple plan, moving towards a moral – '*Remember the giver*' – which is Eucharistic in its simplicity and which, like the quotation from Coventry Patmore which clinches 'The Harvest Bow', is even put in italics. The bucket returns in Heaney's later treatment of the same woman:

> The full of a white
> Enamel bucket
> Of little pears:
>
> Still life
> On the red tiles
> Of that floor.
> (*HC* 26– 7)

Here we return to the bucket in a context that recalls one of the most famous of all object-poems. Heaney has acknowledged the influence of William Carlos Williams on the poetry he wrote in *Wintering Out* and we see an affectionate nod towards 'The Red Wheelbarrow' in this poem (the pears may also slightly recall the plums of 'This is Just to Say'). This is partly a matter of its being an object-poem in very short lines but also because of the signalling implicit in the colour scheme of red and white – and the way in which the objects are allowed to speak for themselves. This is a good example of the vulcanic strategy of concentration which we find throughout his work. Here we are invited to remember the earlier phrase, '*Remember the giver*', but without the word 'remember' having to appear.

Notes

1 Italo Calvino, *Six Memos for the Next Millennium* (Cambridge, MA: Harvard University Press, 1988), p. 52.
2 Seamus Heaney, *The Place of Writing* (Atlanta, GA: Scholars Press, 1989), p. 52.
3 Calvino, *Six Memos*, p. 52.
4 Al Alvarez, 'A Fine Way with the Language', *New York Review of Books*, 6 March 1980, pp. 16–17.

5 Calvino, *Six Memos*, p. 52.
6 *Ibid.*, p. 53.
7 W.H. Auden, 'Journal Entry', 1929, in *The English Auden: Poems, Essays and Dramatic Writings, 1927–1939*, ed. Edward Mendelson (London: Faber and Faber, 1977) p. 300.
8 John Haffenden, 'Meeting Seamus Heaney: An Interview', in Haffenden, *Viewpoints: Poets in Conversation* (London: Faber and Faber, 1981), p. 64.
9 Eleanor Wachtel, 'An Interview with Seamus Heaney', 30 September 2013, www.brickmag.com/an-interview-with-seamus-heaney.
10 Helen Vendler, *Seamus Heaney* (Cambridge MA: Harvard University Press, 1998), p. 138.
11 Philip Hobsbaum, 'Craft and Technique in Wintering Out', in Tony Curtis (ed.), *The Art of Seamus Heaney*, 4th edn (Dublin: Wolfhound, 2001; 1st edn 1982), pp. 37–43 (at p. 40).

CHAPTER 11

Proper Nouns

Vona Groarke

Thirteen of fourteen Seamus Heaney collections have a noun in the title.[1] Whilst some are more abstract than others (Death, Dark, North, Work, Light . . .), and a few are proper nouns (Sweeney, Beowulf), most are resoundingly concrete (one, for example, is Things). Taken out of context, as a complete litany, these would read: death, naturalist, door, dark, north, work, island, lantern, things, ground, spirit level, light, district and circle, chain. That's not even counting the poems of *New Selected Poems*, the *Laments* by Jan Kochanowski, the two bags (*Rattle* and *School*), the tongue in *Government of the Tongue*, the preoccupations in *Preoccupations*, or the stones of *Stepping Stones*. Not to mention *The Cure at Troy* or *The Burial at Thebes*.

Admittedly, it's not unusual for a title of a book of poems to deploy a noun, but the marked avoidance of verbs in his titles (there are only two, both of them gerunds – Wintering and Seeing), suggests a body of work that is firmly committed to the material world. It's not just a question of titles: 'Verb, pure verb', proposes 'Oysters' (*FW* 11), and yet so much of the energy of a Seamus Heaney poem derives from its nouns. From anvil to underground; from Conway Stewart to harvest bow; from skylight to tinsmith's scoop, these nouns in their respective poems are typically set to resonate as a kind of linguistic and imagistic tuning fork. Their base notes are certainty and ballast; touchstone and talisman. They earth the thematic considerations of their poems, and their claim on factual reality makes space around them for more abstract or philosophical concerns. They are how the poems remember; Heaney's nouns are a trail of buttons or fairytale breadcrumbs allowing the poem to find its way back to a personal or mythological source.

This essay will consider Heaney's use of nouns in nine cases, and will hold them against an enquiring light in an attempt to measure their effect.

1. A Scoop

Part I. Sunlight – 'Mossbawn: Two Poems in Dedication'. Leave off that first line ('There was a sunlit absence'), and all is as it should be in a family home that is warm, husbanded and provisioned. Water is honeying, the griddle is cooling, the female figure at the heart of the poem stands by the window to take a breather from the baking heat. She is quiet. She hears two clocks. What she cannot hear is the sound of scones rising, and yet *we* do, and that registering, that name-checked cliché (a bun in the oven), rises like yeast to island the image of her in a life that is all busy-ness and gentle kindness for the sake of a family that is hers, but not exactly. A sacrifice has been made, there is an absence, and though it is sunlit, there it sits at the end of the first line, to position the poem that ensues. And it's not just the absence of an implied rough-and-tumble family (an absence that makes this quiet moment possible), but another absence too, a sacrificed life in which she might have been mother instead of aunt, her body rising to a different kind of rhythm and task, that it will never rise to now.

The poem is a dedication, and even if it weren't, there's so much sensitivity in its description that it would clearly be a poem of praise. It even manages to accommodate the word 'love', again at a line-end, where it has a little more elbow-room. The final stanza reads: 'And here is love / like a tinsmith's scoop / sunk past its gleam / in the meal-bin' (*N* 10). It's not, however, entirely uncomplicated: that third line won't allow it to be. In the fact of the scoop (and how it lightly sound-glances against the noun, 'womb', perhaps?) and its being sunk past its gleam in the meal-bin (with that hint of the ongoing requirement of a family to be fed), lies a sense that something about this life, for all the love given and taken there, has involved a sacrifice that must be acknowledged by those who benefit from it, by both poet and poem. And the heavy lifting of that acknowledgement is done by an object that bears it gracefully and tenderly, but bears it nonetheless. 'Love' and 'gleam', the two more abstract nouns, are threaded together through two resoundingly concrete objects, the scoop and the meal-bin. That has rightness to it, given the poem's world and register. The two sets of nouns correct each other, so that the poem can be two things at once – generous and loving, but also candid. The tinsmith's scoop keeps the poem honest in a way the sunlight, with its tendency to idealize, simply can't. It's a functional object in more ways than one: the simile it facilitates is the highlight (the gleam) of the poem, but it is also the poem's shadow, an allowance for sadness and an admission of small guilt.

2. A Bucket

That most resoundingly consonantal object, all clip and business, the central 'ck' being the hollow base onto which the word's other letters fall: Heaney makes music of the sound of buckets. 'A Drink of Water' notices 'the bucket's clatter / and slow diminuendo as it filled' (*FW* 16). The bucket also balances sound and purpose: in 'Terminus' (*HL*), he grows up between two of them, learning the tricky balancing act of where you come from and who you are. In 'Personal Helicon', he could not be kept away from 'wells / And old pumps with buckets and windlasses' (*DN* 57). The bucket dips into metaphor and brings back a purposeful haul. 'All metaphor, Malachi, stilts and all', as Yeats had it in 'High Talk':[2] the bucket may listen with its tin ear to the music of what happens, but it has its own soundscape too, its diminuendo, the kind of sound yielded when it comes down hard on the surface of the real world, and how that rings in the poems. Functional, certainly, the bucket is made to yield its metaphoric resonance winch by winch. 'Usually', wrote Heaney in his essay 'Feeling Into Words', 'you begin by dropping the bucket halfway down the shaft and winding up a taking of air. You are miming the real thing until one day the chain draws unexpectedly tight and you have dipped into waters that will continue to entice you back. You'll have broken the skin on the pool of yourself' (*P*, 47). The bucket's stock in trade is largesse: it makes metaphors even out of spuds, as in 'Clearances' (No. 3) where they are 'Cold comforts set between us, things to share / Gleaming in a bucket of clean water' (*HL* 27). Largesse and magic. The empty bucket is full of nothing. The full bucket empties again at a hand's turn. It has been a while since I held or even saw a bucket; who keeps a bucket nowadays? Perhaps it has slipped through some pinprick hole into the state of pure metaphor. If you'd only ever read Heaney poems, you'd have been ready for that: his buckets always had a hole in them and it was a magic one, a hole of sound through which the bucket itself could disappear while its haul remained, sculpted and resonant as the resined air under chairs in Rachel Whiteread's 'Untitled (One Hundred Spaces)'.

3–4. Two Lorries

I once heard Seamus Heaney introduce 'Two Lorries' at a reading: he said it was the most prosaic of all his titles, and he seemed proud of the fact. The sestina is a famously unwieldy sort of form, difficult to manoeuvre in and out of its end-word hairpin bends. 'Two Lorries' takes a few shortcuts by way of the end words: 'load' becomes 'load', 'lead', 'payload' and 'explode', while 'mother' swerves into 'meet her' and 'that other' (*SL* 13–14). Even 'lorry' itself sheds its solidity just long enough to flirt with 'flurry'. (And in that particular little magic act, I see a lorry on a dark road, a cigarette flung out the driver's window to litter a flurry of stars in its wake. You connect the words, and straight away – because they have been chosen with inestimable care – are yielded up these lightly gorgeous connections that shift the poem, ever so slightly, from the physical pedantry of a lorry to a moment of loose transcendence. From lorry to flurry; from a concrete noun to an abstract one, from bulk and mechanics to light.) But certain words do not budge a vowel or consonant: 'ashes', 'Magherafelt' and 'coalman' are maintained solidly throughout. I suppose a place name ought not to be tampered with in a poem that concerns itself with the marking of territory and the consequences of that act. And 'ashes' are ashes, what would be the point of tricking with them? They are an end in themselves, inevitable and fixed, and no two ways about it. And then, the coalman (that Jungian trickster) who morphs, in fact, into two coalmen: one who delivers coal to houses, and one who delivers death ('Death walked out past her like a dust-faced coalman'). The word is maintained, but into it are packed quite widely different possible readings. It is, along with the title's two lorries, one of the poem's two double acts, but it works in a different way: one noun and one noun only, but a noun that is capable of supporting two quite different payloads. Though fixed in meaning, it must also prove slippery enough to subvert that fixity and to bubble up elsewhere (in a conjecture or simile) in a way that allows the poem to provide imagistic answers to narrative questions, to set against violent action (with its absolute definitions) an alternative charged with the possibilities of connection. In the word 'coalman', what appear to be opposites (the very real coalman and his doppelgänger, who personifies death) are set to occupy the space of a single noun, and to do so comfortably and profitably. It's hard not to read this as a political statement in its own right, and it is that coalman, used to heavy loads, who shoulders it throughout the poem.

5. A Car

In 'Postscript' (*SL* 82) there is a car and it is a magic conveyance. Not just for the way so many words throughout the poem ('Clare', 'feathers', 'underwater', 'park', 'capture', 'more', 'here', 'there', 'hurry', 'heart', 'guard') are threaded through its sound so that this one, small, plain word shunts to the centre of the poem's soundscape, but because it is the ways and means by which 'known and strange things pass'. There is a landscape and it is carefully written, observed like a Manet seascape, all light effects and mythic swans and all the rest of it. We know where we are, we're given the co-ordinates of both place name and close-up description. And yet, the whereabouts is almost immaterial: the poem says as much – 'You are neither here nor there.' What matters is not so much the outwith as the within, and the crossing between the two occurs at the car door. The car protects from the 'big soft buffetings' of the wind, but something there is that gets through anyway to affect a moment of transcendence, made all the more dramatic for the simplicity of the language that drives it: those buffetings, with all their consonantal clatter and fuss, 'catch the heart off guard and blow it open'. 'Postscript' finishes *The Spirit Level*: 'open' is the last word, which is fun for a closure, but also deadly in earnest, I think, in terms of what it means. I have tried to imagine the poem without the car in it: narratively, I think that's doable (though it would play fast and loose with the metre and lineation). How about this: 'You are neither here nor there, / A hurry through which known and strange things pass / As big soft buffetings catch the heart off guard and blow it open.' But remove the car and the whole poem is simply blown off kilter. The car is crucial. It absorbs the impact, as it were, so a change (that is both minute and hugely resonant, in comparison) can occur within. Without the car, not alone does the sound pattern of the whole poem fray, but the larger point and intimate meaning of it seem also compromised. The car is the magic place that marks off interior space, where a moment of pure openness occurs. And what is more ordinary than an open car door? We need the earthing notion of it to allow for that piercing transcendence: remove the ordinary and physically factual, I don't think we'd trust the transcendent half as much. Even the sound of it carries us over the threshold from the physical to the ethereal/spiritual – from the open car door to 'heart' and 'off guard' – the links are finely wrought, but necessary. We need the car to get us there: it is the engine of the poem.

6. A Bicycle

The policeman is plenty physical with his 'slightly sweating hair', his upturned cap and heavy ledger, but the real personality of 'A Constable Calls' has to be his bicycle (*N* 61). It is more attentively animated, seeming more alert and present in the first two stanzas than the constable is in the ensuing seven. The constable's purpose is uncovering fact, which he must do by exerting authority and a kind of low-level but serviceable fear: his bulk in the room is buttressed by the weight of authority he bears, making him seem bigger and more physically forceful than he actually is. Sweaty, suspicious and mildly (but judiciously) threatening, the physical presence allotted to him is an aspect of his objective and work. He is a boot, a cap, a ledger, a holster, a revolver, a baton-case and a belt. Above and beyond these objects, there is very little detail offered about the man himself. He is, simply, the equipment he requires to fulfil his office and to try to catch the speaker's father out in lies, or assumed lies.

The bicycle, on the other hand, is all body: its outline is amply filled in with detail, its handlegrips, mudguard, dynamo, pedal and cowl are noticed and name-checked. To each is allotted at least one verb, and often it is a verb that glances against a hint of violence ('cocked back', 'hanging'). This is a bicycle that is all business. And when the constable removes himself (when his boot has 'pushed off', an apt description of the act of setting a bicycle to motion but also, one suspects, a choice of verb entirely aware of its negative connotations), the poem's most dramatic moment occurs via a description of the sound of his bicycle, which 'ticked, ticked, ticked'. The verb, with its hint of violence to come and the associated notion that the constable and bicycle combined are, in effect, a ticking bomb, lifts the poem away from being a narrative account of a family incident (a rather dark narrative, in fact, with its natural father/son dynamic disrupted by the constable's presence, the son unwittingly siding with the constable in assuming his father's small guilts), to an image suggesting powerful historical resonance. In this case, the personal really is political and the negotiation between the two (which occurs, intrusively, in the family home) is worked out, not so much by direct speech or physical description, but by the play of noun and verb, by the unlikely and surprising yoking together of those physical nouns and verbs that suggest, slyly and deftly, what will become of them. The most present noun is the bicycle, and to it is allotted the most portentous and significant verb. In the end, despite the constable's sweat and bulk, it is the bicycle that polices the poem.

7. A Rope

The first poem of *District and Circle* (2006) is 'The Turnip Snedder', and with that compound noun's clatter of consonants is set the tone of a collection that puts out a veritable flea-market array of archaic objects and things that take up various positions along the line that runs from the serviceable to the metaphoric, from the concrete to the abstract. Leaving aside proper nouns and concentrating on ones that seem resolutely concrete, I find 'Polish Sleepers', 'The Aerodrome', 'Helmet', 'The Harrow-Pin', 'A Clip' and a brace of others. And then there are those such as 'Midnight Anvil', 'The Nod', 'Nonce Words', 'Home Fires' and 'The Blackbird of Glanmore' that seem to fix at least one notional eye (the eye, perhaps, that mirrors the shape of the Tube line of the title?) on a less functional register.

In 'Súgán', if there is a fluster and a soft supply, there must also be a ruck and a hook in the kind of winding and binding a Heaney poem knows well how to manage. This poem mentions the poet's left and right hands – one holds the elderberry haft, the other the fashioned wire – and the tug between both hands is also the tension between two kinds of nouns, the down to earth wire, and the haft, with its dash more *élan*. One is the cut, if you like, and the other is the jib. The final phrase, 'a power to bind and loose / eked out and into each last tug and lap' (*DC* 30),[3] binds and loosens its binary connections in a scheme of duality and oppositions. What is bound is also loosened; power is eked out and also (in a daring ninety-degree swerve of reference) eked *into* both a tug and a lap. *Súgán* is a rope, but a rope from another language, a rope slightly abstracted by cultural circumstance. There is a sense that the poem does with the language what it describes the poet doing with hay – that the last tug and lap described is also a reference to a language that must be managed, if it is to survive. In this way, the rope gathers into its making a larger and more resonant scheme of associations which the poet has to manipulate to make the ends of its various constituent nouns mesh into what has strength and utility – the very thing that can convert an emergency into a rescue, or may cause violent harm. As with so much in this tightly bound poem, the deployed central noun occupies a space, a corner of poetic ground, from which several images, associative sets and sound loops may be suggested and explored. And, as in so many Heaney poems, that power (which is, as the poem acknowledges, the power 'to bind and loose'), is made manifest in the real world where all nouns must be handled carefully, that they might earn their place.

8. A Door...

He'd have made a good carpenter, I'm guessing, with all his many planed and fashioned doors. *Door into the Dark* (1969): see how the two nouns face each other, two sides of the same plane of wood, perhaps.

Two four-letter words beginning with the same letter, standing on either side of the phrase: the way the title presents itself suggests that the door is equal to the dark, which is saying something. (Usually, an abstract noun delivers a sucker punch to any other nouns foolish enough to even think of meeting it eye to eye.)

Just as a vase can be smashed or a hunk of wood axe-split, the domestic is a fragile entity. It is fashioned out of the same stuff that can also convert it to dust – time and affection not being fixed or forgiving entities. We know this. We tend to think of the darkness as being more than the door, and the door as some kind of buttress against its overpowering, threatening force.

But the Heaney title confronts this way of seeing things. The door into the dark is also, presumably, the door out of the dark again. It opens both ways. We're not told what's on the leeside of it, but we may conjecture light. And there it is, smuggled into the poem at last, the corrective fact, the haul of reference and resonance, the guide-light and source: *where there is darkness, let there be light*. And let the passage between them be not a passage at all, but a real and solid door, something to be taken in hand, to be closed as well as opened, to protect as well as exclude.

9. … And Then, Another

An architect will tell you that a door is probably the one structural aspect of a house that is encountered, *felt* by the body of the house occupier on a regular basis. Yes, you walk on the floor and you look through the windows, but you touch the door many times a day, you negotiate its tension, swing and heft.

By the time we arrive at Heaney's final volume, *Human Chain* (2010), and its poem in memory of David Hammond, that door stands open onto a dark house. The dark has shifted from noun to adjective. Its proposition is now more intimate and, therefore, more encompassing: it no longer stands as a thing apart, a thing in itself: it has entered the familiar world, and has changed it utterly. In 'The door was open and the house was dark', the enormity of that abstract noun is brought home. It is no longer the door that is central, it is the dark. And though the poem ends with 'summer', offering us a vision of something that might offset that overwhelming darkness, it is a feint: the simile is not equal to what it is asked to moderate and transform. 'Summer' is a stand-alone noun – if it rhymes at all, it is with 'unwelcoming', and the awkwardness of the rhyme undercuts the generosity of the impulse to offer some small corrective release. But it is midnight in this summer, so its summer-ness is of really no account. This is a noun that has forsaken its concrete reality: it seems entirely abstracted, separated from what we understand of summer to such an extent that what it suggests is another form of darkness, and fearful loneliness. That's the thing about things, essentially: they tie us to other people, other usages, other rituals, other times and other lives. And that's why this poem is so successfully forlorn: nothing is real, the door is barely even there – it doesn't even need to be opened, or to be passed through, the streetlamps light nothing, all is darkness (even summer), and in this darkness, nothing can be recognized and nothing can be named. The marvellous panoply of Heaney's nouns has been set aside, and I find I long for something concrete, a touchstone fact, a noun that I might use as a guide or surety, a comfort or kindness, and its absence is terrifying.

It seems the Heaney poem without any assertive, definite and proper noun is a strange, unsettling and disorienting space, a place of loneliness – which is rather the point of the thing, I'll hazard, when it comes down to it.

Notes

1 Though, as if to compensate, *Wintering Out* starts with the word 'fodder' and ends with the word 'hands'.
2 W. B. Yeats, *The Poems*, ed. Richard J. Finneran, 2nd edn (London & New York: Macmillan, 1997), p. 343.
3 Seamus Heaney, *District and Circle* (New York: Farrar, Straus and Giroux, 2006).

CHAPTER 12

Language

Bernard O'Donoghue

One of the most striking things about Seamus Heaney's poetry from its beginnings in the 1960s was the frequency with which it commented on its own procedure in linguistic terms. The first books were admired for the strong physicality of their subjects and language – what might be termed their palpability; yet the very first poem (the poem that stayed first in all later selections of the poems) begins with the pen with which the poet will 'dig'. Access to that palpable world is declared to be a translation of it into verbal terms by the pen. This idea is commonplace enough; what is remarkable though is how consistently Heaney returns to analysis of his own verbal mechanics.

In *Seamus Heaney and the Language of Poetry* (1994) my concern was with the expressly linguistic terms in which Heaney discusses his poetic language; what I tried to show was that those things 'changed throughout his career in a series of deliberate and signalled choices'.[1] A suitable subtitle for the book would have been the phrase from the 'Squarings' sequence in *Seeing Things*, 'an art that knows its mind' (*ST* 97). From the first Heaney's poetic language drew attention to itself by commenting on the kind of sustained departure from norms that is often said to be the definitive quality in poetic language, and then conducted an exploration of those departures. Those devices were sometimes a matter of local usage, sometimes the kind of breach of rule that informs the language of poetry from Keats to Dylan Thomas. Sometimes they brought linguistic terminology, especially from phonetics, into the poems themselves: '*Anahorish,* soft gradient / of consonant, vowel-meadow'; 'the tawny, guttural water / spells itself'; 'To flood, with vowelling embrace, / Demesnes staked out in consonants': 'A vocable'; 'Our guttural muse' (*WO* 16, 25, 23, 33, 31). In Heaney's case this self-observing language served as a reaction against what A. Alvarez called disapprovingly 'the gentility principle', which might be defined as a strict adherence to the practices of the standard language, both poetic and in prose; all critics and reviewers recognized from the first the distinctiveness of Heaney's language, a distinctiveness also evident in the sustained linguistic commentary within the poetry itself.

Since 1994, several critics have turned to examine Heaney's language in the light of developments in linguistic and literary theory, as distinct from the more traditional categories of grammatical analysis and philology which had been the terms in which most critics – and Heaney himself – had previously discussed his work. When Henry Hart's fine book *Seamus Heaney: Poet of Contrary Progressions* was published in 1992, he had the field more or less to himself when he gave the title 'Deconstructions' to his final chapter on *The Haw Lantern* (the last published volume when Hart completed the book in 1991). Since then, there have been several further theoretical analyses of Heaney's poetry, often drawing on his own critical commentary in his prose writings. Three books by Eugene O'Brien, culminating with *Seamus Heaney as Aesthetic Thinker* in 2016, have concentrated on the relations between the prose and the poetry, placing Heaney in the wide context of developments in European aesthetic theory.[2]

Before resorting to such theoretical analyses of the work, though, it may be clarifying to scrutinize further the more traditional relations between Heaney's language and the less articulate world it represented. I will recap briefly the development in his poetic language through the eight volumes from *Death of a Naturalist* in 1966 to *Seeing Things* in 1991 as described in *Seamus Heaney and the Language of Poetry*. The acoustic and descriptive accuracy and evocativeness of the first books were partly replaced by the penetrating short lines of the 'Bog Poems' in *Wintering Out* and *North* which took a narrower focus on the events of the Troubles that seemed to demand a language 'clear as the bleb of the icicle' (*N* 20). The materiality of the early language is replaced by something that seems visually to cut through to what it represents with its awl-like 'skinny quatrains'. *Field Work* was an attempt to broaden out again into what Heaney called a more 'social' language, but the pressure of events in Northern Ireland meant that this attempt at what Yeats called an escape was doomed to fail. *Station Island*, especially in the purgatorial sequence that gives the book its title, reverts to matters that are more political than social (if such a distinction can be sustained). *The Haw Lantern* in 1987 takes its bearings partly from the political poetry of the eastern bloc, writers like Miłosz, Herbert and Brodsky. But the major change of theme came with *Seeing Things*, when Heaney claims that his whole perspective shifted. In a much quoted moment in the poem 'Fosterling' the poet reflects in astonishment on 'Me waiting until I was nearly fifty / To credit marvels (*ST* 50). The continuance of this ideal of the celebration of the marvellous rather than the concrete palpable is confirmed by the quotation chosen for the memorial stone on the poet's grave: 'Walk on air against your better judgement' from 'The Gravel Walks' in *The Spirit Level* (*SL* 40).

I want to suggest however that a shift in Heaney's metacommentary within the poetry comes before *Seeing Things*. The word for this practice I used in 1994 was 'verbalisation, a process whereby experience or observation is turned into words'. This is of course the universal process of creating poems through words; what is unusual in Heaney is the insistent way in which he signposts it, for example in the use of conceits such as an opposition between England as verbal action and Ireland as affected noun in such political poems as 'Ocean's Love to Ireland' in *North*. It could be illustrated from many places in the volume *Station Island* which carries on the practice of the earlier volumes in drawing metaphors from the terminology of grammar for commentary: for example the second stanza of 'In Illo Tempore' in *Station Island* continues with such grammatical imagery: 'Intransitively we would assist, / confess, receive' (a kind of transference whereby strictly the adverb 'intransitively' modifies the verbs, not the 'we').

But a striking change in the presentation of language comes in the signpost opening poem of *The Haw Lantern*, 'Alphabets', which traces through the whole learning process of language representation, with the child's recognition of 'the forked stick that they call a Y', and the 'pre-reflective stare' at the plasterer writing the family name with his trowel point. The operative word here is the strange 'pre-reflective'. From his first poems Heaney had been concerned with the process of education, in various senses: for example the Baconian 'Advancement of Learning' which he had adopted as the title of one of his very palpable early poems of learning through an unnerving encounter with rats. The application of education through language and into language, by giving verbal expression to what he will call 'the pre-articulate' in 'His Dawn Vision' in 'Mycenae Lookout' (*SL* 33), was expressed with great exactitude in one of Heaney's finest middle-period poems 'The Harvest Bow': 'I tell and finger it like Braille, / Gleaning the unsaid off the palpable' (*FW* 58).

This is a wonderfully accurate description of Heaney's procedure, and the perfect figure for the technique of the early volumes. Several poems describe a palpable materiality (frogspawn, blackberries), and glean – a farming term – meaning from it by turning it into language, by saying or writing it.

But there is something here more sustained, and more unusual, than this. The line – 'Gleaning the unsaid off the palpable' – describes with extraordinary efficiency what the operation of language rule is in its essence. We encounter palpable, as yet unarticulated things in the world and turn them into language. Heaney has turned from the use of grammatical categories as metaphor to a description of the process of learning language rule itself, an earlier stage in the learning of language which might be called the entry into language. Language usage (as described by Noam Chomsky and others) is mostly a matter of putting into practice rules that the speaker is unconscious of and often cannot state: the 'pre-reflective', 'pre-articulate', what is as yet 'unsaid'. A telling example of Heaney's deployment of this aspect of language comes in one of the most admired personal poems, 'Clearances 4', where the poet and his mother converse through 'wrong grammar' which 'keeps them allied': 'With more challenge than pride she'd tell me, "You / Know all them things"' (*HL* 28). This is formally incorrect because 'them' is a personal pronoun, not the demonstrative adjective ('those'), which is the required form grammatically. But of course the grammatical rule is not stated; both the implicit rule and the breach of it are employed for a kind of theatrical effect.

Braille is a perfect figure for the relations between language and its physical representation, and it is a linguistic medium that Heaney has drawn on more than once to great effect. Through Braille the blind reader gleans meaning from the palpable marks on the page, a process analogous to the way the user of language assigns terminology to the palpable, material world. In his most famous employment of the figure, the young Heaney's familiarity with language is given material form in the Braille books of Rosie Keenan, the blind piano-playing neighbour of 'At the Wellhead', 'books like books wallpaper patterns came in' (*SL* 65). That wonderful poem ends with the great lines about the nature of the blind woman's perception:

> She knew us by our voices. She'd say she 'saw'
> Whoever or whatever. Being with her
> Was intimate and helpful, like a cure
> You didn't notice happening. When I read
> A poem with Keenan's well in it, she said,
> 'I can see the sky at the bottom of it now.'

She cannot literally see it, of course; but the poem with the well in it has made it 'said', impalpable as the reference is in this case. There is a related figure here that we will see Heaney using repeatedly in his later poetry: 'a cure you didn't notice happening'. Again, like the frost's 'secret ministry' in Coleridge's 'Eolian Harp', this cure works like language which achieves its effect without the user being able, or required, to articulate it. 'The Rain Stick' at the start of *The Spirit Level* begins with a variant of the same figure – 'a music that you would never have known to listen for' (*SL* 1).

From these examples it is clear that learning to assign verbal form to what was previously unarticulated or moving between the material and the symbolic through the semi-materiality of writing is a dominant theme of *The Spirit Level*. But, if *Seeing Things* really did, as is claimed in 'Fosterling', mark a turn towards the visionary and the seeing of marvels, the next question to ask is whether the kind of transcendental language this required, a language in Heaney's phrase 'beyond the alphabet', is connected with the examples we have just noted in *The Spirit Level*.

The book opens with the poem I have just mentioned, one of Heaney's most eloquently elusive treatments of language communication, 'The Rain Stick'. At first glance there is a formal continuity from *Seeing Things*: the poem, like the opening section of the second poem, is written in the three-line groups that evolved in the great forty-eight-poem 'Squarings' sequence. The terminology is now musical rather than philological, 'diminuendo' rather than 'intransitively' – but it is still aimed at 'gleaning the unsaid off the palpable'. And it begins with an art that is learning to know its mind: the 'music that you would never have known to listen for'. The experience is being articulated by the same kind of learning process as in 'Alphabets'. The second poem, 'To a Dutch Potter in Ireland', begins its epigraph expressly in the area of grammatical commentary, familiar from the early poems, in the 'strongroom of vocabulary' (*SL* 2). This translation seeks another figure for the sourcing of language in the potter's art, 'words like urns that had come through the fire / Stood in their bone-dry alcoves next a kiln / And came away changed' (*SL* 2).

Another immediately striking feature of *The Spirit Level* there is the use of onomatopoeic forms: the 'snip of scissor blades' in 'Mint', or the '*chooka-chook*' of the pretend railway engine in 'A Sofa in the Forties', and the '*Yippee-i-ay*' of 'The Riders of the Range' in the same poem. As with music in 'The Rain Stick', the auditory imagination – T.S. Eliot's phrase which Heaney was always so taken by – is in the ascendant in those cases. But where the language commentary in the earlier books simply drew attention to difference by various highlighting devices (like the pronunciation-spelling of 'fother' at the start of *Wintering Out*, or the italicizing of '*Broagh*' and its '*gh*'), a more fundamental matter of communication is raised in 'A Sofa in the Forties': the way that linguistic difference is an entry into 'history and ignorance' (*SL* 64), the 'music you would never have known to listen for', the recognition of which is an educational process. The encounter with 'the absolute speaker', the reader of the BBC News, is a recognition of ignorance in the same way that learning a formal grammatical rule identifies as ignorance its previous breach. You don't know you are ignorant of history until you know what history is or how it is constructed. If 'The Riders of the Range' is not exactly pre-articulate, the BBC voice is certainly an intrusion of the dominant articulate into this early language world. 'Between him and us / A great gulf was fixed where pronunciation / Reigned tyranically' (*SL* 64). Heaney has given instances before of South Derry rhymes 'with *hushed* and *lulled* full chimes for *pushed* and *pulled*' (in 'The Ministry of Fear', *N* 57); but it is typical of *The Spirit Level* that the wider issues of 'the sway of language and its furtherings' are explored in a way that is more analysis than demonstration. 'The sway of language' is a more impressionistic, less explicit approach to articulation than the earlier realized sounds and scenes: an approach more in keeping with evocation through the auditory imagination and the artworks that he now turns to.

The painters in this book are involved in the same attempt to derive from the palpable some kind of saying: Fragonard, Brueghel and Memling are proposed as painters of the palpable experience – for example of the pendulum-movement in 'The Swing'. The learning process here is not a matter of language, but it is the same sequence: the necessary external 'push in the back' to send the child in motion is 'Sooner or later . . . learned' (*SL* 58). 'The mellowed silence' of 'The Harvest Bow' is displaced by the sounds of the mocking bird and the dulcimer's 'feminine rhymes' in 'A Brigid's Girdle', a plaited hoop different from the harvest bow.

However, it has often been remarked that that book, published just after Heaney won the Nobel Prize and, even more significantly, after the Northern Irish ceasefires finally came into effect, might have been expected to be more optimistic. Although it contains some of Heaney's finest and most affecting personal poems – such as 'Keeping Going', 'A Call' and 'At the Wellhead' – it centres on one of his fiercest sequences, 'Mycenae Lookout'. There the attempt to get beyond the unsaid in accounting for the palpable – for reality – is altogether less comfortable. Language fails to develop and is ascribed bitterly to the 'Mouth athletes' of 'His Dawn Vision', the third section of 'Mycenae Lookout' where we find 'the war stalled in the pre-articulate' (*SL* 33).

One tactic of articulation which is more marked in this book, though it is not unprecedented in the poems, is a turn towards the informal and conversational. In the relatively formal context of 'Poet's Chair', with its epigraph from Leonardo, the first section ends incredulously: '*Leaves / On a bloody chair! Would you believe it?*' (*SL* 47). An informality that becomes marked from this point on is the introductory 'Then' or 'And', suggesting a continued narrative: 'At Banagher' begins 'Then all of a sudden' (*SL* 67) and the celebrated 'Postscript' begins 'And some time make the time' (*SL* 82). In the same way that the formulation of rules of correctness enabled poets like Keats to achieve poetic effect by breaching them, an explicit recognition of the articulate frees the poet to use vernacular effects that depart from it.

After *The Spirit Level* there appears a text that enables – requires even – Heaney to say exactly what he is doing with language: the translation of *Beowulf* in 1999 with its Introduction's Section 2 which sets out Heaney's *ars linguistica* more fully than anywhere else. He says he noticed when he started on the translation in the 1980s that 'certain lines in the first poem in my first book ['Digging'] conformed to the requirements of Anglo-Saxon metrics ... without any conscious intent' (*B* xxiii) – another kind of pre-articulation. He linked this to the influence of Hopkins, 'a chip off the Old English block', and he went on to relate his 'Hopkins ventriloquism' to 'the speech patterns of Ulster'. Coining a celebrated term, he says '*Beowulf* was part of my voiceright', a highly significant formula because it takes him back to an age-old concern of Irish poets writing in English. The aspiration was expressed in 1846 by Denis Florence McCarthy as follows: 'That we can be thoroughly Irish in our writings without ceasing to be English; that we can be faithful to the land of our birth without being unfaithful to that literature which has been "the nursing mother of our minds"'.[3]

There was never much question of Heaney not showing fidelity to the traditions of English poetry. But here he is extending the sense of linguistic obligation to English itself. Most significantly though, he weaves together the English and Irish traditions by incorporating into his version words from English which occur in his Ulster dialect, like 'thole' from the Old English 'þolian', to suffer. But now it is an even-handed, two-way process: he also uses the word 'bawn' from the Irish *bó dhún*. It is a rationalization of what he had done in 'Broagh' where the opening lines draw on Irish, Anglian Old English ('docken') and Ulster-Scots. And to call *Beowulf* 'part of [his] voiceright' is to concede that the earlier periods of English are part of the child's unarticulated inheritance. In the introduction to his translation Heaney spells out the implications of his mixed linguistic inheritance. The unsystematic introduction of local Irish terms into *Beowulf* is comparable to the way informal vernacular terms were used in *The Spirit Level.*

The book that followed *Beowulf* in 2001, *Electric Light*, shows the direct influence of the Anglo-Saxon poem in a variety of ways, drawing on direct translations of the poem in several places - the beautiful 'The Fragment' which we had been prepared for in the *Beowulf* introduction as 'the lovely interlude that tells of the minstrel singing in Heorot' (*B* xxx), and Sections

3 and 4 of 'On His Work in the English Tongue' (*EL* 62–3). But what is most striking is the even-handedness just noted in the diction of the *Beowulf* translation; the 'Work in the English Tongue' is balanced with the Irish title 'Sruth' (stream) and a torrent of Irish place names: Toomebridge, Bann Valley, Ballynahinch, the Gaeltacht, Clonmany to Ahascragh. As well as by *Beowulf*, we have also been prepared for these lexical developments by 'Tollund' at the end of *The Spirit Level* where the 'tourist signs in *futhark* – runic script / In Danish and in English' could have been 'Mullandstown or Scribe' (*SL* 69). The two local Irish names are particularly parochial (in Kavanagh's approving sense) and new in Heaney's oeuvre; they belong to the pre-articulate, pre-formalized language of place.

Rand Brandes tells us that one of the titles Heaney considered for the whole book was *The Real Names*, from one of the most striking sequence-poems in the book, a poem which could be seen as the book's centre of gravity. Its intention is faithful to Heaney's often cited principle from Lowell's 'Epilogue', which might even be seen as the prompt for Heaney's poem: 'Yet, why not say what happened?'[4] 'The Real Names' has several moments of linguistic dawning of its own, 'The smell of the new book. The peep ahead / At words not quite beyond you', stages that 'everyone goes through ahead of time' (*EL* 46–7), Joe Coulter as Banquo 'entering memory like mitigation' (*EL* 50). And the title poem at the end of the book has one of Heaney's most haunting linguistic failures of communication: the desperate grandmother attempting to comfort the weeping child:

> 'What ails you, child,
>
> What ails you, for God's sake?' Urgent, sibilant
> *Ails*, far off and old.
>
> (*EL* 80)

But the poem in *Electric Light* that deals most directly with language education and the standing of local usage is 'The Loose Box':

> On an old recording Patrick Kavanagh states
> That there's health and worth in any talk about
> The properties of land. Sandy, glarry,
> Mossy, heavy, cold, the actual soil
> Almost doesn't matter; the main thing is
> An inner restitution, a purchase come by
> By pacing it in words that make you feel
> You've found your feet in what 'sure-footed' means
> And in the ground of your own understanding.
>
> (*EL* 14)

To say 'the actual soil / Almost doesn't matter' is, once again, to distinguish the normal representational function of language from a direct evocation of what the thing is in its pre-articulated nature, 'its inner restitution' rather than an outward expression that is divorced from it. Though drawing on Kavanagh, Heaney is giving the same kind of metacommentary here as he has given since 'Alphabets'; the inherited agricultural language, grounded in the child's 'own understanding', had 'worth', just as much as the 'strange' letters learned later by the child in 'Alphabets'.

Concern with language in Heaney's next book, *District and Circle*, follows naturally from the issues raised in this famous passage from 'The Loose Box'. Just as *Wintering Out* began with 'Fodder', translated back into the pre-standard form 'Fother', the book starts with a term which will be unfamiliar to most of its readership, 'The Turnip-Snedder' (new even to most readers in most parts of Ireland where the more general term is 'Pulper'). It has often been remarked that the book's title, as well as referring to the London Underground line, signals an intent to circle back to Heaney's local district in a more sustained way. Other local terms are 'seedling-braird' and '*seggans*' in 'To George Seferis in the Underground', which ends:

> And for me a chance to test the edge
> of *seggans*, dialect blade
> hoar and hoarder and more hand-to-hand
> than what is common usage nowadays:
> sedge – marshmallow, rubber-dagger stuff.
> (*DC* 21)

This claim for the authenticity of the more local usage is echoed by terms like a 'chow' (a chew of tobacco) and 'súgán' (hay-rope), and by the frequent use of italics for marked, local forms. The movement between *Electric Light* and *District and Circle* is a kind of linguistic homecoming, another return to a pre-articulate language that takes its place confidently side by side with Dorothy Wordsworth, Edward Thomas, Seferis, Neruda, Rilke, Auden and Cavafy. It is a reversion which is confirmed throughout *Human Chain*, the book which is most at ease with the ideal of saying 'what happened' in Lowell's terms, in a language 'as clear as the bleb of the icicle'.

Up to *Seeing Things*, the point at which Heaney 'nearly fifty' began to 'credit marvels', his engagement of language was a process of education, as in 'The Advancement of Learning' and 'Alphabets'. But from that point onwards, he explores the pre-articulate not as something to be grown out of but as another language realm, with marvels to be credited as evidence of the entry into language itself, not only its representation. Poems like 'His Dawn Vision' (a striking phrase in the context of language) in 'Mycenae Lookout', where the war was 'stalled in the pre-articulate' (*SL* 33) and therefore irreclaimable through language, suggest that it is not possible after all to learn an articulate route into full understanding.

Notes

1 Bernard O'Donoghue, *Seamus Heaney and the Language of Poetry* (London: Harvester Wheatsheaf, 1994), p. 5.
2 Eugene O'Brien, *Seamus Heaney and the Place of Writing* (Gainesville: University Press of Florida, 2002); *Seamus Heaney: Searches for Answers* (Dublin: Wolfhound Press, 2003); *Seamus Heaney as Aesthetic Thinker: A Study of the Prose* (Syracuse University Press, 2016).
3 D.F.McCarthy, Introduction to *The Book of Irish Ballads* (Dublin: I.M. O'Toole, 1846), pp. 22–3.
4 Robert Lowell, *Collected Poems*, ed. Frank Bidart and David Gewanter (London: Faber and Faber, 2003), p. 838.

CHAPTER 13

Elegy

Brendan Corcoran

The elegy for Seamus Heaney is elemental, practical, salutary. It is also in every sense vocational. The 'poem of mourning and consolation'[1] lies at the heart of both the poetic tradition and Heaney's own body of work. This genre is for him a higher-order calling – a calling occasioned not just by loss and grief but by the mechanisms and demands of poetry itself. Yet, the sheer scale and intensity of Heaney's recourse to the formal elegy and *elegiac* lyrics more generally also represent something simpler and more intuitive that underwrites the elegy's promise as a crucial context for reading his work. Even as he unconditionally stands with Miłosz and Yeats, 'on the side of life', Heaney's writing bespeaks a practice, an essential way of seeing and engaging with the world as it is that stems from this poet's powerful eschatological[2] drive (*RP* 158). From beginning to end, he is aware of the grievousness of existence and drawn to the gravity well of death, loss and concomitant human suffering. Yet, a corresponding conviction that poetry is a 'salubrious', even healing art drives his desire for the 'adequate' poetic response to 'necessity' and allows us to read Heaney as, above all, an elegist (*RP* 191, *P* 56, *RP* 158).

Heaney's daunting elegiac output across his career reflects a pragmatic attitude towards the elegy and the elegiac writ large, much like his stance towards death. The elegy is something Heaney just does – to obviously great effect, as critics like Elmer Kennedy-Andrews, John Wilson Foster and Stephen Regan[3] have variously declared that Heaney has earned the mantle he once bestowed on Robert Lowell: 'the master elegist' (*FW* 23). Neil Corcoran has simply described him as 'one of the great modern elegists'.[4] Helen Vendler says that by *Field Work* (1979), Heaney writes as not only an 'individual man engaged in ordinary domestic and social relations' but as, 'increasingly, an elegist'.[5] Dennis O'Driscoll summarizes Heaney's work as 'a poetry of evocation, yearning and elegy' (*SS* x). And, Fintan O'Toole observed that one aspect of the magnitude of Heaney's untimely death is that there is no one up to the task of adequately elegizing the man who 'was arguably the greatest elegist of our times'. Emphasizing the elegy's central importance to his work, O'Toole adds: 'The elegy brought Heaney's personal grace and compassion into contact with his poetic gift for conjuring vanished things.'[6]

The scope and variety of Heaney's elegiac output reflect his faith in poetry's 'answerability'[7] to the world defined as much by 'atrocity' as by 'beauty', as much by 'suffering' as by 'song' (*N* 29, *GT* xii). Present from the earliest uncollected and collected poems onwards, the elegy is a kind of carrier wave passing through the poetry bearing the signal of the art's responsiveness and responsibility. In his pervasive deployment of the genre, the outlines of broad categories that do not entirely follow any chronological order become apparent. These include poems exploring death in farm life; wide-ranging Troubles poems, including his 'bog elegies';[8] poems mourning his 'familiar dead'[9] – his parents, other family members, friends and acquaintances; poems grieving and memorializing the deaths of fellow-poets; poems grappling with themes like famine, war, terrorism and climate change, where the scale of loss transcends the individual; and poems confronting his own mortality. While Heaney's corpus is peppered with numerous formal elegies responding to the deaths of named individuals, it is saturated with *elegiac* lyrics, poems that may or may not be prompted by a particular death. Such poems are nonetheless in tune with his overall appreciation of death's force, his care for and interest in the living as individuals and as a public experiencing extremity, and his trust in 'poetic answerability or responsibility'.[10] And, to all these must be added the book-length translations that are distinctly elegiac in mood or cast as they overtly address in part or in whole personal and/or cultural catastrophe: *Sweeney Astray*, *The Midnight Verdict*, *The Cure at Troy*, *Laments*, *Beowulf*, *The Burial at Thebes* and *Aeneid Book VI*. Heaney does not merely write occasional poems triggered by his own grief on experiencing loss. Rather, the genre in all its capaciousness, its nuance and complexity, is fundamental to his sense of poetry and its possibilities. Unsurprisingly then, in 1994, when Joe Pellegrino was introduced to Heaney as a scholar working on 'the elegiac Heaney', the poet replied: '"the elegiac Heaney"? There's nothing else.'[11]

And yet, despite the scale of Heaney's production of elegies and elegiac lyrics, he seldom speaks directly about the elegy per se. That said, the constellation of terms and images he uses to describe lyric poetry often fit discussions of the elegy. For example, Heaney consistently privileges poetry's potential as an ultimately 'restorative and salutary' art, effectively tying discourse about poetry's foundations to language pertinent to elegy and the elegiac (*SS* 437). Peter Sacks describes the trajectory of the traditional elegy as 'follow[ing] the ancient rites in the basic passage through grief or darkness to consolation and renewal'.[12] Heaney's practically minded work, whether elegiac or not, maintains the dynamic relationship between these extremes, affirming the immediate and conjoined realities of suffering, death and grief – *and* joy, life and life's continuity across time. Heaney may be read as a far darker poet than is usually assumed, but his poetry and the traditional elegy both drive towards the ideal of restoration or renewal. By being careful to limit his claims about what poetry does, the recuperative energy of his work, knotted to the pervasiveness of loss and grief, attends to a potential for restoration (redress), wholeness, and health.

A fundamentally elegiac term captures Heaney's acute perception of death's entanglement with life: 'mortalia', the fact that 'we must pass away from' various 'people and things' – that also 'have had to pass away from us'.[13] Though he says that Virgil's full line 'Sunt lacrimae rerum et mentem mortalia tangunt' could well serve as the epigraph for his book *Electric Light* (2001),[14] Aeneas's observation might best be a motto for his overall body of work because a life-affirming awareness of 'lacrimae rerum, the tears of things', and a readiness for 'mortalia', pervade Heaney's oeuvre without its succumbing to maudlin complaints or cloying recourse to easeful consolations (*RP* xv).

Consequently, instead of being generically delimiting, the title 'elegist' proves to be as expansive as appropriate. The elegist's peculiar engagement with the ideal and the ultimate is, for Heaney, utterly grounded in the brute commonplace that figures what he calls, borrowing from Hopkins, 'world-sorrow' (*GT* 126). A responsiveness to this 'given note' yields, across his career, an essentially elegiac poetics (*DD* 34). By this I mean an instinct and effort to sustain within his work and his general outlook a 'sense of death'[15] that, in proving to be as honest as pervasive, is equally, if paradoxically, enlivening.

The given world is the place wherein his 'ladders start',[16] and Heaney's subject, in the broadest terms, involves the human capacity to be at once 'self-possessed and overcome', as he says in 'In Bellaghy Graveyard'.[17] With his own burial in this same graveyard, his end arrives at his beginning. And just as Heaney's Mossbawn childhood in Bellaghy's environs yields a near-infinite resource for words, images and framing experiences, so this first world is also centre and source ('omphalos') for his 'sense of death' (*P* 17). Writing about his first encounters with Robert Frost, Heaney heralds 'Out, Out', saying, 'what attracted me then was the familiarity of the world that Frost was writing about. Yard work, farm people, the hard rattling action of a buzz saw.'[18] Regarding the child's mutilation and death in the poem, Heaney observes: 'that kind of thing was part of my own background, a whole rural folklore of sudden deaths, tales of men going through threshing machines or stone crushers or having their legs cut off by reaping machines. "Awful but cheerful", as Elizabeth Bishop would say.'[19]

For all their glaring corporality, the atrociousness of these deaths in Heaney's first world is matched by his matter-of-fact recounting of these events. Heaney describes a childhood exposed to death in many guises. Farm life, of course, as portrayed in 'The Early Purges', offered all manner of raw deaths. He says, 'the earliest pig calls I recollect were screams coming from the Gribben slaughterhouse in Anahorish'(*SS* 8). Similarly, he recalls the second horse the family briefly owned breaking its leg: 'I'll never forget her standing at the gable of the house that evening . . . she was shivering and shivered more vehemently when the man put the humane killer to her brow and dropped her' (9). He points out his early knowledge of the deathbed and 'the vocabulary of dread' the grown-ups used for grave illness (*SS* 21). 'Going to funerals', Heaney says, 'is so much a part of the culture that formed me, part of the ethic of respect' (*SS* 473). And then there is the death in 1953 of his younger brother Christopher, first mourned in 'Midterm Break' from *Death of a Naturalist* (1966). This death traumatized the whole family and haunts Heaney's 'known world' of Mossbawn across his life and poetry (*SS* 16). His sorrow further radiates through various later works such as his translation *Laments* (1995), his compendium of interviews with O'Driscoll (2008) and the concluding poem of *District and Circle* (2006), 'The Blackbird of Glanmore', in which, upon taking note of the bird, Heaney recalls lines from *The Cure at Troy* (1990), his translation of Sophocles' *Philoctetes*, and says:

'I want away
To the house of death, to my father

Under the low clay roof.'
And I think of one gone to him,
A little stillness dancer –
Haunter-son, lost brother –
Cavorting through the yard,
So glad to see me home,

My homesick first term over.
(*DC* 75)

This poem, replete with *mortalia*, allows Heaney's grief over the deaths of father and brother decades ago to coexist with a poignant and concluding wistfulness about his own demise.

Yet, Heaney's childhood knowledge of death's ubiquity may also have mitigated his fear of it. His intimate comfort with death's discomfiting force is characterized by a sanguine equanimity towards the endurance of grief. 'Bear humanly the human lot'[20] defines this ethos. We hear this note as Heaney points out how close to the home lay the bus stop where Christopher was killed. O'Driscoll observes that this 'must have tainted the stop dreadfully for the family'. Heaney replies, 'It did. But what was to be done? My mother still had to get to Castledawson' (*SS* 5).

Heaney's persistent attentiveness to the facts of loss involves much more than the mourner's reflexive embrace or melancholic rejection of 'elegiac conventions'[21] – or the traditional elegist's trust in these conventions' provision of affective consolation – so often the basis for discussion of the elegy. His concern with 'matters having to do with time and death'[22] is, first and foremost, *lyric* in nature, involving an affirmation of poetry's 'responsibility to sing out and make sense and take the measure of reality'.[23] This is a core value for Heaney, and it ties his production of lyric poetry to his commitment to the elegy and the elegiac. Heaney as lyric poet as much as elegist articulates what he finds already present in his materials: the crisis of mortality itself and the possibility of an accommodation with death.

Writing within, not against, the vast elegiac tradition, Heaney's perhaps surprising coolness to the viability of consolation as an elegiac aim or outcome stems from his identification with poetry's 'salubrious' powers (the 'good of poetry'[24]) in contrast to the art's 'placatory and palliative' capacities (*GT* 121). Heaney's grand concern is health over comfort. Part of the problem Heaney has with an elegiac poetry focused on conventions and tropes over a deeper aim 'to be a source of truth and at the same time a vehicle of harmony' (*RP* 193) is that such poetry 'plays into the prepared expectations of our ear and our nature' (*GT* 122). The too-ready 'effect' of such poetry 'will be to offer a sense of possible consolation' (122). When discussing Frost's poem 'Directive', Heaney explicitly disavows the prospect of lyric consolation:

> the poem finally goes beyond the bounds of what poetry can do ... the images presented by the poet are too readily enlisted into his project of consolation, of taking the reader 'beyond confusion' ... One might say that at the moment when the poem should be content with having achieved lift-off, it opts for uplift instead ... it interposes a pre-treated filter which turns the poem from discovery towards effect.[25]

A consolatory fix, though perhaps gratifying, is not realistic – or honest. On his 'contemplation' of the macabre, muse-like Tollund Man and his writing of the poem about the bog body, Heaney says: 'The spirit felt less alone. Not consoled but stayed, in the words of Robert Frost, "against confusion"'.[26] Even 'at times of general distress', like 11 September 2001, when 'people . . . want to be brought beyond confusion', Heaney carefully limits his claims about what the 'do-goodery of poetry' might yield: 'Beauty is transitory, the whole thing comes and goes, life is not solved but there is [in the successful work] a momentary sensation of resolution, a healing moment.'[27] Ideally, poetry offers 'a fair enough answer to what has happened in our own present time'.[28]

Still, Heaney demonstrates utter fluency with the elegy's traditional mourning conventions in masterworks like the sonnet sequence 'Clearances' (for his mother), 'Elegy' (for Robert Lowell), 'Casualty' (for his father-in-law, Louis O'Neill and indirectly the dead of Bloody Sunday) or 'The Strand at Lough Beg' (for his second cousin Colum McCartney, a victim of random sectarian killing) – one of the 'very few modern elegies that observe[s] the conventions of the genre so trustingly'.[29] With 'The Strand at Lough Beg' built around what Heaney describes as the resurrection 'of the dead . . . in a benign landscape',[30] his subsequent 'Station Island' vii revisits this trust as the ghost of the murdered cousin returns to sternly challenge the poet's enthusiasm for such grand generic gestures. As if acknowledging that 'to redeem death in beautiful poetry is to legitimize it',[31] 'Station Island' vii opts for the more melancholic, anti-consolatory mode of elegy. Yet, this later, seemingly more modern poem, does not undermine the poetic or elegiac validity of the earlier recuperative pastoral poem. 'The Strand at Lough Beg' is no 'Spain 1937', a poem decommissioned and denounced by its author, W.H. Auden; as late as the interviews in the RTÉ documentary *Out of the Marvellous* (2009), it still has 'purchase' as a recognition of the human, poetic need to mourn and care for the dead (*HC* 17). Despite the tougher stance of 'Station Island' towards the more consolatory aesthetics of 'The Strand at Lough Beg', Ramazani argues that the later poem ultimately 'salvages these consolatory tropes by curtailing their promise'.[32] As it stands, both poems directly and indirectly critique each other and now, read together, each legitimizes, grounds and *redresses* the other as an effort to grasp a death. The relative success or failure of these two poems' generic conventions rendering some form of affective consolation after McCartney's death misses the point. Though moving, these poems are less about personal affect than how to represent or even strive to apprehend the enigma of random sectarian murder.

These poems' dynamic relationship thus tells us something about the more broadly elegiac energy driving Heaney's poetics and lyric production. Though representing somewhat different approaches to the role of consolation in the formal elegy, the McCartney poems reflect capaciousness indicative of Heaney's more broadly elegiac project governed by the overarching concern for poetry's 'answerability … to what people suffer in the world around it'.[33] Tactical decisions about how to respond to loss elegiacally – in terms of generic conventions, tropes, tones or modes of address – appear to be more incidental aesthetic choices compared to the essential strategic priority that is Heaney's focus on 'answerability'. His devotion to lyric responsiveness and responsibility allows him to follow Emily Dickinson's example to 'both provoke and promote a renovated consciousness of the reality we know and share as a species'.[34] Heaney's writing ultimately presents not a 'defense against [a] consciousness of mortality'[35] – which has always been at least a component of our funerary arts invested in the provision of comfort – but an actual and quite hard-bitten embrace of such consciousness.

> Joseph, yes, you know the beat.
> …
>
> Its measured ways I tread again
> Quatrain by constrained quatrain,
> Meting grief and reason out
> As you said a poem ought.
>
> Trochee, trochee, falling: thus
> Grief and metre order us.
>
> (*EL* 77)

This is from 'Audenesque', Heaney's elegy for the Nobel laureate Joseph Brodsky. The poem conveys through both sound and sense a clear-eyed woundedness as Heaney mourns and extends grief at the loss of a poet into the world and poetry itself. But he exposes himself further when he matches wits with Brodsky's definition of poetry by shifting 'grief and reason' to 'grief and metre'. While there is much to say about Heaney's linkage of reason and metre, I want to draw attention to the impact of Heaney's word 'order'. As the poles around which his poetic world revolves, 'grief and metre' order his poetic life – and not simply his extensive employment of the elegy and the elegiac. These terms embody an organizing principle that possesses its own almost trochaic inevitability, yet they also place a very real demand on all students of poetry. 'Grief and metre' are the forces to which Heaney and his poetry are answerable.

The 'order' engendered by 'grief and metre' is what he calls 'the music of what happens' or 'the music of humanity . . . of an intelligence which has been to school in the world'.[36] In Heaney, both poetry's truth function and pleasure function are umbilically tied to the world as it is – 'hung in the scales / with beauty and atrocity' (*N* 29).

Though he finds a calling in life's contingency, Heaney also displays a subsequent need to produce in poetry an adequate 'response to reality', what he terms 'a beneficent event' (*RP* 2). Vitally, this elegist's access to hope in the prospect of healing – something vital to Heaney's notion of the lyric project – remains dependent still on the piquant acknowledgement that, as Hardy says, 'If a way to the Better there be, / It exacts a full look at the Worst' (*GT* 69). 'The world out there'[37] is replete with 'marvels' (*ST* 52) and the familiar wonders of the 'human chain' (*HC* 17) celebrated by poems, but it is also 'the world of enemies and corpses',[38] in which poetry 'helps us also to endure' (*RP* 185). Indeed, 'human beings, given the right conditions, have an immense and heart-breaking capacity for dignified endurance', Heaney says, 'and to witness such endurance helps the rest of us also to endure'.[39] The poet's role – and the aim of this poet's elegiac poetics – is thus to help us recognize necessity, to adequately mourn and remember, to understand reality in the light of poetry's alterity, and then to help us endure, hold our own, survive. Beckoning his sons to stand as if within the embrace of his arms, as his hands (like his father's once) hold fast to the kite's string, the poet invites his children to share in, trains them to 'take the strain':

> Before the kite plunges down into the wood
> and this line goes useless
> take in your two hands, boys, and feel
> the strumming, rooted, long-tailed pull of grief.
> You were born fit for it.
> Stand in here in front of me
> and take the strain.
>
> (*SI* 44)

And so, recognition of life in need of care underlies the whole business of 'poeting' (*SL* 50). Knowledge of what Keats calls a 'world of pains and troubles'[40] is the starting point for Heaney, from which he 'responds (and exercises [his] responsibility)' – and, through poetry, cares (*RP* xiv). Considering 'the good of poetry' while celebrating Ted Hughes and mourning his death, Heaney wrote: 'At the end of a century which has seen the mushroom clouds over Japan and smoke from the gas ovens over Europe, seen the dustbowls and the melting icecaps, the acid rain and the eroding ozone layer', poetry's fulfilment of its capacity to 'acknowledge all the destructive truths and yet still sing like Caedmon about the glory of creation' is nothing short of the realization of 'our human *raison d'etre*'.[41] The expression of such poetic, indeed, elegiac knowledge presumes a way forward whose hard slog may yet be endured. Here is the ultimate trajectory and difficulty of Heaney's elegiac practice:

> It is easy to descend into Avernus.
> Death's dark door stands open day and night.
> But to retrace your steps and get back to upper air,
> That is the task, that is the undertaking.
>
> (*A* 9)

Notes

1 Peter Sacks, *The English Elegy: Studies in the Genre from Spenser to Yeats* (Baltimore, MD: Johns Hopkins University Press, 1985), p. 2.

2 In 'A Note on the Text', 'Katabasis, Eschatological' is identified as the possible germ of an unfinished afterword to *Aeneid Book VI*. Seamus Heaney, *Aeneid Book VI* (London: Faber and Faber, 2016), p. 51.

3 Elmer-Kennedy Andrews, *Writing Home: Poetry and Place in Northern Ireland, 1968–2008* (Woodbridge: D.S. Brewer, 2008), p. 122; John Wilson Foster, 'The Dominion of the Physical: Reading Heaney', review of *District and Circle*, *Pacific Rim Review of Books*, 5 (2007), www.prrb.ca/articles/issue05-heaney.htm; Stephen Regan, 'Seamus Heaney and the Modern Irish Elegy', in Ashby Bland Crowder and Jason David Hall (eds.), *Seamus Heaney: Poet, Critic, Translator* (New York: Palgrave Macmillan, 2007), pp. 9–25 (at p. 24).

4 Neil Corcoran, 'Seamus Heaney Obituary', *Guardian*, 30 August 2013, www.theguardian.com/books/2013/aug/30/seamus-heaney.

5 Helen Vendler, *Seamus Heaney* (Cambridge, MA: Harvard University Press, 2000), p. 59.

6 Fintan O'Toole, 'Private Memories, Public Traces: A Tribute to Seamus Heaney', *Irish Times*, 6 March 2014, www.irishtimes.com/culture/private-memories-public-traces-a-tribute-to-seamus-heaney-1.1715178.

7 Seamus Heaney, 'Talking Shop 2. "The Weight of Hours"', p. 2. Rand Brandes papers, MS 1100, Seamus Heaney correspondence and manuscripts, 1990–2007, Rose Library, Emory University.

8 Jahan Ramazani, *Poetry of Mourning: The Modern Elegy from Hardy to Heaney* (University of Chicago Press, 1994), p. 338.

9 Heaney, *Aeneid Book VI*, p. 51.

10 Heaney, 'Weight of Hours', p. 5.

11 Joe Pellegrino, 'Biography: Seamus Heaney', Internet Poetry Library, www.ibiblio.org/ipa/poems/heaney/biography.php. With the magnitude of Heaney's elegiac project in mind, including his extensive prose considerations

of issues governing the elegy in general and various readings of canonical elegies, we might go so far as to compare Heaney's elegiac vision to Yeats's seemingly more esoteric *A Vision*, especially in terms of its centrality for the poet and its engagement with poetry's most elemental concerns.

12 Sacks, *English Elegy*, p. 20.
13 Seamus Heaney, '*Lux Perpetua*', *Guardian*, 16 June 2001, 9.
14 *Ibid.*
15 Mick Heaney, 'My Father's Famous Last Words', *Irish Times*, 12 September 2015, www.irishtimes.com/life-and-style/people/mick-heaney-my-father-s-famous-last-words-1.2348525.
16 *The Collected Poems of W. B. Yeats*, ed. Richard J. Finneran (New York: Scribner, 1996), p. 348.
17 Seamus Heaney, *In Bellaghy Graveyard*, broadside (s.l.: s.n., 1996).
18 Seamus Heaney, 'Voices Behind the Door: Robert Frost', in *Poetry Review*, 83/4 (Winter 1993–4), 31.
19 *Ibid.*
20 Jan Kochanowski, *Laments*, trans. Seamus Heaney and Stanisław Barańczak (New York: Farrar, Straus and Giroux, 1995), p. 59.
21 Sacks, *English Elegy*, p. 2.
22 Seamus Heaney, 'Suffering and Decision', in Terry Gifford, Neil Roberts, and Mark Wormald (eds.), *Ted Hughes: from Cambridge to Collected* (New York: Palgrave Macmillan, 2013), pp. 221–37 (at p. 226). Heaney first delivered this lecture in 2007. This phrase is actually Heaney's paraphrase of the Virgilian term *mortalia*.
23 Seamus Heaney, 'The Whole Thing: On the Good of Poetry', in Kevin M. Cahill (ed.), *The Open Door: Art and Foreign Policy at the RCSI* (Dublin: Center for International Humanitarian Cooperation, 2014), pp. 88–108 (at p. 103).
24 *Ibid.*, p. 92.
25 Seamus Heaney, 'Talking Shop 1. 'The Playthings in the Playhouse', pp. 8–9. Rand Brandes papers, MS 1100, Seamus Heaney correspondence and manuscripts, 1990–2007, Rose Library, Emory University.
26 Seamus Heaney, '"Apt Admonishment": Wordsworth as an Example', *Hudson Review*, 61/1 (Spring 2008), 19–33 (at p. 32).
27 Heaney, 'Whole Thing', pp. 95–6.
28 *Ibid.*, p. 107.
29 Regan, 'Modern Irish Elegy', p. 18.
30 *Ibid.*, p. 19.
31 Ramazani, *Poetry of Mourning*, p. 346.
32 *Ibid.*, p. 353.
33 Heaney, 'Weight of Hours', p. 2.
34 *Ibid.*, p. 22.
35 Sacks, *English Elegy*, p. 16.
36 Heaney, 'Weight of Hours', p. 20.
37 *Ibid.*, p. 24.

38 *Ibid.*
39 Heaney, 'Apt Admonishment', p. 27. Similarly, Heaney claims that a poem 'gives true peace only if the horror is satisfactorily rendered. If the eyes are not averted from it. If its overmastering power is acknowledged and unconceded, so the human spirit holds its own against its affront and immensity.' Rand Brandes, 'Seamus Heaney: An Interview', *Salmagundi*, 80 (Fall 1988), 4–21 (at p. 21).
40 Seamus Heaney, 'In Gratitude for all the Gifts', *Guardian*, 10 September 2004, www.theguardian.com/books/2004/sep/11/featuresreviews.guardianreview25.
41 Seamus Heaney, 'The peace of the Word is Always with You', *Sunday Times*, 17 January 1999, 10–11.

CHAPTER 14

Music

Simon B. Kress

Writing sleeve notes for his friend David Hammond's album *The Singer's House* (1978), Seamus Heaney observed that 'the revolutionary power of song itself [resides in] its power to move and pleasure and affect those depths of the personality where attitudes begin'.[1] This notion of music, as preverbal prime mover, suffuses Heaney's work. Few contemporary poets have been as keenly attuned to the aural dimensions of language as Heaney. In many poems, like those exploring place names in *Wintering Out* (1972), the diction seems to yearn for a field of pure sound: 'My mouth holds round / the soft blasting, / *Toome, Toome*' (*OG* 54). The word *music* and its siblings – *song, chorus, rhythm, note*, etc. – appear throughout Heaney's poetry and criticism. Attending to the role music plays in Heaney's poetics is crucial to understanding his work. Music intersects with the central elements of Heaney's work – place, politics, the public voice, the body, the folk, Ireland – marking both its aspirations and its limits.

Arising as it does within the contexts of Ireland and the lyric, Heaney's invocation of music bears a complicated lineage. The lyric, of course, finds its origins in music, from which it became increasingly estranged after the Renaissance. As James William Johnson observes in the *The Princeton Encyclopedia of Poetry and Poetics*, 'Despite the efforts of later writers who were primarily poets and not composers, such as Swinburne, Hopkins, and Yeats, the lyric since the Renaissance has remained a verbal rather than a musical discipline, and the traces of its melodic origin have become largely vestigial.'[2] To invoke music in the lyric mode is to recall this absent tradition, to write belatedly and to foreground that belatedness. Similarly, music is a vital figure in the formation of Irish cultural identity. The association of the Irish simultaneously with barbaric unruliness and with a certain musical genius establishes a paradigm of Irish creativity that can be traced as far back as Giraldus Cambrensis's recognition of the exceptionality of Irish music in his twelfth-century treatise, *Topography of*

Ireland (1188) and persists up to and beyond Matthew Arnold's famous meditations on the Celt and the Saxon.[3] Yet, at least since the 'Celtic Twilight' of Yeats and his generation, Irish traditional music requires the steady stewardship of enthusiasts to keep it alive.

In two senses, then, Heaney's music signals and inscribes a hauntedness into his work, a nostalgia for an earlier wholeness. Something in its twilit status gives music more than a simple figurative sense in Heaney's work: rather, the invocation of *music* is performative, spell-casting. When Heaney cites the 'music of what happens' (*OG* 173), the 'music of the arbitrary' (*OG* 335), the 'shape and music' of a blacksmith's hammering (*OG* 20) or the 'song of a tubular steel gate in the dark' (*SP* 172), he seeks to do more than merely describe reality: he attempts to hallow it, to reclaim it from disuse.

Music appears in Heaney's earliest work as a figure for his most pressing concerns and poetic aspirations: visionary perception, reconciliation of the oral and the literate, and poetic achievement. Heaney's first two collections, *Death of a Naturalist* (1966) and *Door into the Dark* (1969), set the terms of one of Heaney's central dramas: the poet's attempt to align his poetic work with the manual labour of his agricultural forebears. In attempting to make *the work* into labour, labour into *the work*, the collections exhaustively catalogue a pre-literate (or extra-literate) world of seasons and harvests, handiwork and folk wisdom, from which the poet finds metaphors for his poetry – digging, churning, ploughing, thatching, forging, divining. The tradition to which Heaney sought to adjust his individual talent was as much the agricultural world of his rural upbringing as it was the poetic legacy of writers like Yeats, Wordsworth and Kavanagh. Indeed, much of the early work can be read as a brilliant, extended apologia for his choosing the pen over the spade.

Music as structured sound provides the means by which Heaney reconciles the literate tradition of the contemporary poet with the traditions of his rural Northern Ireland. 'Digging', the poem that begins both Heaney's first collection and most selections of his work, depicts the poet seated at his desk, gazing out at his father cutting turf in the field. The poem schematically opposes the artistic work of the poet-son with the manual labour of the turf-cutter-father. 'I've no spade to follow men like them', laments the poet before arriving at his licensing insight: 'Between my finger and my thumb / The squat pen rests. / I'll dig with it' (*OG* 3–4). Rather than prove his claim through polemic, Heaney proves it through sound. The act of description becomes the work: the poet emulates his father's 'rasping sound' when he writes 'a clean rasping sound' – the onomatopoeias of *rasp*, *nick*, *squelch* arguing that a pen can (at the level of sound at least) dig like a spade. Similarly, the poem's percussive monosyllables ape his father's 'stooping in rhythm'. Throughout the early work, manual labour is reconciled with poetic work by the centrality of rhythm and sound in each.

'The Forge', another of Heaney's early canonical poems, makes this musical reconciliation more explicit. Like 'Digging', 'The Forge' stages another scene of exclusion, finding the poet outside a blacksmith's shop, left to conjure knowledge of what goes on inside from the 'anvil's short-pitched ring' or the 'hiss when a new shoe toughens in water'. Sounding it out, the poet imagines an occult scene where the anvil is 'horned as a unicorn', 'an altar / Where he expends himself in shape and music' (*OG* 20). Although the blacksmith's indifference to the world outside contrasts with and even mocks the poet's eager interest in the world inside, they share a devotion to shape and music. Listening, the poet pursues his furtive apprenticeship. Likewise, in his 1978 reflections on childhood, Heaney performs a mastery of shaping and music-making: 'I would begin with the Greek word, *omphalos*, meaning the navel, and repeat it, *omphalos*, *omphalos*, *omphalos*, until its blunt music becomes the music of somebody pumping water at the pump outside our back door' (*P* 17). Here, through the strange-making repetition of *omphalos*, Heaney summons up the work and 'the rhythms of the yard'. The onomatopoeic sound effects that run through all of Heaney's work can be situated within the lyric tradition; but what the early work shows is that the interest in sound registers Heaney's recurrent effort to physicalize poetic work and to sustain his lineal connection with the pre-industrial, manual labour of his rural origins.

Seemingly at odds with the down-to-earth effects in these early poems, sound also operates as a conduit of mystical apprehension. Positing hearing as a way of knowing, of moving into the unknown/unknowable, 'The Forge' exemplifies this fusion of the mystical and the manual at the centre of Heaney's poetics. 'Personal Helicon', an earlier, more overt *ars poetica*, announces the poet's project: 'I rhyme / To see myself, to set the darkness echoing' (*OG* 14). The figures of sound and poetic aspiration return again in 'Station Island', the ghost of Stephen Dedelus/Joyce admonishing the poet to 'fill the element / with signatures of your own frequency, / echo-soundings' – 'you've listened long enough. Now strike your note' (*OG* 245).

Similarly, in 'The Given Note', also from *Door into the Dark*, Heaney employs musical performance as a figure for the more mystical aspects of creativity and artistic achievement, a metaphor he returns to repeatedly in his middle period. The poem depicts an Irish fiddler as visionary, cabined and marooned 'on the most westerly Blasket' drawing airs and 'bits of a tune' out of the night and the weather: 'He took it / Out of wind off mid-Atlantic. // Still he maintains, from nowhere. / It comes off the bow gravely, / Rephrases itself into the air' (*OG* 36). The fiddler represents a vatic otherworldly artist in pure communion with the numinous. He is an exemplar of the artist whose work not only transcends artifice, but circumvents mimesis itself, the weather and the artist breathing the same 'air' – an aeolian circulatory system. Although it lacks the sonic effects of poems like 'The Forge' and 'Digging', the poem's gentle slant-rhymes (island/violin, heard/weather, nowhere/air) still pair the emulative and the expository.

These various strains are wrought into a more integrated poetics in *Field Work* (1979), a collection that finds Heaney actively seeking out new models of the artist. In the years following his major work *North* (1975), Heaney was exhausted and in search of new modes. Heaney's major essays of the period – 'The Sense of Place' (1977, 1980), 'Yeats as an Example?' (1978), 'The Makings of a Music' (1978) and the first sections of his essays 'Mossbawn' and 'Belfast' (1978) – reveal a poet attempting to remake himself, both through a reconsideration of precursors and through a more calculated and self-defining engagement with place and memory than in previous collections. Heaney finds his way back to poetry through music, a recurrent theme in these essays.

Exploring the artistic development of both Wordsworth and Yeats in 'The Makings of a Music', Heaney adopts the figure of music to encompass both the process of poetic composition and the hallmarks of a unique poetic style. As Heaney puts it, he seeks to examine 'the relationship between the almost physiological operations of a poet composing and the music of the finished poem' (*P* 61). Wordsworth, as exemplar of what Paul Valéry called *les vers donnés* – the given line – demonstrates 'a version of composition as listening, as a wise passiveness, a surrender to energies that spring within the centre of the mind' (63). Further: 'It was not a question of the poet's voice performing a part but of the poet's voice being possessed; it was not a question of technical cool, of finding a dramatic pitch, rather a matter of sympathetic warmth' (71). As the notion of *les vers donnés* suggests, there is an unwilled and, because unwilled, a seemingly more natural and immediate quality to such poetry. This is the poet as feeling, sympathetic listener; as between the poet and the subject, there is a perfect sympathy between the poet's instinct and expression.

In *Field Work*, poems on musical artists – Seán Ó Riada, David Hammond and John Field – echo this paradigm of physiological transmission. In 'In Memoriam Sean O'Riada', first published in the summer of 1976, Heaney finds an image of the artist in perfect sympathy with his environment, and through that sympathy able to translate, with hardly any loss of fidelity, the felt reality of experience: 'How do you work? / Sometimes I just lie out / like ballast in the bottom of the boat / listening to the cuckoo' (*FW* 29). The musician works by subordinating the intellect to instinctive apprehension. Similarly, the short lyric 'Song', through a series of mimetic reversals, offers an immediacy unattainable by language:

There are the mud-flowers of dialect
And the immortelles of perfect pitch
And that moment when the bird sings very close
To the music of what happens.
(OG 173)

In a sense, Heaney enacts his own principle of privileged listening: the music of what happens can be heard only by the sensitive artist, and the music of poetry can be heard only by the sensitive reader, or auditor. In this case, the bird is both interpreter and instantiation, for, in the 'very close' space between the subject and the object, the two become interchangeable.

What gives music such force in Heaney's work is its ability to sound in twin registers, both as a Romantic figure for poetic beauty that circumvents the intellect and ideology, but also as a peculiarly Irish inheritance. Indeed, behind a seemingly British Romanticist image like the bird singing close 'to the music of what happens', is the Fenian legend that 'The most beautiful music in the world is the music of what happens.' Or, behind the high art of classical music in Ó Riada is the traditional music of Ireland.

Heaney seeks to recover this heritage most directly in his poem 'The Singer's House', written for his close friend and Irish traditional singer David Hammond, and included as the sleeve notes to Hammond's album of the same name. The poem recounts the local folk belief that 'drowned souls', living on in the form of seals, could be drawn in by the sound of music. The poem offers an image of the singer dissolving Cartesian binaries, effecting a communion of the living and the dead, the human and the natural world: 'his song / a rowboat far out in evening' (*OG* 153). Here we have the artist as singer and Irishman, and music in the poem becomes definitively Irish music. These figures enable the poem's concluding affirmation:

When I came here first you were always singing,
a hint of the clip of the pick

in your winnowing climb and attack.
Raise it again, man. We still believe what we hear.
(OG 154)

Yet this affirmation is accompanied with a sense of loss. Throughout the poem the speaker voices a concern for the preservation of folk tradition and for the preservation, as tradition, of current cultural practices: 'What do we say anymore / to conjure the salt of our earth? / So much comes and is gone / that should be crystal and kept' (*OG* 153). Among those things gone are traditional beliefs and the practice of song that seemed a complement to them. As a meditation on this loss, the question at the back of the poem is one of efficacy and relevance. What justification can a singer of traditional folk songs give for his life and work? And, likewise, has the belief in music's force (and by extension the force of all art) gone the way of an old superstition about seals? And, finally, perhaps the most troubling of all, has tradition itself become a relic? As in 'Digging', the speaker answers by making his own music, becoming a witness to sound: 'So I say to myself *Gweebarra* / and its music hits off the place / like water hitting off granite. / I see the glittering sound' (*OG* 153). The speaker, in an attempt to enact the continued efficacy of language and sound, hovers between the concrete reality of the river, the linguistic reality of the place name, and the metaphorical reality of glittering sound. In such figures, the speaker attempts to recover a lost unity of place, artist and the artistic object, which then becomes the vehicle bearing that unity through to future auditors – 'my quest for definition', Heaney remarks elsewhere, 'is conducted in the living speech of the landscape I was born into' (*P* 36–7). The movement towards music in Heaney's work indicates a complex of associations. It circumvents the discursive and ideological quality of language; it positions the body as the primary mode of apprehension; and it evokes the unifying figure of tradition. The last line of the poem – 'We still believe what we hear' – resonates in each of these registers, and counters the sense of doubt that animates the poem. Tradition and the efficacy of poetry persist acoustically.

In his later work, devoted to 'credit[ing] marvels' (*OG* 331), music remains a figure for access to the numinous past and the numinous beyond. 'Squarings', the long sequence of twelve-line poems that forms the bulk of *Seeing Things* (1991) and to which form Heaney would return again and again in his later work, represents a turning point in Heaney's poetics. Returning to Valéry's notion of *les vers donnés* and his own conceptions of the artistic creation, Heaney later commented that he 'learned what inspiration feels like, but not how to summon it. Which is to say that [he] learned that waiting is part of the work' (*SS* 320).

Ambitiously attempting to construct a vision of the marvellous without recourse to Christian notions of an afterlife, Heaney relies on music as a figure of cosmic and physical order. As in 'The Given Note', music configures a responsivity between the human and non-human. In 'Lightenings' vi, the young Thomas Hardy offers his 'cool brow . . . like an anvil waiting // For sky to make it sing the perfect pitch / of his dumb being' (*OG* 336). Or in 'Lightenings' v, the thumbprints in concrete form 'three stops to play / The music of the arbitrary on' (*OG* 335). In 'Squarings' xlvi, Heaney returns to the fiddler's house of 'The Given Note' and, hearing 'the fiddle going / Like a flat stone skimmed at sunset', asks, 'Was music once a proof of God's existence?' Answering tentatively in the affirmative, the poet directs the reader and himself: 'So let the ear attend like a farmhouse window / In placid light, where the extravagant / Passed once under full sail into the longed-for' (*OG* 364). In 'Squarings', music occupies the outer reaches of Heaney's cosmology. Yet it prescribes an ethic of waiting, of attention, of alert passivity. The human is made to stand in perpetual expectation, a dormant, dust-gathering instrument, whose redemption (if there is such a thing) lies in its potential to make song – even if one is never played upon.

This state of receptive expectancy, which marks early poems like 'Personal Helicon' and 'The Forge', and which is more thoroughly theorized in his middle-period poems both as a model of artistic creation and as a kind of spirituality, becomes the dominant note in his last poems. 'Had I not been awake I would have missed it', he writes in the opening poem of *Human Chain* (2010): 'It came and went so unexpectedly . . . A courier blast that there and then / Lapsed ordinary. But not ever / After. And not now' (*SP* 175). The suddenness of the wind's arrival and the inevitability of its departure shuttle one between bereavement and hope. In an elegy for the musician David Hammond, Heaney calls his friend's name, knowing there would be no answer, and listens to his reverberating voice settle into silence, hearing in it 'only withdrawal, a not unwelcoming / Emptiness' (*SP* 214). Written for his granddaughter, and dated twelve days before his death, 'In Time' forms the coda to the second volume of his *Selected Poems*. The poem dwells in the for-nowness of the everyday, even as the past and the present throw their long shadows: 'Listening to Bach / I saw you years from now / (More years than I'll be allowed) . . . / But for now we foot it lightly / In time, and silently.' The phrase 'in time', of course, references the musician's cardinal imperative and the brute fact of human mortality: the continuity of generations requiring us, for a brief time, to keep time.

What the later poems reveal is that music functions in Heaney's work as ligature. It binds the human to the non-human; it binds the poet to the turf-cutter; it binds the grandfather to the granddaughter. This is not to say something extraordinary about music but to say that music signals Heaney's own reaching for the extraordinary – which, paradoxically, requires a fastidious attention to the ordinary, to the given. Music is both what he hears and what he makes. If done right, there will be little difference between the two. The aspiration is as simple as it is unachievable: to give what has been given.

Notes

1 Heaney's notes here offer many interesting insights into his own aesthetic. For example, Heaney insists that 'a singing voice' must evoke a sense of sentimental nostalgia if it is to be sufficiently effective, and affective: '[it] needs more than efficiency and definition, and the extra dimension in David's singing may come from a longing backward towards his Co. Derry and Co. Antrim ancestry, the line of the melody hankering for the line of what Louis MacNeice called "the pre-natal mountain"'. Likewise, Heaney reveals in Hammond a simultaneously moral and sentimental relation to tradition that may be equally applied to himself: '[Hammond] is not a conservative in his attitude to tradition or traditions, but radically creative. It is not the "purity" of the material that matters to him, not its ethnic culture quotient, its scholarly provenance: rather it is the scope it offers the voice for exultation or repining, for the play of feeling, for human touch. There is a moral vision implicit in the pitch of that voice, an impatience with systems, a calling into the realm of pure freedom.' 'Sleeve Notes', *The Singer's House* [David Hammond] (Dublin: Sruthan Muligan, 1978).

2 James William Johnson, 'Lyric', in Alex Preminger and T.V.F. Brogan (eds.), *The New Princeton Encyclopedia of Poetry and Poetics* (Princeton University Press, 1993), pp. 713–37 (at p. 720).

3 Leith Davis, *Music, Postcolonialism, and Gender: The Construction of Irish National Identity, 1724–1874* (University of Notre Dame Press, 2006).

IV

Publishing

CHAPTER 15

The Belfast Group

Heather Clark

> Culturally in the early 60s, Belfast was a 40-watt bulb. There was hardly anything going on. If a continental film came to Belfast, we queued up in the cold at 11 o'clock at night. So there was this 40-watt bulb which you might call Belfast culture, and this hot spot, which was the Hobsbaum house.[1]
>
> Michael Longley

In 1962, the critic Philip Hobsbaum arrived in Belfast to take up a teaching position in the English department at Queen's University. He came with an impressive array of literary connections. At Cambridge, he had studied with F.R. Leavis, edited the literary magazine *delta*, and befriended Ted Hughes. Later, in London, he chaired a weekly writing group, dubbed 'the Group', whose members included Edward Lucie-Smith, Alan Brownjohn, George MacBeth, Ted Hughes, Peter Redgrove, David Wevill and Peter Porter, among others. These were some of the most prominent young poets and critics in England; such contacts would prove valuable when Hobsbaum convened another literary group in Belfast, where he assembled equally talented, if less confident, young writers. This 'Belfast Group' was a crucial launching pad for the fledgling Belfast poetry scene and the success of one Belfast poet in particular: Seamus Heaney.

Hobsbaum, who had recently finished a PhD at the University of Sheffield under the supervision of the legendary critic William Empson, had doubts about beginning his academic career in a literary and cultural backwater. Belfast was divided along sectarian lines, and the prosperity it had once enjoyed as a centre of the textile industry was waning: unemployment was high at 10 per cent. Louis MacNeice had called it a city of 'hard cold fire'.[2] Hobsbaum found Belfast's arts scene fragmented and, apart from Mary O'Malley's Lyric Theater, stagnant. Almost as soon as he arrived he began searching for talent; he had, as one Belfast Group member put it, a 'Pound-like belief in the existence of village Miltons'.[3] He issued early invitations to his writing group to Edna Longley, his colleague in the English department, and his graduate student Stewart Parker. Later members included Seamus and Marie Heaney, Michael Longley, Stewart Parker, James Simmons, Joan Newmann, Bernard MacLaverty, Norman Dugdale, Michael Allen, Harry Chambers and others.[4]

Seamus Heaney was at this time enrolled in a postgraduate education course at St Joseph's College, where he would soon become a lecturer. He had begun publishing poems that year in the *Belfast Telegraph*, and engaging more seriously with contemporary British and Irish poetry. In November 1962, he experienced a major frisson in the Belfast Public Library as he read Ted Hughes's 'View of a Pig', in *Lupercal*. Hughes's verse, he would later say, gave him the feeling of 'life coming into you and through you' (*SS* 50). Hughes would become one of his most important early poetic models, along with Hopkins and Kavanagh. Heaney had also been deeply influenced that year by the English critic Al Alvarez's anthology *The New Poetry*, which gave him 'more of a charge' than Robin Skelton's competing *Six Irish Poets* anthology (*SS* 51). Alvarez's anthology was an attempt to promote a new style of poetry, later dubbed 'extremism', whose exemplars were Ted Hughes, Sylvia Plath, Anne Sexton and Robert Lowell.[5]

The New Poetry was a response to Robert Conquest's 1956 *New Lines* anthology, which helped launch the Movement poets. Alvarez found much of their poetry staid and dangerously complacent. Among its practitioners were Philip Larkin, Kingsley Amis, Donald Davie, Elizabeth Jennings, D.J. Enright and John Wain. Peter Porter called their stance 'anti-heroic and defiantly unromantic . . . a natural expression of post-war shrinkage in British confidence'.[6] Alvarez's introduction to *The New Poetry*, 'Beyond the Gentility Principle', was an anti-Movement manifesto; he noted that the Movement poets' occupations included librarian, civil servant and university professor, and that their verse was best described as 'academic-administrative . . . polite, knowledgeable, efficient'.[7]

Hobsbaum shared Alvarez's antipathy, which was Leavisite in origin. Leavis had taught that true poetry was a conduit of high feeling and 'dynamic action', and that true poets exhibited 'the higher awareness of the age'.[8] Several of the poets anthologized in *The New Poetry* – Ted Hughes, Peter Redgrove, Peter Porter, George MacBeth – had been members of Hobsbaum's London Group. 'We were all very adverse', Hobsbaum later said. 'We felt the Movement, in terms of poetry, was too circumscribed, too formalistic . . . poetry in Britain, in the early fifties, was at a very low ebb.'[9] Yet Hobsbaum shared certain aesthetic affinities with Movement writers – he too had formalist tendencies, and favoured blunt, plain diction.[10] Yet, like Alvarez, he upheld Hughes's dynamic, muscular rhythms as an antidote to the 'crabbed and moribund' Movement poetry – this 'crop of lyrical pretenders', as Hughes called them.[11]

While the Belfast Group would help foster some of the best poets in Ireland, its contexts were British. Alvarez was then the most important young poetry critic in England, and he had pronounced Hughes's *Lupercal* the best book of the year in 1960.[12] In London, Alvarez had become close to Hughes and Sylvia Plath, whose work he also promoted in the *Observer* and whose posthumous reputation he would help secure. Hobsbaum had been Hughes's contemporary at Cambridge, and though he was part of a rival literary faction, he had no doubts about Hughes's talent: he was 'the lyric poet par excellence and we all knew how good he was'.[13] Hobsbaum had published one of Hughes's first poems in *delta* and had secured him a job reading scripts at a London film studio when Hughes was broke and drifting. Later, Hughes attended the London Group, though he would have distrusted their Leavisite seriousness. (Hobsbaum remembered him reciting Hopkins and singing 'Lord Randall, My Son' so loudly that his landlady complained.)[14] Still, the Group adopted Hughes's 'The Martyrdom of Bishop Farrar' as its banner poem. The poem describes Farrar's burning in graphic detail ('Hear him crack in the fire's mouth', etc.), and symbolized exactly what this 'new poetry' was trying to achieve. *This* poetry did not keep its distance from atrocity or violence: in Hughes's poem, 'sincerity, extreme suffering and extreme death intersect'.[15] Plath's 'Lady Lazarus', and other poems of this generation, would sound similar notes. Edward Lucie-Smith recalled London Group members crashing literary parties at G.S. Fraser's Chelsea flat and 'baiting the company' by reciting 'The Martyrdom of Bishop Farrar' – declaring their 'faith in Hughes' in front of the 'appalled' company.[16] To Hobsbaum, said Peter Porter, it seemed 'that the future of poetry in Britain was dependent on Hughes's work being established as the true model for the age'.[17]

These Leavisite London confluences – called 'the Alvarez generation' by one critic – created the ideological and aesthetic reorientation that so gripped Heaney as he turned the pages of Alvarez's anthology.[18] He called it 'a big stimulus': 'the general sanctioning of a less-polished way with the words and a more head-on encounter with the subject was in tune with my own disposition' (*SS* 64). Heaney also admired the Lawrentian note in Alvarez's introduction, for he was 'under the sway of Lawrence' at the time. (As was Alvarez, who married Frieda Lawrence's granddaughter Ursula.) The anthology was so important to him that on the night he met his future wife, Marie, he loaned her a copy of the book, hoping to impress her. The anecdote suggests how profoundly this anthology shaped Heaney's burgeoning poetic sensibilities.

Philip Hobsbaum was a living link to the poets in Alvarez's pages, and an emissary for a Hughesian sensibility just hitting Ulster's shores: Hughes would provide the crucial aesthetic link between Hobsbaum and Heaney. Hobsbaum had read an early poem of Heaney's, 'October Thought', in the Queen's University literary magazine, and had been impressed by the poet's assimilation of Hopkins and Hughes ('mice mealing in the grain, gnawing strong / the iron-bound, swollen and ripe-round corn-barrel'[19]). Hobsbaum soon sent Heaney a letter of invitation to his writing group. Heaney was already aware of Hobsbaum's presence: in September 1963 he had reviewed Hobsbaum and Lucie-Smith's *A Group Anthology*, which included work from the London Group. 'If', he wrote, 'there was a Group in Belfast, Dublin, Cork and Galway, our young poets would find it easier to meet an audience and above all, interest should increase. Which might not be a bad thing.'[20] Such formal, seminar-like writing groups were not nearly as common then as they are today; Hosbaum's London Group has been called the 'first proper poetry workshop in England'.[21] Creative writing programmes were considered an American phenomenon, and were the object of some derision amongst London's literati: the London Group was known as 'a band of severely puritan teetotalers'.[22]

The first Belfast Group workshop took place in October 1963, not long after Hobsbaum met Heaney. It met on Tuesdays (later Mondays) in Hobsbaum's Fitzwilliam Street flat. The Group was run as it had been in Cambridge and London: about ten people would listen to that week's writer read his or her work, then all would discuss the writing with 'Leavisite rigour'.[23] Heaney remembered how 'Philip introduced each poem on the sheet with a comment, and the discussion took care of itself. It ebbed and flowed depending upon the poem, depending upon the energies that were there at the moment, the animal life of the den ... Hobsbaum was a very good conductor.'[24] They would break for coffee and biscuits, then read selections from their favourite poets' work during the second half. For Heaney, this 'general toning up of the poetry muscles was equally important, maybe in the long run more important' than the Group's explication (*SS* 75). At the evening's close, Hobsbaum would choose the next week's writer, whose work would then be copied onto 'Groupsheets' and mailed to other Group members in advance of the upcoming meeting.

The Belfast Group met for eight eight-week terms from 1963 to 1966. It was here that Heaney met Michael Longley for the first time. Longley had come at Edna's insistence; a 'reluctant joiner' at first, he began to look forward to the meetings.[25] He remembered Heaney asking him, at a party in Hobsbaum's flat, whether he was the author of 'Questionnaire for

Walter Mitty' and 'Emily Dickinson'. 'I was flattered and charmed and our friendship got under way there and then.'[26] Heaney urged him to attend the Group, saying, 'You must have your poems done at the Group. They'll be the best ever discussed there.'[27] Heaney would eventually meet Derek Mahon through Longley; the two had become close at Trinity College Dublin. In the public imagination, Heaney, Mahon and Longley – the Group's most successful poets – would form a triumvirate of Belfast poetry. By the early seventies, the Belfast satirist Michael Foley would refer to the three as the 'Tight Assed Trio';[28] the label, which amused Heaney, revealed their distance from looser aesthetic forms practised by the Beats and other 'pop' poets of the 1960s.[29]

The poet James Simmons felt himself to be on the margins, but understood the value of the Group. In 1963 he told his mentor, Bonamy Dobrée, that he found Hobsbaum's workshop 'very stimulating after much lack of contact with poets . . . The talk is very good on the whole.'[30] That same year, he told the poet Tony Harrison that the workshop 'gives a great fillip [sic] to my confidence. I have seldom felt so much like a real poet since I was at Leeds.'[31] Fiction writer Bernard MacLaverty remembered, 'Here, in a room in Belfast, in the mid-60s, when nothing exciting was happening, Philip came into this and said, "What you're all writing about is as valid and as brilliant as anywhere else." Always Philip was 100% behind the writer.'[32] Heaney agreed: 'He emanated energy, generosity, belief in the community, trust in the parochial, the inept, the unprinted.'[33]

Of course, Hobsbaum did not singlehandedly inspire Belfast's young writers. The success of a previous generation that included John Hewitt, Sam Hanna Bell, W.R. Rodgers and Louis MacNeice had already given Heaney 'a strong sense of local context, of creative endeavour having been there from the start, of high (or highish) artistic ambition proceeding in an Ulster accent'.[34] Yet MacNeice, the most successful of this group, had spent most of his life in England, while Hewitt had left Belfast for Coventry. Michael Longley's memory of late nights queuing up in the cold to see a foreign film typifies this sense of the province's isolation. Simmons certainly felt it: 'You can't believe the loneliness of someone beginning to write, say, in Portrush when I was writing, or Derry, and there's no one to talk to, no one who'll listen or understand.'[35] As a Jewish 'scholarship boy', Hobsbaum understood what it was like to stand on the periphery of metropolitan literary culture. He also knew how to reach the centre; he had made the journey himself, and was determined to guide others. Derek Mahon honed in on what was perhaps the most important aspect of Hobsbaum's presence: 'Here was this man from London, people thought, whose name and whose friends' names appeared in the leading journals, and he's actually taking us *seriously*.'[36] Edna Longley felt similarly: 'It was important in cities like Belfast or Glasgow, where there can be cultural cringe before Dublin or London, that this man had come from England.'[37]

Hobsbaum's Jewishness allowed him to transcend the sectarian divisions that haunted Belfast life. 'I was told by more than one person that Catholics and Protestants would never meet under one roof – for any purpose', Hobsbaum wrote. 'The Belfast Group, among its other achievements, proved these well-wishers wrong.'[38] The Group became not just a place for fellowship, support and critique, but a non-sectarian space in a city where language was closely guarded. Heaney wrote and read several poems at Group sessions that challenged Unionist hegemony, such as 'For the Commander of the *Eliza*', 'Requiem for the Irish Rebels, Wexford, 1798' and 'Orange Drums, Tyrone 1966'. He also presented 'Tweed', an early poem about linguistic dispossession, and 'Soliloquy for an Old Resident', an ironic portrait of a declining Ascendancy family.[39] Longley, too, presented poems exploring his dual English and Irish identities. Yet he 'didn't much care for the Group aesthetic', which drew on the work and ideas of Leavis, Alvarez, Lawrence, Hughes and Robert Lowell. Heaney recalled that 'Lowell was often favoured at The Group', and that Hobsbaum 'inclined in particular' to Lowell's *Life Studies* – the 1959 watershed collection often said to have launched 'confessional' poetry (*SS* 217). Indeed, Heaney noted that at Group meetings, Hobsbaum gave him 'explicit encouragement' to 'roughen up' his poems (*SS* 40). 'I believed then', Longley later wrote, 'that poetry should be polished, metrical and rhymed; oblique rather than head-on; imagistic and symbolic rather than rawly factual; rhetorical rather than documentary.'[40] One Belfast Group member summed up the proceedings: 'Honest-to-God Ulster down-to-earthness was encouraged, poetic flights of extravagant vision and imagination were frowned on as "Pretentious" . . . A bird-watching botanist with a Classical education and a mad uncle who loved stoats would have been the ultimate hero in the ultimate poem in this climate.'[41] Ironically, the former half of the description brings Longley to mind; yet the commentator means to suggest Heaney, who knew he was favoured. The ranking created tension between Heaney and Longley. One night, during a drunken 'flare-up', Longley told Heaney that Mahon was the better poet. Heaney recalled, 'It didn't surprise me to know this was the verdict, but to have it expressed so aggressively was unexpected' (*SS* 77). Mahon and Longley, he said, 'played and read the score by Trinity rules as opposed to Group rules' (76).

The critic Dillon Johnston has contested the Belfast Group's influence, writing, 'It may be that without Hobsbaum's Monday evenings, *Death of a Naturalist* (1966) would not have appeared so early or so impressively as it did. Yet, who can believe that Heaney would have remained a mute, inglorious Milton without the Group's supporting criticism?'[42] Nonetheless, Heaney, unlike Mahon and Longley, was still unsure of his poetic vocation when he met Hobsbaum. His pen name at the time was 'Incertus'. By his own admission, he 'had absolutely no confidence as a writer'[43] and identified with Leonard Bast of *Howard's End*, 'doomed forever to be familiar with the outsides of books'.[44] Hobsbaum remembered that his colleagues in the English department at Queen's 'thought Seamus Heaney to be a relatively slight figure in comparison with the other first-class students of his year'.[45] Hobsbaum's support encouraged Heaney at a time when, he said, Eliot's *Collected Poems* had 'represented to me my distance from the mystery and my unfittedness – as reader or writer – for the vocation it represented' (*FK* 26). After Hobsbaum introduced Heaney to Edward Lucie-Smith at a dinner party, Lucie-Smith showed three Heaney poems to Hobsbaum's Cambridge contemporary, Karl Miller, at the *New Statesman*. Miller published the poems, which came to the attention of Charles Monteith (himself an Ulsterman) at Faber and Faber. Monteith invited Heaney to submit a manuscript to him in 1965, and *Death of a Naturalist* was published the next year by Faber and Faber.[46]

Hobsbaum left Belfast in 1966 to take up an appointment at the University of Glasgow. He bequeathed chairmanship of the Group to Heaney, who was appointed a lecturer in English at Queen's that same year. Heaney remembered that some thought the Group 'had run its course, that it was a Hobsbaum thing' (*SS* 106). Yet he kept it going for the sake of those 'on the outskirts' of literary culture, like Norman Dugdale and Joan Newmann, for whom it had become 'a lifeline'. He convened the meetings in the English department at Queen's, the Four in Hand pub on the Lisburn Road, and, eventually, at his home on 16 Ashley Avenue. In *Stepping Stones*, Heaney downplayed his role as Group moderator, claiming he could not recall the specifics of where they met and who attended, only that he had decided not to run the sessions as a seminar; the feel of the new meetings was to be somewhere between a salon and a 'session in a snug' (106). New members included Paul Muldoon, Ciaran Carson, Frank Ormsby, Medbh McGuckian and Michael Foley.

During this time, the arts flourished in Belfast – so much so that journalists began to speak of an 'Ulster Renaissance'. Heaney himself used the term in 1966 to describe the new landscape, which he credited, in part, to Hobsbaum's presence.[47] His own success, and a sense of political optimism, also buoyed the arts scene. 'The fact that a literary action was afoot was itself a new political condition', Heaney said (*GT* xxi).[48] John Hewitt's departure to Coventry in 1957, as well as the deaths of MacNeice in 1963 and Kavanagh in 1967, emphasized the need for a new generation to revive the place of poetry in the North: according to Heaney, 'we all were brought beyond our highly developed caution to believe that the effort to create new movement and language in the Northern context was a viable project' (*FK* 45).[49] After Heaney left for Berkeley in the fall of 1970, the 'pretence of maintaining' the Belfast Group 'as a living event stopped' (*SS* 106). Two years later, Heaney would move to County Wicklow as sectarian violence increased in Northern Ireland.

The extent of Hobsbaum's influence upon Heaney and the other members of the Group will continue to be a matter of contention. Yet there is no question that Hobsbaum's admiration for Hughes – as well as his personal connections to the poets in Alvarez's anthology – dovetailed with Heaney's preoccupations at the time and encouraged him in the aesthetic direction he was already moving. (Heaney would later say that 'Digging', the first poem in his first collection, was influenced by the 'high-voltage diction of Ted Hughes', *SS* 82.) Hobsbaum also hand-delivered Heaney's poems to the most important editors in London, perhaps sparing him years of frustration. Agent, publicist and – for some – mentor and friend, he gave the Group writers, Heaney said, 'a sense of themselves'.[50] Under Heaney's leadership, the Group model would help inspire the next generation of poets: 'They had us present and talking to them', Heaney said. 'When we were starting out, we didn't have any equivalent elders or exemplars on the ground' (*SS* 106). But they had each other, and Hobsbaum. By linking Heaney to contemporary British and American poetry – and the future of Irish poetry –the Belfast Group was itself a 'human chain'.

Notes

1 'Hobsbaum's Choice', narrated by Roisin McAuley, BBC Radio 3, 30 January 2000.

2 'Belfast', in *Collected Poems of Louis MacNeice*, ed. E.R. Dodds (London: Faber and Faber, 1966), p. 19.

3 Norman Dugdale *et al.*, 'The Belfast Group: A Symposium', *Honest Ulsterman*, 53 (1976), 53–63 (at p. 54).

4 See Heather Clark, *The Ulster Renaissance: Poetry in Belfast 1962–1972* (Oxford University Press, 2006), for further context. Others members

included Paul Smyth, Lucille Gregory, John Bond, Norman Buller, Iris Bull, Jack Pakenham, Hugh Bredin, Michael Mitchell, John Harvey, Maurice Gallagher, Lynette McCroskery, Marilyn Stronge, Dan McGee, Robert Sullivan and Rex Mitchell. See also 'Networking the Belfast Group', http://belfastgroup.digitalscholarship.emory.edu.

5 A. Alvarez, 'Poetry of Loneliness', *Observer*, 14 June 1964, 26. See also A. Alvarez, 'Poetry in Extremis', *Observer*, 14 March 1965, 26. Plath and Sexton were not included in the 1962 edition. They were added in the revised 1966 edition.

6 Peter Porter, 'Ted Hughes and Sylvia Plath: A Bystander's Recollection', *Australian Book Review*, 233 (August 2001). Repr. in Peter Craven (ed.), *The Best Australian Essays 2001* (Melbourne: Black Inc., 2001), p. 398.

7 A. Alvarez, *The New Poetry* (London: Penguin, 1962; 1966), p. 23.

8 William Wooten, *The Alvarez Generation: Thom Gunn, Geoffrey Hill, Ted Hughes, Sylvia Plath and Peter Porter* (Liverpool University Press, 2015), pp. 8–9.

9 Heather Clark, interview with Philip Hobsbaum, Glasgow, 27 October 2000.

10 See Philip Hobsbaum and Edward Lucie-Smith (eds.), *A Group Anthology* (London: Oxford University Press, 1963), p. 121, for a more detailed discussion on the similarities between the two camps.

11 Lucas Myers, 'Ted, Sylvia, and St. Botolph's', unpublished memoir, Ted Hughes papers, Rose Library, Emory University.

12 A. Alvarez, 'Books of the Year', *Observer*, 18 December 1960, 22.

13 Philip Hobsbaum, 'Ted Hughes at Cambridge', *Dark Horse*, 8 (Autumn 1999), 10.

14 Sylvia Plath attempted to join, but was denied admission. Hobsbaum would regret his decision: 'She sent me four meticulously typed poems, but I didn't like her early work at all – real college girl stuff – and I didn't respond appropriately. I was wrong of course ... but I never thought of her as I think now.' (Heather Clark, interview with Philip Hobsbaum, Glasgow, 27 October 2000.)

15 Quoted in Wooten, *Alvarez Generation*, p. 25.

16 *Ibid.*, p. 24.

17 Porter, 'Ted Hughes and Sylvia Plath', 398–9.

18 Wooten notes that 'For all his antipathy to academic analysis, Hughes's interests in Lawrence, Hopkins, Shakespeare, and Yeats' were very much 'the product of Leavisite Cambridge' (*Alvarez Generation*, p. 9).

19 Seamus Heaney, 'October Thought', *Q*, Michaelmas 1959, 27.

20 Seamus Heaney, 'Poetry From a Co-operative Society', *Hibernia*, September 1963, 10.

21 Wooten, *Alvarez Generation*, p. 20.

22 Edward Lucie-Smith, *The Burnt Child: An Autobiography* (London: Victor Gollancz, 1975), p. 172. See also Yehuda Koren and Eilat Negev, *Lover of Unreason: Assia Wevill, Sylvia Plath's Rival and Ted Hughes's Doomed Love* (New York: Carroll & Graf, 2006), pp. 67–8.

23 Michael Longley, *Causeway: The Arts in Ulster* (Belfast: Arts Council of Northern Ireland, 1971), p. 96.
24 'Hobsbaum's Choice'.
25 Michael Longley to Heather Clark, 27 January 2002.
26 *Ibid.*
27 *Ibid.*
28 Michael Foley, review of James Simmons, *Energy to Burn, Honest Ulsterman*, 29 (1971), 40–1.
29 Heaney told O'Driscoll, 'Whatever the Beats and the Liverpool poets were doing, it didn't put me through the eye of my own needle the way "The Bull Moses" or "The Windhover" did' (*SS* 100).
30 Simmons to Dobrée, 11 November 1963, James Simmons papers, Rose Library, Emory University.
31 Simmons to Harrison, 17 November 1963, James Simmons papers, Rose Library, Emory University.
32 'Hobsbaum's Choice'.
33 Dugdale *et al.*, 'Belfast Group', 62.
34 Seamus Heaney to Heather Clark, 24 January 2000.
35 'Hobsbaum's Choice'.
36 Derek Mahon, 'Poetry in Northern Ireland', *Twentieth Century Studies*, 4 (November 1970), 91.
37 Neal Ascherson, 'Great Brain Spotter', *Independent on Sunday*, 28 February 1993, 30.
38 Philip Hobsbaum, 'The Belfast Group: A Recollection', *Eire-Ireland*, 32/2–3 (1997), 173–83 (at p. 173).
39 Seamus Heaney, 'Tweed' and 'Soliloquy for an Old Resident', part of Groupsheet, typed MS, n.d. (circa 1963–4), Michael Longley papers, Rose Library, Emory University.
40 Dugdale *et al.*, 'Belfast Group', p. 56.
41 *Ibid.*, p. 58.
42 Dillon Johnston, *Irish Poetry after Joyce* (University of Notre Dame Press, 1985), p. 52.
43 Frank Kinahan, 'Interview with Seamus Heaney', *Critical Inquiry*, 8/3 (1982), 405–14 (at p. 407).
44 *Ibid.*, p. 27.
45 Hobsbaum, 'The Belfast Group: A Recollection', p. 174.
46 Hobsbaum would also eventually help persuade Macmillan to publish Longley's *No Continuing City*.
47 Seamus Heaney, 'Out of London: Ulster's Troubles', *New Statesman*, 1 July 1966, 23–4 (at p. 24).
48 Seamus Heaney, *The Government of the Tongue: Selected Prose 1978–1987* (New York: Farrar, Straus and Giroux, 1989).
49 See Michael McKeown, 'A Cultural Sahara?' *Hibernia*, July 1968, 12–13, for a discussion of the role the Arts Council played in fostering local talent.
50 Dugdale *et al.*, 'Belfast Group', p. 62.

CHAPTER 16

In Print

Nathan Suhr-Sytsma

Recalling his first encounter with London's leading literary publisher, Faber and Faber, Seamus Heaney reported that he 'hardly thought of 24 Russell Square as an earthly address' and that 'getting a letter from the chief poetry editor of the place was like getting mail from the Almighty God'.[1] That editor, Charles Monteith, who hailed, like Heaney, from Northern Ireland, had seen a trio of Heaney's poems in the *New Statesman* and invited him to submit a full book manuscript of poems. With the acceptance of that manuscript, published in May 1966 as *Death of a Naturalist*, Heaney became the first new Faber poet since the death of T.S. Eliot.[2] While Heaney's comparison of Faber headquarters with heaven wryly acknowledges the naiveté of his younger self, it also foreshadows recent scholarly interest in the persistence of 'an often elusive *faith* in literature as a transcendent category'.[3] Concentrating on the publication of Heaney's poetry in book form, this essay considers how his investments in print have both expressed and furthered such faith in literature.[4] This consideration pairs attention to Heaney's poetic and prose metaphors for publication with a few striking instances of the material forms his work has taken. Heaney deliberately published not only with Faber and its New York counterpart, Farrar, Straus and Giroux (FSG), but also with numerous small presses, foremost among them the Gallery Press in Ireland. Collaborating with such a range of publishers ensured that Heaney's poetry was distributed widely while maintaining a connection with book arts ideals of small-scale production, ideals in keeping with his own commitment to poetic craft and sense of belonging to a long humanist tradition of writing.

Heaney's relationship to the alphabetic and book forms in which his poetry is embodied has been described by Rand Brandes as his 'material mysticism'.[5] Uncovering Heaney's long-standing interest in the esoteric medieval and early modern 'art of memory', Brandes states, 'Through his affiliation with small presses and illustrators, as well as his involvement with the cover designs for trade editions of his work, Heaney joins together the cult of the book, "artificial memory," and ultimately the "marvellous".'[6] A term from Heaney's own oeuvre, the 'marvellous' makes a memorable appearance in a poem about a flying ship appearing over the monastery at Clonmacnoise: the poem ends with one of the ship's crewmen climbing back up, 'Out of the marvellous as he had known it' (*ST* 62).[7] Reading the poem in light of Heaney's decision to conclude his Oxford Professor of Poetry lectures with it, John Dennison identifies the poet's investment in the 'marvellous' not as Catholic-informed mysticism, but as a post-Christian, late humanist faith in literature.[8] In a less well-known instance of a nautical image, Heaney once described the 'publication' of his work as 'rather like pushing the boat out; then the boat/book turns into a melting ice floe and you have to conjure a second boat that turns into a melting floe under your feet'.[9] This dream-like scenario emphasizes the author's loss of authority, as 'the boat/book' becomes less subject to the poet's craft than to an ocean of publishing, marketing, bookselling, reviewing and reading. The scenario also raises the issue of trust – here the poet's trust that his work will remain seaworthy long enough for him to produce new work adequate to new situations – or what Dennison calls 'Heaney's *fiduciary* commitment' to the adequacy of poetry.[10] As another incisive critic, John Wilson Foster, puts it, Heaney's work constructs 'a kind of religious bricolage as the poet senses and seeks a faith that issues in poems but not in organised belief'.[11]

Readers as well as writers habitually have recourse to such faith in poetry. Heaney himself was formed as a reader of literature through his education at St Columb's College in Derry and Queen's University Belfast during the 1950s. Reflecting a half-century later on editing two Faber poetry anthologies directed at students, Heaney wrote that both he and his co-editor, Ted Hughes, had been

> educated at schools and universities where there was still an adherence to Matthew Arnold's faith in literary culture ... Our teachers still proceeded on the basis of the humanist wager. They and we operated in the faith that literary and cultural endeavour was conducted in a disinterested spirit. It was a less sceptical world where the word 'higher' in the term 'higher education' was still credited.[12]

Recent scholarship contends that Arnold's own 'faith' in the 'disinterested spirit' of culture appealed to Victorian readers in part because they were attracted to cultural spaces that provided shelter from the increasing commercialism of their age. According to Günter Leypoldt, 'the emergence of a mass readership' in the nineteenth century created a heightened contrast with 'the practice space of professional writers and artists', who were now seen to operate at 'a level of sacredness that had formerly been monopolized by more traditional forms of (religious, political) authority'.[13] In other words, Heaney's appeal to the 'higher' in 'higher education' taps into a long-standing sense of culture as spatially organized, with 'cultural authority' replacing the sacred as that to which one aspires. Cultural artefacts that have undergone 'singularization' – books, for example, that come to be perceived as unique instances of 'literary culture' rather than simply mass-market commodities – 'invoke a charismatic rather than calculative kind of trust', less a rational investment of time or money than 'the feeling that we are being put in touch with something larger than ourselves'.[14] This charismatic trust or faith is not simply an escape from the material, but an association with certain kinds of materiality.

Heaney develops an almost devotional posture towards the materiality of poetry in a late poem, 'The Bookcase', which revisits the start of his career. Both the bookcase in question and its contents take their place in the pantheon of what John Wilson Foster has called Heaney's 'relishable objects': 'Planed to silkiness, / Mitred, much eyed-along, each vellum-pale / Board in the bookcase held and never sagged' (*EL* 51).[15] As the poet lovingly describes the bookshelves, he also connects them to old and rare books of calfskin ('vellum-pale'), the resilience of the boards seeming to spill over to the resilience of books. The well-made bookcase brings to mind the ideal of the well-made poem that Heaney imbibed through meetings of the Belfast Group during the 1960s, and this poem is itself carefully constructed in three sections of four quatrains each. The poet recalls the colours of book covers by other poets whom Heaney encountered during the sixties and early seventies: Hugh MacDiarmid, Elizabeth Bishop, 'Yeats of "Memory". Hardy of "The Voice"' (51). This reference to Thomas Hardy's poem titled 'The Voice', addressing an absent woman and constructed in quatrains like 'The Bookcase', sets up the final quatrain of the poem's first section. This stanza recalls the voices of now-absent poets – Robert Frost, Wallace Stevens, Dylan Thomas – not in print artefacts, but in a Caedmon Records double LP. In one of his Oxford lectures, Heaney said of Thomas that 'he died at the height of his fame, at the moment when print culture and the electronic media were perfecting their alliance in the promotion of culture heroes'. He recalled the vinyl records of Thomas reading his poetry, 'records which were lined up on the shelves of undergraduate flats all over the world', as 'important cultural events' (*RP* 124).[16] The name of this literary record label, launched in 1952, harks back to the founding event of English-language poetry more than a millennium earlier: the composition of a hymn to God the Creator by an untutored cowherd named Caedmon. The initial solidity of the bookcase is only the prelude, then, to Heaney presenting poetry as 'a transcendent category' that is not bound to a specific medium but moves fluidly between vellum manuscript and printed *Collected Poems*, voice and record, with little discernible loss.[17]

These particular media do, however, seem to be cast in a nostalgic glow by the advent of digital media, unmentioned in the poem. Its final stanzas, as if cueing the death of the book, take the 'measuredness' of the bookcase as an occasion to ruminate on boards as coffins via an early twentieth-century American novel and Irish play, William Faulkner's *As I Lay Dying* and J.M. Synge's *Riders to the Sea*. The 'White boards' that are to serve as a coffin in Synge's play are likened, at the poem's end, to 'the salt salvaged makings / Of a raft for books, a bier to be borne' (52). This line returns to Caedmon in its evocation of Old English alliterative verse: four stressed syllables, the accented 'b' sound repeating across the middle caesura or pause. Finally, the bookcase is transfigured by the imagination into the 'marvellous': 'I imagine us bracing ourselves for the first lift, / Then staggering for balance, it has grown so light' (52). Even in a turn-of-the-millennium collection titled *Electric Light*, the title poem of which dramatizes the poet's first encounter with electricity in a home, Heaney's primary concern is with the light and lift of the imagination.

How did Heaney's own work come to occupy a place on so many bookshelves? As a child in County Derry, Heaney felt that 'the world of print was like the world of proper and official behaviour among strangers ... It was like having to talk to the doctor or the priest, to say yes and no instead of *aye* and *naw*.'[18] By the time he received a letter from Monteith, however, he was well on his way to becoming at home in this professional world. By the time *Death of a Naturalist* appeared in print, he had already published more than fifty poems in periodicals, as well as a pamphlet.[19] This pamphlet, *Eleven Poems*, was published in 1965 in connection with the annual Queen's University Festival (later called the Belfast Festival). Taking its place in a series of more than a dozen Festival Publications pamphlets by poets living in Belfast, including Michael Longley and Derek Mahon, Heaney's poetry could be seen as part of a local resurgence of creativity. In fact, *Eleven Poems* opens with a poem dedicated to Longley, 'Personal Helicon', which would become the final poem in *Death of a Naturalist*. At the same time, Heather Clark observes of such pamphlet publication that 'What began ... as a grass-roots attempt to publish local poetry quickly became an important vehicle for national recognition', particularly as one of the major London weekly papers, the *New Statesman*, reviewed Heaney's *Eleven Poems*.[20]

All but one of the poems from the pamphlet also appear in *Death of a Naturalist*, establishing a pattern whereby Heaney would publish work in pamphlets or fine press editions before gathering them into a definitive Faber collection. While the dust jacket of the first edition has a simple design with no images – the title and author's name are set against blocks of 'lime-green and solid-pink', separated by a thin white band – it highlights Heaney's Irishness in other ways (*SS* 61). The front flap describes him as 'a young poet who already has an eagerly-appreciative audience in his native Ireland' and who 'grew up on a farm in Derry', perhaps following the poet's own preference by avoiding mention of Northern Ireland or the Unionist term Londonderry. The back flap advertises *Sailing to an Island* by Richard Murphy, the other living Irish poet whom Faber published. The back cover, which lists the poets published by Faber alphabetically from W.H. Auden to Richard Wilbur, then positions Heaney as a poet full stop. The list includes the first two poets whose *Collected Poems* he bought of his own accord: T.S. Eliot and Louis MacNeice.[21] The appearance of Seamus Heaney between Thom Gunn and his hero Ted Hughes invites readers to trust that they will find Heaney similarly worth their time.

Can the poet's success with so-called ordinary readers and literary professionals alike be attributed to his association with Faber? Not every Faber poet, after all, is a bestseller or even a hit with critics. Patrick Crotty, who distinguishes between 'the context of Heaney's reception' and 'the intrinsic qualities of the poetry', remains 'extremely sceptical of reductive, non-literary explanations of his popularity'.[22] Crotty goes on to elucidate some reasons for the staying power of Heaney's first four books – *Death of a Naturalist* (1966), *Door into the Dark* (1969), *Wintering Out* (1972) and *North* (1975) – published at regular intervals by Faber, with American editions issued by the New York branch of Oxford University Press.[23] With the next collection, *Field Work* (1979), Heaney began to publish American editions with Farrar, Straus and Giroux, the New York publisher of Robert Lowell and Derek Walcott. While what readers continue to find appealing about Heaney's poetry certainly cannot be reduced to his political savvy or alliance with prestigious institutions, it may be equally reductive to ignore how the publication of Heaney's work has shaped which 'qualities of the poetry' come to be seen as 'intrinsic'. As Stefan Helgesson has recently pointed out, 'literary writing and literature' are not identical: 'They overlap, but there is no unmediated relationship between the practice of writing and the printed, commodified, and possibly consecrated text that is displayed in a bookshop or read on a Kindle.'[24] Among other things, the Faber or FSG imprint, with its whiff of Anglo-American modernism, is likely to prompt a reader to approach this 'consecrated text' differently from a broadsheet, mimeographed zine, record jacket or website.

Heaney, for his part, primarily worked within the medium of 'the European print lyric' and its set of conventions, including the transformation of 'a personal voice into a hybrid entity, a set of marks on the page that can be phenomenalized, given sensual and cognitive form in the mouth and mind of a reader'.[25] While Heaney is famous for crafting poems that demand to be richly 'phenomenalized' on the reader's tongue, he rarely put the experimental possibilities of typography and print at the forefront of his poetic practice. One of the few poems in which he did highlight 'the poem's self-conscious construction in print' is 'Broagh'.[26] Referring to the farm where his paternal grandparents had lived, 'Broagh' is often read as part of a series of poems in *Wintering Out* that meditate on place names from his childhood (*SS* 17–18). At a visual level, the poet sees in his addressee's 'heelmark' in soil 'the black *O* // in *Broagh*', figuring a literal print in the ground as a black print letter. At a sonic level, the '*O*' is the sound of rain on this human-made puddle, 'its low tattoo' at once evoking ink and the drumming sound. Nature phenomenalizes a mark on the ground. The conclusion to the poem continues the dense interplay of the visual and sonic, comparing the end of the rain with 'that last / *gh* the strangers found / difficult to manage' (*WO* 27). Bernard O'Donoghue observes that 'the three uses of italics' – '*O*' '*Broagh*' '*gh*' – 'mark off the three terms as phonemes: that is, notional phonic entities that cannot be enunciated'. He refers to the final '*gh*', a shibboleth demarcating outsiders from locals of both Catholic and Protestant persuasions, as 'an English symbol used as an inadequate approximation to represent a Gaelic sound'.[27] Following O'Donoghue, other scholars have seen the poem as highlighting the interchange among languages in Ireland: *Broagh*, derived from *bruach*, the Irish word for riverbank, also evokes *bróg*, the Irish word for shoe, and thus a 'brogue', both a style of shoe and a term for a Celtic fringe accent.[28] At the same time, the italicized terms are inadequate print graphemes for phonetic performance, drawing attention to poetry's intermedial existence not only among languages but also among the material page, the mind and the mouth.

Heaney was rarely so explicit about print, however, and in fact seems to have preferred figures of pre-Gutenberg writing. Brandes has noted recurring 'scribal tropes' in Heaney's poetry through the 1980s, in which the poet repeatedly compares – and occasionally contrasts – his work with that of monastic scribes.[29] Heaney turned so often to the scribal, perhaps, because it implied the individuality of the hand, bodily labour akin to that of his rural upbringing, and a religious past, whereas print has sometimes been understood to be an impersonal, machine-produced, even disenchanted medium. Indeed, Michael Warner writes that as 'a growing number of things have come to count as printing' – very rarely any more does this refer to the letterpress – 'we use the unspoken but increasingly important criterion of a negative relation to the hand'.[30] The scribal tropes of Heaney's career culminate in his final Faber collection, *Human Chain*, which includes a series of poems referring to the sixth-century saint and patron of monastic learning Colmcille or Columba, after whom Heaney's secondary school was named. '*Colum Cille Cecinit*', a triptych of translations from eleventh- or twelfth-century Irish, opens, 'My hand is cramped from penwork' (*HC* 72). While the trope of a scribe copying an authoritative text may seem an odd fit for the post-Romantic poet, Heaney's poetry also attends to moments when the individuality of a scribe is expressed through a gloss or marginalia. 'Hermit Songs' includes a recreation of Colmcille's written complaint about a noisy new arrival to the monastic island of Iona, whose foot, the saint imagines, '*will catch and overturn / My little inkhorn, spill my ink*'. 'Hermit Songs' concludes with a turn from this image of writing as an ancient but vulnerable practice of civilization into an affirmation of 'faith', which the poet puts 'In steady-handedness maintained / In books against its vanishing'. Not any books, however, but the famous hand-copied manuscripts, painstakingly created in Ireland, of 'Lismore. Kells. Armagh' (79).

Even as Heaney affiliated himself with the singularity of 'penwork' in Faber and FSG books with print runs in the thousands, he collaborated with fine and small presses to produce limited editions of his poetry. His first book with a fine press, the Rainbow Press run by Ted Hughes's sister Olwyn, was *Bog Poems* (1975). Consisting of eight poems also published in his controversial volume *North* (1975) – the poem now known as 'Strange Fruit' appears under the title 'Tête Coupée' – and illustrated by Ireland-based artist Barrie Cooke, its one hundred and fifty copies were priced at £40 each (as compared to £2.95 for a hardcover first edition of *North*).[31] In dedicating the book to Cooke and the Hugheses, Heaney suggested that their role was not just to make his poetry valuable to book collectors but to confirm the value of the work to the poet himself.

There is one 'small press' with which Heaney above all associated himself: the Gallery Press, founded and edited by Irish poet, publisher and farmer Peter Fallon. Fallon began publishing in 1970 and first issued Heaney's work in broadside form in 1971, using the name Tara Telephone Publications. In 1978, the Gallery Press co-published with the Deerfield Press in Massachusetts a limited illustrated edition of new poetry by Heaney, *After Summer*. Building on the work of earlier Dublin-based literary publishers, the Cuala Press (est. 1908) and Dolmen Press (est. 1951), the Gallery Press has made its mission to publish beautifully designed books by Irish writers from a base in rural Co. Meath; its bull emblem recalls the pictorial emblems of Cuala and Dolmen, even as Gallery strives to sell books 'at reasonable prices' compared with those of its predecessors.[32] Unlike Dolmen's Liam Miller, who missed the opportunity to publish Heaney's first book (then titled 'Advancements of Learning' rather than *Death of a Naturalist*), Fallon has made a deliberate commitment to Irish poets who could otherwise publish in London.[33]

While Heaney did not leave his London publisher for Gallery, he entrusted Fallon with limited editions of original poetry, translation projects such as *The Midnight Verdict* (1993), centred on a rendering of Brian Merriman's long eighteenth-century Irish-language poem 'Cúirt an Mheán Oíche', and his Nobel Lecture *Crediting Poetry* (1995), as well as poems printed for private circulation, including Christmas cards. Echoing his formulation in the Nobel Lecture, Heaney has praised Fallon for 'crediting publishing by crediting poetry, crediting the poetry of others as much as his own'.[34] Heaney's language restores the sense of an act of faith, of credence, to the monetary sense of 'credit'. While Fallon's own self-descriptions are decidedly more down-to-earth, he has called his editorial work the 'church' aspect of Gallery, as distinct from 'the "state" of the business side'.[35] If he does not stand in for 'Almighty God', as Faber's Charles Monteith did for a young Heaney, he is at least one of the Muse's ministers.

Just days before Heaney died on 30 August 2013, he saw the proofs of his last project with Gallery, *The Last Walk: Translations from the Italian of Giovanni Pascoli*. His final Faber collection, *Human Chain*, ends with a poem 'after' Pascoli, 'A Kite for Aibhín'. Extending that interest in Italian poet and classicist Pascoli (1855–1912), *The Last Walk* translates an entire sequence of sixteen 'madrigals', a ten-line cousin of the sonnet formed of a rhymed pair of tercets and a quatrain. Accompanied by line drawings and paintings of rural life by Irish artist Martin Gale, who also collaborated with Heaney on *The Riverbank Field* (Gallery, 2007), the poems return full-circle to the concerns of Heaney's early books. The first, 'Ploughing', shares a gerund title with the first poem in *Death of a Naturalist*, 'Digging', as well as the subject matter of another poem from that volume, 'Follower'.

Throughout his career, Heaney recurred to the origins of 'verse' in Latin *versus*, meaning the turn of a plough at the end of a furrow as well as a poetic line.[36] This ploughing-as-poetry metaphor even sponsored the title of one of his most widely circulated volumes, *Opened Ground*, a generous selection of poems published by Faber and FSG after he received the Nobel Prize.[37] Poignantly, the last poem of *The Last Walk*, 'O Vain Dream!', ends with an extra couplet: 'The blackbird's warbling and the snipe is drumming / And I, in my native tongue, return to versing.'[38] Published posthumously in a limited edition of 575 copies, the book is bound in green linen with the title and part of the colophon also in green, a colour that fittingly evokes Ireland and Heaney's lifelong attentiveness to the natural world. Heaney once spoke of Gallery poets as having 'extended and enhanced a tradition that goes back a millennium, and then another half millennium, back to that moment when Irish poetry becomes part of the written record'.[39] Even as Heaney's poetry joins that written record, it is worth continuing to ask how the poet has made his mark not only in writing, but specifically in print.

Notes

1 Seamus Heaney, 'Charles Montgomery Monteith: Address delivered at the Memorial Service at St George's Church, Bloomsbury, on Thursday 21 September 1995' (publisher not identified), n.p.

2 *Ibid.*

3 Stefan Helgesson, 'How Writing Becomes (World) Literature: Singularity, the Universalizable, and the Implied Writer', in Stefan Helgesson and Pieter Vermeulen (eds.), *Institutions of World Literature: Writing, Translation, Markets* (New York: Routledge, 2016), p. 23.

4 I discuss the appearance of Heaney's poems in print periodicals in Nathan Suhr-Sytsma, *Poetry, Print, and the Making of Postcolonial Literature* (New York: Cambridge University Press, 2017).

5 Rand Brandes, 'Seamus Heaney's Working Titles: From "Advancements of Learning" to "Midnight Anvil"', in Bernard O'Donoghue (ed.), *The Cambridge Companion to Seamus Heaney* (Cambridge University Press, 2009), pp. 19–36 (at p. 35 n2).

6 Rand Brandes, '"Letter by Strange Letter": Yeats, Heaney, and the Aura of the Book', *New Hibernia Review / Iris Éireannach Nua*, 2/2 (Summer/Samradh 1998), 28–47 (at p. 35).

7 The untitled poem is part viii of the 'Lightenings' sequence, itself part of 'Squarings'.

8 For Dennison, Heaney's 'commitment to poetry's *adequacy* derives, first and finally, not from Christian belief, but from an Arnoldian substitution of that

orthodoxy with an expansive trust in the arts'. John Dennison, *Seamus Heaney and the Adequacy of Poetry* (Oxford University Press, 2015), p. 8.

9 Quoted in Brandes, 'Seamus Heaney's Working Titles', p. 20.

10 Dennison, *Adequacy of Poetry*, p. 9.

11 John Wilson Foster, 'Crediting Marvels: Heaney after 50', in O'Donoghue (ed.), *Cambridge Companion*, pp. 206–23 (at p. 214).

12 Seamus Heaney, 'Bags of Enlightenment', *Guardian*, 25 October 2003, www.theguardian.com/books/2003/oct/25/poetry.highereducation. The anthologies are titled *The Rattle Bag* (1982) and *The School Bag* (1997). Cf. Dennison, *Adequacy of Poetry*, pp. 209–11.

13 Günter Leypoldt, 'Singularity and the Literary Market', *New Literary History*, 45/1 (Winter 2014), 71–88 (at p. 79).

14 *Ibid.*, p. 75.

15 Foster, 'Crediting Marvels', p. 210.

16 Seamus Heaney, *The Redress of Poetry* (New York: Farrar, Straus and Giroux, 1995).

17 Helgesson, 'How Writing Becomes (World) Literature', p. 23.

18 Seamus Heaney, *Poems and a Memoir* [selected and illustrated by Henry Pearson] (New York: Limited Editions Club, 1982), p. xvii.

19 Rand Brandes and Michael J. Durkan, *Seamus Heaney: A Bibliography 1959–2003* (London: Faber and Faber, 2008).

20 Heather Clark, *The Ulster Renaissance: Poetry in Belfast, 1962–1972* (Oxford University Press, 2006), p. 74.

21 Heaney, *Poems and a Memoir*, p. xvii.

22 Patrick Crotty, 'The Context of Heaney's Reception', in O'Donoghue (ed.), *Cambridge Companion*, pp. 37–55 (at p. 44).

23 *Ibid.*, pp. 44–7.

24 Helgesson, 'How Writing Becomes (World) Literature', p. 24. Leypoldt, similarly, questions 'the sense that the reality of literary objects somehow precedes cultural institutions and commercial markets' ('Singularity and the Literary Market', p. 82).

25 Carrie Noland, *Voices of Negritude in Modernist Print: Aesthetic Subjectivity, Diaspora, and the Lyric Regime* (New York: Columbia University Press, 2015), p. 3.

26 Rand Brandes, '"Inscribed in Sheets": Seamus Heaney's Scribal Matrix', in Catharine Malloy and Phyllis Carey (eds.), *Seamus Heaney: The Shaping Spirit* (Newark: University of Delaware Press, 1996), pp. 47–70 (at p. 52).

27 Bernard O'Donoghue, *Seamus Heaney and the Language of Poetry* (New York: Harvester Wheatsheaf, 1994), pp. 63, 10.

28 Kate Brennan, 'Bilingual Publication and the Poetry of Michael Hartnett/Mícheál Ó hAirtnéide, Seamus Heaney, and Nuala Ní Dhomhnaill', Modern Language Association annual convention, Austin, TX, January 2016.

29 Brandes, 'Inscribed in Sheets', p. 48.

30 Michael Warner, *The Letters of the Republic: Publication and the Public Sphere in Eighteenth-Century America* (Cambridge, MA: Harvard University Press, 1990), p. 7.

31 Brandes and Durkan, *Seamus Heaney*, pp. 16–17.
32 Peter Fallon, 'Notes on a History of Publishing Poetry', *Princeton University Library Chronicle*, 59/3 (Spring 1998), 546–58 (at p. 552). Fallon also discusses Cuala and Dolmen on pp. 547–9.
33 Brandes, 'Seamus Heaney's Working Titles', p. 20, and Fallon, 'Notes', 549.
34 Seamus Heaney, 'Gallery at the Abbey: An Introduction to the 40th Anniversary Reading', in Richard Rankin Russell (ed.), *Peter Fallon: Poet, Publisher, Editor and Translator* (Sallins: Irish Academic Press, 2014), pp. 23–26 (at p. 23).
35 Fallon, 'Notes', p. 552.
36 Jason David Hall, *Seamus Heaney's Rhythmic Contract* (Basingstoke: Palgrave Macmillan, 2009), p. 8.
37 Faber planned to print 10,000 hardcover copies, while FSG printed 11,000 – astounding numbers for a poetry book, even without additional paperback runs. See Jane Feaver to Seamus Heaney, 25 June 1996, Seamus Heaney Papers, Stuart A. Rose Manuscript, Archives, and Rare Book Library, Emory University; and Brandes and Durkan, *Seamus Heaney*, p. 102.
38 Seamus Heaney, *The Last Walk: Translations from the Italian of Giovanni Pascoli* (Oldcastle: Gallery Press, 2013), n.p.
39 Heaney, 'Gallery at the Abbey', p. 25.

CHAPTER 17

Field Day

Marilynn Richtarik

In September 1983, the Field Day Theatre Company reinforced its claim to more than theatrical significance by publishing the first set of Field Day pamphlets – including *An Open Letter*, addressed to the editors of *The Penguin Book of Contemporary British Poetry* (1982) by Seamus Heaney, a member of the company's board of directors. Through thirty-three stanzas of humorous verse, Heaney protested the use of the adjective 'British' as applied to himself. Not everyone was amused. Eavan Boland, reviewing the series for the *Irish Times*, detected a whiff of 'green nationalism', chiding Heaney, 'I cannot believe that the sudden appearance of the word "British" on the title page came as a rude shock. He has either changed his mind or changed his friends.'[1] Heaney had done neither. His political views had always been 'constitutional nationalist' (*SS* 176), and he collaborated in the Field Day collective with some of his oldest and closest friends. In a 1989 interview with me, Heaney asserted that the formation of the Field Day board before the company's second tour merely formalized a structure that preceded Field Day, and archival sources confirm his statement. As early as October 1974, playwright Brian Friel had responded excitedly to Heaney's account of an evening he had spent with poet and critic Seamus Deane and playwright Thomas Kilroy, during which there had been talk of a 'commune' involving the four of them: 'it's high time the articles of constitution of Lit. in this country were redefined, and I think we could forge them. We have each an affinity & an affection & a respect that would make a working party possible.'[2]

These four men, in addition to actor Stephen Rea (who initiated the actual Field Day project in 1979), film-maker and folk-singer David Hammond, and poet and critic Tom Paulin, would eventually work together on the Field Day board, but each, as Heaney explained, had 'a different version or vision of the thing'.[3] In addition to his service on the board and his pamphlet, Heaney's contributions to Field Day included *Sweeney Astray* (a translation of the medieval Irish poem *Buile Suibhne*),

The Cure at Troy (a version of Sophocles' late play *Philoctetes*) and editorial work on the Yeats section of *The Field Day Anthology of Irish Writing*. In return he got camaraderie, the sense of addressing himself to his country's urgent needs at a critical point in its history and the challenge to do things he would not have done otherwise. This essay will focus on the personal context of Heaney's involvement with the company and the two works most directly inspired by it: *An Open Letter* and *The Cure at Troy*.

Heaney's 'version' of Field Day owed its shape to his relationships with Friel and Deane. Heaney had known Friel since the older writer initiated their acquaintance with a congratulatory letter upon the publication of Heaney's first book, *Death of a Naturalist* (1966), but their literary friendship intensified after Heaney published his third collection, *Wintering Out*, in 1972. Friel sent him a draft of his play *Volunteers* in October 1974, and it had a galvanizing effect on Heaney, who had had no idea that Friel, like himself, had been 'delving into the archaeological regions'. '[W]hen I read the play', he later recalled, 'I immediately started typing out all the bog poems and Viking Dublin poems that were to hand, plus the "Singing School"/St Columb's poems ... and by the end of a weekend I found I had a manuscript that I could send to Faber as well as to Brian. That's how *North* got assembled' (*SS* 177, 179). When *Volunteers* opened at the Abbey in March 1975, it was, Heaney recounted, 'so resisted and downgraded by local reviewers' that he, Deane and Kilroy mounted a public defence in the form of a 'post-performance discussion' (*SS* 414), and Heaney wrote a piece about it for the *Times Literary Supplement*. Friel dedicated the play to him upon publication.

Heaney's and Friel's corroborating effect on each other continued through the late 1970s, as both embarked on new phases of their respective careers. In December 1975, Friel thanked Heaney for his editorial suggestions regarding an early draft of part of *Faith Healer* but confessed that he might 'let it lie in the drawer for a while. Because for some time now I've had a growing sense of new directions ... you know yourself that much of what we do is a kind of propagation by layering; and my feeling these weeks is that I want to work from completely new plants & perhaps by different techniques'.[4] He sensed a similar mood in his friend when Heaney sent him, in the autumn of 1979, a section of the Station Island sequence. Friel wrote back immediately to assure him that the 'intelligence of the imagination' told him Heaney was on to something big. 'I think it's going to take a lot of work and, when it's finally full, maybe more rewriting than you've ever done because it's reaching for something larger than the perfection (your forte) of its individual parts. Trust that reach now. Trust it to the end – wherever or whenever that is.'[5] When the poems finally appeared in *Station Island* (1984), Heaney dedicated the volume to Friel.

If Heaney's friendship with Friel stemmed from their mutual recognition of a shared sensibility, his even older friendship with Deane took its charge from the frisson of difference. They had met as scholarship students at St Columb's College in Derry, where Deane grew up in the Catholic ghetto known as the Bogside and where they learned to define themselves in contrast to each other. Deane commented that 'Each of us could caricature himself happily: Heaney slow, calm, solid, country-cunning; Deane quick, volatile, city-smart ... Each could be the other's Other, the other Seamus.'[6] Since both were young to go straight to university, they remained at St Columb's for an extra year of instruction in English literature (*SS* 184–5, 404–5). United by their genuine investment in the subject, they became 'fast friends'. They were invigorated as well, Deane recalled, by their understanding that 'advancement was now to be achieved on the basis of merit, not on sectarian affiliation ... Learning had an extra dimension to it, an extra pleasure; it now carried a political implication, a sense of promise.'[7]

In 1957, the two proceeded to Queen's University Belfast, where they enrolled in the Honours English Literature course. Both had begun writing poems in addition to studying them, exchanging drafts by post during university breaks, as Heaney describes in 'The Ministry of Fear', a poem from the mid-1970s dedicated to Deane (*OG* 126–8). Already, Heaney recollected, Deane had 'a sense of a calling' as a poet, while he himself remained 'far from confident' (*SS* 185). '[C]autious as a cat' by nature, in Deane's view of him,[8] Heaney must have been alternately impressed and appalled by the other Seamus's propensity to say exactly what was on his mind. Heaney also realized that abstract thought came more naturally to Deane than it did to him, noting 'that side of him got great reinforcement when he went to Cambridge University to do his PhD' (*SS* 185). Heaney, during the same period, stayed in Belfast to teach at a secondary school, then became a lecturer at a teacher training college before accepting a similar position at Queen's in 1966, the year he published *Death of a Naturalist* to instant acclaim (*SS* xxi–xxii).

The two saw little of each other during the ten years after completing their undergraduate studies but began to meet again after Heaney resigned from Queen's and moved to County Wicklow in 1972. As he learned to navigate the life of a full-time writer, he turned increasingly to Friel for advice. Since Friel had become friends with Deane during the period when Deane and Heaney had drifted apart, coming more firmly into Friel's orbit also entailed a reconnection with Deane, by then based at University College Dublin. Friel, Heaney sensed, took 'a kind of mentor's interest' in both Seamuses. Heaney, for his part, saw their tripartite alliance metaphorically as 'a swing of the pendulum ... from Belfast back to Derry' (*SS* 178).[9]

Though pleased to renew his friendship with Deane, Heaney remained aware of their differences. He found Deane, a decade on, paradoxically both more cosmopolitan and more parochial than himself. Years of studying Enlightenment intellectuals and teaching in the United States accounted for the former, but Heaney attributed the latter to their divergent experience of life within Northern Ireland. Whereas he himself had mixed with 'the other side' both in the country and, later, in Belfast and become quite comfortable even in the 'official' circles of the Northern Ireland Arts Council, the education bureaucracy, and BBC Northern Ireland, Deane's attachment to the North had always been strictly to his deprived native city. 'From the age of twelve', Heaney reflected,

> I was that bit detached from the place where I'd grown up, whereas Seamus lived on his home ground and kept his ear to it. His Ulster had always been politically more melodramatic than mine anyhow, more Manichaean even, more hard-edged Republican and Loyalist. He never had Protestant neighbours in and out of the house, no day-to-day experience of come and go between the two communities. (SS 186)

When Dennis O'Driscoll asked Heaney if he had felt pressured by Deane in the 1970s 'to be more political' in his poetry, Heaney responded, 'To say "yes" to that would be to overstate, but to say "no" would be to misrepresent the reality of the situation' (*SS* 186–7). This 'reality' is illustrated in Deane's 1977 interview with Heaney, 'Unhappy and at Home'. Heaney ventured, to Deane's obvious dismay, to agree with Conor Cruise O'Brien about the danger of an 'unhealthy intersection' between art and politics, but he also maintained that 'the poet incarnates his mythos and must affirm it'.[10] Perhaps the apparent dissonance between them came down to their variant definitions of 'politics' at the time. Heaney might truthfully disclaim any interest in *party* politics, but his entire body of work demonstrated his instinctive grasp of the political minefield represented by unspoken assumptions and everyday words. Exposing such habits of thought and speech *as* political so they could be subjected to analysis and critique would be one of Field Day's defining accomplishments. Heaney finally answered O'Driscoll's question by saying that he did not feel 'pressured' by Deane, but rather 'extended, awakened, called upon to take in more of the Northern experience we both shared' (*SS* 187).

Heaney's closeness to Friel guaranteed him an insider's perspective on Field Day's inaugural production. Friel sent Heaney a draft of *Translations* shortly after he finished writing it at Rea's request, explaining that they hoped to produce it the following year with money from the Northern Ireland Arts Council.[11] He described the play ironically to Heaney as 'Set in Irish-speaking hedge-school in Donegal in 1833. I think it's about language(s). Anyhow pure Broadway material.'[12] Heaney, though, knew at once that it could be a hit, replying within the week, 'It is all working at the haunting level ... trust "Translations" – I think it's going to be a powerful exciting "event" as well as the deeply conceived work that it is.'[13] Heaney continued to lend support through the production process, contributing a poem to the programme at Friel's request and writing an article on the play for the *TLS*.

Heaney's prediction proved correct. During the last months of 1980, the play captivated audiences and critics everywhere on the Field Day tour through Northern Ireland and the Republic. Heaney remarked that 'What happened on the stage woke something in the collective consciousness. The play is peopled with stereotypical characters ... but the art of the thing is in the way Friel subverts the response that all those stereotypes invite.' *Translations* 'was both a crowd-pleaser and a critique ... It was a unique kind of success, so we urged Brian not to let the excitement pass but to ride it and do something more' (*SS* 414–15). As he wrote to Friel a few months after its première, 'We all feel bigger and stronger for what you are doing.'[14]

Heaney contributed the poem 'Chekhov on Sakhalin' to the programme for Field Day's second production, Friel's version of *Three Sisters* (1981), and listened sympathetically to his friend's complaints about the uncongenial demands of theatre management ('So much of the effort is in ugly pursuits ... And it's prizing me out of a privacy I worked for and valued. And teaching me to haggle and strut. And all real work, of course, has gone by the board'[15]). '[I]t will be worth it', Heaney insisted: 'there was the Abbey and the early Gate and now there's this – nothing else significant, to my knowledge'.[16] How, then, could he refuse when Friel asked him to join Field Day's board of directors in the summer of 1981? 'I got involved', he recalled, 'out of solidarity with the effort Brian and Stephen had put into the initial enterprise, and because of the surge of excitement produced by *Translations*'; there is no reason, however, to doubt Heaney's assertion that 'I probably regarded it as belonging more in the sphere of cultural service than in my creative life' (*SS* 416, 419).

Still, the new members of Field Day expected to contribute materially to the company's output. Heaney knew Friel hoped 'that the poets on the board might branch out and do something for the theatre' (*SS* 416), but he and Deane resisted this notion (the prospect struck Heaney as 'risky for all') – instead, he suggested, they might do something in 'a literary/publication' vein.[17] At the Field Day board meeting on 24 October 1982, members considered, among other possibilities, a pamphlet series, expressing enthusiasm for the idea of inaugurating it with the open letter that Heaney was contemplating to the editors of the Penguin anthology.[18] Despite this endorsement, Heaney hesitated, sending Friel in early November the text of *Among Schoolchildren*, his upcoming John Malone Memorial Lecture, to ask if he thought it might do instead. Friel observed diplomatically that its politics might be overly subtle for the intended audience: 'it is a Minority (within the North) statement. Could/should we be bolder . . . ?' He believed 'the net should be cast wider than the TLS/Crane Bag/London Review of Books readers': 'I think there is a large and intelligent community out there to be spoken to – and adjusted.'[19]

Heaney saw the force of Friel's arguments but nonetheless felt 'awkward'. An insider on the British literary scene, he had appeared in anthologies of British literature before. He was featured prominently in the Penguin volume, and one of its editors, Blake Morrison, had written a study of his work (*SS* 416–17). He realized, moreover, that he should have made his misgivings about the title known by the proof stage, at the latest. By now, the book had been out for months. It seemed to him, though, that readers outside the Northern nationalist community needed a reminder that 'People from the minority in Northern Ireland always felt there was an element of coercion when the "British" word was applied to them' (*SS* 417). This general feeling had recently grown stronger. In 1983, when he wrote his pamphlet, 'we were in the bitter aftermath of dirty protests and hunger strikes, in the middle of the IRA's campaign, and . . . I had the feeling that if my British audience were not kept apprised of my stand-off with the "British" nomenclature, and indeed if my unionist readers were not kept reminded of it, I would be guilty of more than evasiveness' (*FK* 401). To put the matter bluntly, 'I didn't want to fly Margaret Thatcher's Union Jack for her' (*SS* 417).

Heaney solved his problem formally – making his point unmistakably, but in a light verse format that drew much of its sting.[20] Friel, though surprised, reacted with delight: 'I had thought a prose piece was coming. But the verse is so much better – the form for the bull-dancer.'[21] Deane felt otherwise, objecting that Heaney's pamphlet, by personalizing the political issues and being written in verse, made his and Paulin's seem more polemical in comparison and predicting that Field Day's critics would fasten on an apparent division on the board between critical and creative, or extreme and moderate, elements. To what extent, he asked, should 'collective responsibility' apply to Field Day's productions? Was there to be a 'Field Day position' on any topic?[22] In this instance, the other directors overrode Deane's reservations, but the questions he raised continued to bedevil the board. According to Heaney, Deane 'was the most passionate and eloquent in the articulation of a Field Day agenda, and we were all grateful for his brilliance and provocations, if not always for his excessiveness' (*SS* 419). Though Deane thought Heaney understated the nationalist case, he might not have published *An Open Letter* without a little push from his friends. In any case, he never regretted publishing it (*SS* 419).

The Cure at Troy, the other Heaney text to derive directly from his membership in Field Day, realized Friel's hope that the company might inspire poets to write for the stage. Paulin had set an example for his colleagues on the board with his version of Sophocles' *Antigone* in 1984, which appeared on a double-bill with a Molière translation by Derek Mahon. At a meeting in July 1985, Heaney intimated that he might be persuaded to do a play, and later that year he mentioned *Philoctetes* as a possibility. By the following June, though, he was having second thoughts, worried that the Sophocles play might be too literary for the purpose, and for the next couple of years he considered, inconclusively, adapting a Lorca play instead.[23] Friel knew the surest way to persuade Heaney was to appeal to his sense of duty, but for some time he resisted this tactic, confining himself to gentle nudges (including a note in 1988 urging Heaney to reconsider Sophocles).[24] Finally, in the spring of 1989 and with no theatre prospects for 1990 in sight, he made an uncharacteristically direct plea, urging Heaney to write '*something*' for the theatre side of Field Day: 'a translation, a version, a dramatization ... You are needed.'[25]

Heaney had first encountered *Philoctetes* through Edmund Wilson's *The Wound and the Bow*, struck by Wilson's observation that Sophocles 'shows himself particularly successful with people whose natures have been poisoned by narrow fanatical hatreds'.[26] With respect to Northern Ireland, Heaney saw the character of the Greek hero Philoctetes, so obsessed with an old wrong that has left him maimed and bitter that he risks forfeiting both his destined glory in Troy and the opportunity for healing, as 'an aspect of *every* intransigence, republican as well as Unionist, a manifestation of the swank of victimhood, the righteous refusal, the wounded one whose identity has become dependent upon the wound, the betrayed one whose energy and pride is a morbid symptom'.[27] The dilemma faced by Neoptolemus, a younger warrior directed by Odysseus to trick Philoctetes into coming to the aid of his erstwhile comrades besieging Troy, also captured Heaney's imagination, since 'people on both sides of the political fence in Northern Ireland' faced situations like Neoptolemus's 'when the political solidarity required from him by the Greeks is at odds with the conduct he requires from himself if he's to maintain his self-respect' (*SS* 420).

Heaney produced his version during the first half of 1990, with the aid of three English translations of the play (*SS* 420). He approached the work chiefly as a careful craftsman, preserving Sophocles' sense while converting most of the dialogue into blank verse, inflecting the script with his distinctive idiolect. He changed the title at Friel's suggestion,[28] settling on *The Cure at Troy*, although audiences see neither cure nor Troy in the play, because 'in Ireland, north and south, the idea of a miraculous cure is deeply lodged in the religious subculture' (*SS* 422). He also downplayed the *deus ex machina* aspect of the ending, where Hercules commands Philoctetes to return to the Greek army, as he explained in a programme note for the Field Day production: 'I have attempted to present the conclusion as the inevitable culmination of an honestly-endured spiritual and psychological crisis rather than as the result of a supernatural intervention.' Most notably, Heaney injected the chorus speeches with his own voice, even inserting a few topical references (a 'hunger-striker's father', a 'police widow in veils') that he regretted almost immediately. He later reflected that 'the choral mode, allows for and almost requires a homiletic note that you would tend to exclude from personal lyric. So the quotable element in the lines comes in part from that unrestrained rhetoric' (*SS* 421). This effect is heightened in the most famous speech of Heaney's play:

> History says, *Don't hope*
> *On this side of the grave.*
> But then, once in a lifetime
> The longed-for tidal wave
> Of justice can rise up,
> And hope and history rhyme.[29]

These six lines, according to Aidan O'Malley, represent 'the most frequently cited passage' of Field Day's 'entire output'.[30] This seems a fitting observation on which to conclude the present survey of Seamus Heaney's involvement with Field Day, an enterprise that he both helped to shape and that helped to shape him.

Notes

1 Eavan Boland, 'Poets and Pamphlets', *Irish Times*, 1 October 1983. For a narrative of Field Day's early years, see Marilynn Richtarik, *Acting between the Lines: The Field Day Theatre Company and Irish Cultural Politics 1980–1984* (Oxford University Press, 1994). I wish to thank the Hambidge Center in Georgia, where I drafted this essay. I am also grateful to the Heaney and Friel estates for permission to quote from unpublished correspondence and to Lindsey Eckert, Audrey Goodman, Mark Noble, LeeAnne Richardson, Michael Parker and Jonathan Williams for editorial advice.

2 Brian Friel, letter to Seamus Deane, 13 October 1974, Seamus Deane papers, MS 1210, b1/f10, Rose Library, Emory University.

3 Marilynn Richtarik, interview with Seamus Heaney, Oxford, 23 October 1989.

4 Friel, letter to Heaney, 1 December 1975, Seamus Heaney papers, MS 960, b39/f9, Rose Library, Emory University.

5 Friel, letter to Heaney, 8 November 1979, Seamus Heaney papers, MS 960, b39/f9, Rose Library, Emory University.

6 Seamus Deane, 'The Famous Seamus', *New Yorker*, 20 March 2000, 54–79 (at p. 56).

7 *Ibid.*, p. 62.

8 *Ibid.*, p. 66.

9 Although Friel had lived in the Republic since 1967, he had spent nearly thirty years of his childhood and youth in Derry and, like Heaney and Deane, had attended St Columb's. Paul Delaney (ed.), *Brian Friel in Conversation* (Ann Arbor: University of Michigan Press, 2000), pp. xvii–xviii.

10 Seamus Deane, 'Unhappy and at Home: Interview with Seamus Heaney', *Crane Bag*, 1/1 (Spring 1977), 61–7 (at pp. 62–3).

11 Friel, letter to Heaney, 21 November [1979], Seamus Heaney papers, MS 960, b39/f9, Rose Library, Emory University.

12 Friel, undated postcard to Heaney, Seamus Heaney papers, MS 960, b39/f9, Rose Library, Emory University.

13 Heaney, letter to Friel, 26 November 1979, Brian Friel papers, MS 37, 247, National Library of Ireland.

14 Heaney, letter to Friel, 31 December 1980, Brian Friel papers, MS 37, 247, National Library of Ireland.

15 Friel, letter to Heaney, 24 January [1981], Seamus Heaney papers, MS 960, b39/f9, Rose Library, Emory University.

16 Heaney, letter to Friel, 2 July 1981, Brian Friel papers, MS 37, 247, National Library of Ireland.

17 Heaney, letter to Friel, 27 September 1982, Brian Friel papers, MS 37, 247, National Library of Ireland.

18 Minutes of the Field Day board meeting of 24 October 1982, Tom Paulin papers, MS 880, b52/f1, Rose Library, Emory University. Although the minutes do not record who proposed the pamphlet series, Friel later credited

Deane with the suggestion: Friel, letter to Deane, [17 March 1989], Seamus Deane papers, MS 1210, b1/f9, Rose Library, Emory University.

19 Friel, letter to Heaney, 9 November 1982, Seamus Heaney papers, MS 960, b39/f9, Rose Library, Emory University.

20 Seamus Heaney, *An Open Letter* in *Ireland's Field Day* (London: Hutchinson, 1985), pp. 19–30.

21 Friel, letter to Heaney, 23 February [1983], Seamus Heaney papers, MS 960, b39/f9, Rose Library, Emory University.

22 Seamus Deane, 'A Comment' on the first series of Field Day pamphlets, considered at the Field Day board meeting of 5 June 1983, Tom Paulin papers, MS 880, b52/f1, Rose Library, Emory University.

23 Minutes of the Field Day board meetings of 7 July 1985, 9–10 November 1985, 14 June 1986, 21 September 1986 and 30 August 1987, Tom Paulin papers, MS 880, b52/f1, Rose Library, Emory University.

24 Friel, postcard to Heaney, 1988, Seamus Heaney papers, MS 960, b39/f9, Rose Library, Emory University.

25 Friel, postcard to Heaney, [1 May 1989], Seamus Heaney papers, MS 960, b39/f9, Rose Library, Emory University.

26 Edmund Wilson, *The Wound and the Bow* (Boston: Houghton Mifflin, 1941), p. 278.

27 Heaney, quoted in Richard Rankin Russell, *Seamus Heaney's Regions* (University of Notre Dame Press, 2014), p. 291.

28 Friel, letter to Heaney, 22 February 1990, Seamus Heaney papers, MS 960, b39/f10, Rose Library, Emory University.

29 Seamus Heaney, *The Cure at Troy* (London: Faber and Faber, 1990), p. 77.

30 Aidan O'Malley, quoted in Russell, *Heaney's Regions*, p. 304.

CHAPTER 18

Translation

Aidan O'Malley

> You can legislate to your heart's content about how translation should be done, but the practice is going to ignore or outflank the theories.
>
> (*SS* 297)

While an interest in translation can be traced through Seamus Heaney's work, the majority of his extended translations were published in the second half of his career, after 1990.[1] They are, on one level, an expression of Heaney's evolving sense of his place in the poetic world and of his mature confidence in his abilities to measure up to, in particular, the classics and do them some justice. On another, more mundane, level, a number of his later translations came into being because publishers and other producers of texts wanted to secure the name of the best-selling Anglophone poet and Nobel laureate on these works. *Beowulf* (2000) was commissioned by Norton and, by Heaney's own account, was a labour, and hardly one of unmitigated love (*SS* 440); he would never have translated Leoš Janáček's piece *Diary of One Who Vanished* (1999) had he not been approached to do so in late 1997 by Neil Wallace, a Scottish theatre producer, and was intrigued by the prospect of working with Deborah Warner;[2] Heaney was initially more inclined to offer a version of *Oedipus at Colonus* rather than *Antigone* (*The Burial at Thebes*) when he was invited to produce a play for the Abbey Theatre's centenary celebrations in 2004 (*SS* 422); his work on Jan Kochanowski's *Laments* (2009) was a favour to his friend Stanisław Barańczak who had translated the poems and asked Heaney to supply some finishing touches (*SS* 427–8). Translation, moreover, served Heaney as a form of aesthetic workout, a way of keeping his poetic muscles flexed and trim. He embarked, for instance, on his version of *Buile Shuibhne* (*Sweeney Astray*, 1983) to ensure the poetry continued when he moved from Northern Ireland to Wicklow in 1972: it imposed a drill that helped him ease into the cottage at Glanmore and develop it as a place of writing.

Heaney's translations push at the borders of the definition of the term translation. Many were from languages he had no knowledge of, such as classical Greek, Polish and Czech. And while he had varying degrees of competence in Irish, Old English, Middle Scots, Latin and Italian, his translations from these languages were also, for the most part, guided by cribs and other translations. As such, the majority of his translations might more properly be labelled versions, adaptations, reworkings or transpositions. Having said that, with perhaps the notable exception of *Beowulf*, which was produced to function as an academic work, readers do not approach a Heaney translation simply to have the source text decoded (were such a thing ever possible). For the most part, the appeal of these translations lies in the ways Heaney revoices and puts his poetic stamp on them. In other words, they have generally been considered constituent parts of Heaney's oeuvre, and this sets his work apart from that of a professional translator, who would habitually strive for less visibility.

'In the final analysis', Novalis claimed in a 1797 letter to A.W. Schlegel, 'all poetry is translation'.[3] No doubt this is a questionable assertion, but an overlapping of these activities can be detected in Heaney's thoughts on his work as a translator and as a poet. In a 1988 interview Heaney outlined what he saw as two fundamental modes of translation. The first, and 'highest', form is a 'pure' variant that looks to transmit the beauty and wonder of a literary piece written in another language that one knows well. An act of 'impure translation' is the other option, which he describes as the effort to relay something that one can dully rather than fully comprehend. In this case, which almost invariably describes Heaney's situation, the translator is 'listening through the wall of the original language as to a conversation in another room in a motel'.[4] Cognizant that he can never completely capture the entire sense of what he hears, Heaney nonetheless has no doubt about the value of finding a way of breaking through the wall to import these new sounds into his world. What Heaney is silently calling on and adapting for the scene of translation is Robert Frost's notion of the 'sound of sense': the ways in which the tones and the patterning of words, not just their meanings, form the bedrock of poetry. Heaney develops this in a 1981 interview with Frank Kinahan: it is

> As if you're listening through a wall: you don't hear the meanings, but you hear the amorousness, or the rage, or the intimacy, or the desultoriness. Now it seems to me that poetry operates at its very first and last level in making those intimate noises, moods, intonations, touches, making them active in the language.[5]

These direct echoes suggest that Heaney understood his translation work in the same light as he viewed his poetry: both involve bringing into one's own language that which has an audible if not completely comprehensible existence beyond it.

In an attempt to locate these generative pulses, Heaney, in the interview with Kinahan, supplemented his thoughts on Frost's 'sound of sense' by invoking T.S. Eliot's conception of the 'auditory imagination'.[6] For Eliot this spoke of the innate 'feeling for syllable and rhythm ... far below the conscious levels of thought and feeling' that 'invigorat[es] every word'.[7] In his essay 'Englands of the Mind' Heaney parses this in terms of 'the cultural depth-charges latent in certain words and rhythms ... the relationship between the word as pure vocable, as articulate noise, and the word as etymological occurrence, as symptom of human history, memory and attachments' (*P* 150).[8] Sound, this intimates, exceeds consciousness and speaks of profound affinities; indeed, as a *dinnseanchas*-style poem such as 'Broagh' indicates, for Heaney a place and its history can be heard: its roots are in its sounds. Therefore, in order that his translations should, like his own poetry, sound right, Heaney had to find ways of faithfully rendering the music of the original in English. In general, Heaney negotiated this fundamental displacement in a radical fashion, by (re)creating harmonies between the cultural and linguistic roots not only of the two languages directly involved in the translational exchange, but often by also calling upon a third language to help open up a passage from the source to the target language.

'Without some melody sensed or promised', Heaney unequivocally noted, 'it is simply impossible for a poet to establish the translator's right of way into and through a text' (*B* xxxvi). In some cases, this melody emanated directly from the sound of the original: introducing his work on Robert Henryson, for instance, Heaney noted how its Middle Scots immediately resonated with him, leading him 'back into what might be called "the hidden Scotland" at the back of [his] own ear'.[9] But if these Scottish tones had a familiarity that facilitated Heaney's reworking, a more circuitous route was required to uncover the 'enabling note' that permits translation when the original was in a language in which Heaney was not so well versed (*B* xxxvi). A thorough description of the process of finding this key is provided in his account of translating *Antigone* into *The Burial at Thebes*. Faced with Antigone and Ismene's opening encounter, Heaney sought out 'a metre to make the love and panic of the two sisters pulse with a certain ritual force'.[10] From the depths of his auditory imagination a note was rung that sounded right, as Heaney heard 'the opening lines of a famous eighteenth-century Irish poem, "Caoineadh Airt Uí Laoghaire"'.[11] 'The Lament for Art O'Leary', to give it its English title, is a poem in the voice of O'Leary's widow as she grieves over her husband's body, which has been left unburied by the forces of the state who had murdered him. Sanctioned by the echoing scenarios, Heaney 'picked up the note of Eibhlín Dhubh's three-beat line', which not only 'established a tune [he] could carry' and 'play variations' upon, but also brought forth other rhythms and harmonies that established the soundscape of his translation.[12]

Describing how 'Theme and tone coalesced', this process also provides an insight into how Heaney construed translational fidelity, as the central theme of the drama is an act of translation.[13] In one of its meanings, translation refers to a process of burial or reburial and, viewed thus, *Antigone* is a drama of translation that brings conflicting conceptions of fidelity into play. At its heart is an *agon* about how to deal faithfully with the body of Polyneices: should its translation be governed by man-made regulations or by what Antigone calls the 'Unwritten, original, god-given laws'?[14] Should the translation, in other words, be faithful to the letter or the spirit of the original? The way in which this dynamic is performed in *The Burial at Thebes* would suggest that Heaney's emphasis on capturing the sound of sense above the literal sense could be read as privileging the spirit above the letter of the original. In this version it is difficult to perceive why Hegel claimed that the tragedy of *Antigone* emerges from the equal validity of the claims of Antigone and Creon, especially as Heaney's Creon is a money-obsessed anti-feminist who parrots the crude simplicities of George W. Bush's so-called war on terror and whose reading of the letter of the law is explicitly partial.[15]

Other political and cultural associations were also at play in this drama of fidelity for Heaney. In 1968 he was moved by Conor Cruise O'Brien's invocation of the justice of Antigone's position at a lecture held in the immediate wake of a Civil Rights march that had been violently disrupted by the forces of the state in Derry.[16] Heaney also linked the action of the tragedy with his attendance at the funeral of Francis Hughes, one of the H-Block hunger strikers, in 1981. For Heaney, his participation was an act of familial and communal loyalty that exceeded political considerations, and he registers this Antigone-like act under the Irish term *dúchas*.[17] Verging on untranslatability, *dúchas* could be said to speak of the realm of the auditory imagination, as it gestures towards 'inheritance, patrimony; native place or land; connection, affinity or attachment due to descent or long-standing; inherited instinct or natural tendency'.[18] In *dúchas* these characteristics are elevated into 'a kind of ideal of the spirit, an enduring value amid the change and the erosion of all human things'.[19] Translating *dúchas*, therefore, was a way of coming to terms with Sophocles' text: the very 'word "burial"', as Heaney read it, 'carries with it something of ... *dúchas*', as it incorporates 'those "Instinctive Powers of Feeling, Love and Kinship" which authority must respect if it is not to turn callous'.[20]

This vision of an authority forged into justice by the qualities Hegel associated with Antigone encapsulates the terms of Neoptolemus's rebellion against Odysseus's unscrupulous manoeuvrings for the state in Heaney's other Sophocles translation, *The Cure at Troy*. Neoptolemus is, however, no Antigone: while she is inflexible in her allegiance to the immemorial gods of the underworld, he never loses sight of the daylight needs of his nation, but knows that it will be badly served if its ends are achieved by the underhand means urged by Odysseus. As a result, the drama of fidelity in *The Cure at Troy* centres on Neoptolemus's attempts to effect the translation of Philoctetes and his bow in a manner that acknowledges the claims of the letter of the law as well as those of the spirit of higher emotions, even if it prioritizes these. Yet even this more equilibrated perspective fails before the Chorus and its invocation of hope and trust makes an *ex-machina* intervention.[21]

Translation is always difficult and if, for Heaney, being faithful to the sound of sense of the original can be articulated through a fidelity to what one understands as the spirit of one's own inheritance, this never describes a straightforward process with foreseeable results. From his inaugurating statement of intent, 'Digging', the link between fidelity and the work of excavation ran deeply through Heaney's work, and in his translations Heaney's chthonic *dúchas* regularly dispatched him to 'unveil things profoundly beyond us / Mysteries and truths buried under the earth' (*A* 29). In different ways, these journeys to the underworld further enact the necessity and impossibility of executing a faithful translation.

Dante's *Commedia*, and the possibility of translating it, long haunted Heaney. 'Ugolino', a Lowellian 'imitation' of the episode from the *Inferno*, provided a way of articulating the flesh and blood of the 'Troubles', and the 'Station Island' sequence is indebted to 'Dante's example', as it permitted him to negotiate with the shades of writers who had been to Lough Derg before him.[22] His translation of the first three cantos of the *Inferno* was published in 1993, and these portray an *Incertus*, a mid-life Dante havering before undertaking his translation into 'the realm of things hidden'.[23] Ultimately, the translation itself faltered, as Heaney found his lack of Italian defeated any attempt to compose a coherent and faithful soundscape for the whole poem: he 'couldn't gauge tone' or 'establish a measure that combined plain speaking with fluent movement' (*SS* 425). In this light, his translation of Book VI of Virgil's *Aeneid* can be thought of as a return that burrows an even deeper route into the tradition that inspired Dante's voyage.

There is an eerie appropriateness to the posthumous publication of this translation, as Book VI of the *Aeneid* is concerned with the afterlife, in the dual sense of those who have predeceased Aeneas and those who will come after him. Heaney, indeed, acknowledges in his 'Translator's Note' that the impulses that brought him to this text came both from his father's death and from the birth of his first grandchild, to whom he dedicated the 'Route 110' sequence from *Human Chain*, an earlier engagement with this book of the *Aeneid*.[24] The more intimate re-visioning of the second half of Book VI in 'Route 110' speaks perhaps more directly to contemporary readers than the apparition of Rome's future glory that Virgil offers, which means that Heaney's translation proper necessarily concludes on something of a decrescendo of imperial boasting. Having said that, there is also the pervasive sense that this future is ephemeral. Images of windswept leaves blow through this book, and Aeneas is granted a vision of his descendants (Romulus, Julius Caesar and others) in the underworld. They are as spectral as his past, which is most forcefully manifested for him in the figure of his father, Anchises, whom he tries and fails to embrace three times. Aeneas, in other words, experiences the traumatic realization that what thought of as his own inheritance is also always other, and cannot be fully grasped. In a corresponding fashion, a translator must acknowledge and register the essential otherness of what she/he might consider her/his own if she/he is to offer a faithful translation.

'Dante's great literary contribution', according to Heaney, 'was to write in the vernacular and thereby to give the usual language its head.'[25] Emboldened by this authorization, Heaney's translations, to borrow and adapt Dipesh Chakrabarty's term, serve to 'provincialise' English.[26] Confidently declaring the right of his vernacular to function as a legitimate bearer of the cultural heft of canonical texts, Heaney's translations disrupt easy assumptions about the sort of English that such texts should be sounded in, and gesture to the fact that 'standard' English is but one form of the language. At the same time, the operations of what Jacques Derrida called 'the very law of . . . translation' dislodge the possibility of fully possessing a language by unveiling that even if '*We speak only one language*', '*We never speak only one language.*'[27] In enacting this law Heaney's translations bring into play a series of split loyalties, especially with regard to what might be accounted his own languages – English, Irish and Scottish. His most noted translation from Irish, *Sweeney Astray*, hardly describes a scenario of secure domesticity but rather tells the fractured tale of an itinerant outcast, 'a mad scuttler on mountain peaks, / a derelict doomed to loneliness' in his native Ireland and Scotland (*SA* 68). Sweeney's curse, though, was a blessing for Heaney, who returned to and adopted the 'inner émigré' (*N* 67) voice of this 'Ulster lunatic' (*SA* 73) in the 'Sweeney Redivivus' section of *Station Island*, an entirely liberating poetic masquerade by his own account (*SS* 262). In fact, Heaney held that hearing one's work as somewhat other was a way of gauging its worth: 'if a poem is any good, you can repeat it to yourself as if it were written by someone else' (*SS* 197). Furthermore, his employment of Ulster dialect words in his translations can serve to underscore a fundamental tension between the calls of home and those of elsewhere. So, if terms such as 'scaldies' and 'boor trees' find a home in his version of *Diary of One Who Vanished* because they translate 'the rural speech of [Janáček's] childhood', they also function to amplify the conflict at the heart of this suite of Czech poems between the stability of roots and the erotic appeal of the peripatetic – the dynamics of translation, in other words.[28]

It is in this displaced light that Heaney's most acclaimed act of cultural reappropriation – bringing home the foundation poem of English literature, *Beowulf* – might be approached. In the course of his correspondence with Al David, who was appointed by Norton to oversee the scholarly quality of the translation, Heaney makes his case for employing Irish terms by calling on the echoing depths of Eliot's auditory imagination: 'the choice of vocabulary has often deeply personal significance . . . it is the Grendel of pre-literate wallsteads and bottomless bogs who is calling my tune'.[29] While this refers to specific notes that have an (in)direct political valence such as 'Gap of danger' (line 1378) that, as Heaney notes, 'translates the Irish *bearna baoil*, which . . . appears in the Irish language version of the Irish national anthem',[30] his rendering of *Beowulf* was founded on the basis of a fundamentally familiar tone. As he read it, the world of the poem is populated by an unflinching, taciturn people who discourse in a lapidary fashion, qualities he associated with relatives of his, 'the big-voiced Scullions', who spoke 'as if they were announcing verdicts rather than making small talk' (*B* xxxvi). The access that this 'Hiberno-English Scullion-speak' provided Heaney with is evident from the very first word of his translation where, in place of the usual 'archaic literary' renderings of *Hwæt* – 'lo', 'hark' and the like – Heaney employs the much more immediate and familiar 'So' (*B* xxxvi).

Lawrence Venuti proposed that translators adopted one of two fundamental strategies: either they 'domesticated' the source text by rendering it in such a manner that it read fluently and without a trace of otherness in the target language, or they 'foreignized' it by developing ways in the target language of inscribing the foreign nature of the original in the translation.[31] Heaney complicates this very broad distinction, because while acts of domestication are clearly inscribed in many of his translations, these also work to render the texts somewhat foreign. With rare exceptions, such as his renderings of Nuala Ní Dhomhnaill's 'Féar Suaithinseach' ('Miraculous Grass') and 'Mo Mhíle Stór', Heaney did not translate contemporary poetry.[32] Translation for him was almost exclusively an engagement with literary history and, by sounding the archaic roots of language, his Hiberno-English and Ulster dialect words bestow an historic tone on the translations and so foreignize them in an appropriate fashion.

At the same time, Heaney also discovered that the process of translation profitably foreignized these domestic terms. He entitled his introduction to the *Beowulf* translation 'Fretwork' so that it might, amongst other things, capture an echo of the fretfulness felt by Stephen Dedalus after his discussion about the tundish with the English Dean of Studies in *A Portrait of the Artist as a Young Man*. While translating *Beowulf*, Heaney had a commensurate 'thole' moment: he encountered this word for 'suffering' with its defamiliarizing thorn in the original and recalled his aunt using this Old English expression. This connection helped him come to terms with *Beowulf*, not simply because it brought the text home to him, but also through the ways in which the word, as Heaney uncovers it, embodies a 'multicultural odyssey': it speaks of the links between Ireland and Scotland, and between them and the 'American South', turning up as it does in the work of John Crowe Ransom (*B* xxxiv). Ringing with these polyphonic linguistic and cultural harmonies heard in the substratum of the language, 'thole' unearths the relationship between Heaney's vernacular and Old English and supports his asseveration that *Beowulf* is a 'part of [his] voice-right' (*B* xxxiii). This claim, though, is staked not on the grounds of a hermetic definition of his culture, but on the shifting dynamic inscribed in 'thole' that gestures towards what Heaney, citing Osip Mandelstam, called 'a "nostalgia for world culture"' (*B* xxxv). Taking the foreign home, as Heaney's translations record and celebrate, inevitably puts the domestic in motion.

Notes

1 Maristella Gatto points out that every collection since *North* (1975) contains a translated piece. Maristella Gatto, '"Through the Wall": Heaney's "Impure" Translation in "Ugolino" and *Sweeney Astray*', *Bells (Barcelona English Language and Literature Studies)*, 11 (2000), 65–78 (at p. 66).

2 Fax from Neil Wallace to Seamus Heaney, 1 December 1997. Seamus Heaney Literary Papers, MS 49,493/215, National Library of Ireland. Heaney gave a tentatively positive response on 3 December 1997, seeing the commission as a form of relief from the 'heavy-duty' work he was doing on *Beowulf*, which he was finishing.

3 Cited in Antoine Berman, *The Experience of Translation: Culture and Translation in Romantic Germany*, trans. S. Hayvaert (Albany: State University of New York Press, 1992), p. 14.

4 Rand Brandes, 'Seamus Heaney: An Interview', *Salmagundi*, 80 (Fall 1988), 4–21 (at pp. 11–12).

5 Frank Kinahan, 'An Interview with Seamus Heaney', *Critical Inquiry*, 8/3 (Spring 1982), 405–14 (at pp. 413–14).

6 *Ibid.*, p. 413. Frost himself uses the term 'audial imagination' in the letter to John Bartlett (4 July 1913) in which he expounds on the 'sound of sense'. (See http://udallasclassics.org/maurer_files/Frost.pdf, pp. 1–2.)

7 T.S. Eliot, *The Use of Poetry and the Use of Criticism* (Cambridge, MA: Harvard University Press, 1964), p. 111.

8 Seamus Heaney, 'Englands of the Mind', *Preoccupations: Selected Prose 1968–1978* (New York: Farrar, Straus and Giroux, 1981).

9 Seamus Heaney, 'Introduction', in Robert Henryson, *The Testament of Cresseid and Seven Fables*, trans. Seamus Heaney (London: Faber and Faber, 2009), p. xiii.

10 Seamus Heaney, 'Title Deeds: Translating a Classic', *Proceedings of the American Philosophical Society*, 148/4 (December 2004), 411–26 (at p. 424).

11 *Ibid.*, p. 423.

12 *Ibid.*, pp. 424, 425. In a commensurate fashion, the Choral intervention that Heaney employs in place of Hercules' *ex-machina* diktat in *The Cure at Troy* is more a translation of how Heaney heard the tone of Eastern European poetry in translation (which he outlines in 'The Impact of Translation', *GT* 36–44) than it is a translation of Sophocles.

13 Heaney, 'Title Deeds', p. 423.

14 Seamus Heaney, *The Burial at Thebes: Sophocles' Antigone* (London: Faber and Faber, 2004), p. 21.

15 For an exploration of the role of *Antigone* in Hegel's thinking, see George Steiner, *Antigones* (Oxford University Press, 1984), pp. 19–36.

16 O'Brien's lecture and Heaney's reflections are in the same issue of the *Listener*: Conor Cruise O'Brien, 'Views', *Listener*, 80/2065 (24 October 1968), 526; Seamus Heaney, 'Old Derry's Walls', 521–3.

17 Heaney, 'Title Deeds', pp. 411–13.

18 Cited *ibid.*, p. 413.

19 *Ibid.*

20 Cited *ibid.*, p. 426.

21 For an assessment of how Heaney employed this famous Choral ode to solve a problem of translation, see Aidan O'Malley, *Field Day and the Translation of*

Irish Identities: Performing Contradictions (Basingstoke: Palgrave Macmillan, 2011), pp. 128–31.
22 Seamus Heaney, 'Envies and Identifications: Dante and the Modern Poet', *Irish University Review*, 15/1 (Spring 1985), 5–19 (at p. 18).
23 Daniel Halpern (ed.), *Dante's Inferno: Translations by Twenty Contemporary Poets* (New Jersey: Ecco Press, 1993), p. 12.
24 For a reflection on how these two texts relate to Heaney's political and religious environment, see Florence Impens, *Classical Presences in Irish Poetry after 1960: The Answering Voice* (Cham: Palgrave Macmillan, 2018), pp. 74–9.
25 Heaney, 'Envies and Identifications', p. 12.
26 Dipesh Chakrabarty, *Provincializing Europe: Postcolonial Thought and Historical Difference* (Princeton University Press, 2000).
27 Jacques Derrida, *Monolingualism of the Other; or, The Prosthesis of Origin*, trans. Patrick Mensah (Stanford University Press, 1996), p. 10. Italics in original.
28 Seamus Heaney, 'Introduction', in Leoš Janáček, *Diary of One Who Vanished*, trans. Seamus Heaney (London: Faber and Faber, 1999), pp. v–vii (at p. vi).
29 Typescript letter to Prof. Al David, 17 October 1997. The Seamus Heaney Beowulf Manuscript Collection, MS 20/5/1, Queen's University, Belfast.
30 *Ibid.*
31 Lawrence Venuti, *The Translator's Invisibility: A History of Translation* (London and New York: Routledge, 1995), pp. 17–39.
32 Nuala Ní Dhomhnaill, *Pharaoh's Daughter* (Oldcastle: Gallery Press, 1990), pp. 32–5 and 48–9.

V

Frameworks

CHAPTER 19

Catholicism

Kieran Quinlan

Seamus Heaney has engaged extensively, intensively, explicitly and implicitly with religious matters in his poems and essays, and spoken about his relationship with Catholicism on numerous occasions in interviews. Nevertheless, his preoccupation with the subject probably hasn't registered with his readers as much as T.S. Eliot's 'Ash Wednesday' and 'Little Gidding', or even, in an opposite direction, as Philip Larkin's 'Church Going' did with an earlier generation.[1] There are two main reasons for this: a waning in the importance attached to religious issues in most Western countries in the late twentieth and early twenty-first centuries; and a degree of ambiguity on the topic from a poet who has confessed that 'There was never a scene / when I had it out with myself or with another', and that 'Catholicism provided a totally structured reading of the mortal condition which I've never quite deconstructed' (*SS* 471).[2] Moreover, Heaney's initial lapse from Catholic practice in the 1960s was part of a public slide as much as it was a personal slip. And yet, in spite of the foregoing, the 1984 poem that might be said to demarcate the two major periods of Heaney's artistic output, the early digging down and the later rising up, is set in Lough Derg, a site at the very heart of the Irish Catholic tradition for over a thousand years; there, in 'Station Island', the poet makes a genuinely sacred pilgrimage even though the result is his becoming more openly secular. He has claimed too that Catholicism was 'everything' to him in his youth, and, at the backend of his life, noted a renewed awareness of 'something far more important in my mental formation than cultural nationalism or the British presence . . . namely, my early religious education'.[3] Heaney even mirrored his entire religious trajectory in the arrangement of anthologized poems in *The School Bag*, published with Ted Hughes in 1997, a collection that begins with a piece by an Irish pagan poet of the sixth century lamenting 'the arrival of Christianity in Ireland', followed by 'Matthew Arnold's "Dover Beach", a work from the other end of the age of religion', and immediately afterwards by an Elizabeth Bishop poem 'in which one witnesses the rebirth of a religious impulse in a post-religious sensibility'.[4]

Certainly, Heaney lived through times of unusual upheaval in religious matters. He was formed in an era when the Roman Church, even in Protestant Northern Ireland, exercised enormous control over its faithful members; then, in his early twenties, the Second Vatican Council, in an attempt at religious renewal, called much of the familiar Catholic devotional and theological past into question. This unexpected openness was followed, in 1968, by the equally unexpected reiteration of the long-standing ban on artificial contraception, a restriction that inflicted an immense and alienating burden on married couples, dramatically increasing their awareness of a gap between doctrine and life. Meanwhile, the political troubles that broke out in Northern Ireland at about the same time had the consequence that, irrespective of personal religious beliefs, everyone was inescapably identified with their denominational origins. Always uneasy with such constrictions, in the 1970s and afterwards Heaney nevertheless found imaginative sustenance in the example of the exiled Polish Catholic poet Czesław Miłosz and other Eastern European writers battling oppressive regimes. Finally, Heaney witnessed an Ireland that had been relatively poor and religious leap to one that was prosperous and sceptical, and a Church that had been revered and feared become scandal-ridden and, not infrequently, reviled. In all, Heaney went through several reorientations on his way to a post-religious understanding of the human experience. At every stage, however, Catholicism inflected his poetry and provided a context for his creative explorations.

Seamus Heaney's large, rural family was typically Catholic though at least one ancestor in the nineteenth century was a convert from Protestantism and he himself attended a mixed primary school. Unlike the average southerner in the Republic who was unlikely to know very many Protestants, Heaney was surrounded by such from the very beginning. His childhood home was full of religious bric-a-brac – a lamp-lit picture of the Sacred Heart, St Patrick driving the snakes from Ireland, the Eucharistic Congress of 1932 – items that he remembered with affection in later years when they had largely disappeared from even observant homes. He was responsive to the acoustics of the rosary and its accompanying litanies that referred to the Virgin Mary as a 'House of Gold' and a 'Tower of Ivory', while serving as an altar boy nurtured his sense of sacred spaces as well as making him familiar with the 'bark' of clerical authority (*SS* 327). It is especially striking how keenly aware Heaney was of the unmarked boundary between his Derry diocese and its neighbour, the minute differences between their respective catechisms, and, above all perhaps, his ten-year-long worrying over the 'particular judgement', the one-on-one interrogation of the soul thought to be conducted immediately after death (*SS* 319–20; *OG* 332).[5] It was also still the age of miracle and wonder, of residual pagan customs, Lourdes pilgrimages and pulpit invocations of the Fatima apparitions of 1917 that suggested an ongoing intervention of the deity in temporal affairs. At a more practical level, it was the age of meticulously counting indulgences and attending other punishment-reducing or heaven-meriting devotions of the type that had provoked the Protestant Reformation. Like all his fellow Northern Irish Catholics, Heaney too was acutely conscious that a historical wrong had been done to his community overwhelmingly on the basis of its religion; Catholics had a prior right to the local territory where now they were being reminded constantly of their second-class status by the Stormont government and a policing system which was almost entirely Protestant.

Winning a scholarship to a Catholic boarding school in those days, as Heaney acknowledged, run almost like a seminary marked a step up in the world and an even more constant round of pious practices beginning with Mass each morning and prayers throughout the day; pubescent sexual desire, meanwhile, was a regular cause of concern as it was believed that assent could lead to eternal damnation. Oppressive, however, as was the Catholicism that 'embraced' – a telling word – Heaney back then, he too embraced it without, apparently, any of the misgivings of his Clongowes predecessor.[6] Like Joyce too, he passingly contemplated entering the priesthood, though his eventual rejection of it was never as dismissive. Heaney may not have been that engaged with the details of Aquinas's five proofs for the existence of God, but he took delight in the consonantal sacramentalism of the Jesuit convert Gerard Manley Hopkins, and his own first poems would be in 'Hopkins-speak' (*SS* 37).

At Queen's University Belfast, Heaney was a very active member of the Chaplaincy and while there – astonishingly – made three pilgrimages to Lough Derg, another to Lourdes. He enjoyed the outings, observed the pieties, and, cannily, racked up the indulgences. Queens, however, represented 'the world', and Catholics weren't completely at ease with the latter. The professoriat – many of its members from the British mainland – were often religiously indifferent (though with a whiff of post-Protestant imperial entitlement) and, unintentionally or otherwise, were bound to disdain certain Catholic orthodoxies. But while Heaney was becoming ever more aware of challenges to the faith – taking his mother to Benediction at one moment, being shown what Joyce had done with such practices at another;

delving into the Victorian crisis of belief, and being exposed to Matthew Arnold's solution in substituting the truth of poetry for the uncertainties of religion – he was also reading the Catholic mystics, including the sixteenth-century St John of the Cross, as well as such contemporary religious writers as the monk convert Thomas Merton and Jewish almost-convert Simone Weil, well-known names in informed Catholic conversation of the late 1950s. In other words, he was well aware of a vibrant intellectual Catholic discourse of a contemplative bent, one reinforced by the many literary converts to the Church since the days of John Henry Newman and the Oxford Movement, a tradition, it should be noted, that tended to view seemingly unchangeable Catholicism as a rock of stability amid the chaos of modernity. Heaney emerged from Queen's with his Catholicism relatively intact, still marching to the drum of his own 'inner priest', and still 'a humble client at the lattice of confessionals' (*SS* 46).[7] A split was developing, however, between what he perceived as the truth of the human experience and the claims of the Church, especially the guilt and submissiveness its teachings induced. In the 1960s, he would try to 'secularize' himself as he went along with a 'generational assent to the proposition that God is dead', thereby 'screen[ing] out the first visionary world' (*SS* 471–2).

The Beatles era brought several disruptions to the staid tenor of British and Irish cultural life, challenging in particular received norms of sexual behaviour; in its way, the Second Vatican Council, which began in 1963, brought even more (in Ireland at least). While the Council does not appear to have had any direct impact on Heaney's quietly rebellious thinking, its 1965 declaration, for example, that the Church 'rejects nothing of what is true and holy in [other] religions', created an atmosphere more sympathetic to the construction of his own religious mythos.[8] When Heaney was young, Catholic dogmas were presented as truths so obvious (even if faith was required to believe in them) that their rejection was routinely attributed to intellectual dishonesty or human pride, eternal punishment being the consequence for getting things wrong; now the grounds for those old anxieties had been authoritatively relaxed. Thus Irish paganism could be matched and mixed with elements of Catholicism and with borrowings from Ted Hughes, Robert Graves and later, Carl Jung and Mircea Eliade, and especially from the classical worlds of Homer and Virgil and, indeed, the whole smorgasbord of ancient mythologies represented in Sir James Frazer's *The Golden Bough*.

Of course, deciding that Catholicism was simply another mythology, a projection of human aspirations from inside the universe rather than a revelation from a deity beyond it, was one thing; living with the reality of one's own childhood immersion in the faith, its churches and institutions everywhere in sight, its ministers among one's friends, mentors, employers and, after Heaney joined the American lecture circuit, welcoming hosts, was something else. It is hardly surprising, therefore, that Catholicism's 'undying . . . draw' tugs at Heaney at several junctures on his path with rather different resonances on each occasion (*SS* 234). Indeed, in the long tradition of Irish writers rebelling against Catholicism – William Carleton, James Joyce, Austin Clarke, Seán Ó Faoláin, Thomas Kinsella (not to mention those from the Protestant tradition such as W. B. Yeats, George Bernard Shaw, Seán O'Casey and Samuel Beckett) – Heaney appears much more sympathetic with the ideals and vision of the institution; that is also true in relation to his younger contemporaries such as Paul Muldoon and Eamon McCann. In 'Station Island', the Heaney persona admits, 'The angry role was never my vocation' (*OG* 227).

'In Gallarus Oratory', inspired by Heaney's 1966 visit to a famous sixth-century monastic stone hut on the Dingle Peninsula in County Kerry, provides an early instance of his distancing himself from his inherited faith: 'When you're in it alone' you become 'a reduced creature' (*DD* 10). He commented later, 'I felt the weight of Christianity in all its rebuking aspects, its calls to self-denial and self abnegation'; emerging, he experienced 'a lift of the heart, a surge towards happiness' (*P* 189).[9] Penitential practices are no longer to be automatically commended as surely the monks would have done; what for them had been a reminder of their creaturely status in this earthly place of exile, for him becomes an unwelcome and possibly unjust deprivation of its joys. The personal note is also present in 'Limbo' in *Wintering Out* (1972) where a young woman drowns her illegitimate, unbaptised baby to hide her shame: 'She waded in under / The sign of her cross. / He was hauled in with the fish. / Now limbo will be // A cold glitter of souls' (*OG* 72). A very cold eye is cast on a powerfully real place in Catholic iconography – though an invention of theologians to explain the fate of unbaptised infants and others 'invincibly ignorant' of the faith – up until recent times.

The onset of the Troubles in the late 1960s, however, forced Heaney to engage with Catholicism as quasi-tribal identification along with the old dilemmas of submission and sacrifice. Originally inspired by the example of the Rev. Martin Luther King, Jr's civil rights marches in the American South, Northern Irish Catholics began to seek justice in housing and voting independently of their traditional nationalist agenda only to be rebuffed and attacked by militant loyalists. The sending of British troops to quell the violence, and the resultant revival of a dormant IRA, led to shootings, bombings, torture and imprisonments becoming the order of the day. Unlike the Catholic poets of the 1916 Easter Rising who found their inspiration in the legacy of Christian redemptive suffering, the religious metaphors that Heaney employs to represent the terror of the times come from P.V. Glob's account of recently discovered ancient sacrificial burials in Northern European bogs. Still, a Catholic inflection occurs when 'The Tollund Man' is compared to a saint, and words such as 'blasphemy', 'consecrate' and 'holy' have a real presence in the gruesome narratives here and in the bog poems of *North* (1975).

By the time 'The Tollund Man' appeared in *Wintering Out* (1972), Heaney had departed for what the *Protestant Telegraph* described as his 'spiritual home in the popish Republic'.[10] If not altogether 'popish', the Republic was still relatively conservative in its religious outlook, a fact that didn't go unnoticed with this northerner who, though himself teaching at a Catholic institution, had 'certain knowledge' that he 'was a hell of a lot more emancipated from Catholic practice ... than many a star in the [University College Dublin] firmament' (*SS* 230). His scepticism is present, for example, in his 1979 'Elegy' for one-time Catholic convert Robert Lowell which ends with '"I'll pray for you"' (*FW* 23), the common phrase significantly in quotation marks, 'an affectionate and mocking assertion of the fact of their mutual lapsed religion' according to Helen Vendler.[11] It is also present in his setting himself to translate *Buile Suibhne* (*Sweeney Astray*, 1983), a Gaelic text from the early Middle Ages that tells of a regional king's revolt against the Church, his attempt at killing a saintly cleric and his punishment of being transformed into a migratory, homeless bird.

The early 1980s saw Heaney ready to assess his position more fully on matters artistic, political and religious. By choosing Lough Derg as the locus of the 'Station Island' poem, he was at once identifying with a traditional Catholic place of pilgrimage and with Dante, the greatest poet in that tradition. But his goal was not to restore his faith but rather to 'clear the head' (*SS* 236). Indeed, in 'Freedman' in 1975, Heaney had declared his liberation through poetry from both British and Roman Catholic subjugation (*N* 56). The mission ten years later is to spell the matter out in more detail. Thus, in the 1984 poem he re-enters this Catholic underworld to encounter a succession of ghosts from his past, both those read about – such as nineteenth-century apostate William Carleton, once a seminarian and pilgrim but later a denouncer of Catholicism's irrationalities – and those that have formed him, among them another Sweeney, a neighbour and early destabilizer of the poet's childhood obedience to Catholic ordinances. If the ghosts sound an awful lot like Heaney speaking to himself, it is because he is encountering them as they are relevant to his situation. The most explicit rejection of the faith comes in Section IV when Heaney meets with a deceased clerical friend whom he had known in his youth: the man's priestly vocation is admitted to be more the result of the culture of the time than of a divine calling since, in any case, 'the god has, as they say, withdrawn' (*OG* 231). Although several of the ghosts berate Heaney for his apparent fidelity to the Catholic tradition, the poet remains a pilgrim throughout his time on the island, his various sins now secularized into real human failings in his relations with others. At a critical point he expresses hatred of 'everything / That made me biddable', while his 'confession' to a Carmelite priest can be justified as a humanly sanctioned, and sanctified, embrace of poetry writing as his true calling (*OG 241*).

At the end of his pilgrimage, an exhausted Heaney meets the ghost of Joyce, the ultimate renegade from Catholicism in twentieth-century life and literature, and the poet's secular saviour. The selection of Joyce here, Heaney has explained, was to challenge the 'solidarity with orthodox ways and obedient attitudes' represented in the original choice of Lough Derg as a setting for the poem.[12] An earlier draft, meanwhile, adds a more overtly Catholic note (common in Heaney manuscripts) to their encounter: 'When I [Joyce] refused to take the sacrament / I made my life an instrument of grace // So all of you had more abundant / life.'[13] Heaney's choice of rejecting traditional faith, then, is meant to serve as a kind of salvation for those that follow. In fact, in the 'Sweeney Redivivus' poems that conclude the collection, Heaney is, presumably, a new Joyce who must in turn liberate his people who were once 'two-faced and accommodating' and are still 'holding on, every bit / as pious and exacting and demeaned' (*OG* 250). Eamon Duffy notes that while 'the presentation of religion in *Station Island* is far from uniformly negative . . . there is no mistaking the fact that the volume as a whole represents and was meant to represent a decisive turning away from any overt or at any rate continuing catholic identity'.[14]

The poems of *The Haw Lantern* (1987), *Seeing Things* (1991) and *The Spirit Level* (1997) tackle the consequences of Heaney's loss of belief, especially those on the deaths of his parents, a circumstance that both liberated him from his Catholic past to think of the transcendent in an independent way, and that also reinforced his sense that there would be no 'next-time-round'; what was experienced with the passing of loved ones was pure absence, their presence continuing on in memory and imagination only (*OG* 332). Yet there is a constant reaching out to some kind of beyond, as we see, for example, in 'The Mud Vision', at once a poem about the persistence of the magical, the superstitious and the religious (as expressed in a kind of retrogressive devotional Catholicism) and a faulting of such naiveté; at the same time, it is a poem of regret for the passing of that visionary impulse into the light of common day. Indeed, with the official Catholic canopy removed, its sacral language proliferates in the crevices of Heaney's poems, its earthly monks and saints part of the marvellous as he has known it.

One could legitimately interpret the last couple of decades of Heaney's life – his 'transcendentalist' period, as many would describe it – as a negotiating between four philosophical and artistic 'draws': the lyric darkness of Philip Larkin; the sceptically assertive Catholicism of Czesław Miłosz (Heaney was reading the Merton–Miłosz 1960s correspondence in the 1990s); the eclectic mythological and religious borrowings – the 'fardel' of beliefs – of Yeats; and the nagging '*non serviam*' of Joyce. Yet in responding to each of these touchstones, Heaney remains his own man and the maker of his own journey. In a 1990 lecture as Professor of Poetry at Oxford, Heaney roundly condemned Larkin's fear of death and dismissal of an afterlife as expressed in 'Aubade', passionately invoking the more upbeat Yeats who proclaimed the possibility of some continuance; if Heaney was being unfair to Larkin – which he was – it was in order to be fair to himself. Heaney also invoked Miłosz as a critic of Larkin and praised him for his continual seeking of metaphysical answers while also being aware that his own belief didn't match that of his Polish 'master'.[15]

The theme of the afterlife comes up again and again in Heaney's later poems as also in his essays and interviews, though that vision again and again too falls back to earth and the delights it offers. The continuing influence of Catholicism was acknowledged ever more even as he indicated his distance from its rituals and beliefs. By then, of course, the position of the Church had weakened so much in Ireland, as elsewhere, that it was hardly any longer necessary to proclaim one's separation from it. Indeed, for Heaney, the values it represented at its best –self-sacrifice, the service of others, a vision that extended beyond the confines of the here-and-now – seemed worthwhile and, in their way, laudable. In the end, however, Heaney affirmed the alternative Arnoldian faith in the power of poetry to comfort and enlighten us as we journey into the unknown. Some have criticized the metaphysical and practical adequacy of Heaney's conclusion, others his continuing belief in the unbelievable, but the poet himself thought that nothing more could be known, nothing less accepted.

Noli timere ('Do not be afraid'), Seamus Heaney's famous final text message in 2013, is the Latin version of a line from a poem on Miłosz as well as a likely reference to St Matthew's Gospel.[16] Heaney too had, as he said of Wilfred Owen in his Nobel Prize speech, 'a New Testament sensibility' (*OG* 417). It surprised hardly anyone, then – though it says something about a changed Ireland and a changed Irish Catholic Church – that the poet of *Station Island* was given a religious funeral. Enda McDonagh, a theologian and friend who partook in the services, wrote afterwards that while he wasn't 'arrogantly trying to gauge' Heaney's beliefs, they were something different from 'what we call explicit creedal faith'.[17] McDonagh's evaluation was infallibly true.

Notes

1 T.S. Eliot, *Collected Poems* (San Diego: Harcourt Brace Jovanovich, 1991), pp. 83, 200; Philip Larkin, *Collected Poems* (New York: Farrar, Straus and Giroux, 2003), p. 58.
2 Seamus Heaney, *Selected Poems 1988–2013* (New York: Farrar, Straus and Giroux, 2014); Dennis O'Driscoll, *Stepping Stones: Interviews with Seamus Heaney* (New York: Farrar, Straus and Giroux, 2008).
3 Robert Druce, 'A Raindrop on a Thorn', *Dutch Quarterly Review*, 9/1 (1979), 24-37; Karl Miller, *Seamus Heaney in Conversation with Karl Miller* (London: Between the Lines, 2000), p. 32.
4 Heaney, 'Bags of Enlightenment', *Guardian*, 25 October 2003, 4–6.
5 Seamus Heaney, *Opened Ground: Selected Poems 1966–1996* (New York: Farrar, Straus and Giroux, 1998).
6 See Gail McConnell's discussion of 'embraced' in her *Northern Irish Poetry and Theology* (New York: Palgrave Macmillan, 2014), p. 74.
7 See Richard Rankin Russell, *Seamus Heaney's Regions* (University of Notre Dame Press, 2014), p. 198.
8 Norman Tanner, S.J., *Vatican II: The Essential Texts* (New York: Image, 2012), pp. 324–5.
9 Seamus Heaney, *Preoccupations: Selected Prose 1968–1978* (New York: Farrar, Straus and Giroux, 1980).
10 See Michael Parker, *Seamus Heaney: The Making of the Poet* (Iowa City: University of Iowa Press, 1993), p. 120.
11 Seamus Heaney, *Field Work* (Farrar, Straus and Giroux, 1979); Helen Vendler, *Seamus Heaney* (Cambridge, MA: Harvard University Press, 1999), p. 62.
12 Seamus Heaney, 'Envies and Identifications: Dante and the Modern Poet', *Irish University Review*, 15/1 (Spring 1985), 5–19.
13 Seamus Heaney, draft of 'Station Island', Seamus Heaney Literary Papers, MS 49, 493/63 (folder 2), p. 51, National Library of Ireland.

14 Eamon Duffy, 'Seamus Heaney and Catholicism', in John Walker (ed.), *The Present Word: Culture, Society and the Site of Literature* (London: Legenda, 2013), p. 176. In addition to Duffy, Vendler, Parker, Russell and McConnell, see Daniel Tobin, Henry Hart, Michael Cavanagh, John F. Desmond, John Dennison, Peggy O'Brien and Andrew J. Auge for helpful discussions of Heaney's religious views. Also see Kieran Quinlan, *Seamus Heaney and the End of Catholic Ireland* (Washington, D.C.: Catholic University of America Press, 2020).

15 See Seamus Heaney, *The Redress of Poetry* (New York: Farrar, Straus and Giroux, 1995), 146–63.

16 *OG* 256; Matthew 28:10.

17 Enda McDonagh, 'The Word Made Flesh', *Tablet*, 7 September 2013, 13.

CHAPTER 20

Classical Roots

Florence Impens

In 'A Grand Tour', which he wrote to celebrate the award of the Cunningham Medal by the Royal Irish Academy to Seamus Heaney in 2008, Paul Muldoon sees in his elder the poet who had 'instruct[ed] us . . . to entertain Rasharkin as Rome, Toome as Tomis, / the Bann itself as the Bosphorus'.[1] The year before, Heaney had published 'Route 110', a rewriting of Book VI of Virgil's *Aeneid.* He had already reappropriated Virgil, as well as many other Latin and Greek writers, including Horace, Ovid, Aeschylus and Sophocles, but this, in many ways, was the culmination of his lifelong poetic engagement with the classics: it was in 2008, apart from two dramatic commissions, his longest classical piece to date, based on a work that had fascinated him since his teenage years. Sixteen years after the publication of his first adaptation of the same book in *Seeing Things* (1991), it stressed the importance that Virgil, and more generally, the classics, had assumed in the poet's career since the early 1990s.

Classical Presences from *Death of a Naturalist* to *Station Island*

Heaney was deeply familiar with Latin, which he had studied at school – at Anahorish, and St Columb's in Derry – and he had very fond memories of this education. It was during those years, for instance, that he had discovered Virgil, and the *Aeneid.*[2] But until the late 1980s, ancient Greece and Rome only sporadically resurfaced in his poetry, in the form of images and mythological narratives. Often, they represented for the poet a source of metaphors from which he could draw in his work, notably to help universalize a personal situation or memory, as is the case in 'The Underground' (*Station Island*, 1984).

Earlier, in the mid-1960s, however, Heaney had engaged on a deeper level with the classics, and defined his *ars poetica* with mythology in two poems, 'Personal Helicon' (*Death of a Naturalist*, 1966) and 'Antaeus', where he asserts the originality of his voice. Rewriting Greek myths, he had, like

Patrick Kavanagh in 'Epic' and in 'On Looking into E.V. Rieu's Homer', used classical material to increase the literary capital of his poetic project.

In 'Antaeus' (1966), the myth associated with the giant is retold in the form of a dramatic monologue. The son of Gaia, who derives his strength from contact with the soil, is defeated in Greek mythology by Hercules, when the latter cunningly holds him up in the air. But Heaney's poem does not focus on the famous fight and its dreaded outcome, celebrating instead the regenerative power of the earth. The giant 'cannot be weaned / Off the earth's long contours, her river-veins'; he is 'cradled in the dark that wombed [him] / And nurtured in every artery / Like a small hillock' (*N* 3). In those images, Heaney identified an echo of the earthiness of his poetic voice. As he told the audience at the Royal Hospital in Kilmainham, Dublin on 13 April 2009 on the occasion of his seventieth birthday: 'I identified with this earth man because I saw myself as something of an earth man ... I therefore regarded Antaeus as something of a guardian spirit, something who could sponsor whatever poetic gift I might have.'[3]

But the history of the poem's publication also reveals how Heaney, witnessing the onset of the 'Troubles', attempted at an early stage to use classical material for a different purpose, to reflect on the conflict and on Ireland's colonial past. 'Antaeus' was indeed only first published in *North*, nine years after its composition, along with another rewriting of the same myth, 'Hercules and Antaeus'. The poems share many phrases and images, suggesting that both were intimately connected in Heaney's imagination. But while 'Antaeus' celebrates the giant's strength, 'Hercules and Antaeus' focuses on their fight, and on the victory of the hero, who 'lifts his arms / in a remorseless V' (*N* 46). Two lines also suggest historical parallels with stories of colonial struggle ('Balor will die / and Byrthnoth and Sitting Bull'), inviting the reader to hear potential resonance with postcolonial Northern Ireland, and with the civil war that was well under way by the mid-1970s. Placed on either side of the first section of the collection containing Heaney's bog poems, both rewritings illustrate an apparent evolution in his work from poetic to historical readings of mythology under the pressure of contemporary events.

This early attempt to read the 'Troubles' with the classics was, however, a failed, or at least unconvincing, one. Criticized for his ambiguous use of mythology in the collection,[4] the poet soon thereafter insisted that both poems were to be read primarily as poetic rather than political allegories, and that the rootedness of his poetic voice 'is what [he] had in mind at the end of the first section of *North* in 'Hercules and Antaeus'.[5] Very reluctant to be seen to comment on the conflict, Heaney would thus leave the potential of Greek and Latin literatures to echo Northern Irish violence unexploited for another fifteen years, until the beginnings of the peace process, concentrating instead on the universalizing power of classical images to transform topical and local experiences.

Heaney's Classical Turn in the late 1980s

The classics remained a relatively discreet presence in Heaney's work until the late 1980s and early 1990s, when he successively started to rewrite Virgil and Sophocles, both of whom he would explore in greater depth over the following decades. This return to the classics was the result of a complex set of circumstances, and in part, a response to political and personal crises.

The poet's first rewriting of Virgil appeared in *Seeing Things* in 1991. Based on Book VI of the *Aeneid*, lines 98–148, it narrates the episode in which the Sibyl of Cumae details what Aeneas needs to do to gain access to the underworld, and meet the ghost of his father Anchises. Placed as an epigraph to the collection and echoing some of its poems, such as 'Man and Boy', the rewriting resonates as an allegory of the poet's attempt to reconnect in the volume with his father, who had died in 1986. Like Michael Longley with Homer around the same time, Virgil 'gave [Heaney] a new emotional and psychological vocabulary',[6] helping him to address personal grief in his work.

Of course, Virgil was not a 'new' figure for Heaney – he had first appeared in his poetry in the late 1970s as Dante's guide from *The Divine Comedy*, and as a model for the poet in troubled times.[7] But Heaney's relationship with his literary predecessor had changed. From a character in a medieval epic illustrating Dante's Catholic worldview, he had by the late 1980s fully emerged as the classical author of the *Aeneid*.

This transition from a Dantean to a classical Virgil, as well as from a figurative to a textual approach, can in part be explained by the poet's re-engagement with classical literatures while at Harvard in the mid to late 1980s, where under the influence of Robert Fitzgerald, he 'reacquaint[ed himself] with the material' (*SS* 293). His eclectic readings of that period would certainly be reflected in the multiplication and variety of classical allusions in *The Haw Lantern* (1987).[8] It also coincided, on a deeper level, with a moment in Heaney's life when he experienced a crisis of religious faith.[9] At a time of family deaths and personal doubts as to his religious beliefs, Heaney rediscovered the other cultural paradigm he knew best, in an attempt to structure a difficult experience into words. As Helen Vendler writes in 'Seamus Heaney and the Classical Past', the poet 'in his adolescent reading of the *Aeneid*, [had] found a compelling poetic account of pre-Christian myth that would counter the Christian narratives of his Catholic upbringing'.[10] In the late 1980s, Heaney returned to Virgil's epic as an alternative to the Catholic description of the underworld, which enabled him to address his personal grief outside a religious framework. In Book VI, he found a text that could provide solace in the evocation of an imaginative contact with his father and in its promise of life after death, but that was also, and crucially so, secular.

If Heaney's rediscovery of Virgil was motivated by personal and poetic reasons, it also concurred with a moment in Irish literary history when many artists began assiduously to adapt classical texts, notably for the stage, indirectly spurring even further the poet's engagement with similar material.[11] His first version of Sophocles, *The Cure at Troy* (1990), is thus the result of a commission from Brian Friel, on behalf of the Field Day Theatre Company, who suggested he contribute a new *Philoctetes* to their programme. Like 'The Golden Bough', *The Cure at Troy* would prove a crucial adaptation for Heaney, enabling him to revisit the potential of the classics to echo history, and providing an imaginative distance from which to address contemporary violence.

Field Day had already staged a Greek tragedy: Tom Paulin's version of *Antigone*, *The Riot Act*, in 1984. In Paulin's play, parallels with the Northern Irish conflict are rife, from the title to Creon's speech, who, to quote the author, is a 'kind of puritan gangster, a megalomaniac who speaks alternatively in an English public school voice and a deep menacing Ulster growl'.[12] As suggested by this description, Paulin's is a political adaptation, displaying his nationalist sympathies.

The choice of *Philoctetes* was markedly different. The play revolves around the efforts by Neoptolemus and Odysseus to regain the trust of Philoctetes, whom they have previously betrayed and abandoned on Lemnos. As such, it echoed particularly well the growing need for compromise in Northern Ireland on the eve of the peace process, making it a very attractive text for Field Day. Heaney's version of the play emphasizes this need for compromise and sidelines the darker motives that lead the Greeks back to the island, and the prospect of their return to war. It is also framed by two new choruses that invite explicit parallels with the Northern Irish situation. While Paulin's *The Riot Act* mirrored the dichotomy of Northern Irish society, *The Cure at Troy* is a play with a message of hope for its audience, which highlights the notion of forgiveness and the possibility of reconciliation. This message was received to great acclaim, and the line 'and hope and history rhyme'[13] from the second chorus has since been quoted many times by politicians and public figures, including Gerry Adams, Mary Robinson, and Bill Clinton.

On a visit to Derry on 30 November 1995, a little over a year after the ceasefire, the latter for instance famously used the play in his speech to promote a vision of a peaceful and prosperous Northern Irish province. First quoting the second chorus, Clinton concluded:

> Well, my friends, I believe. I believe we live in a time of hope and history rhyming. Standing here in front of the Guild Hall, looking out over these historic walls, I see a peaceful city, a safe city, a hopeful city, full of young people that should have a peaceful and prosperous future here where their roots and families are. That is what I see today with you.[14]

By all accounts, *The Cure at Troy* had become closely associated with the peace process and chimed with public discourse.

The Classics and History after *The Cure at Troy*

Heaney continued to explore the potential of the classics and Greek drama to address contemporary conflicts in the following years. But after *The Cure at Troy,* which, with its message of reconciliation, contributed to the public dialogue on the peace process, his next such classical rewriting, 'Mycenae Lookout' (*The Spirit Level,* 1996), comes as a surprise, as a delayed reaction to the violence of the 'Troubles'. Its 'impulse', Heaney explains, 'was to give a snarl rather than sing a hymn . . . It wasn't a matter of what was happening just then, more a rage at what had gone on in the previous twenty-five years' (*SS* 349).

Heaney, after the first performances of *The Cure at Troy*, had come to the conclusion that the extra choruses framing the play in a Northern Irish context were too explicit, and that to impose such clear interpretative guidelines was 'almost like patronizing the audience' (*SS* 421). His play had been a success, but it had also, arguably, been instrumentalized for political purposes. In that perspective, 'Mycenae Lookout' resonates as the poet's attempt to reclaim his artistic freedom, and to denounce the idea that Northern Irish writers had a public responsibility to condemn the 'Troubles', and now that the peace process seemed to be underway, to celebrate the latter.

Daringly rewriting Aeschylus' *Agamemnon* in five poems, 'Mycenae Lookout' focuses on the passive participants in the Trojan War, allowing alternative voices to be heard. In the Watchman, Heaney found an image mirroring the position of the poet, as a helpless witness of violence. In 'Cassandra', he 'allowed a violence of language that he had for years restrained in himself so as not to feed the hatreds in the North',[15] and whose explicitness, in phrases such as 'camp-fucked' (*SL* 31), 'to do it to her / there and then', 'cunt' (32) and 'they nearly rode each other' (35), has no equivalent elsewhere in his work. Despite concluding with 'His Reverie of Water' and its hint of reconciliation, the sequence, overall, challenges the reader and tears apart the official and self-congratulatory narrative of the peace process. A cathartic experiment, 'Mycenae Lookout' was also a reaction to the pressure that had weighed on Heaney and his contemporaries to make public pronouncements that betrayed the private nature of their art.

By the time the sequence was published, Heaney had indeed become a poet of truly international reputation, and an involuntary spokesperson for Irish writers, having won the Nobel Prize for literature in 1995. When a few years later, in 2003, the Abbey Theatre in Dublin was putting in place their Centenary programme, he would thus be called upon to contribute, as one of the most famous living Irish writers. Asked whether he would write a new *Antigone*, Heaney first hesitated, unsure of what his version would add to an already long list of adaptations.[16] This as well was a commission with a highly public visibility.

What triggered the reappropriation was Heaney's sense of the play's echo with recent and ongoing conflicts in Ireland *and* abroad, illustrating the poet's growing awareness of his global reputation.[17] Sophocles' tragedy resonated locally with the hunger strikes of the early 1980s and, on the global stage, with the American war in Iraq at the start of the twenty-first century.[18] But unlike *The Cure at Troy*, *The Burial at Thebes* (2004) does not establish direct parallels with the contemporary world, which only discreetly resurfaces in the choice of certain phrases and metres. While there is 'at least one Bushism, where [Creon] says of subversive elements, "I'll flush'em out"' (*SS* 423), echoes with Northern Ireland are even more subdued, transposed into the rhythmic patterns chosen for some of the characters. As Heaney explains in his notes to the American edition of the play, the 'three-beat line' of the first dialogue between Antigone and Ismene was inspired by the eighteenth-century *Caoineadh Airt Uí Laoghaire*, and its echo of Antigone's situation at the outset. In contrast, the Chorus and Creon are associated with the English poetic tradition: the former, with 'the four-beat, alliterating, Old English line', and the latter, with the 'traditional iambic pentameter'.[19]

With *The Burial at Thebes*, Heaney composed a multi-layered text. Combining two sets of references, the play was not written as a response to any *one* situation, and remains open to interpretations in multiple settings. Under the direction of Lorraine Pintal in Dublin in 2004, it was made to echo South America. In its revival at the Abbey in 2008 by Patrick Mason, World War Two became the main subtext, while a year later, at 'Writers for Peace', an event organized in Dublin in January by Poetry Ireland, Trócaire and

Amnesty International, the 'among the many wonders' chorus became Heaney's response to the Israeli invasion of Gaza. With *The Burial at Thebes*, Heaney had written a modern version of *Antigone* for the globalized world, which as part of the Abbey celebration successfully illustrated the strong position Irish literature held on the world stage.

Virgil in the Late Heaney

If Heaney participated in the revival of Greek drama in Ireland at the turn of the twenty-first century, in his more private work, however, he remained most fascinated by Virgil, with whom he increasingly identified.[20] The Latin poet provided him over the years not only with a secular representation of the underworld, but also with the model of a writer who too 'had known the brutality of war'.[21] Part of the Latin poet's attraction lay in what Heaney saw as his successful combination of intertextuality and contemporaneity, which allowed him to address historical circumstances while remaining true to the literary nature of his art.

Reappropriating the *Eclogues* in *Electric Light* (2001), Heaney updated the form to reflect both contemporary Ireland and its own literary history. While 'Virgil: Eclogue IX' retains a strong classical dimension, and 'Bann Valley Eclogue' casts the poet as learning the trade in a step-by-step transposition of the Fourth Eclogue into an Irish context, 'Glanmore Eclogue' emulates the qualities Heaney praised in Virgil. On the one hand, it abounds with allusions to the Heaneys' move to County Wicklow, as well as to the rapid transformation of rural Ireland over the last hundred years in Myles's speech. On the other, it is also a palimpsest that reworks pastoral conventions through multiple references to English and Irish literatures. The 'stranger on a wild night, *out in the rain falling*' (*EL* 36) is a figure directly taken from Act I, Scene 1 of J.M. Synge's *In the Shadow of the Glen* (1903). The song, a convention of the pastoral, is reminiscent of the Middle English poem 'The Cuckoo Song', and the name of 'Augusta', most obviously a reworking of Augustus, indirectly refers to Ann Saddlemyer, who introduced the Heaneys to the region, at the same time as it unmistakably recalls Lady Gregory. Combining references to Heaney's English and Irish literary heritage with historical references relevant to his own circumstances, 'Glanmore Eclogue' reproduces Virgil's achievement in the twenty-first century, as the poet who, as Heaney noted in 'Eclogues in Extremis' (2002), had 'in spite of the literary nature of the performance', successfully maintained 'the covenant with life and the times' in his own work.[22]

This delicate balance between the literary and the extralinguistic is at the heart of Heaney's Virgilian poems in *The Riverbank Field* (2007), which inspired Muldoon with the lines quoted at the beginning of this essay. After a step-by-step transposition of *Aeneid* VI, lines 704–15 and 748–51 in the version that gives its title to the volume published by the Gallery Press,[23] which gradually rewrites the underworld into County Derry, 'Route 110' over twelve sections develops the motif of Aeneas's journey among the dead as one in time and memory. Inviting the reader to establish correspondences between each section and episodes of Aeneas's adventures, the poem reads like an overview of personal and political contemporary history under the guise of a classical rewriting, and makes us travel first in the landscapes of the poet's childhood and adolescence, through to the 'Troubles', and finally towards a brighter future with the birth of his granddaughter Anna Rose.[24] A compelling long poem in which Heaney emulates a poet and text he had first encountered at school, and rediscovered in his adult life, 'Route 110' has since been accompanied with a version of the whole book, which Heaney was finishing at the time of his sudden death in the summer of 2013. Published posthumously by Faber in 2016, *Aeneid VI* illustrates yet again the depth of the poet's imaginative relationship with the classics, fifty years after the early 'Personal Helicon'.

The Riverbank Field and *Aeneid VI* are essential poems in Seamus Heaney's oeuvre, and mark the culmination of a sustained creative engagement with classical material that had been part of his imagination from a young age, and resurfaced in his work at a time of personal and political crises. The classics, and Virgil in particular, appealed to the poet for their ability to transcend cultural and religious differences. As secular narratives as well as texts belonging to both the Irish and English literary traditions, they powerfully resonated in the Ireland of the peace process, enabling the poet, who belonged to 'the last generation that learned Latin, that read Virgil, that knew about the descent into the underworld' (*SS* 295), to address in his work the complex transition of the island towards a more secular and inclusive definition of its identity.

Notes

1 Paul Muldoon, 'A Grand Tour', in Seamus Heaney, *Articulations: Poetry, Philosophy and the Shaping of Culture* (Dublin: Royal Irish Academy, 2008), p. 1.

2 On the other hand, Heaney never learnt Greek. For details about Heaney's classical education, see *SS* 295.

3 'Arts Show Special', with Seamus Heaney, narrated by Seán Rocks, RTÉ Radio One, 13 April 2009.
4 See, for instance, Ciaran Carson, 'Escaped from the Massacre?', *Honest Ulsterman*, 50 (Winter 1975), 183–6.
5 John Haffenden, *Viewpoints: Poets in Conversation with John Haffenden* (London: Faber and Faber, 1981), p. 69.
6 Peter McDonald, 'An Interview with Michael Longley, "Au Revoir, Oeuvre"', *Thumbscrew*, 12 (Winter 1998/9), 5–14 (at p. 10).
7 For more information on Heaney's Virgils, and the evolution of Virgilian presences in his oeuvre, see Florence Impens, '"Here are the words you'll have to find a place for": Virgilian Presences in the Work of Seamus Heaney', *Irish University Review* 47/2 (Autumn 2017), 251–65.
8 For more information on classical presences in the collection, see John Dillon, 'Classical Allusions in Seamus Heaney's *The Haw Lantern*', *Classics Ireland*, 2 (1995), 55–66.
9 See *SS* 287.
10 Helen Vendler, 'Seamus Heaney and the Classical Past', in Seamus Heaney, *Stone from Delphi: Poems with Classical References* (San Francisco: Arion Press, 2012), pp. 8–25 (at p. 10).
11 See Marianne McDonald, 'Seamus Heaney's *Cure at Troy*: Politics and Poetry', *Classics Ireland*, 3 (1996), 129–40 (at p. 129), where she counts ten new versions of Greek tragedy by Irish poets between 1984 and 1996.
12 Tom Paulin, 'Antigone', in Marianne McDonald and J. Michael Walton (eds.), *Amid Our Troubles: Irish Versions of Greek Tragedy* (London: Methuen, 2002), p. 167.
13 Seamus Heaney, *The Cure at Troy* (London: Faber and Faber, 1990), p. 77.
14 Bill Clinton, 'Remarks by the President to the Citizens of Londonderry', 30 November 1995, http://cain.ulst.ac.uk/events/peace/docs/pres2.htm.
15 Helen Vendler, 'Seamus Heaney and the Classical Past', p. 21. See also Helen Vendler, 'Seamus Heaney and the Oresteia: "Mycenae Lookout" and the Usefulness of Tradition', *Proceedings of the American Philosophical Society* 143/1 (March 1999), 116–29.
16 See Seamus Heaney, 'Title Deeds: Translating a Classic', *Proceedings of the American Philosophical Society*, 148/4 (December 2004), 411–26 (at p. 415).
17 A few years earlier, Heaney had already addressed a historical event of global significance, when he rewrote Horace's *Ode* 1.34 in response to 9/11. The poem, 'Horace and the Thunder', was first published in the *Irish Times* on 17 November 2001, before being reprinted as 'Anything Can Happen' in *District and Circle* (2006).
18 For more details on Heaney's sense of the historical relevance of the play, see Heaney, 'Title Deeds', p. 412; and Seamus Heaney, 'A Note on *The Burial at Thebes*', *The Burial at Thebes* (New York: Farrar, Straus and Giroux, 2004), p. 76.
19 Heaney, 'Note on *The Burial at Thebes*', pp. 78–9.

20 Like many other poets, including Michael Longley, Heaney was also inspired by a commission for the anthology *After Ovid: New Metamorphoses*, edited by J. Lasdun and M. Hofmann (1996), to develop his engagement with Ovid, resulting in *The Midnight Verdict* (1995), a combined adaptation of the tale of Orpheus and of Brian Merriman's poem, *The Midnight Court*.

21 Gerald Dawe, interview with Seamus Heaney, *The Poetry Programme*, RTÉ Radio One, 31 January 2009.

22 Seamus Heaney, 'Eclogues in Extremis: On the Staying Power of the Pastoral', *Proceedings of the Royal Irish Academy*, 103C/1 (2003), 1–12 (at p. 3).

23 The Virgilian sequence was later reprinted with minor revisions in *Human Chain* (2010).

24 For a detailed analysis of the poem, see Michael Parker, 'Back in the Heartland: Seamus Heaney's 'Route 110' sequence in *Human Chain*', *Irish Studies Review*, 21/4 (2013), 374–86.

CHAPTER 21

Politics

Jonathan Allison

Seamus Heaney once described himself as 'Jungian in religion, and torpid in politics'.[1] In torpidity there is perhaps an element of self-protection for the artist and his art, and Heaney had his fair share of suspicion of what he called 'a national theme' as well as 'the caution that came upon us in the late 1960s, early 1970s because of the collusion between high national rhetoric and possibly low, dangerous activities – the IRA and so on'.[2] The quarrel within himself between poetry and politics, between writing and political commitment was a dominant theme of his writing throughout his life. In 'Terminus' he wrote: 'Two buckets were easier carried than one. / I grew up in between' (*OG* 272). He came to regard being culturally and even geographically 'in-between' as a formative influence: 'I grew up between the predominantly Protestant and loyalist village of Castledawson and the generally catholic and nationalist district of Bellaghy' (*FK* 50). Once portrayed by the *Sunday Times* as 'an accomplished tightrope walker' and an equilibrist who 'has balanced the burdens and benefits of two cultures, Celtic and Anglo-Saxon',[3] he later claimed the poet in Northern Ireland, often torn between solitude and solidarity, is 'stretched between politics and transcendence' (*FK* 119). Clearly, the relationship between Heaney's writing and his politics is complex but insistent.

Although raised in a Catholic, nationalist family his parents were not politically active and were constitutional nationalists rather than Republicans.[4] He once characterized two kinds of Catholic households in the North of his youth, the 'papish' and the Republican. The latter implied support for the physical force tradition of Irish separatism associated with Sinn Fein and the IRA. The former implied support for reform through parliamentary means, associated with the Nationalist Party, later the SDLP: 'Our house fell into the papish rather than the Republican class. I never had any hint of blistering Republican dogma. For example, I knew very little about 1916.'[5] When he sang rebel songs, they did not commemorate the Easter Rising but the 1798 rebellion which he would later invoke in poems like 'Requiem for the Croppies' and the verse play *Munro*.[6]

It's too obvious to need emphasis, but Heaney, like everyone else of his generation in Northern Ireland, was from an early age alert to social, political and sectarian difference. His family was on good terms with Protestant neighbours, although he regarded families with links to the B-Specials as 'beyond the pale' (*SS* 18.) Growing up as a member of the Catholic or nationalist minority in predominantly Protestant or unionist Ulster, this sense of a divided world was acute, and it pervades his work. Sectarian difference is discussed in several autobiographical sketches, and portrayed in many poems such as 'Docker' (*DN*), 'The Other Side' (*WO*), 'An Ulster Twilight' (*SI*) and 'The Nod' (*DC*).

As a student at Queen's, he wasn't politically engaged, and in retrospect wonders how anyone could have been – 'I don't know how you'd have gone about it then' (*SS* 44). However, he acknowledges there was clearly 'a political colouring' to cultural activities such as Ceilidhs or Irish-language plays organized by An Cumann Gaelach (the Irish Language Society at Queen's) and travel to the Donegal Gaeltacht, although generally he feels his pre-Troubles generation at that time lived 'under the guardian angel of passivity' (*SS* 44).[7] Nevertheless, he recognized within himself a broadly 'anti-Partitionist stance', and although he felt within himself a 'them-and-us attitude' towards Unionist culture, he was resigned to the sense that 'the whole gerrymandered life of the place was set to continue' (*SS* 65–6.) He would later take the view that being called 'Seamus' was 'a badge of honour' and 'if it entailed provocation for the Unionists, well too bad' (*SS* 29). In his poem 'Singing School' he describes harassment by members of the Royal Ulster Constabulary, taunting him because of his name, concluding that 'all around us, though / We hadn't named it, the ministry of fear' (*OG* 128). This sense of menace informs many of his most memorable poems about the Troubles in the 1970s, although he was initially reluctant to address politics as a major theme, and worked to avoid becoming a political spokesman. When he began writing in earnest, that underground tension started to emerge, and 'once a literary aspiration developed, it took account of the hurtful conditions' (*SS* 65).

He first wrote seriously about those conditions in a sketch commissioned by the *New Statesman* in 1966, where he warns that 'the atmosphere of the Troubles has been growing'.[8] Written just after publication of *Death of a Naturalist* and with a new job as lecturer at Queen's University beginning in October, this was an eventful time for Heaney and for the province. Nelson's pillar had been bombed in Dublin in

March, followed by the Easter Rising anniversary celebrations in April and rising loyalist violence in Belfast. In describing the urban landscape of Belfast, Heaney points out that many local names such as Falls and Malone Roads are 'anglicized forms of Gaelic names, indicative of former pastoral conditions'. Giving a nod to Patrick Kavanagh's distinction between provincialism and parochialism, Heaney depicts Unionism, with its emphasis on the relationship with Britain, as a form of cultural provincialism and dependency, and warns of the nationalist confidence that 'we'll outbreed them in the end'. He describes the imminent arrival of the Queen to open the new Queen's Bridge, and mentions the annual marching season and the build-up to the Twelfth. He portrays Ian Paisley, founder of the Free Presbyterian Church and future leader of the Democratic Unionist Party as one who 'resents toleration, ecumenism and, it seems, a quiet life. Riots and rallies are what he thrives on', and he predicts that his movement may 'set the political and religious question back 40 years'. Presciently, he notes the possibility of 'an explosion', and he speculates on the effects of political unrest on the cultural life of Belfast, which he supposes 'might concentrate a man's energies on the immediate dramatic complex of tension and intrigue'. Clearly, the divisions he sees around him will become crucial to his own work.

In a 1968 article for the *Listener*, 'Old Derry's Walls', he gave an account of the confrontation between civil rights demonstrators and the Royal Ulster Constabulary in Derry-Londonderry on 5 October 1968.[9] His tone is markedly different, for the predicted 'explosion' has come to pass, and he speaks of the 'grievances of the Catholic majority: unemployment, lack of housing, discrimination in jobs and gerrymandering in electoral affairs'. He predicts that attitudes must change, and 'will have to risk the charge of wrecking the new moderation and seek justice more vociferously'. Catholic attitudes have hardened and 'there are many shattered ivory towers among educated and articulate people who had opted out of political affairs from embarrassment or disillusion'. Clearly, Heaney's political commitment has sharpened. As it turns out, he did not attend many marches, but he has the rare distinction of having retorted 'calm down' to Bernadette Devlin as she rushed towards a police cordon.[10]

A month later, he published an article in *Hibernia* on John Hume, then a civil rights leader in Derry, praising his intelligence, tolerance and 'sympathy for his opponent'.[11] He notes the politician's understanding of local people: 'His understanding of the community is his understanding of himself. His ambition to set Derry's house in order is altruistic and whole because it is obviously the extension of an inner achievement of tolerance and concern.' He links Hume's authority to his 'self-knowledge' and he makes him sound a little like the writer Heaney wanted to become. When the Troubles began, Heaney decided (he later recalled) that his writing must address the growing storm: 'From that moment the problems of poetry moved from being simply a matter of achieving the satisfactory verbal icon to being a search for images and symbols adequate to our predicament' (*FK* 23–4). The term 'verbal icon' is taken from W.K. Wimsatt's influential critical study of 1954, now seen by Heaney as superannuated in terms of what critics might expect of poets, and what poets might expect of themselves. He suggests that his new images will take the form of 'emblems of adversity' – Yeats's phrase from 'Meditations in Time of Civil War' – to suggest a wartime poetic.

One source of emblems was to be found in the landscape itself. In 'Bogland', Heaney attempted to suggest the history of the landscape as an emblem for national history, to construct a myth of national memory, and to 'make the preserving, shifting marshes of Ireland a mythical landscape, a symbol of the preserving, shifting consciousness of the Irish people. History is the soft ground that holds and invites us into itself, century after century.'[12] The speaker contrasts the expansive American west with the limited horizons of Ireland where our 'pioneers' are archaeologists (or poets), not frontiersmen. Due to continuous settlement, 'Every layer they strip / Seems camped on before', and although the ground seems unstable ('the wet centre is bottomless') the bogland is a storehouse of memory. The portrayal of the land as layered, with a historical human settlement, perhaps offers consolation at a time when the landscape of Northern Ireland during the Troubles (which nobody guessed would last thirty years) was increasingly becoming contested terrain.

This metaphor of bogland was later developed in 'The Tollund Man' and other poems, based on imagery suggested by a reading of *The Bog People*, an illustrated archaeological study of exhumed corpses from Scandinavian bogland.[13] Later he would write, 'The unforgettable photographs of these victims blended in my mind with photographs of atrocity, past and present, in the long rites of Irish political and religious struggles' (*P* 57–8). In 'The Tollund Man', the speaker vows to visit Aarhus to see the preserved corpse which resembles 'a saint's kept body'. He identifies with the doomed man who will be sacrificed to the goddess, as he travels to his place of execution, with a 'sad freedom'. The speaker finally declares, 'I will feel lost, / Unhappy and at home' in Jutland's 'man-killing parishes'. That phrase, combining the religious, the parochial and the murderous, links the Iron Age sacrifice to murder victims in Northern Ireland at the time of writing, and the poem attempts to bring past and present atrocities together. In 'Punishment', Heaney concludes with the chilling observation that if he had been a contemporary of the murdered girl he too would have ostracized her, as everyone else did, and 'cast the stones of silence'. It's a moment of self-recognition and confession. He castigates himself as an 'artful voyeur' of the girl's exposed body, even as he recognizes that he failed to stop the paramilitary punishment of her 'betraying sisters' in Northern Ireland, tarred and feathered for fraternizing with British troops. He confesses that he might 'connive with civilized outrage', but nonetheless understands the tribal revenge. Some critics argued that this meant he supported IRA violence, although Blake Morrison explained that it merely showed 'his instinctive understanding of the laws and needs of the tribe'.[14] Nonetheless, it is a moment in the poems which perhaps prompted Charles Moore later to remark, soon after Heaney's death, that he was somehow culpable for never condemning the IRA outright.[15]

These Iron Age/Troubles poems might be called mythic method poems in their attempt to align contemporaneity with ancient patterns, but Heaney wrote various types of political poetry, including ballads ('Craig's Dragoons', 'The Road to Derry'), historical poems ('For the Commander of the Eliza', 'Requiem for the Croppies'), language and place name poems ('Broagh', 'Anahorish'), allegorical poems ('Act of Union'), parable poems ('From the Canton of Expectation', 'The Mud Vision') and elegies for murder victims, including John Lavery, Louis O'Neill, Sean Armstrong, Colum McCartney and William Strathearn.[16] Various poems fall in other categories, including ghost poems ('Station Island'), or the choric poem in *The Cure at Troy*, the now famous 'Human Beings suffer', quoted widely by many politicians to convey the aspirations for peace in Northern Ireland and elsewhere. A moving and defiant poem of place, 'The Toome Road', concludes with the dramatic image of the untoppled *omphalos*, representing the poet's townland, suggesting the defiance of the nationalist community of South Derry: 'O charioteers, above your dormant guns, / It stands here still, stands vibrant as you pass, / The invisible, untoppled omphalos' (*FW* 15).[17]

In an early essay, Heaney associated the *omphalos*, the navel of the world, with the 'water pump outside our back door', which supplied water to five local households (*P* 17). Through what novelist Brian Moore called Heaney's 'omphaloskeptic vision'[18] the poet contrasted this invincible water pump as a symbol of permanence in wartime with the transient American troops stationed nearby: 'but all of that great historical action does not disturb the rhythms of the yard'. However, in 'The Toome Road' the troops are British, not American, which conveys a different political significance, as they patrol his townland in armoured cars (Saracen APCs, or 'pigs' as locally known):

> All camouflaged with broken alder branches,
> And headphoned soldiers standing up in turrets.
> How long were they approaching down my roads
> As if they owned them?

We note the jarring contrast between 'broken alder branches' and 'headphoned soldiers' and the proprietary tone of 'my roads'. He expresses solidarity with the locals, those 'Sowers of seed, erectors of headstones', people associated with the cycles of growth and death. Heaney later recalled his aggravation at such patrols: 'There was an affront to *dúchas* in being questioned about my name and address by these uninformed cubs in uniform at the end of my own loaning' (*SS* 212). The *omphalos* represents a sense of place and an alternative authority linked to a nationalist argument. This is one of his most defiant poems of the period, notably different from his elegies and from the bog poems of the early 1970s.

Again, although Heaney was willing to speak out on occasion, to declare that 'my passport's green', he was often wary of being co-opted by a political argument or a one-sided opinion.[19] The poem must emerge from the self, and from personal feelings. It must not be a mere vehicle for ideas. His best political poems are shaped by the power of his deepest emotions. In an essay on Mandelstam he warned that 'the idea of poetry as an art is in danger of being overshadowed by a quest for poetry as a diagram of political attitudes' (*P* 219). He would balk at the very idea of writing 'political poetry' and told Karl Miller 'your presence as a poet, and your voice within the polis, is a political effect'.[20] When he meets the ghost of Joyce in 'Station Island', the shade urges him to reject 'that subject people stuff', since 'You lose more of yourself than you redeem / doing the decent thing' (*SI* 93). In a later poem, 'The Flight Path', the speaker responds to a senior figure in the IRA who asks when will he write 'Something for us?' He replies: 'If I do write something, / Whatever it is, I'll be writing for myself' (*SL* 25). (He later recalled, 'I simply rebelled at being commanded. If anybody was going to pull rank, it wasn't going to be a party spokesman' (*SS* 257–8.) In a poem of 2011, he describes three delusions which the King of the world presented to Buddha: 'After the first of desire / And the second, terror of death, / That of social obligation'.[21] In each case here, what is paramount is the artist's freedom to refuse an obligation, political or social, to follow his own lights, to assert freedom of the will and personal agency.

In summer 1994, Heaney and his wife returned to Denmark and visited the site where Tollund Man had been exhumed. Their visit coincided with the historic IRA ceasefire, announced on Wednesday 31 August. In the poem 'Tollund', written in the immediate aftermath of that announcement, there are various echoes of the 1972 poem, as for example, 'We stood a long time out in Tollund Moss', a clear echo of his earlier vow that he would 'stand a long time' at Tollund. The poem's conclusion is radiant with hope for a better future, delivered with an off-the-cuff colloquial ease ('unfazed', 'make a go of it', 'not bad'.) They were like ghosts 'who'd walked abroad': 'Unfazed by light, to make a new beginning / And make a go of it, alive and sinning, / Ourselves again, free-willed again, not bad'. It is now possible to explore new possibilities for Northern Ireland and Ireland. Embracing his sinning self, he declares they are themselves again, returned to free will, as opposed to the 'sad freedom' of the doomed Tollund Man, or the restricted-choice determinism of the Troubles, when identities were reduced to sectarian roles shaped by background and affiliation: 'Like Shakespeare's Richard II, we were tempted by the bright air to believe that we were ourselves again, recovered from a time when we had been less than ourselves.'[22]

Despite Heaney's caution about political obligations, he was a supporter of causes upholding artistic freedom and social justice, and he signed the declaration of support for Salman Rushdie in 1989 after Ayatollah Khomeini had issued a death sentence against him.[23] In 1985, a local branch of Amnesty International asked Heaney to write something to mark International Human Rights Day. Initially he refused, but later wrote 'From the Republic of Conscience', published as a pamphlet. He later expounded his theory of 'the redress of poetry' in an article to mark the sixtieth anniversary of the UN Declaration of Human Rights (*Irish Times*, 15 March, 2008.) In 2013 he made a rare intervention in the ongoing debate about displaying the Union Jack on public buildings in Northern Ireland. Recalling the words of nationalist politician Eddie McAteer, who urged that both sides in Northern Ireland were 'entitled to their pageantry', Heaney remarked: 'There's never going to be a united Ireland. So why don't you let them fly the flag?'[24] After the terrorist attacks on New York and Washington on 9/11, he published a poem with Amnesty International, 'Anything Can Happen', based on an ode by Horace:[25]

> Anything can happen. You know how Jupiter
> Will mostly wait for clouds to gather head
> Before he hurls the lightning? Well, just now
> He galloped his thunder cart and his horses
>
> Across a clear blue sky. It shook the earth . . .

The poem laments the effects of violence, while also conveying a sense of awe in the face of Jupiter's overwhelming power. The language of the poem, with its bold, simple diction and clusters of active verbs ('galloped', 'shook', 'overturned', 'daunted') suggests the god's might, before which human agency seems frail. The poem presents a relentless series of images of violence falling from the sky. By drawing upon ancient myth, Heaney suggests an interpretive framework in which violence is linked to some of the oldest accounts of divine intervention in our literature. However, if out of elegy some counterforce arises, here it is the voice of the storyteller (using informal phrases like 'You know how' and 'Well, just now') who tries to provide narrative order in the face of tragedy.

In the later poetry, you hear the tones of pity and compassion for the dead, including those who have suffered from political systems, as in 'Route 110' where he meditates on the 'bodies / Unglorified' of men killed by bombs and bullets, brushed into plastic bags, or reduced to bits: 'And what in the end was there left to bury / Of Mr. Lavery, blown up in his own pub / As he bore the primed device and bears it still . . .' (*HC* 55). He 'bears it still' because he lives in a limbo of repetition, like some purgatorial modernist drama, or maybe it's the imagination of the author himself, for whom the memory is on a perpetual loop. He remembers Louis O'Neill, elegized in the poem 'Casualty', and the thirteen dead men, none of whom have military or paramilitary burials presided over by 'units drilled and spruce and unreconciled'. The poem is a lament for the dead and for their unceremonious departures, and in the context the unreconciled ones appear to lack the qualities which the poet has put into his poetry. After the 1994 ceasefire, Heaney wrote about Václav Havel's concept of hope, and this kind of hope somehow runs throughout all of Heaney's political writing: 'It is not the expectation that things will turn out successfully but the conviction that something is worth working for, however it turns out. Its deepest roots are in the transcendental, beyond the horizon' (*FK* 47).

Notes

1 James Randall, 'Interview with Seamus Heaney', *Ploughshares*, 18 (Fall 1979).
2 'A Soul on the Washing Line: An Interview', *Economist*, 22 June 1991; repr. 5 September, 2013).
3 'Portrait of a Poet', *Sunday Times*, 14 May 1989, A14.
4 'Neither my father nor my mother was actively republican' (*SS* 28). Cf. 'I'd be better described as coming from the "constitutional nationalist" tradition', from *Seamus Heaney in Conversation with Karl Miller* (London: Between the Lines, 2000), pp. 51–2.

5 Monie Begley, *Rambles in Ireland, and a County by County Guide* (Old Greenwich, CT: Devin Adair, 1977), p. 161.
6 Seamus Heaney, 'Munro', *Everyman: An Annual Religio-Cultural Review*, 3 (1970), 58–65.
7 The reference is to 'From the Canton of Expectation' (*OG* 296).
8 Seamus Heaney, 'Out of London: Ulster's Troubles', *New Statesman*, 1 July 1966, 23–4.
9 Seamus Heaney, 'Old Derry's Walls', *Listener*, 24 October 1968, 521–3.
10 He attended a civil rights march in Belfast the following week (Wednesday, 9 October) when he intervened to say 'calm down' to Bernadette Devlin and Michael Farrell, who were intent on crashing the barriers: 'I was being as mollifying as I could be.' Mark Carruthers, *Alternative Ulsters: Conversations on Identity* (Dublin: Liberties Press, 2013; repr. *Belfast Telegraph*, 28 October 2013).
11 Seamus Heaney, 'John Hume's Derry', *Hibernia*, 21 November 1968.
12 Seamus Heaney, 'Bogland', in James Gibson (ed.), *Let the Poet Choose* (London: Harrap, 1973), p. 72.
13 P.V. Glob, *The Bog People: Iron-Age Man Preserved*, trans. Rupert Bruce-Mitford (London: Faber and Faber, 1969).
14 Blake Morrison, *Seamus Heaney* (London: Methuen, 1982), p. 64.
15 Charles Moore, '"Sly" Seamus Heaney Failed to Condemn Terrorists', *Daily Telegraph*, 6 September 2013, www.telegraph.co.uk/news/celebritynews/10289455/Sly-Seamus-Heaney-failed-to-condemn-terrorists-says-Charles-Moore.html.
16 John Lavery was killed in 1971, while carrying an IRA bomb out of his own pub in Belfast; Louis O'Neill died in a bombing in Co. Tyrone in 1972; Sean Armstrong, peace worker, was murdered in Belfast in 1973; Colum McCartney (a second cousin) was murdered in Co. Armagh in 1975; William Strathearn was murdered in Ahoghill in 1977. See David McKittrick et. al., *Lost Lives: The Stories of the Men, Women and Children who Died as a Result of the Northern Ireland Troubles* (Edinburgh: Mainstream, 1999).
17 The *omphalos* is a navel or centre of the world, associated with the oracle at Delphi. In Joyce's *Ulysses*, it is associated with Buck Mulligan's bid to 'Hellenise the island'.
18 Moore praised 'the clarity of this omphaloskeptic vision', which shows 'there are more ways of making it new than are known to those critics of poetry who simply follow current fashions'. 'English Fame and Irish Writers', *London Review of Books*, 2/22 (20 November 1980), 5.
19 In *An Open Letter* (Derry: Field Day Theatre Company, 1983), he voiced his protest at being called British and included in the *Penguin Book of Contemporary British Verse* (ed. Blake Morrison and Andrew Motion).
20 *In Conversation with Karl Miller*, p. 51.
21 'Of All Those Starting Out', in *Dàin Do Shomhairle: Poems for Sorley* (Sorley MacLean Trust, 2011; repr. *Guardian*, 17 June 2011).

22 Seamus Heaney, 'Further Language, *Studies in the Literary Imagination*, 30/2 (Fall 1997), 7–16.
23 Coordinated by the anti-censorship body, 'Article 19', this declaration appeared in many newspapers on 2–3 March 1989, including the *Irish Times*.
24 Deborah McAleese, 'Seamus Heaney: I may not toast the Queen, but allow loyalists to fly Union flag if they want to', *Belfast Telegraph*, 30 January 2013.
25 Seamus Heaney, *Anything Can Happen* (Dublin: Amnesty/Town House, 2004).

CHAPTER 22

Education

Rosie Lavan

More than once, Seamus Heaney recalled the story of the day he went to enrol his sons in a local primary school in County Wicklow, shortly after the family's move to Glanmore Cottage in 1972. The headmaster needed to record Heaney's occupation, and quite unbidden he wrote down *file* – 'poet' – committing Heaney on the page and in Irish to the poet's life he had chosen.[1] It is singularly appropriate that this moment of ratification should have taken place in a school, given that education and poetry, and their associated identities, were complementary and arguably indivisible for the greater part of Heaney's career. Before he was a poet, Heaney was a teacher; before that, he was a student who gratefully and consistently acknowledged the opportunities which had enabled his educational progress and literary achievement. Surely and subtly, forms of education and models of teaching and learning recur in his writing; they are personal – taking us from classrooms in Anahorish or St Columb's – and intertextual, summoning and crediting the great formative presences in his poetic imagination, from Virgil and Dante, through to Wordsworth, Yeats and Eliot, or Kavanagh, Miłosz and Hughes. Most often, of course, they are both: 'If you like', he wrote in a now-famous line in 1972, 'I began as a poet when my roots were crossed with my reading' (*P* 37). To attend to the question of Heaney and education is to encounter that crossing in its most essential and lasting forms.

Indeed, it is not too much to state that the varied meanings and experiences of education in Heaney's career form not so much a framework as a bedrock for his writing of both poetry and criticism. His experiences as student, teacher and professor enable us to locate and understand him in ways at once familiar and refreshed. There are political and institutional dimensions to consider. His success in the eleven-plus examination which took him to St Columb's College in Derry in 1950 points back to the delayed implementation of the Education Act in Northern Ireland, which was passed in Westminster in 1944 but did not clear Stormont until 1947, and forwards to the decisive social shift which these reforms had effected in the North by the 1960s, with the emergence of a newly educated and politically conscious Catholic middle class. For those children from Catholic, nationalist backgrounds with no family tradition of higher education who then found themselves the beneficiaries of liberalizing British reforms translated into Unionist Northern Ireland, there were certain anomalies which offset the familiar post-war narrative in which education at once transforms and isolates the working-class child from their background. In 'Among Schoolchildren', an important lecture delivered at Queen's University Belfast in 1983, Heaney spoke of 'the learning experience as both challenge and liberation', emphasizing for his audience the specific conditions of that experience for children of the North: 'I hope you will bear with me if I adduce myself as an example of the bewilderment and attempts at resolution the sensibility can undergo in this country as it tries to grow into a coherent personality.'[2] Post-war progress is only one half of the story, of course. In his first job, at St Thomas's Intermediate School in Ballymurphy, Heaney was teaching in the midst of broken promises – himself embarking on what he later ironized as 'the generic life of the newly upwardly mobile eleven-plus Catholic', but faced with boys from a staunchly working-class and chronically deprived area of Belfast, which would be further challenged by the violence and upheaval of the Troubles.[3] But it was through this work that he earned the support of Michael McLaverty, the writer, headmaster of St Thomas's and an early literary champion. In mid-1960s Belfast, too, he met his great friend David Hammond, also a teacher, and in his collaborations with Hammond for the BBC Schools Service in Belfast, particularly the radio series *Explorations*, Heaney advanced and developed some of the principles of literary pedagogy which remained central to his approach to the critical discussion of poetry.[4]

Crucially, that freelance work for the BBC, through which Heaney remained closely involved in contemporary educational policy and practice, was economically enabling. In 1963 he left St Thomas's to take a post in St Joseph's College of Education in Belfast; in 1966 he joined the School of English at Queen's University, and his years spent lecturing there were accompanied by growing success in poetry. His decision, in 1972, to leave his post at Queen's and commit to writing presented practical challenges, which freelance broadcasting work, in Dublin as well as Belfast, went some way towards answering. Similarly, when he accepted a post on the teaching staff at Carysfort College of Education in Dublin in 1975, the professional move was practically enabling. He remained at

Carysfort until his resignation in 1981; in 1982 he entered into a temporary teaching arrangement with Harvard, which in turn led to his appointment as Boylston Professor of Rhetoric in 1984. His place in the international academy was assured. So, already, was his place on school syllabi in Ireland and Britain, and this dual profile – a kind of cross-constituency credibility – is relatively rare among modern and contemporary poets.

In 1989, amid rumours of his imminent election as Professor of Poetry at the University of Oxford, Heaney sought to quell speculation by identifying himself, simply and firmly, in the terms of his own first profession. 'I'm a teacher', he told the *Irish Times*. 'My professional life has been about teaching and the pleasure I have got from opening poems to people.'[5] *Finders Keepers* (2002), the major selection of his prose, bears this out. In the preface, Heaney explained the title of the volume by returning to the space in every school which is reserved for fun: 'In the playground the phrase "finders keepers" probably still expresses glee and stakes a claim, so in that sense it can apply as well to the experience of a reader of poetry.' He returned, too, to *Preoccupations*, his earlier collection of prose, explaining that *Finders Keepers* had 'the same shape' as that book. Once again, he had chosen to group his prose in three sections, the first with 'an autobiographical or topical slant', the second with 'a more specifically literary focus', and the third 'a kind of kite-tail' of miscellaneous writings (*FK* ix, x). In *Preoccupations* the first section comprised two of Heaney's most widely cited prose pieces, each of them composites of several articles on related themes, which narrated aspects of his childhood and youth: 'Mossbawn' and 'Belfast'. In the expanded Part I of *Finders Keepers*, Heaney's selections emphasized his experiences of learning and teaching, as well. 'Feeling into Words' (1974), an early essay about discovering the capacity for poetry, appears here where in *Preoccupations* it had stood at the opening of the literary Part II. It is followed by 'Learning from Eliot' (1988), an illuminating retrospective on his experiences of being taught and teaching T.S. Eliot's poetry, and Part I concludes with two pieces gathered under the title 'On Poetry and Professing'. In inviting us to regard the opening section of *Finders Keepers* as 'autobiographical', Heaney was indirectly asserting the central significance of these scenes and observations from a life spent fully in learning: these essays appear alongside others rooted in his native south County Derry –'Mossbawn', and 'Something to Write Home About' – and those which bear witness to the complexities of his time – 'Belfast', 'Cessation 1994' and 'Earning a Rhyme', about translating between Irish and English. Heaney's life in education, then, is not distinct from his life in poetry: in all senses, education is there from the start, inextricable from the life and the work which it shaped.

Collecting the poems that focus on education might similarly begin with those that remember Heaney's schools: in *Death of a Naturalist*, the title poem, or 'The Play Way', set in St Thomas's; two of his poems in the 'Five Derry Glosses' sequence, which remember 'river vigils at high college windows' and the map of the world on the classroom wall; 'The Real Names' in *Electric Light*, which reassembles his St Columb's contemporaries playing their parts in school Shakespeare, and advances towards St Thomas's.[6] School words are promising metaphors for Heaney, too: from the allusive 'An Advancement of Learning' in *Death of a Naturalist*, to 'the hedge-school of Glanmore', the name given to the domain of his new dispensation in *Field Work* which applied associations of the cherished, ad hoc, rural world of learning to the home where Heaney, *file*, first immersed himself totally in the life of poetry (*DN* 18–19; *FW* 29).

Notably, it was during the 1980s, the middle decade of his writing life, that Heaney fully explored the uncomfortable distance that education had opened up between him and his background, and particularly his parents. This is most tenderly and acutely expressed in two poems in *The Haw Lantern* (1987). The opening 'Alphabets', the Phi Beta Kappa poem at Harvard in 1984, begins with his father's shadow puppets, which the watching son knows he will outgrow: 'He understands / He will understand more when he goes to school.' Famously, the fourth sonnet in the 'Clearances' sequence, written in memory of his mother, recalls her affected 'inadequacy' in 'Pronouncing words "beyond her"', which leads to Heaney's own *naws* and *ayes* and 'the wrong / Grammar which kept us allied and at bay' (*HL* 1, 30). Mindful of these different currents of personal experience which work their way into the poetry, this essay will instead chart Heaney's work in a role distinct from, yet intimately related to, his poetry – as co-editor, with Ted Hughes, of two anthologies of poetry, *The Rattle Bag* (1982) and its successor, *The School Bag* (1997). Heaney's commentary on his work with Hughes, offered in an uncollected essay, 'Bags of Enlightenment' (2003), permits us to examine the way he approached and performed the role of teacher, not just in the school, college or university, but in the broadest possible sense of the term.

Published in the *Guardian* in October 2003, 'Bags of Enlightenment' began life as a lecture Heaney delivered at the Prince of Wales Summer School in Norwich in July that year.[7] This occasion marked a brief reprisal of Heaney's role as a teacher of teachers: the summer school, then in only its second year, is an initiative of the Prince's Teaching Institute, which supports teachers in the state sector in the UK. Heaney used this opportunity to speak in detail about his work with Hughes on the two Faber anthologies.[8] He began with a memory which, in a transition characteristic of his rhetoric, gave way to insight. He recalls the neighbours he and his wife had known in Belfast in the late 1960s, an elderly couple, the Wilsons, with whom their young sons spent a great deal of time. Mrs Wilson would often say to Michael, the elder of the two boys, 'You and Christopher are growing up, Granda Wilson and I are growing down, and your daddy and mammy are standing still.' Heaney continues:

> Mrs Wilson's way of seeing things has a bearing on the teaching of poetry and on any consideration of the part literature may play in the classroom or in the culture generally. To what end, after all, do we teach literature, if not for the present delight of those who are growing up? But we also teach it for the future nurture of the mature person, the person 'standing still'. And for the tranquil restoration – perhaps the disturbing recollection – of the person 'growing down'. We teach it for the now of perception and the then of reflection.[9]

That first-person plural may simply be a manner of speaking, commensurate with Heaney's unfailing ease and generosity in communication before all audiences, yet bearing in mind his assertion on the eve of the Oxford Professor of Poetry election in 1989 – 'I'm a teacher' – it would be entirely justified to accept that with that 'we' Heaney was involving himself directly in the enterprise of the teachers he was addressing, continuing to identify and define his work in terms of teaching. His language evokes the curative potential of literature to which he constantly, if always tough-mindedly, returned: 'delight', 'nurture' and 'restoration' are necessarily tempered by 'disturbing recollection'. There is often a sense of happy transgression in Heaney's accounts of the pleasures of reading, and here his convictions deliberately extend beyond the classroom out into 'the culture generally' – a very Eliotic move, reminding us that T.S. Eliot was one of the guiding forces behind Heaney's pedagogy. In 1974, in the Teacher's Notes he wrote to accompany his BBC Schools series *Explorations*, he asserted that 'The first programme aims to stimulate what T.S. Eliot called "the auditory imagination"', and in 'Bags of Enlightenment' he cites a passage from *The Use of Poetry and the Use of Criticism* (1933) which was of formative significance for the editing project.[10]

However, in 'Among Schoolchildren', almost exactly contemporary with *The Rattle Bag* and drawing Yeats, via allusion, into the discussion, Heaney had recognized that teaching philosophy necessarily cohabits with 'other expectations which the state will lay upon its educators'.[11] The curation of poetry in *The Rattle Bag* too occurred in a contemporary educational context in which both policy and commerce were involved, as he acknowledged, 'The books did not set out to be textbooks but they still were part of what might be called the educational-services industry and were intended as an intervention.'[12] We expect an intervention to change or redirect a course of action or a state of affairs, and in a very real sense these anthologies were deliberately, if subtly, radical. Moreover, they were informed by the editors' own attitudes towards and experiences of formal secondary education. Hughes was nine years older than Heaney, and though he was already at secondary school by the time the reforms of the Education Act were introduced, still the poets shared comparable experiences – Yorkshire grammar school followed by a Cambridge Exhibition for Hughes; St Columb's followed by a scholarship to Queen's for Heaney. As Heaney remembered, too, they were products of the same educational atmosphere, schooled in literature according to the same principles,

> at schools and universities where there was still an adherence to Matthew Arnold's faith in literary culture as a means towards the general dissemination of sweetness and light. Our teachers still proceeded on the basis of the humanist wager. They and we operated in the faith that literary and cultural endeavour was conducted in a disinterested spirit. It was a less sceptical world where the word 'higher' in the term 'higher education' was still credited and where the word 'education' was respected in and of itself because it promised to raise what Robert Frost once called 'the plane of regard'.[13]

This is old-school aspiration, remote from contested and sometimes hollow applications of the word in contemporary political discourse. The matter Heaney raises with it is complex, and beneath it lies an equally complex sense of nostalgia. On the one hand, he and Hughes recognized what this approach to a literary education missed – an approach which, crucially, they saw as being broadly the same as that still pursued by the teachers of the 'younger people' imagined as readers of *The Rattle Bag*, who were moving through the British school system in the seventies and eighties. It was a robustly canonical diet: Chaucer, Shakespeare, the Metaphysicals and perhaps Milton; Austen, Dickens, Hardy and perhaps T.S. Eliot. The omissions they detected, and the formalized way of close reading – the kind of literary education which 'turns a student's ear into a poetic bugging device', as Heaney described it in 'Feeling into Words' – were in part what *The Rattle Bag* sought to address (*P* 43).

At the same time, Heaney recognized the merits in this traditional approach: this is clear in his choice of that word 'credited', which cannot fail to recall the Nobel lecture which found him 'crediting' poetry in the most extraordinary sky-borne terms. In Heaney's way of seeing things such credit, based on honest and well-informed conviction – or indeed 'faith', another word he uses here – is unambiguously creditable. He gestures towards those merits, too, in referring to the unassailable respect which the very word 'education' commanded: this recalls his own etymological exploration of the noun in 'Among Schoolchildren'.[14] Respect for those principles is evident elsewhere in tributes Heaney paid to his own teachers and colleagues. There is Sean B. O'Kelly, who taught the final-year English class at St Columb's: 'He was involved and disinterested. He actually relished the stuff he was teaching, there was spontaneity as well as strictness in the way he handled the class' (*SS* 404–5). Or Michael McLaverty, whom Heaney described as 'compulsively a teacher' (*FK* 68). Most recently, in the translator's note to his posthumously published *Aeneid Book VI* (2016), he begins and ends with Father Michael McGlinchey, his Latin teacher at St Columb's 'who sighed for his favourite Virgil in that 1950s classroom', regretting that he was bound to teach the boys Book IX, and not Book VI, of the epic. McGlinchey made of his pupil Heaney 'an inner literalist', who offered his last work as 'classics homework, the result of a life-long desire to honour the memory' of his teacher (*A* ix, vii). It is tempting to wonder whether these matters were in Heaney's mind when he proposed *The School Bag*, the second anthology, conceived from the outset to be a more ordered supplement to what he called the 'random, whimsical' *Rattle Bag* (*SS* 397). 'We wanted this anthology to be different from *The Rattle Bag*, less of a carnival, more like a checklist. It would be a school-book in the usual sense', he wrote.[15]

Highlighting these aspects of the Heaney–Hughes intervention points towards other, tougher admissions which both poets made about the practice and profit of teaching literature. Their faith in its worth did not anticipate universal success. Hughes said as much in the preface to *Poetry in the Making*, which accompanied his BBC series of that name, stating that his 'basic assumption' that 'the latent talent for self-expression in any child is immeasurable . . . is very likely false', and it lay beyond the practical means of a teacher to elicit this in every pupil.[16] Heaney considered related difficulties in recollection of McLaverty's buoyant assertions at St Thomas's that poetry was in all senses bettering, even when 'the boys in the class knew that the whole thing was a masquerade'. But he recognized that McLaverty 'was drawing upon two and a half millennia of western aesthetic and educational theory':

> From Plato to the present, from the Athenian academy to the parent-teaching meeting at your local primary school, there has been an ongoing debate about the place and the point and the choice of imaginative writing, and about the relevance of such material to the formation of the good citizen's sensibility and behaviour. (FK 68–9)

The moral challenge to sustaining this belief in the 'humanizing' potential of literature faced with the evidence of history is compounded by practical, professional and circumstantial issues – the challenges involved in teaching itself, which Heaney experienced most acutely, and with a large measure of disillusionment, during his year at St Thomas's.

Difficulties around 'the place and the point and the choice of imaginative writing' are evergreen, and they have recently been explored by another poet and contemporary of Heaney's. David Constantine, born in 1944 and writing in 2013, was struck when reading Heaney and Derek Mahon that what was once, and not so very long ago, instilled and accepted as a common literary inheritance, is being lost:

> I have to concede that, reading Derek Mahon lately, his *Selected Poems* of 1990, and Seamus Heaney, his *Human Chain*, 2010, I had the uneasy feeling that the ground they spring from and have thriven in and assume their readers share may be withdrawing and disintegrating under forces as irresistible as those working on the glaciers and the ice-caps in the warming world.[17]

It is a sensitive area, and Constantine – who is anything but conservative in his cultural commentary – is serious and candid in working through it. His extensive discussion of Mahon and Heaney leads him to state:

> In the United Kingdom, particularly in England, we don't have and can't even honestly desire a unitary or coherent culture any more. In reality we never did have one, it was always class-bound, and hierarchical, and mostly excluded women from among its makers. Now the disintegration (to use a pejorative term) or the variety (to view it cheerfully) is staggering.[18]

Quite apart from the fact that *Human Chain* was one of the books which led Constantine to these ruminations, there are further points of relevance to the present discussion. Heaney recognized, valued and critiqued 'English' literature, with all its problems and promises, on many occasions throughout his career. His place in the modern canon of poetry in English, while assured, was not uncontested and he required it to be carefully qualified – most firmly and famously in *An Open Letter* to Blake

Morrison and Andrew Motion, on their well-meaning but ill-judged inclusion of him in *The Penguin Book of Contemporary British Poetry* (1982). He also understood that the forces which shape our engagement with and appreciation of literature, as individuals and as educators, are 'personal and social, and personal because social', to borrow a phrase from G.H. Bantock's analysis of T.S. Eliot's writings on education.[19] They are bound to change, and are themselves subject to consistently changing pressures. Finally, Constantine's remarks place Heaney in a generation shaped and defined by its educational experiences, locating him as surely as the eleven-plus, his university scholarship or his undergraduate enthusiasm for Dylan Thomas. By extension, they contextualize the aims and ambitions of *The Rattle Bag* and *The School Bag*. A poet compiling a comparable anthology for 'younger people', who themselves sound endearingly old-fashioned to the contemporary ear, could not, and indeed probably would not, work from the same assumptions which underpinned the Heaney–Hughes projects.

By the time *The School Bag* was published in 1997, Heaney had already used the title for a poem of his own. 'The Schoolbag', in memory of John Hewitt, was first published in 1987 and then collected, with revisions, in *Seeing Things* (1991).[20] It is a poem that makes a number of significant returns. First, to the title object itself: Heaney looks back across forty years to his 'handsewn leather schoolbag . . . half-full of blue-lined jotters'. In those days Hewitt, here addressed as 'Poet', was '*nel mezzo del cammino*' – in the middle of his life, in Dante's words (*ST* 30). It matters that Heaney should see Hewitt at this age in *Seeing Things*, his own self-consciously mid-life book. Moreover, the poem is clearly in dialogue with Heaney's lecture 'Learning from Eliot', delivered at Harvard in 1988, which begins, 'It was the middle of my own life before I began to grow up to T.S. Eliot, but the story necessarily starts far earlier. As a schoolboy in a Catholic boarding school in Derry . . .' (*FK* 26). 'The Schoolbag' takes us back still further, to the road to Anahorish School and the cheerful advice from family friends and neighbours which Heaney had earlier remembered in 'Feeling into Words': '*Learning's easy carried!*' (*ST* 30). Already in the 1940s the County Derry neighbours were teaching the boy the lesson he learned in 'Digging'. Though he did not realize it until later, the first poem in his first collection was underpinned by the 'almost proverbial common sense' of his childhood home, just as we might say his convictions about the purpose of teaching poetry owe much to Mrs Wilson in Belfast (*P* 42).

Heaney offers Hewitt the schoolbag as a bearer of both literary potential and good luck: 'So take it, for a word-hoard and a handsel.' The poem itself is a hoard of Heaney's own. He had chosen the Anglo-Saxon compound, 'word-hoard', to begin 'Words Working', the first episode of *Explorations*, in which, with T.S. Eliot in mind, he sought to introduce his listeners to the singularities of literary language.[21] In the lecture which is directly contemporary with 'The Schoolbag', he wrote of Eliot, and in echo of Yeats: 'You begin and end with the words alone' (*FK* 38). Passing the schoolbag to the poet is an attempt to keep the words coming, from the place where the acquaintance with words first became lasting. 'Perhaps the final thing to be learned is this', Heaney wrote in the lecture: 'in the realm of poetry, as in the realm of consciousness, there is no end to the possible learnings that can take place' (*FK* 38). Learning from Eliot, Heaney was teaching us, too.

Notes

1 See Charlie McCarthy (dir.), *Seamus Heaney: Out of the Marvellous*, Icebox/RTÉ, 2009; and Charlie Rose, Interview with Seamus Heaney, *Charlie Rose*, 19 April 1996.
2 Seamus Heaney, *Among Schoolchildren* (Belfast: John Malone Memorial Committee, 1983), p. 4.
3 Neil Corcoran, *Seamus Heaney* (London: Faber and Faber, 1986), p. 19.
4 See Rosie Lavan, '*Explorations*: Seamus Heaney and Education', *Irish Review*, 49–50 (Winter–Spring 2015), pp. 54–70.
5 Eileen Battersby, 'Oxford Poetry Post for Heaney Likely', *Irish Times*, 3 June 1989, p. 1.
6 See *DN* 15–16, 56; the second and fourth of the 'Five Derry Glosses', in Donovan Wylie, *32 Counties* (London: Secker & Warburg, 1989), pp. 70–1 (the former appears, comprehensively revised, as 'Squarings' xli in *ST* 101); *EL* 45–50.
7 There is some discrepancy over dates: the *Guardian* records that the lecture was delivered in July 2003, but in *Stepping Stones* Dennis O'Driscoll indicates that it was delivered in 2002. As 'Bags of Enlightenment' is uncollected elsewhere, the dates given in the *Guardian*, the only published version which exists, are followed. See also *SS* 398.
8 The subject matter was particularly appropriate: he first met the Prince of Wales at Westminster Abbey, after the memorial service for Hughes in 1999, at which he delivered an address. Prince Charles subsequently wrote to him, and this and other direct contact with the Royal family came in the midst of speculation about the appointment of Hughes's successor as Poet Laureate. Heaney then met the Prince again, at the first summer school in 2002. See *SS* 398–9.
9 Seamus Heaney, 'Bags of Enlightenment', *Guardian*, 25 October 2003, pp. 4–6 (at p. 4).

10 Seamus Heaney, *Explorations: Teacher's Notes* (London: BBC, 1973), 3; Heaney, 'Bags of Enlightenment', p. 5. Renewed thanks are due to Evelyn Ellison and her colleagues at BBC Northern Ireland who were able to recover copies of the Teacher's Notes and Pupil Pamphlet in spring 2013.
11 Heaney, *Among Schoolchildren*, p. 5.
12 Heaney, 'Bags of Enlightenment', p. 4.
13 *Ibid.*
14 Heaney, *Among Schoolchildren*, p. 5.
15 Seamus Heaney and Ted Hughes (eds.), *The School Bag* (London: Faber and Faber, 1997), p. xvii.
16 Ted Hughes, *Poetry in the Making: An Anthology of Poems and Programmes from 'Listening and Writing'* (1967; London: Faber and Faber, 1969), pp. 11–12.
17 David Constantine, *Poetry* (Oxford University Press, 2013), p. 121.
18 *Ibid.*, p. 128.
19 G. H. Bantock, *T. S. Eliot and Education* (London: Faber & Faber, 1970), p. 25.
20 The poem first appeared in *A Poet's Pictures: A Selection of Works of Art Collected by John Hewitt* (Hillsborough: Shambles Art Gallery, 1987), n.p.
21 Seamus Heaney, *Explorations* [Pupil's Pamphlet] (London: BBC, 1973), n.p.

CHAPTER 23

War and Peace

Richard Rankin Russell

Seamus Heaney grew up in Northern Ireland at the start of World War Two, a fact that has occasioned relatively little critical interest in contrast to the astonishing amount of work dedicated to his poetry about the so-called Northern Irish 'Troubles'. It is easy to think of Heaney as a Troubles poet, but in fact, that is only one aspect of his writing about war and peace, which nonetheless often has driven even astute assessments of the topic of violence in his poetry. Moreover, he established his poetic voice before the outbreak of conflict in 1968–9 and his poetry both outlasted the end of that conflict and went well beyond its confines in its imaginative treatment of violence. Both World Wars conditioned his thinking about war in general, but World War One proved more pivotal to his consideration of the poet's role in a time of violence. This essay begins with Heaney's experience of war through his poems and prose about those conflicts, then moves into more familiar territory, treating 'The Tollund Man', 'Punishment', 'The Harvest Bow', 'Tollund' and 'A Kite for Aibhín' in relationship to the Troubles, along with his essays 'Belfast', 'Cessation 1994' and 'The Whole Thing: On the Good of Poetry'. Heaney was especially concerned with the violence committed during times of war (particularly the Troubles) and he often struggled with how to aesthetically depict such religiously inspired violence. In seeking how his art might imagine peace, he turned sometimes to the authority wielded by sacred figures like the poet, and at other times to the positive vulnerability art can offer to us as human beings connected by our joint frailty.

Heaney has spoken of how the material things of World War Two – gas masks, blackout blinds, ration books and later, German prisoners of war – gradually entered his later poetry. The local aerodrome, for example, had 'a touch of wonderland about it, what with the planes coming in and rising up and the pilots and the ground staff . . . Menace and marvel equally in the air' (*SS* 358).[1] 'The Aerodrome' recalls the Toome Aerodrome and its 'wartime grey control tower', its 'B-26 Marauders', its 'Hangars, runways, bomb stores, Nissen huts, / The perimeter barbed wire, forgotten and gone' (*DC* 11).[2] The aerodrome brought war and a promise of a different kind of violence –mass and dehumanized – from the more intimate violence the young Seamus would have seen growing up on his parents' farm such as the drowning of unwanted animals or the putting down of aged animals. But 'The Aerodrome' finally only functions as background for a narrative about the young boy's relationship with his mother and how her deep love for him anchored him and allayed his fears that she might 'rise and go // With the pilot calling from his Thunderbolt' (*DC* 12). Heaney here represents World War Two and its American pilots as menacing only in the sense that they threaten to upset the young child's sure foundation of love.

Another poem from *District and Circle* (2006), 'Anahorish 1944', features American soldiers bound for the beaches of Normandy coming upon workers at a slaughterhouse killing pigs. The slaughter house workers, bathed in pig blood, silently watch the soldiers, 'Two lines of them, guns on their shoulders, marching. / Armoured cars and tanks and open jeeps. / Sunburnt hands and arms' (*DC* 7). Objectified into browned 'hands and arms', these soldiers throw the workers chewing gum and candy and continue on their mission. The soldiers on their mission seem the adults, while the butchers are rendered briefly akin to children catching candy at a parade.

World War Two, as Heaney figures it in these two poems, seems simultaneously distant and exotic, near and quotidian, but finally seems so far in the past as to be withdrawing in front of our eyes even as the poet tries to represent it. When he discussed World War Two early in his Nobel lecture, 'Crediting Poetry', he recalled hearing on BBC Radio 'the names of bombers and of cities bombed, of war fronts and army divisions, the numbers of planes lost and of prisoners taken . . . But . . . none of the news of these world-spasms entered me as terror . . . [and] there was something positive about the security I inhabited as a result of it' (*CP* 10).[3] It would take other conflicts to bring war home to him.

Heaney's engagement with World War One crystallized for him much of his thinking about identity and the poet's conflicted and complicated role in a time of violence. And the English poet-soldier Wilfred Owen, 'and others like him in the trenches of Flanders, are among the first of a type of poet . . . who looms as a kind of shadowy judging figure above every poet who has written subsequently'. Owen represents '"the poet as witness"', and just as important, 'poetry's solidarity with the doomed, the deprived, the victimized, the under-privileged'. Such figures combine 'the truth telling urge' and 'the compulsion to identify with the oppressed' in the 'act of writing itself' (*GT* xvi).[4] Owen had 'earned his right to his lines by going up the line' (*GT* xv), and there may persist in Heaney's writing about him and other World War One poets such as Francis Ledwidge, in his 'Tommy's uniform' and 'haunted Catholic face, pallid and brave', an unexpressed wish that he himself could have seen combat, problematic as this notion is for Northern Irish Catholics (*FW* 60).[5] Gerald Dawe convincingly argues that 'Heaney's poem in honour of Ledwidge is itself an important historical marker, since it has only really been from that time, in the early 1980s, to quote George Boyce, that "rightly, if belatedly, the Great War" has been seen "as central to the forging of Irish identities".'[6] Heaney might have felt more authentic as a poet had he been a soldier since he would then have been even more of an eyewitness and truth teller. Because Owen's 'poems have the potency of human testimony, of martyr's relics ... any intrusion of the aesthetic can feel like impropriety' (*GT* xiv).

I want to suggest here that Heaney himself strove for just this 'potency of human testimony' in his own poems about war – particularly about the violence in Northern Ireland from 1968 to 1994 and beyond – and that he remained troubled his whole career about the 'impropriety' of the aestheticization of violence even as he remained increasingly convinced that this representation was a crucial part of his role as poet. Moreover, he sought to imagine what a future Northern Ireland free from war might resemble – a place characterized by dialogue between members of formerly opposed factions and a slowly forming trust between them.

Ledwidge's importance as 'one of the central voices of an emerging Ireland: Catholic yet liberal, nationalist yet non-sectarian, Irish yet fully alert to the world beyond the island's shores',[7] brings us closer to Heaney's own conflicted position as a Catholic from Northern Ireland committed to Irish constitutional nationalism as well as ecumenism. He made occasional, telling revelations about the conflict that suggest he did sometimes harbour the hope that the violence itself might birth a united Ireland. For instance, he concludes his 1969 essay on the documentary film *John Hume's Derry* by remarking, 'There was a hint of the phoenix-flame in some of those petrol-bomb shots.'[8] Such language about 'the phoenix-flame' draws upon Irish republicanism's hopes for a united Ireland springing from the ashes of war-torn Northern Ireland; it recalls iconography and language from the 1916 Easter Rising in Dublin and anticipates such imagery on republican wall murals in the North beginning in the early 1980s. More disturbing was Heaney's admission in his Nobel Prize address about a thought he had concerning a friend imprisoned in the 1970s for a political murder: 'I shocked myself by thinking that even if he were guilty, he might still perhaps be helping the future to be born, breaking the repressive forms and liberating new potential. . .' (*CP* 18).

In his poems that deal with war, particularly the conflict in Northern Ireland, he often recognizes the potency of mythical violence, even if he sees through that violence and rejects it. 'The Tollund Man', 'Punishment' and 'Strange Fruit' offer an intimate knowledge of the war raging on the streets of Northern Ireland and reject the abstractions for which terrorists on both sides fought. In this sense, they accord with Peter McDonald's argument about Northern Irish poetry and violence that 'poetry makes sense of things in distinctive ways, which defeat the patterns offered by rhetorical and political coherences'.[9] They also follow Wilfred Owen's example and offer testimony to war's effect on the human body, mind and soul. By virtue of dwelling upon the wounded condition of the Northern Irish body politic, by giving witness through specific, telling details, Heaney's work, even as it struggles with the aesthetic representation of violence, categorically disavows the siren song of war and points towards peace.

Consider 'The Tollund Man', published in *Wintering Out* (1972) at the height of the Troubles, which tries to vivify this body, beginning with his precise description of the figure. The man's head is 'peat-brown', his eyelids are 'mild pods', and he wears a 'pointed skin cap'. Quickly, deftly, Heaney sketches in these details, showing how the man has become 'a saint's kept body' (*WO* 47). He admits how easily one can get caught up in the culture of violence in ancient Jutland or then-contemporary Northern Ireland – even if one speaks for the victim as he attempts to do here. Thus, he is tempted to 'pray / Him to make germinate' a whole series of victims in the present and past. But to risk this prayer troubles the poet's desire to maintain artistic integrity. The artist's gaze at this body, then, can become a veneration and thus a recognition of the violence's religious power that runs the risk of tacitly endorsing it. When Heaney concludes the poem by imagining travelling to Jutland, not speaking the language but feeling 'lost / Unhappy and at home' (*WO* 48), he certainly does not seem bewildered, as McDonald feels poets writing meaningful poems about the Troubles should be.[10] In fact, his knowingness and intimacy with the victims here and in other bog poems led to criticism that Heaney somehow endorsed the violence.

In his essay 'Christmas, 1971', Heaney wrote wearily of living in the war zone that was then Belfast, bemoaning how 'I am fatigued by a continuous adjudication between agony and injustice, swung at one moment by the long tail of race and resentment, at another by the more acceptable feelings of pity and terror.' Again, a yearning sense of not being on the front lines emerges when he remarks, 'We live in the sickly light of TV screens, with a pane of selfishness between ourselves and the suffering. We ... live on among the families of the victims, those blown apart and those in cells apart' (*P* 30).

Two years earlier, Heaney had read Danish archaeologist P.V. Glob's study *The Bog People*, which led him to write a series of bog poems, including 'The Tollund Man', based on photographs of those bodies. Studying these bodies made him feel closer to the violence, but in writing poems about the bog bodies, Heaney was working with a double disadvantage – both attempting to write aesthetically about violence and doing so through meditating on the medium of photography. Additionally, as George Watson pointed out, he faced the 'temptation (perhaps especially potent for a Catholic religious sensibility) of myth-making'.[11]

Walter Benjamin wrote in his 'Critique of Violence' that 'mythical violence in its archetypal form is a mere manifestation of the gods. Not a means to their ends, scarcely a manifestation of their will, but first of all a manifestation of their existence.'[12] In the bog poems and even in 'Anything Can Happen', his poem about the September 11 attacks carried out by radicalized Muslims, Heaney comes uncomfortably close to acknowledging mythical violence and therefore implying that there is no human agency in such murders – only the gods manifesting their existence in ways uncontrollable by us. He rejects the notion of mythical violence, in the bog poems, if not in 'Anything Can Happen'. Thus he largely salvages the role of the poet in these poems by not only giving us detailed specifics of these heinous crimes in the role of witness, but also, in the bog poems, by questioning the concept of the poet *as silent witness*, not active rejecter of violence. Through this process, Heaney admits the suasive power of reading violence mythically, but finally turns away from it and finds his moral foundation in poetry's authority and at other times, in its instantiation of human vulnerability.

'Punishment', probably Heaney's most well-known bog poem, effectively shows how group violence in the past and present scapegoat society's most vulnerable in its portrayal of the so-called 'Windeby Girl' pictured in Glob's book (whose body has now been proven to be that of a young, undernourished teenaged boy).[13] Heaney terms 'her' a 'Little adulteress' and muses that 'your / tar-black face was beautiful' (*N* 30, 31). He then famously indicts himself for being 'the artful voyeur // of your brain's exposed and darkened combs', invoking his insider's knowledge of the violent punishment of tarring and feathering committed against Catholic women who consorted with British soldiers. Usually in his rejection of violence, Heaney turns to either poetry's authority or to its ability to render us all vulnerable in an egalitarian and thus connected way: here, he offers a rare combination of these two tendencies in one poem by alluding to the narrative of the woman taken in adultery from John's Gospel, Chapter 8, and admitting his own frailty in the face of such ferocious violence: 'I who have stood dumb' (*N*, 31).

Heaney references this scriptural episode in his essay 'The Government of the Tongue', substituting poetry for Jesus' writing in the sand and remarking upon its power:

> In one sense the efficacy of poetry is nil – no lyric has ever stopped a tank. In another sense, it is unlimited. It is like the writing in the sand in the face of which accusers and accused are left speechless and renewed. I am thinking of Jesus' writing as it is recorded in Chapter Eight of John's Gospel. (*GT* 107)

He then posits that poetry, like Jesus' drawing in the sand which prevented the Pharisees from stoning the woman for adultery because they recognized their own sin, can establish an interim space that forces us to reflect on our own capacity for violence: 'In the rift between what is going to happen and whatever we wish to happen, poetry holds attention for a space, functions ... as pure concentration, a focus where our power to concentrate is concentrated back on ourselves' (*GT* 108).

Crucially, by restoring the agency of the 'Beheaded girl, outstaring axe / And beatification, outstaring / What had begun to feel like reverence' (*N*, 32), 'Strange Fruit', the only sonnet of all the bog poems, rejects the mythical violence whose manifestation Benjamin articulates and along with it, its 'power, the principle of all mythical lawmaking'.[14] Instead of this power, Heaney began privileging frailty in addition to poetry's power as an answer to the mythical violence he had associated with the conflict in Northern Ireland. He offers this frailty most evocatively in 'The Harvest Bow' and in a gesture of a squeezed hand during an atrocity in Northern Ireland he describes in *Crediting Poetry*.

'The Harvest Bow' perhaps too optimistically ventures that the bow woven by the poet's father out of wheat could sport a motto that 'The end of art is peace', yet the fragility of that 'frail device' implies that art's ephemerality might be the best antidote to death-dealing certainties in wartime (*FW* 58). Poetry's power, that is, does not cohere in its obduracy of form or message, but rather in its openness. James Longenbach articulates this theory best when he argues that 'the power of a poem inheres in the realization that we cannot count on it. Its ephemeral consolation depends precisely on its being ephemeral, open to the vicissitudes of self-doubt.'[15]

In *Crediting Poetry*, Heaney recounts the story of the massacre in Kingsmill, County Armagh of ten Protestant textile workers on 5 January 1976, one of whom squeezed the hand of the only Catholic man among them when the terrorists, whom the workers assumed were members of a Protestant loyalist paramilitary group, asked Catholics to step forward. When the Catholic worker made to step forward, 'he felt the hand of the Protestant worker next to him take his hand and squeeze it in a signal that said no, don't move, we'll not betray you, nobody need know what faith or party you belong to' (*CP* 18). When he stepped forward anyway, the IRA killed his Protestant co-workers. Heaney argues for the human frailty and connection of that squeeze of the hand, stating, 'The birth of the future we desire is surely in the contraction which that terrified Catholic felt on the roadside when another hand gripped his hand, not in the gunfire that followed, so absolute and desolate' (*CP* 19). That human chain of frailty that betokens hope for the future, figured again in the title of his final volume of new poetry, *Human Chain* (2010), offers a way forward by its affirmation of our common humanity.

That future arrived in Northern Ireland with the temporary ceasefire of the Irish Republican Army on 31 August 1994, followed by the ceasefire declared by the Combined Loyalist Command on 13 October. Heaney's essay written in September of that year, 'Cessation 1994', complements the tentative hope expressed in a poem written then as well – 'Tollund'. In his essay, Heaney suggests that 'the cessation of violence is an opportunity to open a space ... where hope can grow'. Going on to cite the definition of hope offered by former Czech dissident, then President of the Czech Republic, Václav Havel, Heaney argued that hope 'is a state of the soul rather than a response to the evidence ... the conviction that something is worth working for ... Its deepest roots are in the transcendental, beyond the horizon', concluding, 'The self-evident truth of all this is surely something upon which a peace process might reasonably be grounded' (*FK* 50).[16]

'Tollund' registers not so much that transcendental hope 'beyond the horizon', however, as a changed landscape in the ancient bogs of modern-day Denmark and on the ground in Northern Ireland given the ceasefires of 1994. He sees himself and others visiting this strange new landscape that now slowly morphs into a post-ceasefire Northern Ireland as 'More scouts than strangers, ghosts who'd walked abroad ... to make a new beginning / And make a go of it, alive and sinning, / Ourselves again, free-willed again, not bad' (*SL* 69). The rhyme of 'beginning' and 'sinning' suggests a potential harmony at starting over in imagining a new beginning to political and cultural life in Northern Ireland even while admitting they will make mistakes, an admission compounded by the flatness and refusal of the last line's end rhyme ('bad') to chime with 'abroad', which implies that concord will be difficult. And yet by reinscribing human agency into the situation, Heaney refuses to privilege mythical violence and instead focuses on our ability to treat each other as precious, unique selves, a necessary precondition for peace and future reconciliation. That recognition of our angular singularity pierces abstractions invoked to justify violence and war. It also suggests how art founded on specific images and expressed in particular forms can in turn evoke our individuality.

More recently, Heaney argued that the poem itself can exemplify wholeness and healthiness, and that the poet can potentially bring healing to his society. In his 2001 lecture, 'The Whole Thing: On the Good of Poetry', he posits, 'The virtue of poetry, of art in general, resides in the fact that it is first and foremost a whole thing, a hale thing, a thing formally and feelingly sound, right within itself.'[17] Poetry, he concludes, gives us 'a momentary sensation of resolution, a healing moment'.[18] And he finally argues, resorting to medical language, that poetry 'is like the immunity system of the spirit; it works for good but it cannot always withstand assault . . . poetry is a kind of drip feed, and when it works it percolates down out of its refined element into the common speech and understanding of a whole society'.[19] Thus poetry can potentially protect us from harm, and its wholeness can slowly work itself into the larger world, spreading health, a prerequisite for peace.

Heaney concludes *Human Chain* with a translation of Giovanni Pascoli's poem '*L'Aquilone*' as 'A Kite for Aibhín', in honour of his granddaughter. 'A Kite' begins with 'Air from another life and time and place, / Pale blue heavenly air is supporting / A white wing beating high against the breeze' (*HC* 85).[20] The poem subtly rewrites the sudden appearance of the terrorist-controlled airplanes in the New York sky on September 11, 2001, represented in 'Anything Can Happen' as Jupiter and 'his thunder cart and his horses' that rage 'Across a clear blue sky' (*DC* 13). Heaney now replaces that image of horror coming out of 'a clear blue sky', rendering even the sky itself 'heavenly', symbolizing freedom and joy with the kite.

As it sails above us, and after 'string breaks and – separate, elate – // The kite takes off, itself alone, a windfall' (*HC* 85), this tail end of the poem conveys Heaney's utter self-fulfilment he imagines in his death, while the phrase from the last line, 'itself alone', modifies a phrase from the end of 'Tollund', 'Ourselves again'. It also references the political party Sinn Fein, whose motto is 'Ourselves alone'. Finally occupying a solitary space, he views himself as soaring away from such sectarian attitudes. In so doing, the poem offers this hope for Northern Ireland as a whole and conveys both the spiritual tenor of Heaney's poetry and his emphasis on human agency as antidotes to the poison of mythical, seemingly unending war.

Notes

1 Dennis O'Driscoll, *Stepping Stones: Interviews with Seamus Heaney* (New York: Farrar, Straus and Giroux, 2008).
2 Seamus Heaney, *District and Circle* (New York: Farrar, Straus and Giroux, 2006).
3 Seamus Heaney, *Crediting Poetry* (Loughcrew: Gallery Press, 1995).
4 Seamus Heaney, 'The Interesting Case of Nero, Chekhov's Cognac, and a Knocker', *The Government of the Tongue: Selected Prose, 1978–1987* (New York: Farrar, Straus and Giroux, 1988).
5 Seamus Heaney, 'In Memoriam Francis Ledwidge', in *Field Work* (New York: Farrar, Straus and Giroux, 1979).
6 Gerald Dawe, *Of War and War's Alarms: Reflections on Modern Irish Writing* (Cork University Press, 2015), p. 59. Dawe is citing George Boyce, *The Sure Confusing Drum: Ireland and the First World War* (University College of Swansea, 1993), p. 24.
7 Dawe, *Of War and War's Alarms*, p. 57.
8 Heaney, 'John Hume's Derry', [orig. in *Hibernia*, 21 November 1969] in David Pierce (ed.), *Irish Writing in the Twentieth Century: A Reader* (Cork University Press, 2000), p. 766.
9 Peter McDonald, *Mistaken Identities: Poetry and Northern Ireland* (Oxford University Press, 1997), pp. 65–6.
10 *Ibid.*, pp. 64–5.
11 George Watson, 'The Narrow Ground: Northern Poets and the Northern Ireland Crisis', in Marasu Sekine (ed.), *Irish Writers and Society at Large* (Totowa, NJ: Barnes and Nobles Books, 1985), pp. 207–24 (at p. 214).
12 Walter Benjamin, 'Critique of Violence', in *Reflections: Essays, Aphorisms, Autobiographical Writings*, trans. Edmund Jephcott (New York: Schocken, 1986), p. 294.
13 Karen E. Lange, 'Tales from the Bog', *National Geographic*, September 2007, 80–93.
14 Benjamin, 'Critique of Violence', p. 295.
15 James Longenbach, *The Resistance to Poetry* (University of Chicago Press, 2004), p. 108.

16 Seamus Heaney, 'Cessation 1994', in *Finders Keepers: Selected Prose 1971–2001* (New York: Farrar, Straus and Giroux, 2002).
17 Seamus Heaney, 'The Whole Thing: On the Good of Poetry', *The Recorder: A Journal of the American Irish Historical Society*, 15/2 (Spring 2002), 5–20 (at p. 8).
18 *Ibid.*, p. 10.
19 *Ibid.*, p. 16.
20 Seamus Heaney, *Human Chain* (New York: Farrar, Straus and Giroux, 2010).

VI

Critical Contexts

CHAPTER 24

The Feminine

Laura O'Connor

This essay explores Heaney's concept of the feminine, a key term in the elaboration of his poetics, and contextualizes his gendered poetics in relation to the philosophical and material changes brought about by second-wave feminism. Heaney began to use 'the feminine' as a central theoretical concept in the early seventies. Although this coincided with the launch of the Irish Women's Liberation Movement in 1971, Heaney's early literary criticism neither heralds nor engages with radical feminism. It is widely acknowledged that the Troubles in Northern Ireland were a major influence on, and a significant hermeneutic framework for, the tone and content of Heaney's oeuvre and the critical reception of his work. The impact of the radical changes wrought by the women's liberation movement on the poet's work as well as his critical reception, is a far less prominent, but nonetheless crucial, theme of Heaney criticism.

Heaney's use of 'the feminine' and of feminism needs to be considered in relation to its changing status as a loaded 'keyword' that 'virtually force[s] itself on [our] attention because the problems of its meanings [seem] inextricably bound up with the problems it [is] being used to discuss'.[1] In other words, the concept of Heaney and the feminine must be historicized as well as problematized. Feminism has radically transformed women's lives and Ireland's social and cultural ethos since the 1960s. Significant advances include equal pay legislation; increased professional opportunity and political agency; the proscription of sexist terminology and stereotypes; greater sexual autonomy and reproductive control; the dismantling of compulsory heterosexuality; men's increased participation in child-raising and domestic labour; and growing public intolerance for sexual abuse and violence against women. The improved material conditions of (some) women's lives and changes of outlook modified the nuances of the critical vocabulary used to analyse gender across various feminist constituencies. Feminists seeking equal pay and opportunity were antagonistic to how men used 'the feminine' to reinforce separate and unequal domains for the sexes. Moreover, praise for 'feminine' accomplishments was regarded as an ideological trap used to reconcile women to subservient roles as homemakers and professional subordinates to men. Such scepticism often proved divisive: some women felt slighted by feminist disdain towards 'feminine' conduct and disavowed 'feminist' values. Writers, philosophers and artists, for their part, intent upon reimagining a symbolic order and cultural ethos that were not predicated upon male privilege and patriarchal assumptions, idealized the feminine as a yet-to-be-realized desideratum. '*Écriture feminine*' epitomizes this utopian strain of feminism. Thus, while materialist feminists regard an emphasis on alterity as polarizing, and a potential impediment to securing 'the same' entitlements, those committed to exploring women's radical difference from men might object to a male poet usurping their prerogative.

Heaney's early criticism theorizes a stark gender dichotomy in 'modes' of creative endeavour:

> In the masculine mode, the language functions as a form of address, of assertion or command, and the poetic effort has to do with conscious quelling and control of the materials, a labour of shaping . . . Whereas in the feminine mode the language functions more as evocation than as address, and the poetic effort is not so much a labour of design as it is an act of divination and revelation; words in the feminine mode behave with the lover's come-hither instead of the athlete's display, they constitute a poetry that is delicious as texture before it is recognized as architectonic. (P 88)

Elsewhere he ascribes a sectarian and colonialist provenance to this gendering of his bicultural heritage and to the hybrid blend of staccato consonants (Protestant/settler/masculine) and rolling mellifluous vowels (Catholic/native/feminine) in spoken Ulster English (*P* 44–5). The feminized come-hither readily maps onto a gendered myth of poetic inspiration, in which an implicitly male poet gives form and voice to the intuitive wisdom imparted by a silent female muse. Fran Brearton[2] claims that Robert Graves's *The White Goddess* directly influenced Heaney's early poetics, overlapping and blending with Jungian archetypal psychology, Yeats's gyring cosmology, and the *aisling* myth in the Irish political imaginary. The task of integrating the Gravesian goddess/Jungian anima into the poet's creativity entails anxious assertions of masculine difference from and heroic mastery over 'the feminine'. One of the ironies of Heaney's dalliance with 'the feminine' is that it is cited, reprovingly, by editor Harold Bloom, and several contributors, in *Modern Critical Views: Seamus Heaney* (1986). They opine that if Heaney is to attain premier representative status, he must first wrest himself free from 'the treachery of wetness', as Moynagh Sullivan argues.[3] Moreover, Heaney's categorical representation of gender binaries invited critique because contemporary feminists, in Ireland and elsewhere, were themselves conflicted about delineating the feminine in relation to the masculine.

The first section of this essay, 'Becoming Canonical', examines how Heaney conceives a poet's labour, representative function and affiliation to a literary tradition in patrilineal terms. The next section, 'The *Aisling* Revisited', examines the *aisling* (dream-vision poem) as a flashpoint both for the critical controversy surrounding *North* (1975) and for the ensuing feminist critique of patriarchal poetry and of gendered nationalist iconography. Finally, in 'Heaney as Foremother?' I discuss the ascription of a maternal ethos to Heaney and suggest how this complicates our understanding of what constitutes 'the feminine'.

Becoming Canonical

The earliest of Heaney's many self-reflexive poems about poetry proclaim the indebtedness of his craft to his father's arduous farm labour. The memory of his father 'mapping the furrow exactly' in 'Follower' offers a template for verse-making and delineates his future field work. The portrait of his father and grandfather 'stooping in rhythm' to lay potato drills and to cut turf in 'Digging' stresses their masculinity, suggesting by association the manliness of the son's chosen métier. The domestic tasks of skilled churning and bread-making are also observed with filial appreciation, but they are not beheld as arts to be emulated. At a time when the domain of women's work expanded rapidly, it is significant that the family farm remains a presiding representation of labour, divided by gender, in Heaney's oeuvre.

The filial emulation devoted to his forefathers' craft also colours how Heaney undertook to become a canonical poet along the lines theorized and practised by the high modernists. Heaney's criticism, like T.S. Eliot's, reflects how he revised and reconfigured the tradition from which he emerged as an individual talent. The intensive reading entailed by his translations – *Beowulf*, *Sweeney Astray* and *The Cure at Troy* – cultivated the mixed Anglo-Saxon, Gaelic and classical strands that Heaney saw as integral to his tradition. His commitment to tradition dovetails with the post-war pedagogy of literary studies, making his work congenial to like-minded critics such as Bloom and Helen Vendler.

From the publication of *Death of a Naturalist* in 1966, Heaney was recognized as a Northern Catholic minority, as well as an Irish national, poet and spokesperson. He became a respected critic, reviewer and anthologist; a Professor of Poetry at Oxford and Harvard; and a multiple award-winner before he became a Nobel laureate in 1995. His public profile as a representative voice for the Northern Catholic minority increased after the outbreak of the Troubles. The layered ironies of 'Whatever You Say, Say Nothing' address the ethics – and the effort – of speaking responsibly to the media. Heaney understood from the example of Yeats and Joyce that twining his home locale and community into the trellis of world literature would carve out a distinctive 'place' for him in the world's literary imagination. He dons the Yeatsian mantle of the national bard, a poet-representative who speaks for and to the nation on an international stage and weaves public controversies and personal life struggles into an autobiographical oeuvre. Heaney underscores how his religious and farming background sets him at an antagonistic distance from the 'overbearing' tone of Yeats's Ascendancy posturings; at the same time he expresses wholehearted admiration for the '[majestic] gift of cultural authority' that enables Yeats to 'rebuke the culture because he was its most intense representative' (*PW* 11). His own devout Catholic upbringing and education enhance his sense of poetry as a vocation, not unlike a priestly 'calling', that reinforces the masculinist bias of bardic authority and of the hierarchical flow of cultural capital that, in turn, determines canonical rankings.

The poet-persona's path to becoming canonical is dramatized in the title sequence of *Station Island* (1985), which works a variation on Yeats's sprezzatura performance of self-canonization in 'The Tower'. 'Station Island' draws on a wealth of religious, historical, political and literary intertexts associated with 'St Patrick's Purgatory', an island pilgrimage site in Lough Derg, Donegal. The poet-pilgrim merges with the penitents circuiting the stations, drawn in by 'Habit's afterlife . . . I was back among bead clicks and the murmurs / from inside confessionals' (*SI* 67). Station Island is on the southern side of the border dividing Ulster, an apt location for Heaney's dilemma of twice finding himself on the 'wrong' side of the sectarian divide: first as a member of the Northern Catholic minority and then, after migrating to the South in 1972, as a poet-spokesperson on the Troubles despite having 'Escaped from the massacre' (*N* 73). Conversely, because Lough Derg's long history connects the 1980s Ulster poet-persona with pre-partition, and even pre-Reformation, Ireland, the site obliquely registers both the political provenance of Ireland's sectarian state-formation in 1922 and Heaney's claim on dual representativeness as an Irish, and as a Northern Catholic minority, poet. Heaney accentuates the sectarian divide by reserving the interlocutory role for the shades of his

Ulster precursors, William Carleton and Patrick Kavanagh; the accusatory shades of three (Catholic) victims of the Troubles; and the admonitory shade of Joyce who enjoins him to quit 'doing the decent thing' (*SI* 93). World canonical precursors (including Yeats, Eliot and Dante) are honoured through formal allusion alone. None of his twelve interlocutors are women. Few women precursors mattered deeply to Heaney, and the predominance of men in the tradition to which he subscribes is evident from the intertextuality of his oeuvre.

Heaney's smooth path to literary and cultural eminence offers a useful comparative framework for understanding contemporaneous feminist endeavours to contest and undo the sexism that determines how literary reputations are cultivated and literary canons are established. Poet-critic Eavan Boland was a leading figure in challenging the homosociality of Ireland's literary scene. She denounced the sexist under-representation of women in *The Field Day Anthology of Irish Writing* (1991) and the exclusively male composition of its editorial board (which included Heaney). Like Heaney, Boland makes a double-gesture of self-differentiation from, and filiation to, Yeats: she invokes her status as a representative minority voice for women to validate her entitlement to assume the bardic authority to speak for, and to, the nation. The dual role linked both poets with transnational campaigns for civil rights and lent them the literary cachet of the 'Irish' brand garnered by Irish modernists.

The *Aisling* Revisited

Among Heaney's works, *North* is the most dependent upon gender binaries as well as being the most controversial. Heaney telescopes Ireland's colonial history into a stark juxtaposition between contemporary sectarian violence and ekphrastic images of Iron Age victims of blood sacrifice, culled from P.V. Glob's *The Bog People*. Colonization is figured as rape. 'And I am still imperially / Male', the speaker of 'Act of Union' declares, apostrophizing Ireland, 'leaving you with the pain, / The rending process in the colony, / The battering ram, the boom burst from within' (*N* 49). In 'The Betrothal of Cavehill', the North of Unionist hegemony, impregnable as 'basalt', 'maintains its stare / South: proud, protestant and northern, and male. / Adam untouched, before the shock of gender' (*N* 51). The overly schematic dichotomies arise in part, as Edna Longley observes, because 'the gap has narrowed between Heaney's creative and critical idioms', inscribing the categorical gender divide of the early critical prose onto the verse.[4]

A major reason why *North* has proved so controversial is because it tapped into, and stoked, two vigorous cultural debates persisting from the 1960s through the 1990s: the revisionist debate over national historiography, and feminist debate about the patriarchal bias of nationalist ideology. Participants in these two distinct yet indirectly related discursive movements turned to a foundational Irish myth, the *aisling* mode, in order to interrogate the atavistic rage they saw as fuelling the Northern conflict and the 1980s counter-insurgence against women's liberation. The *aisling* (dream-vision poem) extends from its early medieval status as a functional sovereignty myth, through its remaking as Jacobite political allegory in the eighteenth century, to its transformation into a literary vehicle for the messianic republican ideology of the 1916 Rising and its aftermath. The *aisling* was a primary vehicle for transmitting *the* 'Story of Ireland', a tale of an oppressed but unvanquished nation whose apotheosis (for some) was the 1916 Rising. The Jacobite *aisling*, which circulated primarily through song, figures Ireland's colonial history as the rape of the sovereignty goddess/muse – personified as Cathleen Ni Houlihan and Róisín Dubh, among others – on whose behalf the poet rallies the people to overthrow the foreign usurper. Yeats and Lady Gregory's *Cathleen ni Houlihan* (1902) became 'a kind of gospel' for the Irish Volunteers; their leader, Eoin MacNeill, felt obliged to remind them that 'Cathleen Ni Houlihan is an abstraction' when he countermanded Patrick Pearse's order for an insurrection on Easter Sunday.[5] The Rising was timed to coincide with Easter as a sacramental sign of how the insurrectionists' blood-sacrifice would fulfil their tryst with destiny. The messianic republicanism of Pearse's influential speeches and poetry reinforces the conflation of Catholicism with republicanism in the Rising's symbolism, compounding the sectarianism that led to the 1922 partitioning of the island. Critiques of the ideological currents underlying diehard republicanism gained traction in the run-up to the fiftieth anniversary of the Rising in 1966, and became more urgent and heated after the outbreak of the Troubles in 1969.

The *aisling* mode in *North* connects ancient myth about a tutelary bogland goddess – the 'Insatiable bride' and 'mother ground . . . sour with blood / of her faithful' in 'Kinship' – with 1970s republican ideology. Revisionists detect an 'as before, so again' fatalism in the bog-people allegory, a typological model of history that aligns it with Jacobitism and with the 1916 Proclamation's treatment of the Rising as one of a series of generational revolts destined to recur until freedom is attained. The alarmed contemporary censure of *North*'s atavism contains genuine fear of the *aisling* mode's ideological appeal. The atavism charge also reacts to the baleful 'devouring mother' aspect of the magna mater archetype, an obverse image of Pearse's long-suffering, acquiescent and steadfast mother. As Elizabeth Butler Cullingford argues, Pearse's masochistic homoeroticism and veneration for the mother (suffused with Catholic devotion to Mary) 'desexualize[es]' the *spéirbhean* and replaces her with a chaste *Pièta*.[6]

Patricia Coughlan contends that *North*'s primary motivating force is the drive 'to wrest a self from the "feminine" unbounded indeterminacy of the bog'.[7] Her argument shifts the focus away from nationalist/republican politics in order to make the politics of gender, and gender hierarchies, paramount instead. '[T]he bog-goddess is imagined as both mother and spouse, and as destroyer and provider' Coughlan notes, 'but it is still persistently (and in both senses) the *ground* on which the speaker's self and his very identity is predicated.' A great strength of Coughlan's close literary analysis is how it negotiates between the figural and the material and accentuates how effectively the ambiguous nature of bogland – detritus and fuel; land and water, swallower and preserver – represents the malign/benign dualism of the magna mater. It is wryly appropriate that Coughlan's 2007 riposte to Heaney's defensive reaction to her critique is conducted through an analysis of their contrary interpretations of Brian Merriman's late eighteenth-century *Cúirt an Mheán Oíche* (*The Midnight Court*', a parodic *aisling* in which the male poet-persona is roasted by a chorus of ribald women.[8]

It is telling that during this 'key moment for feminist literary criticism' (1989–91), several Attic Press Lip pamphlets – by Boland, Longley and Gerardine Meaney – turned to the *aisling* to theorize the 1980s backlash against women's liberation.[9] The concerted effort to restrict women's reproductive autonomy and restore them to a subordinate place in the patriarchal household was conducted through the public pillorying of 'fallen' women, including the woman honoured in Heaney's 'Limbo'. It was epitomized by the 1983 referendum, a successful bid to amend the Constitution in order to pre-empt the European Court from legalizing abortion in Ireland. Moynagh Sullivan argues that the coterminous moral panic over Ireland's reproductive futurity and the 'critical fixation' on Heaney's yet-to-be-realized status as the (manly) national poet both respond to a repressed unpalatable reality: neither the personified Eire nor the national poet prefigure a unitary nation-to-be but function instead to mask its failure, the partitioning of the island into two states.[10]

Nevertheless, Heaney's working concept of the feminine seems more heterogeneous when considered abreast of contemporary poetics by women, especially in relation to the *aisling* mode. Boland's LIP pamphlet, 'The Woman Poet in a National Tradition' (1989), argues that women poets have transformed what she generalizes as 'the Irish poem' by refusing the passive role of emblematic muse and boldly assuming the representative role of national poet. She enacts the performative coup in 'Mise Eire' ('I am Ireland'), an overt revision of Pearse's eponymous poem. The poet-speaker asserts her superior prerogative to speak for 'Eire' by inflecting 'I am the woman' with proprietary female representativity. Unlike Boland, who foreswears the *aisling* –'I won't go back to it', 'Mise Eire' begins – Gaelic poet Nuala Ní Dhomhnaill is profoundly engaged with it, and not only because of the genre's centrality to Gaelic literature. The presiding trope and structural principle of Ní Dhomhnaill's *Feis* (1991) is the perfect complementarity symbolized by the sacred marriage of the sovereignty myth (*flaitheas*). Like Heaney, she envisions a poetry of redress in Jungian terms. She adapts the negative aspect of the magna mater archetype, the *cailleach* persona, as a means to confront and work through matrophobia (both personal and societal). For Ní Dhomhnaill and Medbh McGuckian, the idealization of an archaized mother tongue has generative potential for imagining an alternative symbolic order to their received traditions, a utopian conjecture of what their literary vernaculars might be if the enmeshed patriarchal and colonialist bias pervading them could be undone. The *aisling* mode of McGuckian's 'The Dream Language of Fergus', for instance, plays with a primal mother tongue in relation to a hypothesized proto-language culled from Osip Mandelstam's (and Heaney's interpretation of Mandelstam's) reflections on translating Dante. 'Fergus' portrays the quest for primal linguistic purity in a spirit at once sceptical and utopian. The intertextual intimacy between Heaney and McGuckian displayed in this and other poems attests to their mutual influence. Because the voluptuous indeterminacy of McGuckian's verse resonates with French feminist theory, critics repeatedly characterize it in terms of feminine alterity. Heaney's blurb on her *Selected Poems* (1997) eloquently portrays her poetic idiom as a form of (endometrial) *écriture feminine*: 'Her language is like the inner lining of consciousness, the inner lining of English itself, as it moves amphibiously between the dreamlife and her actual domestic and historical experience.' Thus, while feminism apprised Heaney of male privilege in ways that sometimes made him defensive, it also affirmed his proclivity to treat the feminine as the unknowable Other.

Heaney as Foremother?

One of the more remarkable appraisals of the feminine (and the maternal-feminine) dimension of Heaney's poetics occurs in the course of a published dialogue I moderated between Ní Dhomhnaill and Medbh McGuckian in 1992. McGuckian observes that Heaney was 'a wonderful mediatrix' and 'the first person who didn't make her [feel] that poetry was a closed shop' when she studied with him at Queen's in 1972.[11] Ní Dhomhnaill concurs, adding that Heaney's 'great strength is that he is actually a woman – a great big benevolent mountain, standing protectively behind you, like your mother should do'.[12] The representation of Heaney as muse (mediatrix) and perfect mother is striking in the context of a conversation that ranges over how both poets feel they were hurt into poetry by their mothers' inadequate mothering of them, and how this motivates them to foster a 'different [kind of subject/object] reciprocity', based on the experience of maternity, to that practised by their male peers.[13] The portrayal of Heaney as a benevolent literary foremother accords with widespread evidence of Heaney's unstinting hospitality and inclusive generosity towards his contemporaries and readers. Building on Coughlan's close analysis of the materiality of the bogland-as-mother trope, and Moynagh Sullivan's use of object-relations psychoanalysis in her criticism of McGuckian and Heaney, I propose that the munificent-mother tribute pertains not only to the warm and inviting Heaney persona, however, but also to formal aspects of Heaney's oeuvre.

Heaney relates to bogland less as stakeable property than as an encompassing ecosystem of which he is a constituent part, a habitat undergoing continuous change. The 'Ruminant' bog germinates and decomposes as it 'holds / and spreads, / sump and seedbed, / a bag of waters / and a melting grave' (*N* 41, 43). Bogland is readily associated with abjection, and the death-dealing properties of the *cailleach*, but these perturbing associations are counterbalanced by a nurturant beneficence. The poet-speaker's palpable sensual pleasure and evident 'love [for] this turf-face . . . [and for] the spring off the ground' indicate that he also feels buoyed up by the womb-tomb terrain (*N* 40). According to object-relations psychoanalyst Christopher Bollas, formal features of an evocative object (a bog, a blankie or a poem) stimulate uncanny memory traces of the infant's neonatal 'holding' environment that later inhabit language as the 'unthought known' at the core of the aesthetic.[14] A transformational evocative object (person, place, text) exerts a pull because it induces an archaic feeling of being 'held' redolent of the innumerable metamorphoses the newborn experiences even before she can recognize the mother as an other. When bogland, or P.V. Glob's *The Bog People*, quickens the 'unthought known' for Heaney, an aesthetic awakening he especially experiences when '[his] roots cross with [his] reading' (*P* 37), it evokes textures of feeling that seem somehow strangely familiar. Heaney's tactile imagery, and his preoccupation with equilibrium as theme and formal feature, aims to recreate in the poem the subliminal sense of being cradled that accompanies aesthetic satisfaction. Thus a Heaney poem may impart to the reader a sense of being held and balanced in a manner that is often perceived as maternal and feminine.

Second-wave feminism raised the public's, and Heaney's, awareness of sexist bias in language and literary institutions. It confronted him with how the habitual use of gender analogies potentially reinforces sexist depictions of woman as the subordinate partner in a couple and of subjugated groups as feminine. Accordingly Heaney distanced himself from several early pronouncements about gender by not reprinting them. While feminist consciousness-raising ultimately didn't exert decisive influence on Heaney's development as a poet, it did transform the perspectives readers bring to bear on his poetry. And for as long as 'the feminine' remains a loaded 'keyword', with proliferating meanings thwarting conceptual precision, readers shall continue to discover fresh angles for discussing its salience for reading Heaney.

Notes

1 Raymond Williams, *Keywords* (Oxford University Press, 1985), p. 15.
2 Fran Brearton, 'Heaney and the Feminine', in Bernard O'Donoghue (ed.), *The Cambridge Companion to Seamus Heaney* (Cambridge University Press, 2009), pp. 73–91.
3 Moynagh Sullivan, 'The Treachery of Wetness: Irish Studies, Seamus Heaney and the Politics of Parturition', *Irish Studies Review*, 13/4 (2005), 451–68.
4 Edna Longley, *Poetry in the Wars* (Newcastle-upon-Tyne: Bloodaxe, 1986), p. 163.
5 Elizabeth Butler Cullingford, '"Thinking of Her ... as ... Ireland": Yeats, Pearse and Heaney', *Textual Practice*, 4/1 (1990), 1–21 (at p. 11).
6 *Ibid.*, pp. 16, 14.
7 Patricia Coughlan, '"Bog Queens": The Representation of Women in the Poetry of John Montague and Seamus Heaney', in Claire Connolly (ed)., *Theorizing Ireland* (Basingstoke: Palgrave Macmillan 2003), pp. 41–60.
8 Patricia Coughlan, '"The Whole Strange Growth": Heaney, Orpheus and Women', *Irish Review*, 35 (2007), 25–45.
9 Margaret Kelleher, 'The Field Day Anthology and Irish Women's Literary Studies', *Irish Review*, 30 (2003), 82–93 (at p. 83). See also Eavan Boland *et al.*, *A Dozen LIPs* (Dublin: Attic Press, 1994).
10 Sullivan, 'Treachery of Wetness', p. 452.

11 '*Combrá:* Medbh McGuckian and Nuala Ní Dhomhnaill, with a foreword and afterword by Laura O'Connor', *Southern Review*, Special Issue on Irish Poetry, 3/3 (1995), 581–614 (at p. 592).
12 *Ibid.*
13 *Ibid.*, p. 599.
14 Christopher Bollas, *The Shadow of the Object: Psychoanalysis of the Unthought Known* (New York: Columbia University Press, 1987), pp. 17, 51–2 and *passim*.

CHAPTER 25

Heaney in Between

Kevin Whelan

A cliché of Heaney criticism is to divide his poetry into two phases: an earlier one of bog and body, a later one of air and spirit, a movement from gravity to grace. Less observed is that a third phase emerged in the superb efflorescence of magnificent poems in the late Heaney: 'District and Circle', 'The Blackbird of Glanmore', 'The Tollund Man in Springtime' and 'Miracle'. These poems are no longer about body or spirit as a binary but about the catalytic relationship between them, about the constant movement, between time and eternity, between the past and the present, between the represented and the representation, between history and memory, between filiation and affiliation. Heaney made all these things come alive in each other through the sheer power of his representation. Representation, the only mode of cognition for writers, is not secondary – representation for a poet is always the primary act of self-consciousness, not a belated second-best thing that occurs in the aftermath of what we call 'living'. 'I grew up in between', as Heaney recounts in the poem 'Terminus', and his in between-ness became the space from which he spoke, in a voice poised between an inherited vernacular and an acquired literary speech (*OG* 272).[1] He had a sense of growing up 'in suspension between the archaic and the modern', with his own life span bridging the medieval and the postmodern.

The transition from the first life to the second life is a significant threshold in lyric poetry. The first life is where experiences serve a pragmatic purpose and an immediate need while the second life is where they fulfil a need that is psychic and spiritual, a chewing of the imaginative cud. Memories provide a locus where human affections can attach themselves: they provide contours for the inner landscape as well as the outer one.

Heaney retained a sense of his life as a nested circle of overlapping spheres, like the skins of an onion, protecting an inner core, 'concentric ripples widening from the original stir at the centre'.[2] His poetry sought to connect with and exalt what the Nobel citation called 'the living past', but also to connect this public political realm (the history of the hurt) with his interior life (the history of the heart), the world of emotion. Heaney maintained a prodigious access to and receptivity towards the emotional register of that earlier childhood world, sealed hermetically by his family moving from Mossbawn to Bellaghy when he was thirteen, and his own move around the same time to boarding school in Derry, and by the fact that his was an exceptionally unblemished childhood. For Heaney, the child occupies a pristine world – a seamless web of total life – a parochial, hallowed world, simple, innocent and timeless: the child is a primitive – at one with his material, not detached from it. Heaney's writing too is drawn from visible elements, clear but resonant, and possessed of a suggestive aura.

In 1970, Heaney and his family moved to Berkeley for a sunlit, laidback year and his positive reception there by established poets, his friendship with the writer Thomas Flanagan, as well as the congenially relaxed atmosphere of 'the warm-planked, democratic wharves' among 'the twilights and guitars / of Sausalito' (*FW* 19), freed and steeled Heaney the writer. He returned to Ireland in September 1971 with a reinforced sense of writerly purpose and made the decision to commit to the vocation of being a full-time writer.

The resultant move in 1972 to Glanmore Cottage in County Wicklow was greeted with a portentous *Irish Times* headline ('Heaney moves south'), and as good riddance to a 'Papish propagandist' by the *Protestant Telegraph*. Heaney always stressed that the move to Glanmore was not a retreat from the North but an advance in his commitment to writing and his growing sense of certitude as a poet. The four years spent there from August 1972 until November 1976 were hugely conducive to his creative life – it was here that *North*, with its sedimentary, grounded poems was incubated – and Heaney often likened his experience to the Wordsworths at Dove Cottage.

North (1975), Heaney's most controversial book of poetry, attends to the dead of Jutland, the dead of Denmark, the dead of ritual slayings. On a visit to Denmark, he explored the Vikings, and encountered the bog bodies in the museum at Aarhus in Jutland. For him, this experience stirred a recognition of an archetype of violence that had once dominated Northern Europe, including Ireland. The Vikings indulged in the ritual slaughter of young men and women, often by strangulation, and then sacrificed their bodies in the bogs. The bog preserves that which is buried in it. Heaney took this burial and preservation, and sought to make it a paradigm of regeneration. Then he extended the idea of the 'old man-killing parishes' from Scandinavia to the north of Ireland. The catalytic relationship becomes the one between the victims of the Northern

'Troubles' and the assassinated victims of these ancient societies. Critics, notably Ciarán Carson, accused Heaney here of replacing history by destiny: 'It is as if he is saying suffering like this is natural; these things have always happened; they happened then, they happen now, and that is sufficient ground for understanding and absolution. It is as if there never were and never will be any political consequences of such acts.'[3]

Violence surges into Heaney's poetry as painful, disruptive and wounding divisions, for which his poetry is applied as a healing ointment. If Heaney's poetry has one supreme action within it, it is healing. The poet takes something shot, knifed, torn, divided, whose wound is still leaking and bleeding, and his poetry acts as a salve, a bandage, a suture that will mend that which has been torn, not so much to make it whole again but so as to reduce the pain, to make the wound capable of being borne.

This therapeutic function is fundamental to Heaney's poetry. His poetry never erupted into a fulminating rage against the killings of the Troubles as an inevitable consequence of a rancid politics. Rather, he intimated that ritual killings have persisted for centuries, and that these sectarian murders are an updated version of this ancient violence. That tack opened Heaney to the accusation that he was turning the historically specific into something preordained, of converting history into destiny.

In 'Punishment', Heaney gazes at the women who had been tarred and feathered, and tied to the railings of a Catholic church: as he contemplates them, they metamorphose from being two particular women, in a specific and horrific incident, into icons and archetypes of the earlier Viking corpses upon whom he has also gazed. Thereby, Heaney's critics claimed, he extracted the harm out of the horror; he dissolved the historical atrocity and substituted a pallid and melancholy vision of a human destiny indelibly stained by violence.

In 'Funeral Rites', the poet argues that all this violence must be converted into a ritual: you could not live then in Northern Ireland without becoming a connoisseur of funerals. Because Northern Ireland is a tiny place, the casualty rate was proportionately very high: over three and a half thousand deaths in a population of one and a quarter million. Heaney is not considering an individual death, but a generic death - multiple deaths that are consolidated under one aegis. We know that these are the coffins of dead relations, that this is a ritual that has been repeated endlessly, and the poem wants that seepage of ritual repetition to enter into the reader's sensibility: ritual is centred on repetition. 'Sorry for your troubles.' This ritual has been repeated, is being repeated, and will be repeated over and over and over again.

I knelt courteously
admiring it all

as wax melted down
and veined the candles,
the flames hovering
to the women hovering behind me.

And always, in a corner,
the coffin lid,
its nail heads dressed
with little gleaming crosses.
(*N* 6–7)

The ritual effect depends on those deceptive little words like 'the' and 'it'. Death has always been handled this way, this is how his people have always buried their dead. The poet in the middle of it all does not repudiate the conventional, but seeks to render it sacrosanct, hallowed by repetition. He is genuflecting before the dead, because only the observation of someone humbled before a corpse can observe the minute details - the crosses on the nails in the coffin, how the flesh around the knuckles is puffed up in a corpse that has the rosary bound tightly around its fingers. Heaney asks his reader to recognize that this is not just a County Derry funeral, but a generic act of courtesy towards the dead, and that there is a form of redemption in that courtesy: there is no fear of death as a final erasure or extinction – the taboo of the secular world.

With the line 'Now as news comes in / of each neighbourly murder / we pine for ceremony, customary rhythms' (*N* 7), he highlighted the intimate hatred that characterizes Northern Ireland. A Northern Ireland murder is always a neighbourly murder because this is a small, even asphyxiated community. Heaney intimates that we pine for 'customary rhythms', trying to find a way of taking these 'random' killings, and elevating them into some broader understanding that confers a sense of meaning.

'Exposure', the final poem in *North*, responded to Heaney's move south in 1972 as the violence escalated. 'My responsible tristia' (*N* 66) echoes the title of Osip Mandlestam's second book, whose influence Heaney was absorbing at this time. 'A hero on some muddy compound' (*N* 66) is Mandlestam in the Gulag at Veronezh 1934–7, although the phrase also evokes the cages at the Maze internment camp. The poem is suffused with awareness of other exiled poets – Ovid in Tomis, Dante banished to Verona from his beloved Florence, Chekhov on Sakhalin Island. The 'beautiful prismatic counselling' is from Heaney's school and university friend Seamus Deane. The then longhaired Heaney reached back to the Elizabethan displacements of the Gaelic order in the late sixteenth and early seventeenth centuries for his central image:

> I am neither internee nor informer;
> An inner émigré, grown long-haired
> And thoughtful; a wood-kerne
> Escaped from the massacre . . .
>
> (*N* 67)

These wintry lines recall the escape of the young northern leaders O'Neill and O'Donnell in 1592 from Dublin Castle and their flight south to the mountain safety of the O'Byrne territory in south Wicklow, which included Glanmore, where Heaney was then living. There is a further link through Heaney's wife Marie Devlin: the Devlins of Wicklow, prominent in 1798 as associates of Michael Dwyer, were descendants of a northern Devlin who settled here at that time at Ballysimon near Ashford.

Another referent for the 'hero on some muddy compound' is found in 'Hercules and Antaeus' (*N* 46–7), a poem that marked a major transition in his poetry. From now on, Heaney forsakes his poems about shapes that dissolve and are reconstituted: he pursues instead another kind of poetry in which it is not the ground that predominates but the air: he pursues a poetry of the spirit as opposed to a poetry of the body. Heaney considered Hercules and Antaeus as 'a dangerous poem to have written': 'Hercules represents the balanced rational light while Antaeus represents the pieties of illiterate fidelity.'[4] That up–down, drag–lift, earth–air, Hercules–Antaeus, sky-at-the-bottom-of-the-well motif recurs throughout the work.

Antaeus in Greek myth was the giant that could not be beaten while he stood Heaney's ground. Hercules defeated Antaeus by the simple tactic of lifting him off the ground, 'in a remorseless V' (*N* 47) where he loses his power. Heaney's early work emphasized the strength and vitalism that come from staying grounded, from belonging, from keeping close to roots and origins. From the mid 1980s, Heaney's poetry is written as if in the aftermath of being lifted from the ground. Human existence is pre-eminently not physical but spiritual, not grounded but immaterial. Heaney knows that the opposite of materialism is idealism. When his Hercules lifts his Antaeus off the ground, it is as if Heaney is admonishing himself: 'Enough of me located down there; come out of your farm in Co. Derry, leave your mosses and mud and muck, and see the great world. Let yourself be raised up by Hercules in this V (a sign for victory) and become a ridge of mountains, become "pap for the dispossessed"' (that ferocious line).

Hercules lifts his arms
in a remorseless V,
his triumph unassailed
by the powers he has shaken

and lifts and banks Antaeus
high as a profiled ridge,
a sleeping giant,
pap for the dispossessed.
(*N* 46–7)

There was a similar transition in Heaney's own style, fully present in *Seeing Things*, the 1991 volume that marked a profound shift in his poetry. The geometrical rigidity of the square-shouldered four-line stanza that Heaney had relied on in his earlier collections relaxed dramatically. The formal and metrical rigour loosens and the musicality deepens – as if Heaney had abandoned the penny whistle and taken up the uilleann pipes. The poetry itself, especially after *The Haw Lantern* in 1987, was becoming lighter, elevating off the sodden ground and into the air. Milosz, Brodsky and Walcott became his new mentors for the complicated passages that he was tracking from the conditions of oppression to those of freedom, from dispute, clamour and violence to serenity, ocularity and wisdom, from the stasis of memory into the vision of reverie, a Yeatsian manoeuvre.

Heaney's enduring strategic vocabulary had been of ground and the earth from which everything grows but a ground which has simultaneously the quality of being solid and the quality of being deliquescent, as fluid as water. He grappled with the actuality of things that are rooted in the ground, the personal, local and domestic experience of his own growing up, and then the phenomenon of growing out of that towards another world, the element of air and light. The migration in his poetry is from earth, with its pretensions to solidity, towards a light that is dissolving, a lightness whereby every thing that was material is converted into air. And yet, even as it is converted into light, it does not lose or break contact with the earth from which it initially grew.

Heaney's particular favourite 'air' poem of sudden reversals was 'Lightenings' viii from the 'Squarings' sequence in *Seeing Things* (1991). In it, the realms of the real and the marvellous intersect as the earthbound monks are amazed by the air ship caught in their altar rails. But when the ship is released successfully, the perspective changes as the man climbs back 'Out of the marvellous as he had known it' (*OG* 338). Heaney often invoked the courage and flexibility of the crewman in his poem as the ideal position of the poet, 'between the ground of everyday experience and the airier realm of an imagined world', while also stressing the need for wisdom to solve difficulties, as displayed by the abbot.[5]

This new turn in his poetry was accentuated by the death of Heaney's parents (Margaret in 1984, Patrick in 1986), and of his three beloved aunts – Mary in 1980, Grace in 1991 and Sarah in 1995. As he said in an interview with George Morgan, 'The important moment for me was the death of my parents and the freedom that gave me to use a more numinous vocabulary. You need the words to tackle death. You are at the death-bed and they are alive this moment, they are dead the next. What has disappeared?'[6] These deaths, a searingly personal encounter with the most profound human experience of presence and absence, as the embodied becomes the ethereal, triggered a searching response in Heaney's poetry, an effort to find spiritual meaning in his post-Catholic but not secularized vision.

Heaney characteristically did not research or fact search before writing; he was a poet, not a historian, answerable only to the protocols of the imagination. A favourite 'touchstone' of the poet, which he often used when signing his volumes, came from *Timon of Athens*: 'Our poetry is as a gum which oozes / from whence 'tis nourished.' Heaney always regarded his poetic talent as a gift: something external given to him, something that mysteriously expressed itself and breathed through him (the original meaning of inspiration). 'The Given Note' expresses that sense of being grounded and grateful:

> He took it
>
> Out of wind off mid-Atlantic.
> Still he maintains, from nowhere.
> It comes off the bow gravely,
> Rephrases itself into the air.
>
> (*DD* 46)

In 'District and Circle', Heaney entered the London Underground and compared it to the journey in Virgil's *Aeneid*, when Virgil enters the underworld. He also remembers Dante descending into the Inferno, going into hell. In the Christian as well as the pagan centuries, the dead descend into the underworld, only to rise again, not into this world, but into a transfigured world. The journey into the underworld is fraught with danger and fright: its fatal attraction is that while you may be able to see again those loved ones who have died before you, you will not encounter them as they once were. They reveal themselves to you as revenants, ghosts by whom you will be haunted for the rest of your life, but who also void your existing world, rendering it spectral and hollow. Note the title of Heaney's collection *Seeing Things*.

A repeated image in the poem 'District and Circle', is of people in the carriage of a subway train hurtling along between the walls of the tunnel: Heaney insinuates the possibility of a sudden explosion. While fearing a blackout-like death, the people are also seeing fragmented, shimmering, shuddering reflections of one another in the windows of the carriage of the train against the tunnel walls. When Heaney sees himself in the fractured image in the train window, he suddenly recognizes a resemblance between how he now looks and how he remembers his father. So he recalls his famous early poems about his father. He reverts to the idea of not just seeing yourself in the past but also of seeing into the past. His Viking poems are about the Jutland killings of all those centuries ago but they are equally about the Northern Irish killings of the Troubles. When you find a way of positioning one in relation to the other, when you realize that one is recognizable in terms of the other, that familiarity becomes a new way of knowing.

In 'District and Circle', he used the phrase 'human chain', the title of his next book, as he enters the Underground and the metaphorical underworld:

> Another level down, the platform thronged.
> I re-entered the safety of numbers,
> A crowd half straggle-ravelled and half strung
> Like a human chain, the pushy newcomers
> Jostling and purling underneath the vault . . .
> (*DC* 18)

As he descends to the second level of the underground, a new crowd rushes through another entrance and mixes with the swirling crowd already there. It is rush hour, trains are packed, everyone is tensed to enter as quickly as possible through the train doors. Heaney described these people as only a random straggle lacking connection with one another. But then he reconsiders: maybe they are part of a human chain, maybe even this most miscellaneous crowd is a connected chain of human beings. This is the human chain – every human community in space or in time is connected as the links of a chain are connected.

Co-existent with that concept, and just as strong, is the desolate notion that these people are no longer connected in any chain of communal fraternity. We must regard ourselves as completely insignificant creatures among millions of others: in our termite condition, we are mere underground insects scurrying about on trivial tasks. 'A crowd half straggle-ravelled and half strung': we are unravelled because no community binds us together.

The poem proposes, on the one hand, that there is the possibility of a human chain, belonging, community, shared experience, transfigured experience, but on the other hand rebukes this possibility with equal vehemence to the point where the poem simply stops, because there Heaney can deliver no credible resolution to this dilemma:

And so by night and day to be transported
Through galleried earth with them, the only relict
Of all that I belonged to, hurtled forward,
Reflecting in a window mirror-backed
By blasted weeping rock-walls.
Flicker-lit. (*DC* 19)

Heaney abruptly terminates the line and jumps to the last foot of the last line (4/5 of which is blank) and just inserts 'Flicker-lit'. 'Flicker-lit' is perfect here. This is a poem flicker-lit by hope but surrounded by darkness. 'Galleried earth' reminds us of the victims of the London Underground bombing, of all the Viking dead, of the sacrificial bog people, of the megalithic tombs of Brú na Bóinne. Heaney evokes a human ritual designed to confer or represent meaning, the power of a community bound together by a sacrifice (which is the root meaning of religion – to bind together).

When you enter into the underworld, the hope is that you will eventually re-emerge out of it with the idea of human community ever more indelibly stamped, like Aeneas's descent into the underworld carrying the golden bough or the Christian funeral where the body becomes part of the faithfully departed 'marked with the sign of faith'. Virgil's and Dante's magnificent descents insist that the underworld is ultimately not the real world. The underworld remains subterranean, below our human level. In contrast, Heaney is haunted by the idea that once you descend, only the memory of an exit remains. Remembered exit is an invention, a desperate fiction that is not actually endorsed by experience. Heaney generates a brooding claustrophobia in *District and Circle* – coffined under the ground in a rock-encased tunnel, flicker-lit walls, distorted human faces reflecting on the glass like the shades of the classical underworld, recognizable people, yes, but lacking substantial presence. They are the living dead and we must reach the melancholy conclusion that this journey and their journey will go on forever. No Dantean moment, no consoling light, rescues the moment when Heaney re-emerges into the light, 'E quindi uscimmo a riveder le stelle.'[7]

Heaney's great poems, situated between the life and the writing of the life, will remain part of the imaginative resources of the world as long as people read poetry.

Notes

1 *OG* in this chapter refers to Seamus Heaney, *Opened Ground* (New York: Farrar, Straus and Giroux, 1998).
2 Seamus Heaney, 'The Art of Poetry No. 75', Interviewed by Henri Cole in May 1994, *Paris Review*, 144 (Fall 1997), www.theparisreview.org/interviews/1217/the-art-of-poetry-no-75-seamus-heaney.
3 Ciarán Carson, 'Escaped from the Massacre?' *Honest Ulsterman*, 50 (1975), 183–6 (at p. 184).
4 Seamus Deane, 'Unhappy and at Home', interview, *Crane Bag*, 1/1 (1977), 61–7 (at p. 62).
5 Esther de Groot, 'Seamus Heaney', in Sheila Clarke (ed.), *Ashford Writers in Residence* (Dublin: Ashford, 2006), pp. 102–19 (at p. 115).
6 George Morgan, interview with Seamus Heaney, *Cycnos*, 15/2 (July 2008), http://revel.unice.fr/cycnos/?id=1594.
7 'The guide and I entered by that hidden path, to return to the clear world: and, not caring to rest, we climbed up, he first, and I second, until, through a round opening, I saw the beautiful things that the sky holds: and we issued out, from there, to see, again, the stars.'

CHAPTER 26

Critical Audiences

Justin Quinn

This essay begins with the moment when Seamus Heaney's reputation spread from Ireland and the United Kingdom, where he became established in the late 1960s, to the United States, as it allows us to understand some of the ways in which his critical audiences relate to one another. It will also consider Heaney within the emerging critical context of global Anglophone poetry. This may appear to be a task of mapping the poet's reception, yet the terms of that reception influenced the turns of Heaney's poetry. Yeats's definition of poetry as 'the quarrel with ourselves' is singularly unhelpful in Heaney's case, as the later poet was necessarily aware of his poems' international readership. This acclaim – and where it brought him and whom it brought him into contact with – became integral to his imaginative world. Thus if we consider some of the critical contours of Heaney's reception, both at home and abroad, we also learn more about the poetry itself.

As Heaney's fame spread beyond Ireland and England to the United States, and as several American critics, publications and institutions consolidated his position, a counter-argument questioned this international fame. In a review of *The Spirit Level* (1995), Peter McDonald asked, 'Are Heaney's most enthusiastic fans those who know least about his artistic, political, and historical contexts?'[1] Yet a representation of those contexts was integral to his reputation beyond Ireland; as Edna Longley remarked, 'There are pressures on poets to emphasize their Irishness in America, and according to pre-existing categories.'[2] Heaney's poetry has always been deeply engaged with the social, cultural and political history of Ireland and England; this is manifest on linguistic, formal and thematic levels. It is thus natural that some critics question the terms of his reception in the United States. McDonald goes as far as to say that 'praise from Belfast means more, and reveals much more, than celebration from American academe'.[3]

The most prominent US advocate of Heaney's work is Helen Vendler. She wrote reviews of his books on several occasions, and also an introductory study, *Seamus Heaney* (1998). The terms of her praise are instructive. Acknowledging that most readers appreciate his treatment of autobiography and the Irish political context, she nonetheless claims that the sources of his power lie elsewhere: 'Lyric is not narrative or drama; it is not primarily concerned to relate events, or to reify contesting issues. Rather, its act is to present, adequately and truthfully, through the means of temporally prolonged symbolic form, the private mind and heart caught in the changing events of a geographical and historical epoch.'[4] Along the way she does sketch in some historical and autobiographical background, in order to give an idea of the conflicts – both military and hermeneutic – that Heaney negotiates in his poetry. But the terms of this are troubled: one of Heaney's central *themes* is the effort to win freedom for lyric poetry in the face of adverse circumstances. Vendler is a fine explicator of poetic form, but she fails to register the extent to which she finds in Heaney's poetry a retelling of critical debates in the US from the 1950s onward.

For Vendler is an exponent of New Criticism, a practice that designates biographical, historical, psychological and other contexts as of secondary importance to the study of poetry. Underwritten by humanist values, it fought a long rearguard action in the US academy against politicizing tendencies – first from the old Left in the 1950s (which it won), and then against multiculturalism (which it lost). Necessary to her reading is a flattening out of the specificity of Irish historical circumstances. For instance, when she remarks how '"The Troubles," like all complex historical events, have produced rival explanations',[5] one might wonder at the sub clause. She must not consider the way in which the Troubles were *unlike* other historical events, in order to read Heaney as, like her, an advocate of lyric poetry. Of course, Heaney was such an advocate, but Vendler's *parti pris* creates a blind spot in her criticism: time and again it is precisely certain thematic aspects of his work that she explicates. Her critical work on Heaney is not reducible to this dynamic, but it is a significant and silent element of her engagement.

Like many Irish writers before him, Heaney arrived in the US with a story of colonial oppression. Regardless of his sophisticated treatment of this theme, his poetry could be slotted into a narrative of victimhood, allowing US critics to overlook those aspects of the poetry which they would have questioned in an American writer. Of interest in this respect is criticism of John Updike by feminist critics in the 1980s, in general terms similar to Patricia Coughlan's critique of Heaney in 1991.[6] With accuracy and éclat Coughlan analysed Heaney's uncritical acceptance of gender tropes of the land and colonial victimhood, even as he overturned other political codes.[7] So while Heaney is critiqued for his use of gender by an Irish critic, in the US his postcolonial status precludes it. It would seem that one can be patriarchal as long as one can claim a different victimhood.

It is also helpful here to note the background to the US's relationship with postcolonialism and its authors. At first glance, it seems natural that the US would favour those countries which, like itself, also escaped the British Empire. Common enemies make close friends. However, in the decade or so after World War II, as the United Kingdom's global power was irreversibly reduced, nation-states emerging from colonialism were viewed as inimical to the US. As Frantz Fanon's work in the 1950s made clear, these countries were drawn to communism, suspicious that the US was merely taking over from Great Britain as imperial master. The turn occurred in the 1970s, with the arrival of Heaney, Derek Walcott and others. These poets, through personal friendships and poetic debts, forged links with the dissident writers of the Eastern Bloc, connecting their postcolonial stance with anti-communism. Led by Joseph Brodsky, these writers would often claim that their interest in such work was apolitical and purely aesthetic. However, it is noteworthy that they favoured poets who suffered at the hands of the communist authorities; and their political accommodations, like those of Miroslav Holub (whom Heaney championed), were passed over in silence. Much is made of Heaney's engagement with Eastern European writers, and many critics have emphasized the parallels between the stories of dissent and colony. But this misses a more important linkage: these parallels take on importance in the arena of the United States during the Cold War, as they instructed Heaney's and Walcott's hosts how the postcolonial story could be shifted from the left to the right.[8]

If Vendler's self-described New Criticism floats on strong political currents, Longley and McDonald are New Critics of a different variety. Or rather their writing shows that the nature of New Criticism is site-specific. Like Vendler, they are attentive to the poetry as a discourse different from political speeches and editorials, but they know the ways in which these can be strategically used to engage with politics. Remarking on Vendler's approach, Longley comments that 'as Northern Irish poetry negotiated its political context after 1969, insofar as a New Critical ethos persisted, it was translated into new kinds of concentration, verbal complexity, formal reflexiveness, close reading, arguments about value … From one angle, this restored the historical-political dimension of Yeats – invisible to American poet-critics.'[9] This implies a historically informed criticism that does not scant the rhetorical forces particular to poetry. As a general aim, this is salutary if it now relies too much as foil on the neo-nationalist criticism of Declan Kiberd, Seamus Deane and others, as evidenced by Longley's recent *Yeats and Modern Poetry*, which reiterates many of her positions of the 1990s. It is possible, indeed, that her attacks on neo-nationalism ironically only keep it on life support.

In Ireland, the UK and the US, in different ways, the important framework, then, for understanding Heaney's poetry was postcolonialism. In Northern Ireland, it came with fierce debates about the role of culture in such violent times. Heaney, both as poet and as member of Field Day, was fully involved in these, even while usually seeking an eirenic position. In the UK, at the heart of the former empire, his reception was different again, a little less discerning about the finer details; but this was cross-hatched by other resonances, for instance with Scottish poets and critics. Heaney's engagement with Norman MacCaig, Somhairle MacGill-Eain and George Mackay Brown was long-standing, alerting him to ways in which another Gaelic culture could make forays into the empire; also, the Scottish critic Karl Miller was one of Heaney's earliest advocates in London, as editor of the *Listener* from 1967 to 1973, and then at the *London Review of Books*. As we move across the Atlantic, the historical detailing gets vaguer, and, as Longley implies, becomes part of older sentimental ideas of Ireland's struggle with the British oppressor; it also slots easily into America's quite unsentimental Cold War cultural policy. This is where Heaney's work meets with Vendler's particular type of aestheticism, very different from that of Northern Irish critics' close reading of poems. And both are attempts to establish poetry's position in relation to politics. Each of these contexts engages postcolonialism in different ways; like New Criticism, it too is site-specific.

In recent years, however, a further critical framework has suggested itself, in part due to shifting cultural interests, and in part due to a change in Heaney's later work (the two are doubtless connected). Globalism has become an important area of academic interest, as thinkers have tried to grasp the ways in which, first, capital connects disparate parts of the world, forging new mercurial causative patterns; second, the way that capital has helped culture travel in new ways through different cultures. Often this is vaguely characterized as a homogenizing process, but others have argued that counter-currents are also present, which reconfigure links to local traditions and small languages.

In 'Known World', from the collection *Electric Light* (2001), Heaney tells of his attendance at an international poetry conference in Macedonia in 1978. As he moves into the new global arena that gathers poets from a wide range of countries, he looks back to his own beginnings, figuring his childhood home with uncharacteristic severity, referring to it metonymically as a 'death-trap' and 'a barley-sugar twist / Of glut and loathing' (*EL* 20). The poem ends with him rising into the clouds, transported by a Lufthansa Boeing, and 'took it as my due when wine was poured / By a slight *de haut en bas* of my headphoned head. / *Nema problema. Ja.* All systems go' (*EL* 22–3).[10] Here we have Heaney as comfortable cosmopolitan, circulating along the slipstreams of global airspace, at home in translation, and privileged. In other poems he would fret at such privilege and the distance from his beginnings, but 'Known World' helps us understand how this connection between the local and global becomes one of the central themes of Heaney's work in the second half of his career, especially in the final ten to fifteen years of his life. Ramazani comments on this aspect of his work: 'Rather than merely reacting against various globalizing forces, from the tenth to the twenty-first century, Heaney's poetry participates in and illuminates them. He shows globalization to enter individual lives even in remote rural sites, introduced by radio, electric light, mobile populations, war, travel, poems and different languages.'[11] He continues by demonstrating how such experiences are 'mirrored within the intrinsic binding structures that hold together a poem's teeming patterns',[12] revealing that the global is not merely a theme in Heaney's poetry, but is played out within the internal mechanisms of the poems themselves. Criticism thus continues with close reading, but now against the horizon of the world.

Is Heaney then a cosmopolitan poet? The adjective is associated with both a glossy fashion magazine and a cocktail, both perhaps consumed in a lounge overlooking a global metropolis like New York; whereas Heaney, over his entire career, harks back to his upbringing in the specific locality of Bellaghy, in Northern Ireland. But that wide world, as Ramazani shows, is also one of Heaney's mainstays. His poetry emerges not purely from the local, but in its juxtaposition with more distant horizons – sometimes different climates and countries, and especially from his mid-career, the earth itself, as we see in poems like 'Alphabets' and 'M'. Alexander Beecroft remarks how cosmopolitan literatures 'frequently indulge in the trope of universalizing imagery or themes from [an] earlier tradition, reworking what was once a more local tradition so that it can better serve a larger world'.[13] Transferred to our notional cocktail lounge in New York, this means that its best clientele are those who bring something of their hinterlands with them. There may be some interesting mud on their boots.

While this argues for the importance of the world as a theme (offset against local origins) in Heaney's work, it does not yet mean that Heaney has a global audience, as for instance Allen Ginsberg had (and as Eliot, Byron and Shakespeare before him). Heaney has been translated into many languages, but it does not yet seem that he has influenced their poetries to an extent comparable to the American poet.[14] Taking two examples of poetic traditions that had a strong effect on Heaney himself, we see the conveyance of his own work out of English has not been as easy as most would think. The first Czech translator, Zdeněk Hron, excelled especially in versions of the Metaphysical poets and Tony Harrison, but he had difficulty rendering the tone and play of dialect words in Heaney's poems.[15] One reviewer provided a detailed account of the many misreadings and questionable formal choices in his translations.[16] Ewald Osers and Ivana Bozděchová worked together on the other book-length selection of Heaney's poetry in Czech. Again, the reaction was not positive, and for a later publication Bozděchová was awarded the prize for worst translation of the year by the Czech Literary Translators' Guild.[17] In Poland the situation was different, where two of the country's most talented translators turned their hands to his poems. Jerzy Jarniewicz describes how important Heaney was for the poet and translator Piotr Sommer from the mid-1970s, but Sommer did not publish a book-length selection until 1998, and by this time he had turned his attention to the New York School of poets.[18] The other translator was Stanisław Barańczak, who published another selection in 1995. Jarniewicz describes the different emphases of these two gifted translators, and this might lead one to think that Heaney's presence in Poland was assured. It seems, however, that the country valued him more for what he could do to promote Poland beyond its borders – Jarniewicz remarks that 'Heaney became in fact the cultural ambassador of Poland in the West.'[19] Magdalena Kay remarks that his relationship with Polish poetry 'is not based on reciprocal influence – Heaney has not had great influence on Polish poets'.[20]

More generally, Heaney presents challenges to the translator above and beyond those of many other poets. First, he makes frequent use of traditional devices such as rhyme and metre, and this requires skills that poetry translators increasingly lack. John Dryden, when editing Ovid's *Metamorphoses* in translation, could call upon a large number of mediocre poets who were technically competent; however, now most Anglophone poets and translators would struggle to write a passable stanza in regular metre and rhyme. Of course, such competence is not necessary for a poet – given the major achievements of poets in free verse, this much is clear – but its general lack in poetic culture makes it difficult to secure translations of poets who use such devices. The differing global reputations of Eliot and

Yeats have something to do with their different natures as poets, but a large role is also played by the fact that Eliot's major works for the most part are in free verse, whereas Yeats forged some of his finest poems in the more demanding forms of the European tradition, such as ottava rima.

The next difficulty that a Heaney translator faces is the play of various dialects – as the accent and lexicon of Heaney's birthplace collides with that of the metropolis (dramatized in a poem like 'Making Strange'). As many critics have pointed out, this is one of the central themes of Heaney's work and it is enacted in a consciously tactile way in his poetry. It is also one of the hardest things to convey in translation, as it requires an approximation of the historical, linguistic and cultural history of Ireland and Britain. Nothing of comparable difficulty exists in Ginsberg's or Eliot's poetry. One of the most dramatic effects in the history of cinema occurs in *The Wizard of Oz* (1939), when Dorothy wakes up after the tornado and emerges from a monochrome Kansas farmhouse into the Technicolor environment of Munchkinland. Losing the play of dialect in Heaney's poetry is the equivalent of watching this film on a black-and-white television.

If we restrict our attention to poetry in the English language, a more profitable field of study opens. In *Global Anglophone Poetry: Literary Form and Social Critique in Walcott, Muldoon, de Kok, and Nagra* (2015), Omaar Hena identifies our moment as one caught between the postcolonial and the cosmopolitan.[21] Many of the patterns and structures of colony persist into the present, and indeed created many of the foremost aspects of present globalization (the most salient is perhaps the supremacy of English as a lingua franca). Heaney's work is poised between these, which are both poetic themes and ways of reading. His imaginative mainstay was the farmlands in Northern Ireland where he grew up; again, a shift to cosmopolitanism would seem to suggest a shucking off of that rural background, but the opposite is the case. As Ramazani implies, Heaney gives us new ways to understand the connections between such localities and the larger horizons of the world. Whereas in his earlier work, especially the place-name poems of *Wintering Out* (1972), Heaney inflected these phenomena into the narrative of empire and colony, in the later work, as in 'Known World' above, he is curious about how the intimate knowledge of home (accent, religion, political allegiance) is balanced against the expanse of the world.

Above I argued that use of traditional poetic form can retard a poet's journey into other languages; is this any different when we remain within English for a global audience? Hena argues that 'Because the medium of poetry has a particularly long history, it has the unique advantage of tapping into prior histories of colonial conquest as they are carried in the conventions of form, genre, and intertextuality'.[22] This implies moral responsibilities for the cosmopolitan artist, not merely wine served in a Lufthansa jet at 35,000 feet; equally it demands an allegiance to the craft and tradition of the art of poetry. The two demands can be hard to accommodate. Arguably Heaney has only one category of victimhood, and as he shifts, and his critics with him, to a globalized context beyond that of postcolonialism, he fails to register the responsibilities of such privilege. He feels a measure of guilt about his prerogatives, but cannot identify which persons, elsewhere, are paying for them. This particular blind spot is apparent in 'The Tollund Man in Springtime', where he revisited his earlier poem, now tracing the resonances of the ancient figure through a global metropolis (as opposed to imperial capital). Having established this new environment with characteristic virtuosity, Heaney then seems at a loss and clips the poem shut with a two-word sentence which merely registers one of the phenomenal aspects of his experience (on the Underground the passing walls are 'Flicker-lit', *DC* 19). Heaney had intimations of the world beyond postcolonialism, but the poems provide only partial accounts. He may thus be read best as a poet on the border of these two paradigms, their pressures and easings giving contours to his work in ways we have not fully learned to read.

Notes

I would like to acknowledge the assistance of Alena Dvořáková, Jacek Gutorow, Jerzy Jarniewicz, Jahan Ramazani and David Wheatley when writing this essay.

1 Peter McDonald, 'Levelling Out', review of The Spirit Level, *Thumbscrew*, 5 (Summer 1996), 39–48 (at p. 47).
2 Edna Longley, *Poetry and Posterity* (Highgreen: Bloodaxe, 2000), p. 243.
3 Peter McDonald, 'Faiths and Fidelities: Heaney and Longley in Mid-Career', in Fran Brearton and Eamonn Hughes (eds.), *Last before America: Irish and American Writing* (Belfast: Blackstaff, 2001), pp. 3–16 (at p. 6).
4 Helen Vendler, *Seamus Heaney* (Cambridge, MA: Harvard University Press, 1998), p. 12.
5 *Ibid.*, p. 40.
6 See Mervyn Rothstein, 'In *S.*, Updike Tries the Woman's Viewpoint', *New York Times*, 2 March 1988, C21.
7 Patricia Coughlan, '"Bog Queens": The Representation of Women in the Poetry of John Montague and Seamus Heaney', in Toni O'Brien Johnson and David Cairns (eds.), *Gender in Irish Writing* (Milton Keynes: Open University Press, 1991), pp. 88–112. See also Coughlan's article which explains the subsequent development of Heaney's reaction to her critique: '"The Whole

Strange Growth": Heaney, Orpheus and Women', *Irish Review*, 35 (2006), 25–45.

8 I make this argument at greater length in *Between Two Fires: Transnationalism and Cold War Poetry* (Oxford: Oxford University Press, 2015), pp. 143–94.

9 Longley, *Poetry and Posterity*, p. 249.

10 I discuss this poem and this subject at greater length in 'Regionalism, Globalization, and Seamus Heaney's Latin Lift-off', *Journal of European Studies* 46/1 (2016), 1–14.

11 Jahan Ramazani, 'Seamus Heaney's Globe', *Irish Review*, 49–50 (Winter 2014 – Spring 2015), 38–53 (at p. 49).

12 *Ibid.*

13 Alexander Beecroft, *An Ecology of World Literature: From Antiquity to the Present Day* (London: Verso, 2015), p. 34.

14 For an account of Ginsberg's international reputation, and more generally that of the Beats, see Nancy M. Grace and Jennie Skerl (eds.), *The Transnational Beat Generation* (New York: Palgrave Macmillan, 2012).

15 See Seamus Heaney, *Přezimování pod širým nebem*, trans. Zdeněk Hron (Prague: BB Art, 2002).

16 Alena Dvořáková, 'Poezie v imigraci: Seamus Heaney', *Tvar*, 20 (2003), 23.

17 See Seamus Heaney, *Jasanová hůl*, trans. Ivana Bozděchová and Ewald Osers (Olomouc: Volvox Globator, 1998). By coincidence, or not, Bozděchová had translated Osers' memoirs.

18 Jerzy Jarniewicz, *In the Shadow of Foreign Tongues: Essays on Irish Poets* (Łódź University Press, 2014), p. 84.

19 *Ibid.*, p. 94.

20 Magdalena Kay, *In Gratitude for All the Gifts: Seamus Heaney and Eastern Europe* (Toronto: Toronto University Press, 2012), p. 40.

21 Omaar Hena remarks that 'the binaries held over from colonialism and the Cold War … are far from over and continue to frustrate claims to cosmopolitan culture', in *Global Anglophone Poetry: Literary Form and Social Critique in Walcott, Muldoon, de Kok, and Nagra* (New York: Palgrave Macmillan, 2015), p. 5. For a different account of cosmopolitanism in Heaney, see Michael Cronin, 'Ireland's Fractal Futures: Seamus Heaney and the Cultures of Possibility', in Eugene McNulty and Ciarán Mac Murchaidh (eds.), *Hearing Heaney: The Sixth Seamus Heaney Lectures* (Dublin: Four Courts Press, 2015), pp. 124–35.

22 Hena, *Global Anglophone Poetry*, p. 2.

CHAPTER 27

The Postcolonial

Deepika Bahri

Is Seamus Heaney a postcolonial poet? The assumption of a mutually exclusive relationship between aesthetics and politics, because the 'postcolonial approach . . . sacrifices literary understanding on the altar of politics',[1] long bedevilled debates about the fit of the Irish case within a postcolonial paradigm. While Edna Longley warned of the danger of flattening specific histories in 'the post-colonial pastry-cutter',[2] Dermot Bolger insisted upon its dual obsolescence and irrelevance for 'younger writers'.[3] Critics such as Luke Gibbons, however, stoutly defend a reckoning with Ireland's colonial history in terms that emerge as the staples of the postcolonial condition in almost all ways comparable to many Third World locations. Profiling this history, Gibbons explains that 'conquest was not restricted to military and political subjugation, but involved the classical colonial patterns of confiscation and plantation of land, and systematic attempts to extirpate native law, language, religion, and culture'.[4] Heaney is not a postcolonial poet merely because Ireland was colonized; rather, it is Heaney's ability to inhabit the borders of a colonial cartography while crossing them to create transnational connections that plants his poetry securely within the postcolonial aesthetic imaginary. In this essay, I evaluate the status of Seamus Heaney as a postcolonial poet by arguing for a reading of Heaney's concurrent investment in matters related to colonial politics alongside the burden of aesthetics such that form emerges as sedimented content, and colonial borders yield to a transnational imagination. While rooted in Ireland and a landscape marked by colonialism, Heaney's brand of transnational poetics is marked by *errancy*, a mode of wandering and taking flight that discloses alternative horizons for the postcolonial aesthetic and political imaginary. Along with references to other works, this essay features a close reading of an unpublished poem, 'Errata for BK'.

The installation of a hard line between the political and the poetic forestalls the possibility of grappling fully with 'important intuitions of

Irish identity', through a poetic alembic.[5] It is only when that line is eroded that new relationships between the local and the global begin to loom into view. Then, political cartographies are reimagined through a utopian schema that rises above the here and now to offer new vistas for the imagination. The political Heaney, cast as the poet of the Northern troubles and Irish colonial history, is charged with the burden of representing the experiences and injuries of imperial history; the poet Heaney, *the Nobel Prize-winning poet Heaney*, however, is the colossus who bestrides the world stage of literature through sustained 'fidelity to the processes and experiences of poetry', to use his own words (*P* 56). The occupation of the poet is to be preoccupied with the poetic, whatever else his allegiance. To suggest that in Heaney the poetic and political find felicitous reconciliation is not to render him immune from criticism about his inattention or inadequate response to the injuries of Irish history, but rather to suggest that Heaney finds a way of translating his poetic *and* political burden across the charted borders of politicized and imaginatively foreclosed geographies.

Postcolonial writers have responded variously to imperial history, bemoaning what Molara Ogundipe-Leslie calls 'time's insults' and 'the agonies of flogged races' in her poem 'To a "Jane Austen" Class at Ibadan University'. The poem nonetheless ends with a plea, echoing and restitching into her own the words of Ghanaian poet Kofi Awoonor: 'Sew the old days that we may wear them / to dance through coming storms.'[6] The storms are coming and will continue, she intimates. What does it mean to dance through them, wearing, essentially, a cloak woven with words, one's own *inter*-woven with others, not least those of Jane Austen who dominates the curriculum and obscures from her Nigerian students' view the ruthless colonizer '[Robert] Clive's antics'? The poem reckons with the challenge of living with history while fighting it, with pen as weapon and an ear to the ground for the rumble of storms to come. Is this poetic error, a wandering away from the immediate political context (if etymology is to be trusted, error implies a wandering away or going astray) or an attempt to imagine another destiny than the one in progress in its tethering to colonial geography and history? Or indeed, is it both? Why is this a particularly postcolonial poetics – postcolonial because both local and transnational, poetic because it permits a vision disclosed in the glide between the border and that which is broader than the given political border?

In what specific ways is Heaney's a postcolonial and transnational aesthetic? Trusty staples of a postcolonial condition – place names, religious references and an English that is hoist by its own petard, to name but a few – appear with such regularity in his poetry that it is specious to deny the mooring of his poetry in historical space and time. For Heaney, however, the boundary is also a confluence, the poetic is also political and 'Two buckets' are 'easier carried than one' (*OG* 272). To define this as a *postcolonial* and transnational aesthetic is to commend the particulars of historical and geographical experience to the reader's attention, but to define it as a postcolonial and transnational *aesthetic* is to see how his poems rise above a *particular* geography and a *foreclosed* historical timeframe through an extension of political and poetic reach. Culture, self and identity are at once located and dislocated in this poetic alembic, and the poet's true north seeks its compass from the frontiers of writing and the republic of conscience rather than the geopolitics of nation and the self that is shaped by it. At stake in my essay is a willingness to blur what Jahan Ramazani describes as the traditional foci of transnational analyses, to wit 'formal, national, or regional borders' in the interest of reading poetry 'within, across, and against these groupings'.[7] At stake, moreover, is a reckoning with Heaney's writing as a species of *errancy*, a wanderlust that leads the poet from known, bounded worlds to uncharted poetic provinces, the frontiers of writing and the republic of conscience, with a word-hoard for company.

Heaney's poetic ethic of writing as wandering rather than landing emerges forcefully in a line from his unpublished poem 'Errata for BK': 'For border read broader.'[8] The poem was written on the occasion of Irish writer Benedict Kiely's eightieth birthday in 2000.[9] Heaney composed it in imitation of Paul Muldoon's 'Errata', published in the *New Yorker* in 1998.[10] Taking the form of editorial corrections on the proof copy of the text, 'Errata for BK' is of course a private toast to Kiely, but it might also be read as an experiment in the poet's task of *rectifying*, of setting things straight by finding alliances and substitutions within the realm of words. It begins, charmingly, thus: 'For BK read OK', cleverly suggests that 'For Kiely [we] read kindly', and concludes with a toast, 'For eighty read sláinte.' Cheers. But what begins as a nonce poem exceeds its purpose and its occasion, pointing to something larger: language itself is a mode of error and wandering, fortunate mistakes and misprision, but these movements from local to global, one context to another, are to be cherished and cheered on. The poetic revels are underway in the bespoke world of letters.

Is such revelry warranted in a world of suffering? Heaney addresses the relationship of poetry to the events and troubles of history in two distinct responses that counterpose the aesthetic and the political. In the 1988 publication *The Government of the Tongue*, Heaney describes a meeting in Belfast in 1972 with the singer David Hammond. On their way to the studio to record songs and poems, the two are stopped short by explosions. Against the 'implacable disconsolate wailing of the ambulances', 'music against which the music of the guitar that David unpacked made little impression', the friends fall silent (xi). Heaney claims that 'the very notion of beginning to sing at that moment when others were beginning to suffer seemed like an offence against their suffering'. The moment uncovers an abiding tension between the rival claims of Art and Life, which he 'more melodramatically' redubs 'Song and Suffering' (xii). The pressure at that moment is to bear witness as poet, to join suffering and song, 'to survive amphibiously' in the 'realm of the times' as well as that of 'moral and artistic self-respect', a challenge that is 'immediately recognizable', Heaney says, 'to anyone who has lived with the awful and demeaning facts of Northern Ireland's history over the last couple of decades' (xx).

Like the polis, the aesthetic demands fidelity, but it also issues licence. In the poetic realm, the tongue 'governed for so long in the social sphere by considerations of tact and fidelity, by nice obeisances to one's origin within the minority of the majority, this tongue is suddenly ungoverned' (xxii). In this unfettering, Heaney claims, the tongue 'gains access to a condition that is unconstrained and, while not being practically effective, is not necessarily inefficacious' (xxii). Awkward sentence that, and apologetic. To put it bluntly, it is an unpoetic position statement in defence of poetry. It is this propositional reality expressed in awkward phrasing, 'while not being practically effective, is not necessarily inefficacious', that the poet must wander away from in order to be free of its constraints, imaginative failures and prosaic lockdown.

Before he can pass through to this world of song, the poet must be ready to assume the poetic burden. In 'From the Republic of Conscience', Heaney writes, 'You carried your own burden.' This is not a position of comfort but one in which 'your symptoms of creeping privilege disappeared' (*OG* 276). 'From the Frontier of Writing', Heaney reports that 'suddenly you're through, arraigned yet freed' (*OG* 274). The arraigned poet is called to account. Heaney extols Mandelstam's version of lyric action in *The Government of the Tongue*, explaining that 'obedience to poetic impulse was obedience to conscience' (xix).

'From the Republic of Conscience', the poet reports as follows: here, the 'sacred symbol is a stylized boat' and the ship of poetry moves with 'an ear' for the sail and 'a sloping pen' for the mast. If attention to aesthetics demands the joining of sensation and perception, as the word's etymology in the Greek *aisthisis* suggests, it is fitting that the metonymies of ear and pen are complemented by a stylized boat in which the keel is 'an open eye' and 'the hull a mouth-shape' (*OG* 276). Word, body, pen, symbol, eye, ear, mouth, conscience are all bound by the sacred government of 'unwritten law', the poet a 'dual citizen' of more than one world, bidden to speak on behalf of others, an ambassador who 'would never be relieved' (*OG* 277). Perception must join sensation, affect with observation, the political language of the 'Republic' with the imaginative and moral burden of conscience. In this view of the poetic task, to pass into the frontier of writing is to accept the government of another law, another allegiance than that to which the non-literary world presses the conscience. Here the poet's 'responsibility is to etymology rather than economics', as he says of Mandelstam. Here 'the tongue proceeds headily into its role as governor' as he says of Sylvia Plath, 'by the disciplines of metre, rhyme, etymology, and enjambment' (*GT* xix, 152). The poet is always crossing, a republic of one, assuming the burden of conscience while soaring away from the fetters of a prosaic world and its political borders.

Heaney's commitment to transnationalism emerges in his repeated return to the trope of borders and frontiers in what might be read as poetic displacement of political troubles founded in their overwhelming reality. The idea of borders begins to populate the very medium in which he speaks of them. 'For border read broader' becomes a sort of poetic manifesto in 'Errata for BK'. If the poetic trick is to read broader for border, what does this entail? In viewing poetry itself as 'The Place of Writing', the title of his Richard Ellmann lectures at Emory in 1988, Heaney claims that 'different political and cultural dispositions get expressed in poetry at a level below the professed meanings and espousals of the poems themselves'.[11] In casting poetry as a *place*, Heaney establishes its claims to its own government, sovereignty and laws. If seawater is 'the base of all inks and pigments' in the republic of conscience, and 'seashells / are held to the ear during births and funerals', then the poet's dominant element is more akin to water than land. Seawater must move; it must circulate, lapping this shore and moving on, so that the sound of sea held to the ear speaks of a fluid 'poetics of relation', to use Édouard Glissant's term from an eponymous work.[12] Neither landlocked nor bound by time, the poet hears in the sound of the sea an endless cycle of birth and death that turns away from empty homogenized time towards eternity and a broader, shared fate. Reading for the broader does not deny the border that defines and places the poet, but acknowledges his call to the world from it, as he turns his telescopic lens upon a temporally and spatially broader vista than the mapped world.

This expansive vision is nonetheless born in Heaney's love of his own country, place and ground. In 'Errata for BK', the aforementioned unpublished poem, the poet begins by defining what is one's own: 'For Tyrone, read own turf.' In listing the errata to be corrected, '*amor*' is to be read as 'Omagh' in a clever sonic inversion that signals attachment to place while capitalizing on the vagaries of sound and sense. Love is Omagh, the capital of County Tyrone, the site of one of the worst atrocities of the Troubles,[13] but crucially also Kiely's homeland and part of Heaney's geography of belonging. The poem continues in this mode of using localized references in ways that emplace the poet within the landscape of the Troubles, their prehistory, his own biography and that of his circle of friends. Wandering through space and time, the poet goes on to suggest a series of corrections, 'Carleton' for 'intinn', for instance, referring to William Carleton, the ghostly double from 'Station Island' who informs his mind and intentions. Wandering through words, the poem continues to stray, 'For Burgh Quay read Lagan'; the Quay at Dublin is *mis*taken for the river that runs through Belfast and some fifty miles of Northern Ireland. Having rehearsed the use of metaphor and metonymy in a native context, the poem then begins to wander further away from local geography and history, expressing both preference and misprision in the line, 'For novels read *Ovid*.' Collapsing three big ideas, the relation of part to whole, metamorphoses and becoming as the condition of being, and the trope of the novel and newness in the oldest of stories, Heaney establishes errata and errancy as the poem's guiding spirit. It is from this stance of lurching that he declares, 'For border read broader.' Having issued this injunction, he continues: 'For *urbi* read *orbi*.' The lyric incantation begins to combine the utopic vision of a manifesto with the mysterious benediction of a papal declaration which began in Roman times thus, 'Urbi et Orbi' ('To Rome and to the World').

The poet begins at the ramparts of Omagh, but then moves to the aesthetic frontier of writing and an unbounded polis that expands into the world. When the engines that bore him to the republic of conscience stop, the poet can 'hear a curlew high above the runway' (*OG* 276). In 'Errata for BK', however, the line following 'For *urbi* read *orbi*' is hardly as lofty and uplifting. The listener, now in expectation of some grand pronouncement, ready for some apostolic blessing, next encounters the perplexing directive: 'For mixer read soda.' Given the culminating toast, 'For eighty read sláinte', we are settling down, it seems, with a drink. From *urbi* to *orbi* to the glass in hand, we will now be borne into the arena of invention.

If we have come a long way from County Tyrone and the violence embedded in the evocation of Omagh, we have also been on the classic Heaney flight path. Heaney's initial response to the relationship of song to suffering – 'the very notion of beginning to sing at that moment when others were beginning to suffer seemed like an offence against their suffering' (*GT* xi) – seems to be followed by unspoken questions posed to history itself. I argue that Heaney's mode of wandering from local time and place implies the following: When had the sirens stopped long enough to allow the luxury of song? If they stop in one place, they begin elsewhere. If peace prevailed on earth, and there were no suffering, moreover, what would the poet sing of? 'The end of art is peace', he declares in 'The Harvest Bow', echoing Yeats who was himself echoing Coventry Patmore (*FW* 58). In the essay 'Yeats as an Example?' Heaney suggests that 'the finally exemplary moments [in Yeats] are those when powerful artistic control is vulnerable to the pain or pathos of life itself' (*P* 109). In *The Cure at Troy*, Heaney, also extolling the possibility of the moment in which 'hope and history rhyme', begins nonetheless with the observation, 'Human beings suffer' (*CT* 77). Human history is one of torture and hurt; history lives through us as the sensation of suffering; for the poet perception and sensation, the very definition of *aisthisis*, are allied.

Confronting the violence of history, glass in hand, the poet composes his elegy and his tribute, wandering through the possibilities of the word-hoard to memorialize suffering and hint at an other world. Asked about this predilection, he famously responded, 'The elegiac Heaney? There's nothing else.'[14] In this light, every poem is an elegy, the poet a listening post with ear both to ground and to the curlew high in the sky, fishing through the word-hoard, hoping that the tongue 'has located the source where the fixed stars are reflected and from which they transmit their spontaneous and weirdly trustworthy signals' (*GT* 152). The hope of the poem is to attune itself to the music of what happens, what *is* happening in every moment. 'Poetry can be as potentially redemptive and possibly as illusory as love', Heaney claims, seeking repose in the thought that 'We still believe what we hear' (xxiii).

When the world will not satisfy us, the word must sound out the music of what happens and encode therein the hope of redemption. Heaney's trust in words is most clearly articulated in the essay 'Feeling into Words', where he says that in the poem 'Digging', he felt that he had done more than 'make an arrangement of words', that he had 'let down a shaft into real life' (*P* 41). 'Finding a voice means that you can get your own feeling into your own words', he writes (43). It is in the making one's own of the word that seeks its best home that the poet feels and sounds out his song. Until then, as Bakhtin famously said in *The Dialogic Imagination*,

> The word in language is half someone else's. It becomes one's 'own' only when the speaker populates it with his own intentions, his own accent, when he appropriates the word, adapting it to his own semantic and

> expressive intention. Prior to this moment of appropriation, the word does not exist in a neutral and impersonal language . . . but rather it exists in other people's mouths, in other people's contexts, serving other people's intentions; it is from there that one must take the word, and make it one's own.[15]

Words are pregnant repositories, reborn in context, glossed over, emptied out, repurposed, always demanding a further gloss. The poet moves in the intimate spaces of difference on the borders between words, on the glide from one consonant, one vowel to another, broader for border, *orbi* for *urbi*. The little difference is constantly being invented in the politically conflicted world; the poet chooses the happier invention: 'For Ben read trovato.' Heaney borrows from the Italian saying 'se è non vero, è ben trovato' ('even if it is not true, it is well invented'). Bear it across, translate, he says next, '"For Ben said" read Benedict.' Erring on, the poem begins to ally discovery and diction, returning to the word-hoard as the best of all possible sources.

Heaney's toast to Kiely and his imitation of Muldoon's imitation of a crucial stage of the poetic task, to review and correct errors, establishes his relationship with the word and world as he wanders through possibilities and meanings. Because there is so much to correct in a wrong world, every poem is a sort of 'Errata'. The notion of margins, glosses and errata permeates the space and place of writing, words underwritten by other words and ideas, always ready for another gloss, another tongue put into the mouth of the poet. *This* is the transnational dimension of Heaney's postcolonial poetics, the bearing of meaning from one point of origin to another, the word passed through word of mouth, held for the sound and the music and scattered again: 'For pearls read broadcast.' What makes this a transnational poetics is the joining of the burdens of politics and poetics into the capacity for going beyond the border of known suffering, in order to fathom its broader dimension. To feel one's own suffering is natural, to feel another's is the province of the poetic. Heaney, the world poet, redefines the limits of the polis for which he is accountable. The poet's task as ambassador from the republic of conscience is to cross over and look again in the word-hoard, find the words, say it well, say it better. There is plenty in the word-hoard, and wisdom too: 'For *largesse* read *sagesse*.' The poet chooses from this plenty. It is the politician who insists that the nation is our measured province and not the world. The poetic trick, it would seem, is to reach beyond known experience and visible border: 'For border read broader . . . For *urbi* read *orbi*.' From one's own city and horizon, envision the broader world beyond. Moreover, look into the word-hoard and *Bene dict*. Say it well. The well said is a kind of benediction, the wishful blessing as the sirens continue to wail. It is a particularly *postcolonial* poetic trick to find continuity where there was rupture, to err and overwrite, to translate all origins, and imagine a borderless world of possibility in place of the torn halves and fragments of vanquished cultures given to us in the blinkered narratives of the victors and politicians.

Notes

1 Denis Donoghue, 'Fears for Irish Studies in an Age of Identity Politics', *Chronicle of Higher Education*, 21 November 1997, B4–B5.
2 Edna Longley, *The Living Stream: Literature and Revisionism in Ireland* (Newcastle-upon-Tyne: Bloodaxe, 1994), p. 31.
3 Dermot Bolger, 'Introduction', in Bolger (ed.), *The Vintage Book of Contemporary Irish Fiction* (New York: Vintage, 1995), p. xiii.
4 Luke Gibbons, 'Ireland and the Colonization of Theory', *Interventions: International Journal of Postcolonial Studies*, 1/1 (1998), 27.
5 David Lloyd, *Anomalous States: Irish Writing and the Post-Colonial Moment* (Durham, NC: Duke University Press, 1993), p. 13.
6 Molara Ogundipe-Leslie, *Re-creating Ourselves: African Women and Critical Transformations* (Trenton, NJ: Africa World Press, 1994), pp. 232–3.
7 Jahan Ramazani, *A Transnational Poetics* (University of Chicago Press, 2009), p. 21.
8 Letter to Paul Muldoon, circa 2000, Seamus Heaney papers, MS 960, Stuart A. Rose Manuscript, Archives, and Rare Book Library, Emory University.
9 'Heaney Leads Funeral Tributes to Kiely', *Irish Times*, 14 February 2007, www.irishtimes.com/news/heaney-leads-funeral-tributes-to-kiely-1.1195206.
10 Paul Muldoon, 'Errata', *New Yorker*, 12 October 1998, 86.
11 Seamus Heaney, 'W. B. Yeats and Thoor Ballylee', in *The Place of Writing* (Emory University; Scholars Press, 1989), p. 20.
12 Édouard Glissant, *Poétique de la relation* (Paris: Gallimard, 1990).
13 https://cain.ulster.ac.uk/events/omagh/events.htm#:~:text=Omagh%20Bomb%20%2D%20Largest%20loss%20of,to%2C%20or%20in%2C%20hospital.
14 Quoted in Joseph Black *et al.* (eds.), *Broadview Anthology of British Literature: Concise Edition*, Volume B (Peterborough, Ont.: Broadview Press, 2017), p. 1445.
15 Mikhail Bakhtin, *The Dialogic Imagination: Four Essays* (Austin: University of Texas Press, 1992), p. 294.

CHAPTER 28

The Archipelago

Nicholas Allen

Seamus Heaney's fascination with the boundary places between land and water, and the significance of these littoral spaces for a poetry of historical exploration, are there from his first collection, *Death of a Naturalist*. 'Storm on the Island' is a short poem that has nothing of the later work's imaginative complexity, but it offers a first step towards a longer consideration of islands, coastlines, lough and sea in the evolution of Heaney's thinking about his own cultural moment, and his role as a poet within it, and on occasion without. The poem's imagined community of island people is far from the familiar critical rendering of Heaney's writing, which has focused nearly entirely on the groundedness of his imagery since 'Digging' established a category of reception that insisted on Heaney's relationship with the given place of his birth in rural Derry.[1] This condition corresponded with emerging themes in the mid-century reading of poetry in Ireland, which turned with Patrick Kavanagh towards the rural and the organic and away from the epic abstraction of the late Yeats. The idea of Heaney as a laureate of the known place is compelling but ignores the complex ways in which Heaney employed metaphors of liquidity and water in his descriptions of landscape. These fluid images connect to a principal interest of Heaney's in the sea world of the North Atlantic, which stretches in his work across time and place, from the coast of Europe in *Beowulf* and *North*, easterly to the Americas. Water was always a signal element in Heaney's writing, dripping from the pump at the home farm in Anahorish and flowing as a river of memory into the last collection, *Human Chain*. Its presence troubles the material categories into which Heaney's poetry might be placed and suggests an expanded, and unpredictable, sensory panorama in which to read his work.

The basic units of social association in twentieth-century literary criticism in Ireland were the parish, the region, the nation and the state, the interaction of which has informed the evolution of a critical vocabulary that extends to the transnational and the postcolonial. Heaney's work fits uneasily into these categories, as becomes clear by concentrating on those poems that use images of archipelago and periphery, of islands, coastlines and riverbanks, as points of crossing between historical reality and the imagination. This essay situates Heaney's writing in critical contexts that favour an emerging vocabulary of contingency and migration, two themes that are constant across all his collections.[2] Related to this, archipelago has become a critical tool in the study of literature following an extended conversation between historians about the limits of nationalism as a means to describe complex interactions between fragmentary interest groups over extended time.[3] Their debate grew from discussion of the island wars of the seventeenth century before its later extension into the wider Atlantic world.[4] Heaney returns to this history repeatedly, particularly in his attention to Elizabethan relics of the English language in Ulster dialect, and his related awareness of early poetic figures like Edmund Spenser. The colonization of land, the marginalization of cultures unwilling or unable to be assimilated into emerging orders and the expropriation of antagonistic populations were three strategies of conquest. The consequences of these processes, and the varieties of reaction to them, form a tangled history that takes shape on the margins and often at the boundaries of land and sea, such as happens frequently in Heaney's poetry.

The offshore Heaney is a figure of the shallows and the morning mists and a poet of changing states, his medium the shallows and his abiding metaphor the leaving and return of the eels that inhabit Lough Neagh. This is a poetry of the riverbanks and the foreshore, two locations that persist throughout the body of his work as thresholds in which to test the capacity of art to summon the afterlife from memory. *Station Island* and *Sweeney Astray* are two sustained examples of this accommodation, governed as their key sections are by a speaker in emotional distress, an upset that opens awareness to other territories beyond the familiar. This is a perception that builds up through *Station Island*, a collection of two parts, the first of which are individual poems and the second the series that gives the book its name. 'Away from it All' is a test piece that introduces ideas of the sea, the coast and life beneath the surface, and the poem shares a vocabulary and setting with Heaney's earlier, and more famous, coastal works, like 'North'. The effect was epic in 'North' but more muted here, and not altogether convincing, the poem a step away from the generalizations of the earlier work towards the specific observation of the 'Station Island' sequence. Its basic subject is a day of lobster fishing:

> In full view of the strand,
> the sea wind spitting on the big window,
> we plunged and reddened it,

then sat for hours in conclave
over the last of the claws.

(*SI* 16)[5]

The poem has echoes of other images of sacrifice in Heaney's work. Principally, poetry is witness to a change of element that causes unexpected suffering. Bewilderment is the key response, which may explain Heaney's turn towards the boiling lobster now, and later to the figure of man turned bird in *Sweeney Astray*. The politics of this is suggestive as it means that all victims are innocent of the violence they suffer, in the sense that none of them expects it. This is relevant to a poem like 'Casualty' when Louis O'Neill ignores the warnings to observe a curfew and dies because of it. The crossing of a boundary between community and the individual shares poetic representation in the sea voyage; fishing for eels, lobster, or elsewhere mackerel, sets the scene for a miniature drama that stages the human understanding of memory and death. In turn this offers a key intersection between the understanding of critical terms like archipelago and periphery and the illustration of suffering in Heaney's poetry, which is one reason why the coastal margin is so important a geography.

'Away from it All' bears none of this direct weight even as it exhibits Heaney's general tendency to think of water as a metaphor for dissolution. The motif occurs in 'Chekov on Sakhalin' as the writer sails, 'His head... swimming free as the troikas' (18), and again in 'Remembering Malibu', when the speaker is relieved to find the Pacific cold, 'for I would have rotted / beside the luke-warm ocean I imagined' (30). The seaborne poems are more likely to have adults as their protagonists than the river poems, whose subjects are children and, later, the dead on the far bank. 'A Hazel Stick for Catherine Ann' is a child's education in fishing and a poem comparable to 'Digging' in its initiation of the subject to a sensitive life. These currents all join in the twelve sections of 'Station Island', each of which describes one stage in a pilgrimage to Lough Derg, an inland sea that becomes a site of vision. The liquidity of Heaney's language suggests the alterity of the pilgrimage as a journey to unknown territory, both human and poetic, women 'wading' and the crowd 'slushing through' (62, 63). The visions come in 'a shower of rain' (65), the blustery weather a sign of imaginative disturbance. The figures who appear are themselves in liquid disarray, William Carleton witness to the 'looped slime' of executed rebels, a priest in 'knee-deep mist' (65, 71). The third section connects these images to Heaney's own home life in the speaker's turn to childhood memory. Kneeling among the faithful he returns to the rituals of childhood worship:

A seaside trinket floated then and idled
in vision, like phosphoresecent weed,
a toy grott with seedling mussel shells
and cockles glued in patterns over it.
(67)

This trinket was the possession of an aunt long passed away and prepares the poem for its movement towards personal loss, as in the seventh section when the ghost of William Strathearn appears, beckoning the speaker to 'come to the edge of the water' (77).[6] The weather is steady now, the surface smooth 'as if it were a clear barometer'. The fiction of peace passes with the apparition of the bloody revenant behind the speaker, retelling the story of his murder. The weather changes after this, the 'White waves' rising over 'Black' (81) and 'muddied water' (87), the speaker's attention to wind and water a register of the speaker's difficulty in returning to shore. The voyage from lakeshore to island is taken with the commitment of the pilgrim to undergo the duress of ritual. What cannot be foreseen is the effect of such ritual upon the speaker and his perceptions, the rough crossing a symbol of the imbalance that follows a psychological readjustment. The poem's final section begins with the speaker raising his hand to be lifted from the boat to the jetty, the hand that holds him bony and cold, and belonging to a figure sculpted from the foreshore, walking 'straight as a rush' (92). This apparition of James Joyce is a picture of a man made of water, his 'voice eddying with the vowels of all rivers', the speaker coming to as 'Raindrops blew in my face' (92, 93). Joyce's advice is familiar to Heaney's readers since *North*, the long foray of the artist an isolated pursuit punctured by moments of vision, a light in the darkness signalled as a gleam, an aurora, or here, a 'sunspot'. The idea extends to the speaker's address to Joyce in an earlier published version of the poem:

'Old father, mother's son,
there is a moment in Stephen's diary
for April the thirteenth, a revelation,

set among my stars...
(93)

The passage referred to is the final section of *A Portrait of the Artist as a Young Man*, in which Stephen Dedalus collects in diary form the fragments of a philosophy that will sustain his aesthetic life. The passage Heaney's speaker refers to concerns Stephen's discussion in *Portrait* with the Dean of Studies:

> 13 *April*: That tundish has been on my mind for a long time. I looked it up and find it English and good old blunt English too. Damn the dean of studies and his funnel! What did he come here for to teach us his own language or to learn it from us. Damn him one way or the other![7]

Stephen's conversation with the Dean is emblematic of the linguistic, and so cultural, divide between Ireland and England, the student and his master disputing the meaning of an object used to hold liquid metal. The debate was resonant for the generation of Northern writers around Heaney and chimes with the interests of his fellow Field Day member Brian Friel's play, *Translations*.[8] That Heaney finishes his own poem of pilgrimage with Stephen's recognition that the language he took to be familiar was once and always strange is a recognition that art, like belief, is composed of a set of provisional arrangements, the roots of which run deep into cultural contradiction. If Stephen saw this complexity as damnation, Heaney imagines the loss of national sovereignty as the confirmation of a fluid imagery, the coordinates of which are the waterways before him. So the figure of Joyce directs the speaker to

> '... Keep at a tangent.
> When they make the circle wide, it's time to swim
> out on your own and fill the element
> with signatures on your own frequency,
> echo sounding, searches, probes, allurements,
>
> elver-gleams in the dark of the whole sea.'
>
> (*SI* 93–4)

This is the major synthesis of Heaney's vision of the artist in his middle phase. It contains the dominant elements of his visionary aesthetic in the form of light and water, elements combined in the practice of swimming, an immersion one stage beyond the more common observational state of fishing in other poems. Submersion is a state between life and death, and the experience closest to Heaney's complete attachment to a subject. This is an association beyond the limits of a land-based nationalism (that ground which provides 'alien comfort', (92), when the speaker leaves the boat), and it exists symbolically as squalls of rain, of mists and fogs, just as the 'Station Island' poems end in 'cloudburst' and 'downpour' (94), the old cycle of land, water and sky restored by the speaker's penitence. This is the spiritual substrate of Heaney's poetry and representative of a ritual cycle that is catholic in its elemental inclusivity.

'Station Island' is a high-tide mark of Heaney's poetry and a sequence in which the personal and the aesthetic find historical balance in the practice of devotion. The deep swell behind these lake land poems are the darker depths of 'The Strand at Lough Beg' and 'Casualty', which were first published in *Field Work*. 'The Strand at Lough Beg' shares the Station Island poems' setting in 'lowland clays and waters', the boundary between life and death figured again in the marshland ecology of the inland sea (*OG* 145).[9] The poem's subject is the sectarian murder of Colum McCartney, who was tricked into stopping for a fake roadblock and shot. The light of the early lines is significantly different from Heaney's other poetry, McCartney's killers 'a demon pack / Blazing out of the ground' (145). A 'red lamp' signals entry to a hell the embers of which the poem extinguishes with a liquid salve by its return to Church Island and 'its soft treeline of yew'. The poem's first two stanzas are simple statement and rebuttal, McCartney's killers substituted for the 'scullions' and 'herders' of his home place. This achieved, the last stanza risks all with its insistence that the dead are part of a living equation whose terms reside in the organic growth of the lough side. Heaney can be misread here as a poet who associates tribal belonging with a natural setting, as he was in *North*. Consider instead the many words that bring to mind images of liquidity: 'Drowning', 'dew', 'brimming', 'wash', 'drizzle', 'cloud' and even 'blood' (146). These prepare the poem for a final act of restitution in which water, shore and vegetation wrap the body of the dead subject in organic embrace:

> I dab you clean with moss
> Fine as the drizzle out of a low cloud.
> I lift you under the arms and lay you flat.
> With rushes that shoot green again, I plait
> Green scapulars to wear over your shroud.
> (146)

The poem is an assembly of peripheral visions. The words 'cloud' and 'shroud' bring the heavens to earth in a drizzle of rain, the murdered subject dressed in shooting rushes, the violence of the killing grown into the lough side environment. Heaney's memorial vestments are offshoots, like the poem, of a marginal aesthetic whose landscape is the unsteady border between land and water. A similar impulse propels Heaney's elegy for Louis O'Neill, 'Casualty', a poem full again of liquid images, from the rum and blackcurrant at the bar to O'Neill's work as a fisherman. O'Neill was killed in a bomb planted in retaliation for the Bloody Sunday killings in Derry in 1972. The poem has three sections, the first two of which introduce the person, his conversation, death and funeral. As the third section approaches the move from history to vision accelerates with an increase in images of fishing and water:

He had gone miles away
For he drank like a fish
Nightly, naturally
Swimming towards the lure
Of warm lit-up places . . .
(147)

The speaker admits in the first lines of the third stanza that he missed O'Neill's funeral, a confession that distracts the reader from Heaney's own sleight of hand in substituting the religious ritual for the poem, which is built from the now familiar elements of the coastal margin, O'Neill's mourners

in equal pace
With the habitual
Slow consolation
Of a dawdling engine,
. . . the land
Banked under fog . . .
(149)

If these poems are written at a high pitch of sectarian suffering, they are the sharpest notes in a repertoire that Heaney practised throughout his career. The Northern Troubles changed dramatically in the decades after *Field Work* and *Station Island.* Heaney's own life expanded too: his American sojourns, his family and his public reputation as a poet of global significance all leavened the singular suffering of the early to mid-period poetry, in which the weight of the world sat heavily on the poet's shoulders. This resulted in a remarkable body of poetry from *Wintering Out* to *The Haw Lantern*. After this Heaney's terms changed, the bloody testimonial of the old vision grown into something more calm and clear-sighted. Now, vision is not a stream of images that flow through a river of commas, such as in 'North', but a facility corralled by the poet in a fence of dashes, colons and full stops. In this later phase, Heaney's archipelago is a set of singular islands, not the North Atlantic seaway of Dane and Viking. Relevant to this, the poet adjusts the elegy as the ideal form in which to merge the past and present, the dead and the living, land and water, as in 'An Invocation', Heaney's poem for Hugh MacDiarmid from *The Spirit Level* (a title that suggests slyly the poet's newfound, and hard-won, balance). MacDiarmid is a Sweeney-like figure in Shetland,

Beyond the stony-limits, writing-mad.

That pride of being tested. Of solitude,
Your big pale forehead in the window glass
Like the earth's curve on the sea's curve to the north.
(*SL* 27)

This new geometry of land and sea, and their interrelation, indicates Heaney's own turn towards a clear statement of poetic principles. Where before there were flashes of light in the sky, or bubbles of air in the ice, now there is 'A poetry like the weather, / A shifting force, a factor factored in / Whether it prevails or not' (28). This art is tied still to the old qualities of endurance and self-examination, but takes form in a poetry that no longer equates distance with retreat. This is especially true of the next poem in *The Spirit Level*, 'Mycenae Lookout', which imagines a solitary soldier on watch for the fires that will announce the fall of Troy. The fifth and final section of the poem is 'His Reverie of Water', which is remarkable for Heaney's refinement of his previous aesthetic. It is, like nearly all these marginal works, a poem of regret, except that the shaft from present to past is dug deeper than ever before. It begins, 'At Troy, at Athens, what I most clearly / See and nearly smell / Is the fresh water' (36). The culture of these places is reduced by war to the return to the camp of the bloody hero as 'a stranger' who is restored by the 'filled bath'. There is rebuke in this capture of the epic form in the small space of the interior, the 'splashing' of the blood-dazed man like the untutored swimming of a child, not fit for the open sea. The image turns to the dilution of violence by the action of water, 'the treadmill of assault / turned waterwheel' (37). Where in the earlier poetry the inevitability of violence ran forward through time like a river, now human conflict is one part of a system that sinks deep into a shared history that is a resource of renewed possibility. Heaney imagines the structures that draw from this common well in terms that are strongly reminiscent of the later Yeats, 'the ladder of the future / and the past' a nudge towards the bleak vision of 'The Circus Animals' Desertion'. Yeats considered his poetry as a response to a particular, and violent, turn of the historical wheel. Heaney does too, but earths his work in a different terrain, the muck of rural Derry a vouchsafe for human co-operation:

> men puddling at the source
>
> through tawny mud, then coming back up
> deeper in themselves for having been there . . .
>
> finders, keepers, seers of fresh water . . .
>
> (37)

Experience, as so often in Heaney's poetry, is won by an excursion offshore, or into another element. The sensual optimism of the rushing pump is a clear expression of Heaney's liquid aesthetic, the human forces of history and violence continually washed clean by the natural abundance of water. There is a shift in tone from the earlier poetry in the accommodation the poems make towards squalls and storms, forces that blew the first poems into submission. The 'stealth / and habit' of the later work represents a combination of intelligence and perseverance that the poet cultivated over a long career. This is an art of the riverbank since Heaney rarely sets out for the open sea, as did Yeats in 'Sailing to Byzantium', and the ocean is more often observed as a series of island or continental edges, as in 'Remembering Malibu'. Heaney was mistrustful of a perspective that extended over the horizon of the known world. His speakers are, like the watchman, alert to minor changes in a wide panorama, not makers themselves of that environment. They are keepers and guardians, not architects or visionaries. Poetry is the province of clear sight, a gift given it because it sees history without making it, or so the conceit runs.

This idea settles in the later collections into a reflection on what the poet leaves behind. If the speaker of the early books was looking forward through the lens of antiquity, by *District and Circle* he looks back from the perspective of modernity. 'To George Seferis in the Underworld' and 'Wordsworth's Skates' nestle beside each other in this later collection as two parts of a conversation about art, mortality and the persistence of poetry. The poem for Seferis imagines the Greek poet 'somewhere just beyond / the summit ridge', buffeted by the 'ozone-breeze and cavern-boom' of Cape Sounion (*DC* 22).[10] The coastal edge draws Seferis into a picture of conflict, his poetry imagined by Heaney as 'too black and white' (23), the border between land and sea a metaphor too for liberty and tyranny, of crime and the punishment that poetry offers, of a despotic reputation. Heaney's speaker pictures another landscape. His attention turns to the ground and its carpeting of sedge, which the speaker insists is '*seggans*' (22), a word 'harder and more hand-to-hand' (23) than its modern equivalent. This is in one respect an affirmation of Heaney's long-held commitment to the familiar object, confirmed by touch. But in another it is a refusal of the equally well-established sense of the world as a sinking centre. Here the earth is firm, with give but no liquid surrender. The same is true of 'Wordsworth's Skates', which imagines the poet skimming over Windermere in the freeze. The skates are rotting on display, but the lines they left in the landscape are, like the lines of the poet, marked deep, 'the reel of hem on frozen Windermere / As he flashed from the clutch of earth along its curve / And left it scored' (24). The late horizon of Heaney's poetry represents a complex equation between land, water and the boundary edge. This was a sum the terms of which the poet adjusted throughout his career, and which extends to his two great late poems in *Human Chain*, 'Eelworks' and 'The Riverbank Field', about which I have written elsewhere.[11] Heaney was a writer immersed in the elements, a poet who imagined history as the weather and art as its barometer. Accordingly, ideas of archipelago and periphery illuminate the poetry in ways that the concerns of province and nation do not since the sharpest storm is felt at the coastal edge. Heaney's early imagination was shaped by water from the first and his speakers patrol the water margins at every point of stress in his poetry, an attention to which is made possible by a critical reading moored in the vocabulary of archipelago and periphery.

Notes

A version of this essay was first published in *Ireland, Literature and the Coast: Seatangled* (Oxford University Press, 2020).

1 The academic basis of the critical response to Heaney was established largely by Neil Corcoran's *The Poetry of Seamus Heaney: a Critical Study* (London: Faber and Faber, 1998), and Helen Vendler's *Seamus Heaney* (Cambridge, MA: Harvard University Press, 1998).

2 Connected to this is a significant passage in *Stepping Stones*, in which Heaney remembers the partitioned map of Ireland that hung on his school wall. He is critical of the map's attempt to educate the children in the mentality of a separate state, but the sentence following suggests something of the unintended consequences of unionist dogma: 'So the map was meant to imprint an official Northern Ireland and establish a six-county-centric point of view from the start. I can still see the little boats on their dotted lines across the North Channel from Larne to Stranraer, from Derry to Glasgow, from Belfast to Heysham – all happily bound for the "mainland"' (246). Whatever the intention behind the map, it opened the child's mind to a vision of the northern seaways, which never left.

3 Read, for example, J.G.A. Pocock, *The Discovery of Islands: Essays in British History* (Cambridge University Press, 2005); or John Kerrigan, *Archipelagic English: Literature, History, and Politics 1603–1707* (Oxford University Press, 2008).

4 A version of this can be read in Hugh Kearney, *The British Isles: A History of Four Nations*, 2nd edn (Cambridge University Press, 2006).

5 Seamus Heaney, *Station Island* (New York: Farrar, Straus and Giroux, 1985).

6 Heaney discusses the significance of this object in *SS* 247.

7 James Joyce, *A Portrait of the Artist as a Young Man*, ed. J.P. Riquelme (New York: W.W. Norton, 2007), pp. 222–3. As quoted in Shane Alcobia-Murphy, Sympathetic Ink: Intertextual Relations in Northern Irish Poetry (Liverpool: Liverpool UP, 2006), 240.

8 For an excellent account of these relations, read Marilynn Richtarik, *Acting Between the Lines: The Field Day Theatre Company and Irish Cultural Politics 1980–1984* (Oxford: Clarendon Press, 1994).
9 Seamus Heaney, 'The Strand at Lough Beg', *Opened Ground: Selected Poems 1966–1996* (New York: Farrar, Straus and Giroux, 1998).
10 Seamus Heaney, 'To George Seferis in the Underworld', *District and Circle* (New York: Farrar, Straus and Giroux, 2006).
11 Nicholas Allen, 'Seamus Heaney and Water', *Irish Review*, Seamus Heaney Special Issue, 49–50 (2014–15), 173–82.

VII

Legacy

CHAPTER 29

In Public

Fintan O'Toole

In March 2013, less than six months before he died, Seamus Heaney gave one of his last formal public speeches. It was at the National Museum in Dublin, for the launch of the book version of a project I had been involved with, *A History of Ireland in 100 Objects*. He was, as always, extraordinarily gracious – a grace that had come to be taken for granted in Irish public life. His ability to bring both gravity and warmth to any occasion had by then been recognized on many state occasions, especially those of great symbolic import such as the historic visit of Queen Elizabeth II to Ireland in 2011. He had a great gift for being a 'smiling public man'. He was also, of course, one of the most naturally eloquent people on the planet. It was easy to imagine him turning up at the National Museum with a few rough thoughts in his head and delivering the necessary blessing with his customary fluency and generosity, leaving everyone feeling flattered and delighted and inspired. And yet what was most remarkable was to see just how careful he was. He had written out his speech in full and he delivered it exactly as he had written it. There was no improvisation. He was taking no chances. He was taking care. To use a phrase he played on so beautifully in one of his finest essays, he was governing his tongue.

The care was surely habitual but, in this instance, he was also aware that the speech had a political content. At the time, Ireland was struggling under the weight of the private debts that had been nationalized after the great banking collapse of 2008 in which the hubris of the Celtic Tiger era had reached its nemesis. The Irish government and all of its fiscal policies were still under the control of the Troika of international institutions that led the so-called bailout of the state: the European Commission, the European Central Bank and the International Monetary Fund. In his speech, Heaney picked up in particular on one of the last objects in the book, the sign that had marked the headquarters of the notorious Anglo Irish Bank. He noted and relished the irony that its logo drew on images of early Irish culture that had been subsumed into the bank's corporate identity. This led him on to a reflection on debt and inheritance:

> It is not too much to hope . . . that this admirable imaginative contribution to our national life should open up a new way of thinking about ourselves and the country we live in. It reminds us that we are not simply a credit rating or an economy but a history and a culture, a human population rather than a statistical phenomenon. It is significant, for example, that when we think of things preserved from the past we often use the expression 'handed down' – 'handed down' instead of the more abstract 'inherited'. 'Inherited' is slightly legalistic whereas 'handed down' presupposes the physical handover of a gift; it situates the exchange in a social context, implies a kind of handshake. And it is that sensation of human contact, of a covenant with the past, of an at-homeness experienced in silence and stillness, it is that combination of distance and familiarity which can give us some sense of belonging with those who have gone before. So it might be said that if we have inherited a debt, we have also been handed down a treasury.[1]

It is striking that in this short passage, 'we' appears five times – Heaney had come to occupy with confidence – even with comfort – a position in which he could speak in the plural and seek consciously to articulate a view on behalf of a 'national life', an Ireland that can at least be imagined as a functioning entity. Striking, too, that this articulation, for all its graciousness, is oppositional. The national life on whose behalf the poet is speaking is evoked precisely as one that needs to be articulated outside of the particular economic discourse that was then dominating its realities. It is, indeed, threatened by that other discourse. There is here an unmistakable note of protest, a controlled anger at the reduction of the country to a 'credit rating' or 'statistical phenomenon'.

And through the poet's medium of a reflection on words, there is a highly political counterpointing of legal 'inheritance' – the financial debt accrued by private banks that the state had turned into sovereign debt and was leaving as a burden to future generations – with the 'handing down' of physical things as gifts from human being to human being. A capitalist and consumerist economy of money and debt is reimagined as a gift economy of human relationships and mutual obligations. There is, too, a very clear placing of the poet himself in relation to this dichotomy. Heaney is using the context of the National Museum quietly, modestly but with unmistakable toughness, to place himself within a national life that is not that of the reigning technocracy. And he is doing this with an eye to the future, to the longue durée that is brought to mind by the physical presence of so many ancient objects and the invitation to 'Ireland's history in their lineaments trace'. It would be an exaggeration to think of Heaney in the museum as the equivalent of W. B. Yeats at the Municipal Gallery (the words 'my glory' are hard to imagine on Heaney's lips), but there is an unmistakable element of self-definition in relation to the long unfolding of Irish belonging over time: he wishes not to be part of 'Irish heritage', not to be 'inherited' as an asset, but to be 'handed down' with the sensation of human contact.

Here, then, we see what really defines Heaney's presence. It is not fundamentally a matter of how he did or did not influence public life. It is rather a matter of how he *defined* public life. What he came to embody and articulate is a profound challenge to a shrunken, etiolated and mechanistic idea of what the democratic arena has become in the twenty-first century.

It might be expressed in Derek Mahon's insistence in 'Tractatus' that the world is not merely 'everything that is the case' but also 'everything that is the case imaginatively'. Heaney's constant rebuke is to the notion that the market is everything that is the case and behind his graciousness there is a steely insistence that collective life is an imaginative, compassionate and humane enterprise. Most remarkably, in that museum speech, Heaney posits the somewhat startling notion that collective public identity, the shared sense of belonging over long periods of time, might be best experienced in 'silence and stillness'. A connection is being made between the contemplative space of art and the active space of politics. They are not, he implies, opposites but interdependent arenas. Whether or not he intended this suggestion as an expression of his own political presence, it certainly captures the essence of Heaney's public role.

There is always in Heaney's work a sense of double obligation: to the private and the public, to the relentlessly individual, even lonely, demands of the work itself and to the possibility (sometimes remote, sometimes almost tangible) that it might at some level become a collective benefit. In his Nobel Prize address, he framed this doubleness quite simply: 'I credit poetry, in other words, both with being itself and for being a help . . .' (*OG* 417).[2] In the end, what gave him such a potent public presence was that people understood that he was a help because he was himself, that the stillness and silence he was able to distil into moving language are indeed a kind of civic good, a grounding for that sense of belonging without which nations and democracies cannot sustain themselves.

Yet we have to remember that this reconciliation of the contrary demands of the private and aesthetic on the one hand with the communal and political on the other was very hard-won. The tension was there even when he was known only as the author of his first collection *Death of a*

Naturalist. If we go back to 1967, and a reading at the emergent Project Arts Centre in Dublin, in Anthony Glavin's report for the *Irish Times* we find Heaney, even then, presenting precisely this same tension to his audience: 'Introducing a moving group of autobiographical poems, the poet made the point that, though a poet begins in solitude, and goes on into the arrogance of solitude and self-discovery, he then needs "a community to endorse that arrogance".'[3]

This phrase made Glavin uneasy:

> There is a danger here, one that Heaney is no doubt aware of: the poet who seeks endorsement from a community in the end plays to that community and becomes submerged in its applause. It requires courage to turn from easily earned approval to the difficult task of solving one's own identity: Heaney possesses that courage to no mean degree but must guard it with his life.[4]

This commentary is acute and it reminds us that the dilemma of the relationship between poetic 'solitude and self-discovery' on the one hand and the demands that the 'community' might make in return for its endorsement, predates the outbreak of the Troubles in 1968. It is, of course, implicit in any artistic career and it was bound to become explicit in an artist like Heaney who, on the one hand, chose the minority medium of poetry, and on the other aspired to articulate a common life. The Troubles were a powerful catalyst for making what was implicit explicit, but the reaction would have happened anyway.

What the Troubles did do was to ensure that the reaction would happen under great moral and political pressure. It may be most useful to trace that pressure in a single poem, 'The Last Mummer', which eventually appeared in *Wintering Out* in 1972. It was this poem that Heaney used to explain himself and his way of dealing with the contrary demands of the public need for a response to the explosive crisis and the private need to be true to an aesthetic impulse. Interviewed by Eavan Boland for her series 'The Northern Writers' Crisis of Conscience', in August 1970:

> If I go to sit-downs, if I go on Civil Rights marches, if I see burned-out areas, it's not enough for me simply to retell these things, although a lot of people would like the poet to do this. The poet must in some way encompass these things into his own terms, his own way of looking at things. For me, it'll always be by some kind of analogy. I'd find images. I'd take them out of the community: I'm thinking of something at the moment like Christmas mummers who are a dying race of people. They're an underground movement that's dying out. I wrote a poem called 'The Last Mummer' imagining this fellow going around the suburbs with a kind of anger in him, throwing stones at roofs and beating the walls with a stick.

> I didn't, at the time of writing, mean this to be a poem about Northern Ireland, but in some way I think it is.[5]

This quote is worth dwelling on because it opens up some of the complexities, anxieties and even contradictions of Heaney's self-presentation as a public figure under the pressure of the early years of the Troubles. It evokes both 'the community' and the individual artistic impulse, both the poet's political activism and his need to 'retell' public events by translating them into 'his own way of looking at things'. But it does this in a way that confuses the sequence of his responses. Which comes first – the public need or the poetic image? In the first part of this quotation, Heaney seems to imply that he starts with the need to respond to the Civil Rights marches and burned-out streets and then seeks an image that can serve as an analogy to encompass them in a poem. He suggests, moreover, that this image itself is communal: 'I'd take them out of the community.' However, he then goes on to cite a poem in which the sequence clearly works the other way around – 'The Last Mummer'. He suggests that far from the political context seeking an image to express it, it is the image that has been drawn towards a political meaning. When the poem was written, the meaning of the angry old mummer being ignored by people in a suburban house who are watching TV was broadly social rather than immediately political. It delineates the long process through which rural folk customs are being displaced by consumer-driven modernity, not the immediate crisis of the Civil Rights struggle and intercommunal violence. It was not at first a 'poem about Northern Ireland' – it became one under the pressure of the communal need for a response to crisis. To adapt the expression that Heaney himself famously adapted from W. B. Yeats, it shifts from being a 'satisfactory verbal icon' to being an image or symbol 'adequate to our predicament' (*P* 56).

Of course, this apparent contradiction is really more of a fruitful tension. To use another Yeatsian phrase, the dreams and the responsibilities are not separate: dreams beget responsibilities and responsibilities beget more dreams. The old mummer beating the gate (not in fact the walls) with his stick and throwing his stone at the roof of the suburban house is a dreamlike image that becomes 'responsible' in the old sense: a response to the needs of the community for a poem 'about' its increasingly violent predicament.

What is striking, however, is that 'The Last Mummer' itself changes radically under the stress of this tension. The poem that Heaney had in mind when he was talking to Eavan Boland in 1970 seems almost certainly to be the original version that was presented to the Belfast Group. It is a sonnet and it is tightly focused on that single image of the mummer arriving at the house. He is ignored by the TV-watching family,

And, shrouded, starts beating
The bars of the gate.
His boots crack the road. The stone
Clatters down off the slates.[6]

The poem ends there and its feel is more anthropological than political. It is not in fact 'adequate': Heaney's claim to Boland that the mummers are an 'underground movement' (implying an analogy to the IRA) is too much of a stretch. He clearly understood this himself, for we can see that the degree to which 'The Last Mummer' becomes 'a poem about Northern Ireland' is not just a function of the communal expectation that it be so. Heaney engaged in this process very actively by changing the form and greatly extending the content of the original. In the first place, he de-emphasized its sonnet form, taking the tight fourteen lines and breaking them up into seven discrete two-line sections. The words remain the same but the appearance of serene formality is broken – 'The Last Mummer' now *looks*, in this more fractured form, more like a poem that is responding to the urgency of political turmoil.

Even more radically, Heaney added two whole sections of similar length and appearance. We do not end with the image that Heaney described to Boland of the enraged mummer and his stick and stone – a useless, superannuated artist of a dying world. Instead, the mummer becomes an image of a whole other kind of artist – or rather of two kinds of artist. The new second section takes the mummer back to his older self and evokes mumming itself as a tradition that once crossed the sectarian divide. We find this mummer 'picking a nice way through / the long toils of blood / and feuding'.

It is not that these blood feuds – and their obvious resonance for the 'now' of the Troubles – do not threaten. But the mummer understands the sectarian geography and knows how to present himself in a particular (which is to say, Protestant or Catholic) house. The poem celebrates his acute reading of his different audiences:

he had an eye for weather-eyes

at cross-roads and lane-ends
and could don manners

at a flutter of curtains.

The new third section introduces an explicit creator and consumer of images, a 'you' who is in fact both an 'I' (Heaney himself) and a 'you' (the reader): 'You dream a cricket in the hearth / and cockroach on the floor.' This dream is pastoral, apparently as far removed from the urgency of Civil Rights and burnt-out streets as it could go. But now the mummer-as-artist is fully part of the communal world, and fully armed with the power to infuse the rhythm of the seasons with a sacred energy. In this dreamed-of cottage, the mummer is no longer alone as an isolated figure outside the collective – he is one of a 'line of mummers' and he is inside the house. The tradition, and the artistry he represents, are both fully intact and socially embraced. The mummers are leaving the cottage after their performance and the poem captures a beautiful image of rightful seasonal order and the shared peace they will leave behind:

> melted snow off their feet
>
> leaves you in peace.
> Again the old year dies
>
> on your hearthstone, for good luck.
> The moon's host elevated
>
> in a monstrance of holly trees,
> he makes dark tracks, who had
>
> untousled a first dewy path
> Into the summer grazing.[7]

So here now, in the transformed poem, we can see Heaney not merely (in the second section) remaking an image that is not 'about Northern Ireland' into one that is but (in the third) developing that image as a way of thinking about how to be an artist in the new political context.

The first section, even though it remains in verbal terms substantially the same, is changed by being placed in sequence with the two new ones. In its original form it does not really imply that the mummer is a possible avatar for the poet himself. He seems quite a distant figure, coolly observed within a parable of social and cultural change. In its new form, the mummer does indeed become a possible image of the poet in particular, of the contemporary Irish artist in general. The family turning away to watch TV is the public; the mummer beating the gate and throwing a stone at their roof is a figure of artistic impotence. What, this section now asks, can the poet do but howl in useless frustration? (The gate will no more be affected by the stick than the roof by the stone or than the political conflict by a poem.)

The expanded poem, however, seeks to move beyond this mere frustration with two other images of artistic possibility. The mummer of the second section may be watchful, wary and inclined to temper his art to the demands of his audience, donning and doffing manners depending on who is fluttering the curtains. But this wariness is also a way of picking a path through the long toils of blood and feuding, of navigating a safe course through a dangerous sectarian landscape. And the mummers of the third section, even though they are self-consciously summoned in an archaic dreamworld, suggest a different possibility – that of a numinous art that brings peace through its evocation of timeless rituals in tune with the rhythms of the earth.

It is true, of course, that this third image becomes, in the context of the sectarian conflict, highly problematic. Perhaps unconsciously, Heaney uses a metaphor that could not be more specific to his own Catholic upbringing: the moon and the holly trees become the transubstantiated host and the ornate monstrance in which it is displayed for adoration. (High church Anglicanism uses the same symbolism, but the doctrine of transubstantiation is one of the breaking points between Catholic and Protestant belief.) The implication, deliberate or otherwise, is that the dreamworld in which this wholeness is possible is culturally Catholic. And this of course raises the question that the Troubles and their long prehistory will not allow to be answered: if the poet must move between solitude and the community, what is the community? The truth is that if by a community we mean a shared public sphere, there is no community in Ireland for most of Heaney's life. It is not for nothing that this third section of 'The Last Mummer' in which 'peace' is the gift of the artist is a dream – reality would prove to be much more unyielding.

In a sense, then, the challenge that Glavin posed in 1967 – how would Heaney seek the community's endorsement for his solitary explorations without becoming captive to the need for its applause? – was partly met by the circumstances themselves. On a divided island, applause would come, if it came at all, from one side of a very high fence. At best, 'the community' could be thought of as a project or aspiration, a kind of benign fiction. The danger for Heaney, indeed, was not so much that he would be drowned in communal applause as that he would sink into a kind of naiveté, evoking an ideal of community that was completely out of kilter with political realities. In that same interview with Eavan Boland in

1970, he continues to talk of 'this community' as an overarching entity in a way that borders on wishful thinking:

> I certainly have felt anger. This is something I would like to ... get into words. I have got it into words here and there. But I have also found something else in this community. I have been educated gradually into a notion of all the goodness, the positive energies on either side of the division. So I cannot take up a line of poetry and generalise about Protestants, when I think of all the Protestants I have known that it's untrue about. I would think that it comes in the end to declaring for honesty and openness and goodwill, however abstract these things seem now.

His great challenge as a public figure was to retain that faith without allowing it to soften into mere ingenuousness, to evoke a community without forgetting that it did not exist, to declare for honesty and openness and goodwill without forgetting that they were abstractions. His method for meeting it was to triangulate constantly between the three possibilities elaborated in the full version of 'The Last Mummer': frustrated rage; the open weather eye always alert to the dangers as it tries to plot a way through the long toils of blood and feuding; and the poet's dreamed-of power to bless and make whole. Triangulation is a way of determining an unknown point by forming triangles to it from those points that are known. For Heaney, the unknown point is indeed a national life, a public sphere in which community is not a fiction and goodwill not an abstraction. The known points are his own memories and experiences and perceptions transmuted into images that bridge the gap between private apprehension and public comprehension.

It was perhaps only with his death that the full realization came of how well he had met this challenge. He had done justice to each of the three impulses, to the anger that is proper in the face of cruelty and injustice; to the countervailing need for restraint and calculation in a terrain full of dangers; and to the deep need to have life, however grim it has become, blessed by the dignity and exuberance of imaginative creation. In his absence it became clear that something was missing, not just in artistic life, but in public life. And a public life that can miss a poet so much is a life that has been immensely enriched by his presence.

Notes

1 Seamus Heaney, speech at the National Museum, Dublin, 20 March 2013.
2 'Crediting Poetry', in Seamus Heaney, *Opened Ground: Selected Poems 1966–1996* (New York: Farrar, Straus and Giroux, 1998).

3 *Irish Times*, 27 July 1967, 8.
4 *Ibid.*
5 *Irish Times*, 14 August 1970, 12.
6 'Poems by Seamus Heaney', Belfast Group Poetry Network, Emory Center for Digital Scholarship, Manuscript, Archives, and Rare Books Library, Emory University, http://belfastgroup.digitalscholarship.emory.edu/groupsheets/heaney1_10407.
7 *Ibid.*, http://belfastgroup.digitalscholarship.emory.edu/groupsheets/heaney1_10442.

CHAPTER 30

Exhibiting Heaney

Geraldine Higgins

Readers of the *Guardian* in 2007 may remember a much-loved series called 'Writers' Rooms'. At the top of the page was a photo of each writer's study and underneath a description of that space by the writer in question.[1] The series appealed to our desire to look inside other people's houses and to our curiosity about that most elusive thing: creativity. Obviously, the writers themselves are curators of these spaces, but the conceit of the series was to feature the rooms without the writers. Indeed, the tagline was 'Portraits of the Spaces where Authors Create'.[2] We gaze at the totems and tools in the photograph and are guided through the room by the writer's pen portrait underneath.

Seamus Heaney's attic study in Dublin was featured in August 2007, and he begins the piece by telling us what we can't see – the view from the other skylight outside the frame of the photo:

> This is a corner of the attic room of our house in Dublin. In the down-slope of the ceiling on the other side there's a second skylight, much wider and longer and lower than the one in the picture, and through it I have a high clear view of Dublin Bay and Howth Head and the Dublin port shipping coming and going – or not, depending on the weather.[3]

The skylight frames the writer's room as an exhibition in itself – representing the place where the writing happens and the space that opens up somewhere else – or as Heaney puts it, 'the double sense of here-and-nowness in the familiar place and far-and-awayness in something immense' (*SS* 475). To move from the private room to the public exhibition space is to put pressure on ideas about surface and depth, privacy and creativity, the man who suffers and the mind which creates, as Eliot has it. It also reflects the transition from the jottings and drafts of the pre-archive to 'something intended, complete': the printed text.[4] In framing this chapter with the writer's room, I want to focus attention on the aura of the exhibited space as well as the transformative relationship between Heaney's creative inspiration, his writing process, the poetry and its referents.

It is a truism of exhibition and museum studies that every exhibition must tell a story that unfolds through time and space. In this chapter I have drawn on the experience of curating two exhibitions on Seamus Heaney in two different locations – in Atlanta, Georgia (Emory University, 2014) and the National Library of Ireland, Dublin (Bank of Ireland, 2018).[5] The main focus is *Seamus Heaney: Listen Now Again*, a free public exhibition which will be open at its current location in the Bank of Ireland on College Green, Dublin, for five years before moving permanently to the National Library of Ireland (NLI). The story begins with the donation of Heaney's literary archive to the NLI in 2011.[6] Spanning almost fifty years of poetry manuscripts, the NLI collection (nineteen boxes covering the years 1963–2010) also includes drafts of essays, lectures, plays and reviews. Heaney himself loaded the material into his car and delivered the boxes to the library to join what he called a 'human chain' of Irish writers there.[7]

The title of *Listen Now Again* adds an auditory imperative to the Emory exhibition, *Seamus Heaney: The Music of What Happens*. Both exhibitions reflect on the importance of listening, not just to the sound of Heaney's poetry but to a music 'that you never would have known to listen for' (*SL* 1). This phrase, like 'Listen Now Again', is from 'The Rainstick', a poem that describes how something as ordinary as a cactus stick filled with dry grit or grain can be transformed into something miraculous – the sound of rain. Heaney's mission as a poet is not just to capture the music of what happens, but to urge us to pay attention.

The guiding thread of *Listen Now Again* is the theme of transformation, following the chronology of Heaney's poetry from the earthbound bog poems of his early work to the airiness and uplift of crediting marvels in his later career. This trajectory is reinforced by the use of the four elements – earth, fire, water and air – to disrupt the linearity of the historical timeline and to reflect Heaney's own elemental imagination: 'Let everything flow / Up to the four elements, / Up to water and earth and fire and air' (*SL* 38). These dual strands show the sequential development of Heaney's career volume by volume while tracing some of the circular motifs that recur across his writing life.

The elements also inform the design and layout of the four main sections of the exhibition. Excavations (earth) begins in the fields of Heaney's birthplace in Mossbawn, County Derry, and focuses on the bog as a metaphor for history and memory. This is followed by Creativity (fire), which examines the creative process of forging words into finished poems as well as Heaney's circles of influence as teacher and poet.

Conscience (water) shows Heaney's struggle to write ethically about the violence in Northern Ireland and his engagement with global politics and injustice. The exhibition concludes with Marvels (air), which shows how his later poetry moved towards a sense of uplift and transcendence, and also looks at Heaney's legacy as a beloved public figure.

To read and research Heaney's work is to inhabit his memory, both a dreamscape of sensory impressions and a real landscape of solid objects – pumps and buckets, sofas and meal bins. In *Stepping Stones*, Dennis O'Driscoll asks Heaney if a poem begins when he finds a form and he replies, 'Generally speaking, my poems come from things remembered, quite often from away back, or things I see that remind me of something else. Sometimes the thing has an aura and an invitation and some kind of blocked significance hanging around it' (*SS* 445). The challenge for any exhibition is to recreate that sense of aura and invitation without necessarily showing the 'real' objects themselves. It is not just a question of respecting what Matthew Arnold calls 'the object as in itself it really is'[8] but of showing what poems are made of, how they work rather than what they represent. Each section is anchored by talismanic objects on loan from the Heaney family: Heaney's blackthorn walking stick, his writing desk, a lamp that belonged to W. B. Yeats, his signed copy of the Good Friday/Belfast Agreement, a 1960s bronze bust of Heaney by sculptor Carolyn Mulholland, and a reproduction of his 1995 Nobel Prize medal. These objects act as thematic lodestones but aere not illustrations of particular poems. In designing the exhibition space, we wanted to recreate the intimacy of the writer's room without replicating it[9] in order to stage a meaningful encounter between visitor and writer, text and object, sound and vision.

Heaney's signature poem, 'Digging', contains the two objects that have come to define his writing life: the spade and the pen. One of the earliest decisions, crucial to the curatorial process, was how best to represent this much-loved poem: with an early manuscript draft or a photo of the author writing/digging or with a real spade and a real pen? Our aim was to recreate the written world of the poem without reducing it to a literal rendering of its most obvious meaning. We decided to display the manuscript of 'Digging' alongside a proof copy of the poem from its first appearance in the *New Statesman* as well as a letter from Faber and Faber informing Heaney about the date of publication for *Death of a Naturalist.* This is the first poem the visitor encounters in *Listen Now Again* – as text, context and an audio recording of Heaney reciting the poem – establishing the blend of the familiar and the unexpected that is reproduced throughout the exhibition.

In 'Digging', the first and last stanzas book-ending the poem chart the shifting relationship between the speaker and the two objects. In the first stanza, the cradled pen appears charged with the latent threat of violence in the almost-palindrome 'snug as a gun' (*DN* 1). When the spade is introduced and then described as an instrument of skilled manual labour, it belongs to the world of the speaker's father and grandfather and is associated with the monotony of repetitive work. The pen/gun has the power of transformation (turning swords into ploughshares/the pen is mightier than the sword) but the spade does not turn into the pen – it is replaced by it. The two central objects or instruments co-exist only in the written world of the poem, which masks a moment of rupture with a powerful declaration of continuity – 'I'll dig with it' (*DN* 2).

This manifesto leads the visitor into the familiar territory of Heaney's beloved early poems evoking the traditional concerns of his farming family and the everyday miracles of transforming cream into butter, straw into golden thatch. Describing the writing process of *Death of a Naturalist*, Heaney says, 'the whole effort of the writing was to solidify the thing in language, block it out, make it embossed, until it became a kind of language braille of sorts'.[10] These tactile metaphors resonate with the archaeological theme, accessible but multi-layered, that remains vital throughout his work.

The manuscripts are shown in low trench-like cases so that the viewer looks down towards the ground, encountering displays of real turf, a two-sided turf spade (a sleán), as well as images and quotations about the 'squelch and slap of soggy peat' (*DN* 2). Charting the poet's relocation from the north of Ireland to his rural retreat in Glanmore, Co. Wicklow, we highlight Heaney's discovery of P.V. Glob's book of photos of the bog bodies through a video installation in the floor. These uncanny images of the Tollund Man, Grauballe Man and the Windeby girl accompany the manuscripts devoted to the bog bodies of Heaney's 1975 collection, *North*. We introduce Heaney's fascinating edits of the bog poems by showing an early draft of 'Bogland' in which we see that the ground 'soft as pulp' was once 'soft as banana'.[11] Then we move to drafts of two of the crucial bog poems – 'Strange Fruit' and 'Punishment' – to show why archives matter.

The sonnet 'Strange Fruit' (*N* 39) anatomizes the 'leathery beauty' of a beheaded girl exhumed from the Danish bog and questions the poet's own response to her. When we examine the manuscript drafts of the poem, not only do the form and content change dramatically but we can also see that it was originally entitled 'Triceps', then 'Reliquary', then 'My Reverence' and seemingly finally, 'Tête coupée'.[12] In abandoning the religious implications of the earlier titles and the severed head of 'Tête coupée', the final title, 'Strange Fruit', opens up an entire field of force and of situational politics. The new title invokes the lynched black bodies hanging from the 'southern trees' of Abel Meeropol's song 'Strange Fruit' made famous by Billie Holiday in 1939.[13] The drafts show Heaney's decisive black line striking through 'Tête coupée' and its replacement by the capitalized, handwritten 'Strange Fruit'.

This change of title also binds the poem more closely to the earlier 'Punishment' (*N* 37), perhaps Heaney's most controversial treatment of the kinship between these tribal human sacrifices and the atrocities perpetrated on the streets of Belfast and Derry. Both poems illuminate issues of gender and the male gaze as well as the tension between subject and object, female body and museum exhibit. 'Punishment' compares the ritual killing of the ancient 'Little adulteress' with the tarring and feathering of women who became involved with British soldiers in 1970s Northern Ireland. The poem charts the speaker's response to the exhumed body ranging from empathy ('I can feel the tug / of the halter'), to visualization ('I can see her drowned / body'), to tenderness ('Little adulteress'), to intimacy ('My poor scapegoat, / I almost love you') (*N* 37–8), before the focus shifts from the dead girl to the troubled poet. The final four stanzas of the poem stage Heaney's ethical dilemma about his own artistic practice and his political culpability. The self-accusatory lines, 'I am the artful voyeur / of your brain's exposed / and darkened combs' (*N* 38), follow several revealing drafts of the poem in which the speaker accuses himself of being a 'cowardly spy' and a 'posthumous collaborator'. One draft shows the poem in sonnet form, another with the alternative title, 'Shame'.[14] In these handwritten drafts, Heaney wrestles with how to convey the speaker's complicity with tribal ideas of punishment. In the final version, the ambiguity of 'artful' combined with 'voyeur' resonates throughout the poem and beyond as Heaney weighs up his own role as culpable bystander and as tribal witness.

North received the most controversial reviews of Heaney's career; most focused on the bog poems, particularly 'Punishment'. The volume was hailed by Conor Cruise O'Brien as listening to 'the thing itself . . . the actual substance of historical agony and dissolution, the tragedy of a people in a place: the Catholics of Northern Ireland',[15] and tendentiously reviewed in the *Honest Ulsterman* by Ciaran Carson who called Heaney 'the laureate of violence – a mythmaker, an anthropologist of ritual killing, an apologist for "the situation", in the last resort, a mystifier'.[16] Carson and Edna Longley were foremost amongst the critics who questioned Heaney's employment of Glob's photographs of the Danish bog bodies to address contemporary violence in Northern Ireland.[17] By exhibiting not only the drafts of the poem but also Glob's photograph of the Windeby girl,[18] and a 1970s newspaper cutting of a tarred and feathered girl found amongst Heaney's papers, we highlight the mediated textures and contexts of the poem and invite viewers to consider their own voyeurism.

This idea of making and shaping poetry opens out into the section on 'Creativity' where we examine Heaney's writing process. The guiding poem here is 'The Forge', our symbol of fire, showing the poet at work forging words into finished things.

The centrepiece of this section is Heaney's writing desk – really a wooden board on top of two filing cabinets – that sat under the skylight in the attic of his home in Dublin. This simple workspace relates to Heaney's 'superstitious fear of making a designer study, a film set rather than a bolt-hole' (*SS* 231) and reminds us of the work that goes into every draft. In a specially commissioned video piece projected directly above the desk, we hear Heaney's own voice reading lines or words that we see crossed out or changed on screen. We see the poet's hesitations and uncertainties as well as the evidence of his craftsmanship.

At the heart of the exhibition are Heaney's notebooks, some nondescript jotters filled with drafts, to-do lists and occasional diary entries, others bound and carefully dated. These notes and drafts highlight the aura of the handwritten page in an era of mechanical (or digital) reproduction. In the occasional diary entries, the outside world intrudes on Heaney's working day with important events like the death of poet Robert Lowell or his election to the poetry professorship at Oxford as well as notes scribbled down in a hurry such as '3rd May. Central Garage Bray while VW was being fixed.' My favourite notebooks on display are gifts from the Heaney children, described in this diary entry for Christmas 1973:

> The boys gave me this – one from Michael and one from Christopher so I am writing in them immediately. It's half nine, Chris is still in his pyjamas, Christmas Miscellany is on the radio, Marie is making breakfast and Catherine Ann, 8 months old today is sitting eating her finger with her two bottom teeth saying Ba Ba.[19]

Such moments transport us from our sense of the poet at work to an encounter with the poet at home, full of the joys of being in the present. Ultimately, what we find when we turn to Heaney's notebooks and drafts, letters and printed books is not just the invaluable poetic legacy but the human traces of a writing life unfolding in real time.

Seeing Things

In a fascinating essay on creativity in the *Dublin Review*, 'Sixth Sense, Seventh Heaven', Heaney talks about the three stages of feeling, contemplation and 'harmonic expansion' needed for a poem to 'get up on its own legs'.[20] He points out that these three stages or steps are experienced not sequentially but simultaneously by the poet as 'an awakening of nerve ends and word-slips'. Heaney then gives us an example of such a moment in the confluence of place, space and poetic inspiration when he discovered the twelve-line form of the 'Squarings' poems collected in *Seeing Things*. Revisiting this moment in *Stepping Stones*, Heaney writes:

> The first poem more or less wrote itself one afternoon in the National Library of Ireland. . . . I'd been in the library for about six weeks and, the day I finished, I was sitting in this most beautiful reading room with the rain coming down on the glass dome. Suddenly I wrote a few lines and it became a twelve-line, four three-lines, thing. It felt given, strange and unexpected; I didn't quite know where it came from, but I knew immediately it was there to stay. It seemed as solid as an iron bar. . . . The form operated for me as a generator of poetry. (*SS* 320)

Heaney has always been interested in the alchemical process of turning solid things into language, often at the point of physical contact. In *Seeing Things* alone we find 'the actual kicked ball' (8); 'the small of your back made very solid sense' (99); and 'I was four but I turned four hundred maybe / Encountering the ancient dampish feel / Of a clay floor' (100). But the thrust of the volume is towards buoyancy, even transcendence, in those strange moments described as 'both the door and what came through it' (9) or the pitchfork thrust 'past its own aim, out to an other side' (23). Here too, the form that 'seemed as solid as an iron bar' melts into the air of the written word but has the gravity 'in the scale of things' (100) both to hold the poem in place and to generate more ideas.

Later in *Stepping Stones*, Heaney confesses to being a 'great hoarder': 'I'm a great hoarder of course; I once did a little sequence of poems called 'Shelf Life': things that are kept, picked up, like bits of stone, an iron spike, an old smoothing iron that belonged in our house, and so on' (*SS* 445). 'Shelf Life', like many of Heaney's titles, suggests two meanings: the 'sell-by date' of perishable goods and the timeless quality of the real objects collected and cherished by the poet. This sequence of six poems from *Station Island* is a verbal cabinet of curiosities: a granite chip from Joyce's Martello Tower that hurts the poet's hand and is 'jaggy, salty, punitive'; an old smoothing iron that teaches how 'to pull your weight and feel exact and equal to it'; the 'soft option' of unshowy old pewter; an iron spike from New Hampshire that reminds the poet of a 'harrow pin'; the magical 'morning offering' of the 'Stone from Delphi'; and finally 'A Snowshoe', 'a hieroglyph for all the realms of whisper' (*SI* 21–4).

The objects are unified by their grouping on the shelf of the poet's imagination, but the six poems are more than a mere verbal inventory of the chosen things. All the objects except the last are made of stone or metal, anchoring the poet, keeping him grounded but also pinning him down. In each case the objects are weighed and tested for their efficacy as metaphors, the heaviness of their materiality contrasting with the weightless written artefact.[21] What matters is the poetical riff, not the literal referent. The objects also act as metaphorical vehicles, transporting the speaker through time and space from the Martello Tower to New Hampshire to the oracle's shrine at Delphi. Tellingly, the last and lightest object, the snowshoe, although made to traverse the earth, is likened to 'an old-time kite' (*SI* 24).[22]

This journey from the material to the metaphysical is mirrored by the tension between the poet and the polis or what Heaney terms 'song and suffering' in his political poems. In *Listen Now Again*, 'Conscience' is represented by water to convey the idea of journeys both real and mythological and also to suggest self-reflection and the flow of history. Coming of age as a poet at the onset of the Troubles in 1960s Northern Ireland ensured that Heaney would be alert to the responsibilities of a poet writing in a time of violence. Yet he was careful *not* to overstate the impact of poetry in such times. 'What do I say if they wheel out their dead?' (*WO* 31) he asks in an early poem, and later claims, 'No lyric has ever stopped a tank' (*GT* 107–8). However, Heaney also professes the power of poetry to help by pushing back against reality. The continual questioning and revising of his perspective on the role of the poet in violent times underlies his collaboration with fellow artists in the Field Day Theatre Company as well as the influence of Eastern European poets on his work.

By 1995, when he was awarded the Nobel Prize in literature for works of 'lyrical beauty and ethical depth', Heaney's words had entered the language of the peace process itself. US President Bill Clinton, quoting a passage from Heaney's play *The Cure at Troy*, said, 'One line always leaps out at me – the moment when "hope and history rhyme".'[23] During his acceptance speech in Stockholm, Heaney memorably described the podium on which he stood as a kind of space station. He said it allowed him 'the luxury of walking on air', adding, 'I credit poetry with making this space walk possible.' From this speech too comes the line chosen as Heaney's epitaph, 'Walk on air against your better judgement' (*OG* 416–17).

In his later years, Heaney's work returns to the importance of human connections. He welcomes the 'Age of Births' with poems for his granddaughters, and circles back to the people and places of his own childhood, as well as journeys that intertwine the mythic and the everyday. A month before he died, Seamus Heaney completed his translation of *Aeneid Book VI*, writing of life's final journey from time into eternity. His last poem was the delicate 'In Time', addressed to his youngest grandchild, in which he imagines her dancing into a future that he won't see. The sure-footed poet and the wobbling child are connected by the power that comes up through the ground, 'And earths you here for real'. Dated 18 August 2013, the poem ends, 'But for now we foot it lightly / In time, and silently'.[24]

When we visit the sacred places or the exhibition spaces of writers we love, we are in search of a powerful connection between poet and place, subject and object – a connection 'both matter-of-fact and dreamlike, unexpected and foreknown, like poetry itself'.[25] The aim of *Listen Now Again* is to create this intimate connection between the visitor, the poet and above all, the poems. Returning to the photo of the 'Writer's Room', we realize that the image we want to see is one of Seamus Heaney standing in his study.[26] The slight sense of anxiety or intrusiveness that we feel in examining the empty room is relieved when we see the writer in situ, our guide to the real and the made-up.

As Heaney 'becomes his admirers'[27] or enters his archival moment, we recognize that this space is also about loss and absence. The exhibition closes by showing Heaney's continuing legacy in Irish public life with his last words in a text to his wife, Marie – *Noli timere*, Latin for 'Don't be afraid'. This text inspired the artist Maser to paint the phrase on the gable of a building on South Richmond Street in Dublin. Maser recreated this piece as the final installation in *Listen Now Again*. This time the words 'Don't be Afraid' are illuminated on a wall of blackboard paint so that visitors can leave their own messages for and about Seamus Heaney.

Notes

1 See 'Writers' Rooms: Seamus Heaney', *Guardian*, 31 August 2007, www.theguardian.com/books/2007/aug/31/writers.rooms.seamus.heaney. There were 85 rooms in the series, with photographs by Eamonn McCabe.

2 See also Claire Battershill, 'Writers' Rooms: Theories of Contemporary Authorship in Portraits of Creative Spaces', *Authorship*, 3/2 (2014), 1–14.

3 'Writers' Rooms'.

4 W. B. Yeats, 'A General Introduction for my Work', repr. in *Essays and Introductions* (London: Macmillan: 1961), pp. 30–1.

5 A third major exhibition opened in 2016 at the Seamus Heaney HomePlace in Bellaghy, Co. Derry. See http://seamusheaneyhome.com.
6 Emory University acquired Heaney's archive of correspondence in 2003.
7 From Heaney speech at the National Library of Ireland (hereafter NLI), quoted in Carl O'Brien, 'Heaney Hands Notes to National Library', *Irish Times*, 21 December 2011, www.irishtimes.com/news/heaney-hands-notes-to-national-library-1.889199.
8 Matthew Arnold, 'The Function of Criticism at the Present Time', in *Poetry and Criticism by Matthew Arnold*, ed. A Dwight Culler (Boston: Houghton Mifflin, 1961), p. 239.
9 See April Bernard, 'Here's What I Hate about Writers' Houses', *NYRB*, 11 August 2011, www.nybooks.com/daily/2011/08/11/heres-what-i-hate-about-writers-houses.
10 Seamus Heaney, 'A Soul on the Washing Line', interview in the *Economist*, June 1991, repr. 5 September 2013, www.economist.com/prospero/2013/09/05/a-soul-on-the-washing-line.
11 Seamus Heaney, MS 49, 493/10, NLI.
12 Seamus Heaney, MS 49, 493/38, NLI. The poem was published with the title 'Tête coupée' in the special edition of *Bog Poems* edited by Olwyn Hughes (London: Rainbow Press, 1975).
13 See also Gail McConnell, 'Heaney and the Photograph: "Strange Fruit" in Manuscript and Published Form', *Irish University Review*, 47, supplement (2017), 432–49.
14 Seamus Heaney, MS 49, 493/37, NLI.
15 Conor Cruise O'Brien, 'A Slow North-East Wind', *Listener*, 25 September 1975, 404–5.
16 Ciaran Carson, 'Escaped from the Massacre?' *Honest Ulsterman*, 50 (1975), 183–6.
17 Edna Longley, 'North: "Inner Émigré" or "Artful Voyeur"?' in Tony Curtis (ed.), *The Art of Seamus Heaney*, 2nd edn (Bridgend: Poetry Wales Press, 1985), pp. 65–95.
18 Recent DNA testing has shown that the body is actually that of a sixteen-year-old boy dated to between 41 BCE and 118 CE.
19 Seamus Heaney, MS 49, 493/142, NLI.
20 Seamus Heaney, 'Sixth Sense, Seventh Heaven', *Dublin Review*, 8 (2002), 115–26.
21 Heaney also says that it is possible to think of every poem in 'Squarings' as 'the peg at the end of a tent-rope reaching up into the airy structure, but still with purchase on something earthier and more obscure' (*SS* 302).
22 *Seamus Heaney: The Music of What Happens* at Emory featured a handmade kite as the centrepiece of the exhibition.
23 Bill Clinton, *Between Hope and History: Meeting America's Challenges for the 21st Century* (New York: Random House, 1996), p. 175.
24 Seamus Heaney, 'In Time', *New Selected Poems 1988–2013* (London: Faber and Faber, 2014), p. 218.

25 George Morgan, interview with Seamus Heaney, *Cycnos*, 15/2 (July 2008), http://revel.unice.fr/cycnos/?id=1594 .
26 See Eamonn McCabe's jacket photo for *Human Chain* of Heaney in his study.
27 W.H. Auden, 'In Memory of W. B. Yeats', *The Collected Poetry of W.H. Auden* (New York: Random House, 1945), p.50.

CHAPTER 31

The Archive

Rand Brandes

On 16 March 2016 the 1965 letter from Faber and Faber editor Charles Monteith accepting Seamus Heaney's *Death of a Naturalist* for publication appeared on the Waterstones.com blog.[1] Introducing Monteith's letter on the blog was a note from Hannah Marshall, Faber Members Manager, reminding readers of Heaney's long relationship with the publisher and directing our attention to the posthumous publication of Heaney's translation of Book VI of Virgil's *Aeneid*. As if summoned from below, the letter that had lingered in the Faber archives suddenly appeared out of the electronic netherworld not only to make manifest the fifty-year historical arc of Heaney's publishing life, but also to stir in us the original excitement that Heaney must have felt upon receiving it. The Heaney archive at Faber and Faber out of which this letter arose is certainly extensive, but privately held, as is the archive of Heaney's American publisher, Farrar Straus and Giroux. Other major Heaney archives, however, like those at the National Library of Ireland in Dublin and Emory University in Atlanta, Georgia, are open to the public. In addition, there are institutions with more limited, but significant, Heaney papers, such as the University of California at Berkeley, Harvard University and Queen's University Belfast; commercial entities include BBC Northern Ireland and Radió Teilifis Éireann. As the Faber letter demonstrates, the Heaney archives are a treasure trove of historical and literary documents that have the power to re-energize, refocus and resituate Heaney studies around the world. The theoretical implications and critical potential of the archival materials become clear when one traces the paper trail of the archives from the prenatal attic to the postmortem reading room and into the afterlife of textual studies.

Heaney used his Dublin attic as both a writing space and a warehouse. Until the poet's correspondence was placed in 2003 at the Stuart A. Rose Manuscript, Archives and Rare Book Library at Emory University in Atlanta, Georgia (hereafter Rose Library), the letters and cards sent to the poet filled drawers, files, boxes and even worn-out suitcases in his attic. Heaney also retained the original manuscripts and typescripts of his outgoing correspondence in folders since he often communicated by telefax. Mixed in with the correspondence that travelled to Emory were a variety of other manuscripts, administrative papers and published materials. In 2010 Heaney again worked in the attic, this time not to organize his correspondence but to prepare his manuscripts for placement in the National Library of Ireland. The collection included hundreds of notes, verse fragments and drafts of poems (many unpublished), revised typescripts, Group worksheets, prose pieces, journal entries and materials at various stages of the publishing process. All told, it seems as if Heaney kept every scrap of paper related to his writing life from his days at Queen's University Belfast forward – at least that is what one would think after mining these two substantial archives. Importantly, unlike archives that are compiled posthumously by family members or literary executors, the Emory and NLI archives were assembled by the poet himself, which means that all of the materials in both archives literally passed through Heaney's hands. These archives were shaped by the poet and then reshaped again by the institutional archivists. Both are copious collections, each taking the libraries' archivists approximately two years to process the materials after they arrived directly from the Heaney home in Dublin.

For Heaney scholars writing today the archives contain not only many treasures worth pursuing, but also many truths worth exploring. As Ted Hughes writes of the drafts of Sylvia Plath's poem 'Sheep in Fog': 'What these drafts reveal, then, is more than the working out of a famous poem. They reveal what is essentially a parallel body of poetry . . . These drafts are not an incidental adjunct to the poem, they are a complementary revelation, a log-book of its real meanings.'[2] On the most fundamental level archives provide biographical information that allows the critic to trace important connections between the poet's life and the work as well as to gain a deeper understanding of and appreciation for the creative process. Writing, revising and annotating his manuscripts, typescripts and correspondence by hand (even if digitally born) has infused Heaney's papers with the ancient authority of the archive.[3]

The raw numbers associated with the Emory and NLI archives are instructive and present a clear picture of the size of the collections. Emory lists their Heaney archive at 102 boxes dating from 1951–2004, while the NLI lists their collection at 19 boxes covering the years 1963–2010. The NLI Heaney collection figures can be broken down further into 300 folders containing 10,167 loose sheets (pages), along with

34 notebooks (these include hardback and springback notebooks and exercise books).[4] Emory's Heaney archive is organized into eight series and multiple subseries: Correspondence (General correspondence, Literary correspondence, Outgoing correspondence and Other correspondence); Writings by others (Writing about Seamus Heaney, Other Writings); Printed material (Writings by Seamus Heaney, Writings about Seamus Heaney, Review, and Collected printed materials); Subject files; Photographs; Audio-visual material; Personal papers; and Writings by Seamus Heaney (Poetry and Translations, and Prose).[5] The NLI archive is organized into six series based upon genre, and the subseries are organized chronologically and by volume: Poetry, 1963–2010; Prose, 1970–2005; Verse Translations, 1979–2009; Drama, 1990–2004; Other Papers, 1990–2004. The subseries are too numerous to list here, but the NLI Heaney archive catalogue provides extremely detailed information.[6] In these two archives alone are thousands of manuscripts and letters in addition to the plethora of administrative papers and associated materials – materials that are now open to student and scholar alike.[7]

The origin of the archives begs the question: from where did the archives arrive, under what conditions were they produced and what do they tell us about Heaney the man as well as Heaney the poet? One natural response is to ask, how did he do it? How did Heaney maintain lifelong epistolary relationships with friends, colleagues, fellow writers, scholars, students and public figures, and still write the poems, plays, essays, reviews and translations in addition to editing journals and books? How did he keep the wheels of his publishing life turning, sometimes whirling, from the proofs to the marketing events? How did he edit journals, review books, write for and participate in radio and television programmes, visit schools, give major lectures and teach throughout most of his career? How did he give reading after reading, introduce other writers at public events, launch summer schools, open art exhibitions, give commencement addresses, participate in fundraisers and welcome foreign dignitaries? Where did he find the time to labour over guest lists, organize seating charts and make his own engagement calendars with pen and ruler in hand? How did he produce endless recommendations for students and fellow writers? Where did he find the strength to write elegy after elegy and deliver eulogy after eulogy and still be a gracious, generous host and good company? Part of the answer can be found in the materials held by Emory and the NLI. These materials can be seen as footnotes and confirmations that round out the life Heaney describes in *Stepping Stones* – a life defined by hard work, much writing, constant self-interrogation, arts, activism and inspiration.

Those wanting to know more about Heaney's relationship with other contemporary poets, writers and artists will head to Emory's collection of Correspondence (sixty-four boxes), much of which is comprised of letters written to Heaney. The subseries Literary Correspondence is comprised of seven boxes, and the letters here often mix the personal with the professional. For instance, the seeds of Heaney's version of Sophocles' *Philoctetes*, *The Cure at Troy*, seem to have been planted in a note from Brian Friel: 'May-day – May-day — May-day / Now that you've done Italy and Oxford's in the bag and the Abbey restored, *you have got to do something for the theatre* – a translation, a version, a dramatization. S.R. & I are plotting a 3-play season. You are needed. Okay? Just come half-way down the mountain – theatre is a VULGAR medium. Love ___B.'[8] On another occasion the playfulness and deep understanding of the relationship between Friel and Heaney can be seen: 'Welcome back to Dublin – / and to national responsibilities. B. ____'[9] Another example of the professional mingling with the personal is captured in a circa 1988 letter from Paul Muldoon assessing the closing line of Heaney's poem, xxiv from the 'Squarings' section of *Seeing Things*: 'And I'm not sure you quite get away with the chime of "equilibrium, brim". In fact, I'm sure you don't get away with it. It's much too pleased with itself.'[10] Heaney commented on the complexity of the situation by speculating that the 'chime' sounded too Muldoonian.[11]

In addition to documenting significant moments in Heaney's professional life, the correspondence reveals the workings that supported the personal life. Since Heaney is a poet of place, his creative life would not have grown as it did without Glanmore Cottage in County Wicklow, which his family first rented and then purchased from Ann Saddlemyer. It all begins in a letter from Saddlemyer to Heaney written on 15 January 1972: 'Word has crossed the Atlantic that you might be interested in living in my Wicklow house for the summer, or part of it.'[12] She continues by listing the reasons why she hopes the arrangement will work and concludes: 'And I would like to know that you were out of the north for a while with your family.' The Emory archive drives this point home by including a letter from Seamus Deane dated 2 February 1972 in which he describes looking for Heaney and Brian Friel: 'In the midst of many other things, I decided to drop you this note, for the following purposes: one, to inquire if you enjoyed the Newry march ... I assumed you had been delayed by the troops.'[13] Deane then writes: 'Second purpose – a play by one W. Shakespeare, called *Macbeth*, I believe, reputed to be very good, awaits its introduction to the European world, and I wonder have you yet ejected its rancid poison from your system? Could you send it soon?' Heaney did finally complete the introduction, perhaps his most extensive comment on Shakespeare, but the edition was never published.[14]

Heaney did not deliver to Emory most of the letters from family, friends, renowned writers and public figures that he received congratulating him on being awarded the Nobel Prize; however, a notable exception is the handwritten note of congratulation from Ted Hughes. In a calligraphy all his own, Hughes writes on 8 October 1995: 'Dear Seamus – well there it is. And it's there forever. Like a sea-god on a great wave, you emerged and inevitably took it by sovereignty of nature.'[15] Hughes's letter of congratulation, mythic in image and spirit, was transformed by an accident of nature. The letter had apparently been rained upon so in the file folder one finds Hughes's script in its visionary state: illuminated and the ink alive with blacks, blues, browns and burnt oranges under the plastic protective cover. Visually stunning and personally powerful, Hughes's letter symbolizes the many gems awaiting the archival explorer. A letter to Heaney's long-time friend, Darcy O'Brien, places the Hughes letter in perspective. After describing the agonizing process of trying to decide who would be invited to fill his ten allotted seats at the Nobel Award ceremony, Heaney writes on 31 December 1995: 'The house has turned into a gross mail-box. I keep saying that I must get a fulltime secretary. I keep knowing a life-change has occurred but not quite knowing how to proceed except in the old way. I keep thanking God that *The Spirit Level* was delivered to the publisher before all this got under way.'[16]

Heaney proposed changing the title of his first post-Nobel volume, *The Spirit Level*, to *The Gravel Walks*, according to a letter to Jonathan Galassi, the editor at Farrar, Straus and Giroux, even after the title had appeared in Faber and Faber's spring 1996 catalogue.[17] Obviously the change was not made, but as proof copies of his early volumes will attest, the poet's practice of revising his work all of the way through the printing process was part of his modus operandi from the beginning. On a more intimate, but still significant level, a typescript draft of one of *The Spirit Level*'s most famous poems, 'Postscript', concludes with the phrase 'swings it [the heart] open', while the published version is 'blows it open'.[18] Much can be said about the transformative power of 'blow' versus the more mechanically accurate 'swing', and those interested in Heaney's creative process will find even more opportunities to explore this in Heaney's work in the NLI, whose collection is rich with revisions.

The NLI online catalogue descriptions of the individual manuscript items in the Heaney archives are extremely detailed and easy to navigate.

Beginning with catalogue item 1, 'Typescript drafts of poems submitted by Seamus Heaney to the Belfast Group's poetry workshops, ca 1963–1966', the archive opens to both the known and the unknown. In I.i.1 there are early Group worksheet drafts of Heaney poems that were collected in *Death of a Naturalist*, such as 'Mid-Term Break', 'Personal Helicon' and 'Blackberry-Picking' (unhyphenated), but no 'Death of a Naturalist' or other iconic *DN* poems. Item I.i.1 also includes 'To a Wine Jar', Heaney's translation from Horace's Odes, III, xxi, that was not published until 1994 and was never collected.[19] Heaney's only other Horace translation is the 9/11 poem 'Anything Can Happen'. There is at least one poem included in the Group worksheets that was never published, dating back to the summer of 1959. 'Amputation' is perhaps one of Heaney's earliest attempts at verse and opens with the prophetic word 'squat', as in 'squat pen' from 'Digging'. The Group worksheets, therefore, include Heaney poems that were composed much earlier and are truly works in progress.

The organic energy and ongoing potential of the early poems demonstrate that Heaney rarely gave up on a poem and would stay in touch with the draft for years, if not decades, before publication. This commitment can also be found in the drafts of poems in item I.i.5., described as a 'Hardback notebook, containing manuscript drafts of poems and some prose pieces, 1966–1972'. The NLI catalogue notes that some of the poems in the I.i.5 notebook were revised and published in *Door into the Dark* (1969), *Wintering Out* (1972), *North* (1975) and *Seeing Things* (1991). This emphasizes one practical reason that Heaney kept the majority of his manuscript materials: his sense that even if a draft is not fully realized as a publishable poem in the moment, it might emerge in the long term. While not identified as such in the catalogue, there is a very early draft of a poem, 'Lenten Stuff', in the notebook that becomes part of one of Heaney's most ambitious and successful poetic endeavours, *Station Island*. Heaney published a typescript version of 'Lenten Stuff', taken from the NLI notebook, in a 1986 issue of *ERATO*. Included in Heaney's essay, 'Station Island: Jottings for a Poem', 'Lenten Stuff' begins: 'Now I can only find myself in one place: / Low-backed island on an inland lough. / A cold chapel takes up half the island.' Heaney dates the poem April 1966 and the essay also includes journal entries related to the poem from September 1979, November 1980, December 1981 and January 1982 when the entire 'Station Island' sequence was well on its way to completion in 1984. Of all of the manuscripts in the NLI archive, those related to *Station Island* reveal what a huge undertaking the sequence, and ultimately the entire volume, were for Heaney.

Staying with the earliest poems in the NLI Heaney archive, item I.ii.1., identified in the catalogue as 'Taken from a file originally marked by Heaney as 'Death of a Naturalist', are sixty-seven pages of drafts of poems that would evolve into the *Death of a Naturalist* manuscript sent to Faber and Faber for publication in 1966. Heaney also included in the file a letter from Peter Crawley at Faber and Faber dated April 1966 – thirteen months after the Monteith letter posted on the Waterstone blog – discussing the forthcoming publication. The file contains multiple holograph and typescript drafts of the 'Table of Contents', 'Acknowledgment' and poems. However, not all of the poems that appear in the published version of *DN* are in the file and those that are occasionally have alternative working titles. For instance, 'Blackberry-Picking' is 'Blackberry-Gathering', 'Poem (for Marie)' is 'The Sky's the Limit', and 'Personal Helicon' is 'An Apprenticeship'. The rightness of the published titles is obvious, as are the improvements that come with the revisions, such as those in 'Digging', where 'a rich rasping sound' in the draft becomes 'a clean rasping sound'. The file also contains a holograph draft of 'Trout' written on a torn envelope stamped with the postal date 7-xi-1964. Interestingly, in the Emory archive, Heaney describes in a letter the exact moment when 'Trout' was scribbled down: 'I remember exactly how it ['Trout'] was written – at one sitting, quickly, in my girlfriend's flat when she and her cousins were examining new clothes they'd just brought in.'[20]

Another significant dimension of the NLI 'Death of a Naturalist' subseries file is that there are trace elements of the manuscript titled *Advancements of Learning* that Heaney sent to Liam Miller at Dolmen Press in November 1964 prior to accepting Faber's February 1965 invitation to publish *Death of a Naturalist.* Heaney discusses in general the differences between the two manuscripts in *Stepping Stones*; however, he does not identify poems such as 'Lighting the Lamp' or 'Men's Confessions' that were in the Dolmen manuscript but not the published Faber volume and that can be found in this file (80–3). The ability to drill down in the NLI archive and find unpublished material that sheds light on how Heaney's creative process informs his publishing decisions is exciting and illuminating.

The archives at Emory and the National Library of Ireland are by far the most well known and accessible to Heaney scholars, but other collections will begin to assert their influence as the tide of textual studies rises. While there is little agreement on the tipping point when a collection of papers achieves the status of an archive, and caution amongst Rare Books librarians about overselling their holdings, the Heaney materials at the Bancroft

Library at UC Berkeley are worth noting. In 1971 the Bancroft Library purchased from Heaney a spiral-bound notebook and several loose sheets containing drafts and revised typescripts of poems he wrote while in residence there as a visiting lecturer. The National Library of Ireland has a photocopy of the Bancroft notebook and its contents are listed on the NLI website, which identifies the poems as drafts for *Wintering Out* among others from that era (I.iv.3). Researchers working in the NLI will have to trust that the poet copied every page of the Bancroft manuscripts.[21] The approximately forty loose sheets contain around twenty verse fragments and poems in various states of completion, some of which were published but not collected and others that were collected in *Wintering Out* as noted.[22] Another Heaney archive that will certainly grow in size and importance in the next few years is at Harvard. The majority of catalogued Heaney items held by Harvard are teaching-related and the majority of those are photocopies of teaching materials – photocopies used in class as examples. This archive will certainly take on greater significance once the papers of Heaney friend and scholar, Helen Vendler, are placed there.

When it was announced that the NLI would receive Heaney's manuscripts, his alma mater, Queen's University Belfast, responded graciously and the university spokesperson noted that QUB had already established the Seamus Heaney Beowulf Manuscript Collection.[23] Another Northern Ireland institution with significant Heaney archival materials is the BBC Northern Ireland, which holds not only audio and video recordings of the poet, but also the transcripts for many of the broadcasts Heaney did in the 1960s and 1970s, often in conjunction with his friend David Hammond. Bringing the writing back to its prenatal source, the 'Seamus Heaney Home Place' in Bellaghy, NI near Mossbawn (which opened in 2016) now has a variety of Heaney artefacts, including manuscripts, many of which are used for display purposes.

Established Heaney scholars are revisiting their earlier arguments or modifying works in progress as a result of the manuscripts now available. A new series of biographically guided studies of Heaney's work, if not actual biographies, will soon use the correspondence, journals, diaries and other unpublished texts to explore the relationship between the poet's work and his life in new and interesting ways. Critics will also be able to delve into Heaney's writing process in the many manuscript and typescript drafts behind the poems that seem to be spontaneous creations on the page. Heaney scholars wanting to publish quotations from the manuscripts in both archives, however, must still receive permission from the Heaney estate through Heaney's English publisher, Faber and Faber, which has its own publishing plans. One would expect to see in the next decade new Faber publications, such as a Heaney *New Selected Prose* to complement the 2014 *New Selected Poems*, or a new collection of translations by the poet that has been foreshadowed by the publication of Heaney's translation of Book VI of the *Aeneid*. If one looks at the Faber publications that appeared after the death of Ted Hughes, one might also expect a Heaney *Collected Poems*. We will probably not see a *Complete Poems* in the near future or even a collection of letters that contain any family correspondence for a generation or more. The archives themselves are works in progress, and like the materials they contain, their power to illuminate and transform is boundless.

Notes

1 Hannah Marshall, 'From Faber & Faber's archive: Seamus Heaney's acceptance letter from 1965', Waterstones blog, 16 March 2016, www.waterstones.com/blog/from-faber-and-fabers-archive-seamus-heaneys-acceptance-letter-from-1965.
2 Ted Hughes, *Winter Pollen: Occasional Prose*, ed. William Scammell (New York: Picador, 1994), p. 206. The essay was originally written for Roy Davids of Sotheby's Manuscript Department, to be given as an illustrated lecture to the Wordsworth Trust, Grasmere, 25 February 1988. The passage quoted here also appeared in Roy Davids, 'Manuscripts: An Endangered Species?', *Manuscripts*, 54/2 (Spring 2002). Davids sent an inscribed copy of the essay to Heaney.
3 The term *archive* can refer to both the space in which documents are stored and to the documents themselves. The process of assembling a bona fide archive reflects the etymological roots of the term *archive* derived from the Greek *arkheion*, the building in which government records were stored and processed by the magistracy. Order is imposed on chaos, and the mass of papers that littered the poet's desk, cabinets, shelves and floors move from the worthless to the priceless, from the creative realm to the critical, from the individual to the institutional.
4 Frances Clarke, archivist of the Seamus Heaney papers at the NLI, provided the number of folders, loose sheets and notebooks. Her blog post on the archival process contains a few images of interesting Heaney manuscripts: https://blog.nli.ie/index.php/2013/04/18/the-seamus-heaney-literary-papers.
5 Stuart A. Rose Manuscript, Archives, and Rare Book Library, Emory University, Seamus Heaney papers, 1951–2004, MS 960.
6 The catalogue is accessible here: catalogue.nli.ie/Collection/vtls000358500/CollectionList?lookfor=&type=AllFields&view=list#tabnav.
7 The NLI manuscripts have been available to researchers since the collection was processed. Emory offered limited access to Heaney's correspondence from

2004 to 2016 until the restrictions were lifted by the Heaney estate in the spring of 2016.

8 Brian Friel, letter to Heaney, 1 May 1989, Rose Library, Seamus Heaney papers, MS 960, b39/f9.

9 Brian Friel, letter to Heaney, undated, Rose Library, MS 960, b39/f8.

10 Muldoon, letter to Heaney, circa 1988, Rose Library, MS 960, b42/f9.

11 Brandes, conversation with Heaney, Dublin 1990.

12 Ann Saddlemyer, letter to Heaney, 15 January 1972, Rose Library, MS 960, b1/f12.

13 Seamus Deane, letter to Heaney, 22 February 1972, Rose Library, MS 960, b38/f8.

14 Seamus Heaney, 'Introduction', *Macbeth* (Dublin: Folens, 1973), pp. 5–22. Printed in 150 copies for Consultants and Contributors; no trade edition was published.

15 Ted Hughes, letter to Heaney, Rose Library, MS 960, b40/f14.

16 Heaney, letter to Darcy O'Brien, 31 December 1995, Rose Library, MS 960, b47/f9.

17 Heaney, letter to Jonathan Galassi, 6 September 1995, Rose Library, b6/f9.

18 Heaney, draft of 'Postscript', January–September 1993, Rose Library, MS 960, b45/f9.

19 Seamus Heaney, 'To a Wine Jar', *Honest Ulsterman*, 97 (Spring 1994), 20.

20 Heaney, letter to Massimo Bacigalupo, 5 January 1998, Rose Library, MS 960, b49/f7. Bacigalupo's translation of Heaney's *The Redress of Poetry* into Italian was published in 1999.

21 Heaney obviously wanted to have access to these drafts for future reference after he left California.

22 Bancroft Heaney archive details provided by David Fauls, Curator of Rare Books and Literary Manuscripts, Bancroft Library, University of California, Berkeley, CA.

23 Anne Madden, 'Seamus Heaney's Papers Go to Dublin, But We Don't Mind', *Belfast Telegraph*, 22 December 2011, www.belfasttelegraph.co.uk/news/northern-ireland/seamus-heaneys-papers-go-to-dublin-but-we-dont-mind-insists-qub-28694856.html.

CHAPTER 32

Legacy

Chris Morash

When Seamus Heaney passed away on 30 August 2013, the scale of the response was a signal that any retrospective assessment of his life and work was always going to be weighted with a symbolic power over and above the genuine and intimate grief felt at the loss of a much-loved public figure. On 31 August, for instance, the *Irish Times* turned its entire front page over to Fintan O'Toole so that he might eulogize Heaney. 'Like all great poets', O'Toole wrote, 'Seamus Heaney was an alchemist. He turned our disgrace into grace, our petty hatreds into epic generosity, our dull clichés into questioning eloquence, the leaden metal of brutal inevitability into the gold of pure possibility.'[1] Heaney's picture was on the front page of newspapers around the world that day, from the *New York Times* to the *Guardian*; his funeral in Dublin was a public event, attended by writers, artists and politicians and ordinary members of the public. In the commemorative events that followed around the world, and in everyday conversations, the sense of loss was real. Given the place of poetry in contemporary life, where many poetry publishers struggle to stay in business, it was an extraordinary outpouring, going beyond national pride in a local Nobel Prize winner. It was as if more than a poet, or even an individual, was being mourned; it was as if some collective part of the culture was being laid to rest.

There are many ways in which we could trace the legacy that began to take shape in the months after August 2013. The most obvious way would be to build on the myriad lineages of example and influence (anxious or otherwise) pursued elsewhere in this volume, placing Heaney as a figure in a shifting mosaic that would include Wordsworth and Longley, Miłosz and Mahon, Yeats and Bishop, Kavanagh and Hughes (to name only a few). And, indeed, the meaning of that legacy is already being negotiated by the major figures in Irish poetry. Paul Muldoon opens his 2015 collection, *One Thousand Things Worth Knowing*, with a complex and moving elegy, 'Cuthbert and the Otters' (subtitled 'In memory of

Seamus Heaney'), which insists on Heaney's continued presence in Irish poetry ('like a hauberked warrior laid out on his shield, / may yet be thought of as whole'), while at the same time sharply registering his loss: 'I'm at once full of dread / and in complete denial. / I cannot thole the thought of Seamus Heaney dead.'[2] Likewise, in his 2015 collection *The Days of Surprise*, Paul Durcan recalls hearing the news of Heaney's passing in Achill in the poem 'Breaking News' – 'Something that really happened', Durcan told the *Irish Times*, 'in as much as I was driving up a mountain slope on Achill Island when I accidentally touched the dials on the radio of the car. And a voice said, "It has just been announced that the poet Seamus Heaney has died."'[3] In Durcan's poem, Heaney's voice echoes down the chimney, telling him: 'Calm down, I'm only dead, I'm only beginning / The new life, only hours and minutes into it.' The Heaney who speaks in 'Breaking News' is a figure who has become 'the spaceman I've always longed to be': 'After a lifetime of being neither here nor there – / Of being kidnapped by Time – / I am out in the cosmos / Tramping the Milky Way with my father and my mother – .'[4]

There is another way, however, to begin to understand Heaney's legacy in the context of the acts of mourning in the months that followed August 2013: by attempting to gauge Heaney's legacy outside the tightly knit world of Irish poetry. Early in 2015, the Irish broadcaster RTÉ canvassed audiences to find Ireland's favourite poem of the past one hundred years. Listeners and viewers were invited to nominate poems (which they did in their thousands, ultimately nominating some 130 poems), from which a panel selected a shortlist of ten finalists, which were put to a public vote, producing several thousand more responses. 'This project was all about putting poetry firmly at the heart of the national conversation', the 'Poem for Ireland' website announced. 'Let's keep it there.'[5] On one hand, it is easy to dismiss 'A Poem for Ireland' as simply a media event. On the other hand, if we want to think about legacy in terms of wider cultural resonance, this at least provides us with something like a survey (admittedly, without the checks and balances that would make this anything like a scientific sample) that allows us to ask: what is the place of poetry in Irish life?

The final shortlist for 'A Poem for Ireland' is instructive, in that it was largely made up of poems that, in various ways, looked back to an Ireland that was very different to the Ireland of 2015.[6] Generations of former Irish schoolchildren had memorized Patrick Kavanagh's 'Christmas Childhood', and it is trotted out like fruitcake every Christmas, so its inclusion was little surprise. Likewise, with historical commemoration fever already underway in the run-up to the 1916 centenary, W. B. Yeats's 'Easter 1916' initially seemed like a safe bet. Others poems, such as Paula Meehan's 'The Statue of the Virgin at Granard Speaks', with its reference to the Ann Lovett case in 1984, hearkened back to a more recent (but in some respects equally foreign) Ireland of sexual repression. It would have been surprising, to say the least, if no poem by Heaney had been on the shortlist, but more obvious choices would have been an early, frequently anthologized or taught poem ('Blackberry Picking', for instance, or 'Mid-Term Break'). However, in the end, the poem that was selected – and celebrated – as Ireland's favourite poem of the past century was 'Clearances 3', from *The Haw Lantern*, a poem popularly known by its initial line: 'When all the others were away at Mass'. 'When I read "When all the others were away at Mass"', commented one person who voted for the poem, 'it was the only one to evoke a tear and a memory that flooded me with a sense of love, loneliness for my own mother and then a warm feeling that this is Irish, this is Ireland, *albeit* in a time that is fading.'[7]

The poem that 'flooded' this reader with her own memories, and 'a warm feeling' about 'a time that is fading' can point us towards what was being mourned in the months after August 2013, for 'Clearances 3' is, in the first instance, a poem of mourning and remembrance. 'When all the others were away at Mass / I was all hers as we peeled potatoes' (*HL* 27). The poem's first word – 'When' – situates the octave in a past that is prior to the sestet: 'So while the parish priest at her bedside / Went hammer and tongs at the prayers for the dying'. Poised between 'when' and 'while', between past perfect and continuous past, we start to recognize that this is not simply a poem of remembrance; it is a poem in which a memory is remembered: 'I remembered . . .', the poet tells us, locating the act of remembrance itself in a past that is superimposed over the remembered moment of potato-peeling. What is more, this moment itself is delicate, precarious: 'Her breath in mine, our fluent dipping knives – / Never closer the whole rest of our lives'. That which is remembered is not only fleeting in itself (breath, the movement of knives); the phrase 'the whole rest of our lives' carries a double charge, for the 'rest of our lives' here is a projection into a future that has passed; after death, there is no 'rest of *our* lives'. Finally, for all of the clarity and precise materiality of the imagery of the opening stanza – the potato peels dropping 'like solder weeping off the soldering iron' (*HL* 27) – this is a poem that enacts absence. As readers, we assume that the 'her' around which the poem centres is the poet's mother (and, as we shall see in looking at Heaney's manuscripts, this was originally the case); however, the pronoun is never pinned down as such (although the sequence as a whole is dedicated 'in memoriam M.K.H., 1911–1984', *HL* 24). Likewise, we assume that the memory of peeling potatoes takes place in the family home, but again this is never actually stated. In other words, this is a poem in which 'mother' and 'home' are both powerfully present and absent at the same time. It is a poem that enacts multiple forms of homelessness.

'Clearances 3' had been published almost thirty years before it was chosen as Ireland's favourite in *The Haw Lantern* (1987). Considering the arc of Heaney's career retrospectively, *The Haw Lantern* now seems like a pivotal collection. It was the point at which, in parable poems such as 'From the Frontier of Writing' or 'From the Republic of Conscience', earlier meditations on the role of the poet in the specific context of the Irish conflict from collections such as *North* (1975) and *Field Work* (1979) became more universal public statements. At the same time, there was a revisiting (the memory of a memory) of the private and family concerns of collections such as *Death of a Naturalist* (1966) and *Door into the Dark* (1969). The difference between the two directions in which Heaney's poetry was moving can be noted in the initial places of publication of two of the key poems in the collection: before it appeared in *The Haw Lantern*, the 'Clearances' sequence had been printed in 1986 in a numbered edition of eighty hand-sewn copies, of which 'twenty copies, unnumbered, are meant for kin and kith of the poet and the printers'.[8] By contrast, 'From the Republic of Conscience' appeared first as a pamphlet published for Amnesty International on Human Rights Day, 1985.[9] These might seem like bibliographic poles of the private and the public; however, they are not entirely unconnected. In a deleted stanza from an early draft of the poem 'Parable Island' (included in *The Haw Lantern*), Heaney makes it clear that the form of the parable itself is a way of addressing some of the same problems of time passing that emerge in 'Clearances'. 'If they only could', he writes in the abandoned stanza, 'they would deal with this / in the usual way – construct a parable – / except that now the vengeful god's one eye / is burning history up and has decreed / parables a doomed species like the rest.'[10]

The sense of 'history' (and the past more generally) 'burning up' runs throughout the poems gathered in *The Haw Lantern* with a force that is both private and public. What is more, the manuscript drafts of the poems in the collection show that this was a fire not easily harnessed. In 2008, Heaney told Dennis O'Driscoll that he had begun 'Clearances 3' before his mother, Margaret Heaney (to whom early drafts of the poem are addressed), passed away in 1984, but was only able to complete them later. At that point, he recalled, 'I actually enjoyed writing those sonnets, and did them quickly' (*SS* 312). In the early stages, however, the poem was much more recalcitrant. Indeed, for such a fully achieved sonnet, the poem did not begin as a sonnet at all. Among the early drafts is a poem of five six-line stanzas, entitled 'A Chaplet: For My Mother'. The opening line of the published sonnet is present and runs through all of the extant drafts, as does the central image of potato-peeling: 'When all the others were away at Mass / I was all yours, peeling the potatoes.' However, the second stanza of this early draft moves in a different direction, giving the falling potato peels a much more precise correlative in Catholic devotional practice: 'Earlier you let fall memorial cards / Out of your missal, between the kneeling boards.'[11] In this (and other) early drafts of the poem, what is being staged is an anguished encounter between a kind of proleptic mourning for his mother (the early drafts predate his mother's death in 1984), and a different (and angrier) mourning for a lost (or at least inadequate) Catholic faith. In the final published version of the poem this is still present, particularly in the image of the parish priest going 'hammer and tongs at the prayers for the dying' (*HL* 27). However, it is not foregrounded in the same way that we find in the draft called 'A Chaplet', keeping in mind that a chaplet is a set of prayer beads, for which the emerging orbs of the peeled potatoes become secular equivalents not quite able to shed their origins, even after the image of the chaplet is dropped from the later drafts. Here, as elsewhere, we can see what Eamon Duffy means when he tells us that 'the symbolic world of Catholicism saturates Heaney's imagination', and that Catholic devotional practice exists as (using Nicholas Boyle's words) a 'presence in absence' in Heaney's work.[12]

'A Chaplet' culminates in a pair of lines with a raw anguish we rarely find in Heaney's published work: 'O mother, mother, in each departing kiss, / The lents, the christenings, the rosaries'.[13] A later draft amends this, so that 'each *departing* kiss' becomes 'each *homing* kiss', and 'the lents, the christenings, the rosaries' become a desperate question: 'what lents, what christenings, what *last ditch* rosaries'.[14] This later version also changes the basic structure of the poem yet again, by introducing an epistolary frame, and adding his aunt, Mary Heaney, to the poem's addressees. This draft, no longer called 'A Chaplet', but now called 'Dear Mam and Aunt Mary', is at least partially spoken in the voice of the poet's younger self ('Tell Daddy I was asking for him') writing a letter home from St Columb's College. Little remains of this epistolary device in the final poem; however, it was part of the search for a literary form to contain a constellation of loss that tied together mother, home and belief – all of which can be understood as forms of homelessness, whether personal, physical or philosophical. In the end, in this poem Heaney was only able to 'give thought to his homelessness' (as Heidegger puts it)[15] through language itself, and the breakthrough only came when Heaney finally hit upon the phrase that appears in the penultimate line of the final version – 'fluent dipping knives'. At that point, the poem came together as the sonnet that he would remember writing 'quickly' more than twenty years later.[16]

'Intellectually speaking, the loss of faith occurred offstage', Heaney later told Dennis O'Driscoll, when speaking of his own falling away from belief. 'There was never a scene where I had it out with myself or with another. But the potency of those words remains for me, they retain an undying tremor and draw; I cannot disavow them. Nor can I make the act of faith' (*SS* 234). The rawness of some of the early drafts of 'Clearances 3' suggests that there may have been at least one 'scene' where he 'had it out' with himself – at least on paper. Whether in the poetic persona of the schoolboy Heaney writing to an absent home from which he now comes and goes 'at the set times', or in the 'homing' kiss to his absent mother and aunt ('you whimpering, and she incontinent'), buried in the writing of 'Clearances 3' is a lost home, a place where belonging was once possible, if only 'When all the others were away at Mass'.

This image of the lost or abandoned home haunts Seamus Heaney's poetry in the years that follow *The Haw Lantern*, from the 'bare wallstead, and a cold hearth rained into' that opens what is arguably his most sustained poetic achievement, the 'Squarings' sequence from *Seeing Things* (1991), to the central image of his poem for David Hammond, '"The door was open and the house was dark"' from *Human Chain* (2010). Like 'Clearances', the poems in 'Squarings' are triggered by the image of a lost home, a house derelict but dizzyingly free, the roof open to a 'Bright puddle where the soul-free cloud-life roams' – 'Just the old truth dawning: there is no next-time-around', scoured by the 'Knowledge-freshening wind' (*ST* 55). Living with the recognition that 'there is no next-time-around' shapes 'Squarings', which moves through a sequence of sixty-eight poems from a ruined house to the River Bann glimpsed from a roadway, shimmering in sunlight: 'Out in the channel between the painted poles', homelessness can be inhabited, if only fleetingly, and it is possible at last to 'be in step with what escaped me' (*ST* 108).

When Heaney died in 2013, homelessness had a more than usually powerful referent in Irish society. The same issue of the *Irish Times* that published Fintan O'Toole's front-page eulogy also followed up on a story that had dominated headlines over the previous week, concerning a homeless man, Hendryk Piotrowski, whose body had been found in a refuse skip;[17] later that week, the paper reported that seven more people were becoming homeless in Ireland every day.[18] This was the tangible image of an economic crisis that often seemed to escape representation in abstract concepts such as bank liquidity and unsecured debt. Underlying such images were historical memories of nineteenth-century evictions, of roof-trees being thrown down; but underlying this again was a recognition that to be homeless, to be nomadic was also utterly a condition of late modernity, visible in 2015 as a crisis of migration reached epic proportions on Europe's borders. 'Our house is our corner of the world', Gaston Bachelard once argued. 'As has often been said, it is our first universe, a real cosmos in every sense of the word.'[19] If there was a pair of images that seemed to encapsulate the state of Ireland at the time of Heaney's death, it was the ghost estate, the silent wasteland of half-built homes; and its corollary, the homeless person huddled in a sleeping bag in a doorway – precisely the images with which Heaney had opened 'Squarings' twenty-seven years earlier: 'bare wallstead, and a cold hearth rained into', and 'a beggar shivering in silhouette', images whose genealogy goes back to the absent homes of his poetry from the mid-1980s, including 'Clearances 3'.

In years to come, as the Irish economic recession of the early twenty-first century becomes a matter of historical record, this echo of current affairs in poems written twenty or thirty years earlier might seem like little more than a footnote in Seamus Heaney's legacy. However, any legacy is ever thus: a legacy must always exist in (and on behalf of) its own present moment, shaped by present concerns. In the three decades between the first drafts of the poem that became 'Clearances 3' and its emergence as Ireland's favourite poem in 2015, Ireland underwent a period of unprecedented transformation, from a country that saw itself as insular, underdeveloped and theocratic, to being a determinedly secular nation of nomads that is now among the most globalized in the world. In the course of an interview for the *Paris Review* conducted in 1994, when Heaney was asked about another poem about belonging and loss from *The Haw Lantern*, 'The Mud Vision', he replied in terms that illuminate the forces gathered in 'Clearances 3':

> I was wanting to write about contemporary Ireland, the Republic of Ireland, as a country with a religious subconscious but a secular destiny – at the point of transition from the communality of religious devotion to the loneliness of modernity and subjectivity. The community in the poem has lost the sense of its own destiny and of any metaphysical call. And it is exposed to the challenge of making a go of it in a more secular world.[20]

In 2013, in a piece that appeared shortly after his death, Heaney commented again on 'The Mud Vision', framing this sense of existential homelessness in the context of the economic crisis of the time. The community in the poem, he wrote,

> had belief and a unique revelation; now they are left with the trappings of modernity in a world they understand but are no longer at home with. Alienated from what has been brought upon them, they "crowd in for the big explanations", rather like the Irish population in the wake of the Celtic Tiger, listening, bewildered, to experts. Economists. Regulators. Apologisers. Apologists.[21]

When the Irish people attempted to 'thole the thought of Seamus Heaney dead' after 2013, 'Clearances 3' flared into a new life, illuminating not only a transient financial crisis, but revealing that crisis as a symbolic expression of a more profound homelessness, now arguably the dominant feature of Irish life. 'After a lifetime of being neither here nor there', Paul Durcan's Heaney reassures us, 'Of being kidnapped by Time – / I am out in the cosmos.' This may be the true legacy of Heaney's work, the one that will be rewritten to meet changing circumstances in years to come: the invitation to live homelessness as necessity, to be alive to the materiality of the world and to language, not as a victim of time or of memory, but attuned to the 'pleasant splashes' produced by the 'fluent dipping knives', as that which once constituted home drops away like potato peelings into a bucket.

Notes

1 Fintan O'Toole, 'Comfort Is Best Found in His Poems', *Irish Times*, 31 August 2013.
2 Paul Muldoon, *One Thousand Things Worth Knowing* (London: Faber and Faber, 2015), pp. 3–4.
3 Arminta Wallace, 'Paul Durcan: The Most Playful Poet in Ireland', *Irish Times*, 17 March 2015.
4 Paul Durcan, 'Breaking News', *The Days of Surprise* (London: Harvill Secker, 2015), pp. 125–6.
5 The jury was composed of a mixture of broadcasting, entertainment, publishing and academic figures: Caitriona Crowe, Damien Dempsey, Maria Johnston, Anne Doyle, John Fitzgerald and Ríóna Ní Fhrigril. See http://apoemforireland.rte.ie.
6 The full shortlist was 'A Christmas Childhood', Patrick Kavanagh; 'A Disused Shed in Co. Wexford', Derek Mahon; 'Dublin', Louis MacNeice; 'Easter 1916', William Butler Yeats; 'Fill Arís', Seán Ó Ríordáin; 'Filleadh ar an

gCathair', Ailbhe Ní Ghearbhuigh; 'Making Love Outside Áras an Uachtaráin', Paul Durcan; 'Quarantine', Eavan Boland; 'The Statue of the Virgin at Granard Speaks', Paula Meehan; 'Clearances 3', Seamus Heaney.

7 The comment is attributed to Deirdre Halpin. See http://apoemforireland.rte.ie.

8 Seamus Heaney, *Clearances* ([Amsterdam]: Cornamona Press, 1986).

9 Seamus Heaney, *From the Republic of Conscience*, illus. John Behan (Dublin: Amnesty International, 1985).

10 Seamus Heaney, draft of 'Parable Island', Seamus Heaney Literary Papers, MS 49, 493/80 (34), National Library of Ireland.

11 Heaney, 'A Chaplet: For My Mother', MS 49, 493/80 (50), National Library of Ireland.

12 Eamon Duffy, 'Seamus Heaney and Catholicism', in John Walker (ed.), *The Present Word: Culture, Society and the Site of Literature: Essays in Honour of Nicholas Boyle* (Oxford: Legenda, 2013), pp. 166–83 (at pp. 166–7). The phrase 'presence in absence' in this context is from Nicholas Boyle, *Who Are We Now? Christian Humanism and the Global Market from Hegel to Heaney* (Notre Dame University Press, 1998), pp. 309–10.

13 Heaney, 'A Chaplet: For My Mother', MS 49, 493/80 (50).

14 *Ibid.* (54).

15 Martin Heidegger, 'Building, Dwelling, Thinking', in *Poetry, Language, Thought*, trans. Albert Hofstadter (New York: Harper, 1975), p. 159.

16 Marie Heaney, conversation with the author, Dublin, 1 December 2015.

17 Daniel Lowry, 'Death of a Homeless Man', *Irish Times*, 31 August 2013.

18 Peter Murtagh, 'Seven More Homeless Every Day, Says Focus Ireland', *Irish Times*, 10 September 2013.

19 Gaston Bachelard, *The Poetics of Space*, trans. Maria Jolas (1958; Boston: Beacon, 1994), p. 4.

20 Seamus Heaney, 'The Art of Poetry No. 75', interviewed by Henri Cole in May 1994, *Paris Review*, 144 (Fall 1997), www.theparisreview.org/interviews/1217/the-art-of-poetry-no-75-seamus-heaney.

21 Seamus Heaney, 'The Home Place: The Mud Vision', *Irish Times*, 28 September 2013.

Index

For EU product safety concerns, contact us at Calle de José Abascal, 56–1°,
28003 Madrid, Spain or eugpsr@cambridge.org.

www.ingramcontent.com/pod-product-compliance
Ingram Content Group UK Ltd.
Pitfield, Milton Keynes, MK11 3LW, UK
UKHW022300171225
466163UK00008B/416
9781107180147